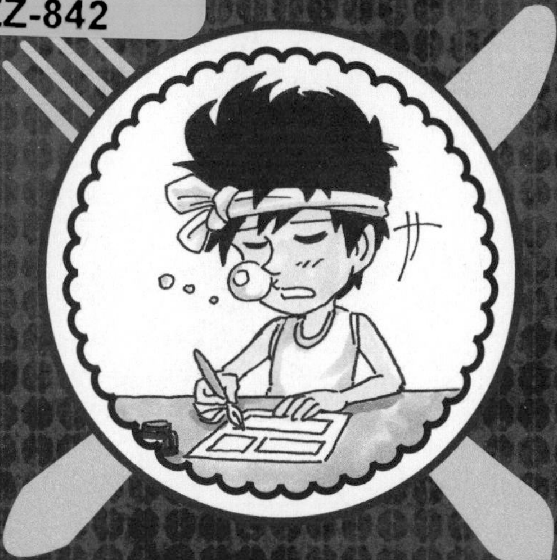

If I'm passionate enough about something, I can pull an all-nighter for it. When you're deeply focused on something that you really enjoy, everything else, including the need for sleep, becomes unimportant. At least that's what I thought when I was younger. I used to be able to pull all-nighters off. But not anymore. People need sleep!! (Ha!) (My current weight is…69 kg!! What, what?!)

–Mitsutoshi Shimabukuro, 2014

Mitsutoshi Shimabukuro made his debut in **Weekly Shonen Jump** in 1996. He is best known for **Seikimatsu Leader Den Takeshi!**, for which he won the 46th Shogakukan Manga Award for children's manga in 2001. His current series, **Toriko**, began serialization in Japan in 2008.

TORIKO

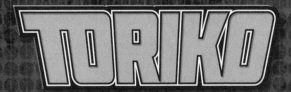

TORIKO VOL. 31
SHONEN JUMP Manga Edition

STORY AND ART BY **MITSUTOSHI SHIMABUKURO**

Translation/Christine Dashiell
Weekly Shonen Jump Lettering/Erika Terriquez
Graphic Novel Touch-Up Art & Lettering/Elena Diaz
Design/Matt Hinrichs
Weekly Shonen Jump Editor/Hope Donovan
Graphic Novel Editor/Marlene First

Printed in the U.S.A.

Published by VIZ Media, LLC
P.O. Box 77010
San Francisco, CA 94107

10 9 8 7 6 5 4 3 2 1
First printing, December 2015

viz media
www.viz.com

RATED T FOR TEEN
PARENTAL ADVISORY
TORIKO is rated T for Teen and is recommended for ages 13 and up. This volume contains realistic and fantasy violence.
ratings.viz.com

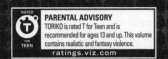

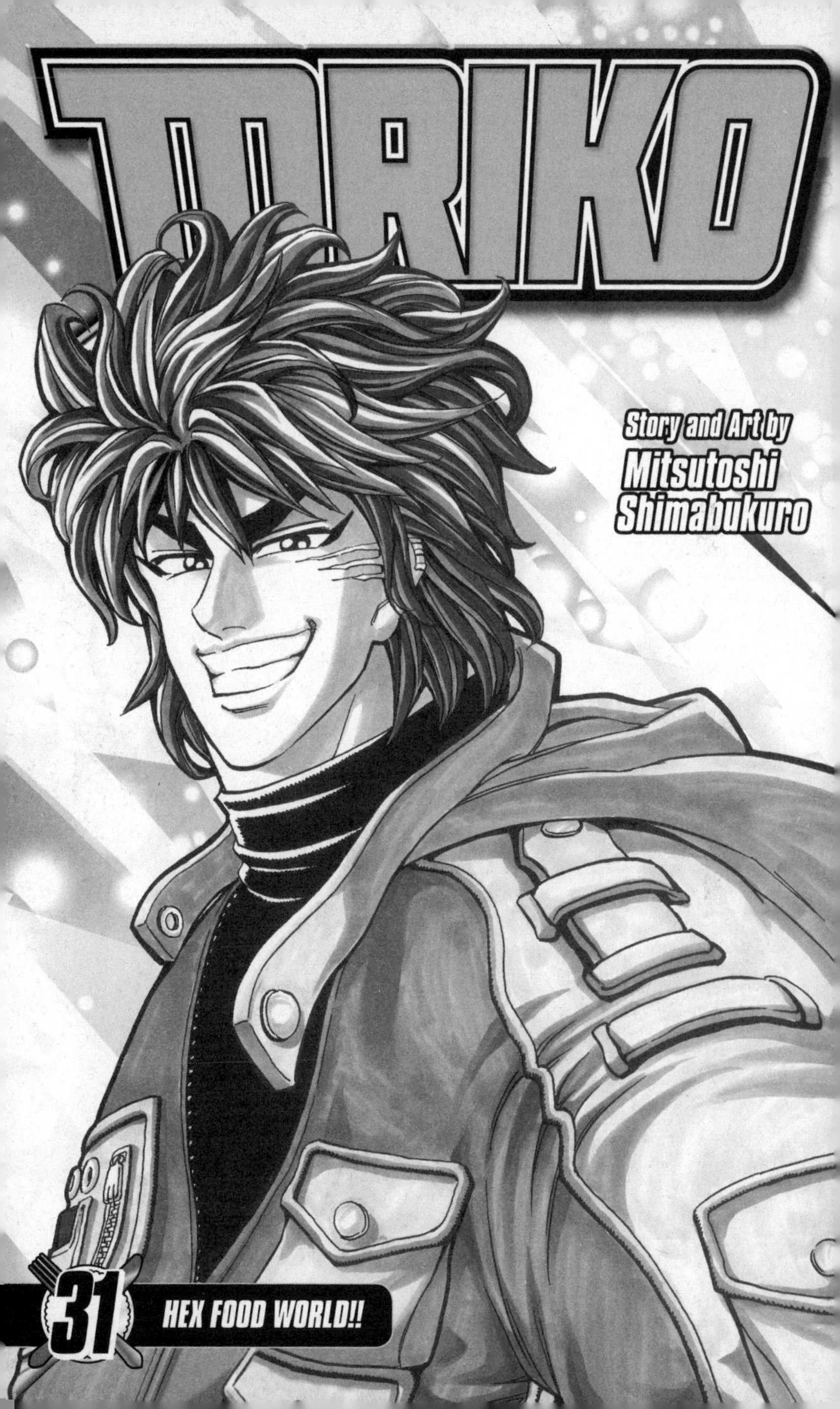
TORIKO
Story and Art by
Mitsutoshi
Shimabukuro
31
HEX FOOD WORLD!!

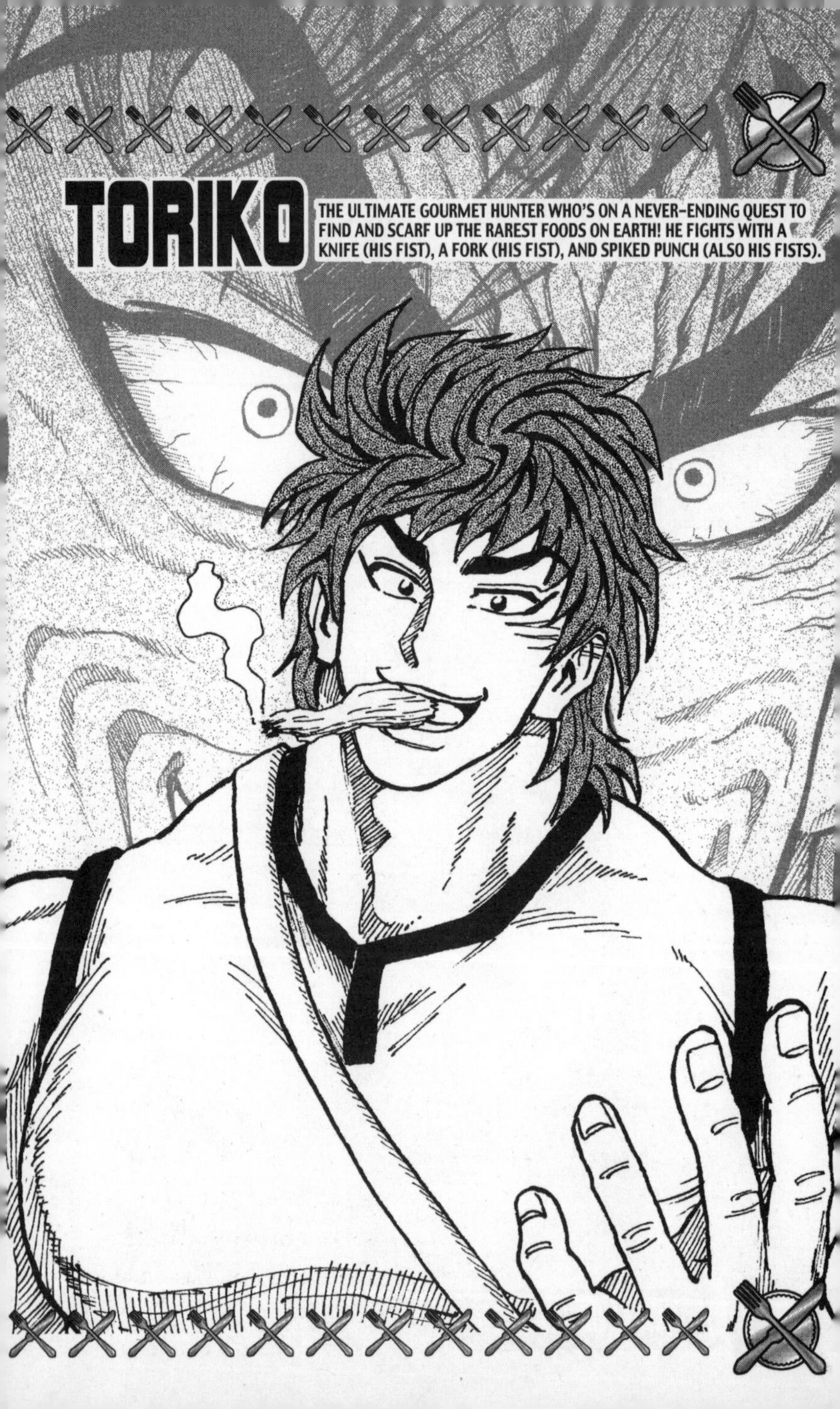
TORIKO
THE ULTIMATE GOURMET HUNTER WHO'S ON A NEVER-ENDING QUEST TO FIND AND SCARF UP THE RAREST FOODS ON EARTH! HE FIGHTS WITH A KNIFE (HIS FIST), A FORK (HIS FIST), AND SPIKED PUNCH (ALSO HIS FISTS).

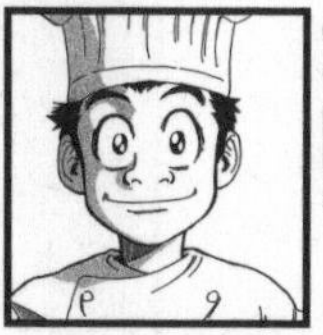

●KOMATSU

TALENTED IGO HOTEL CHEF AND TORIKO'S #1 FAN.

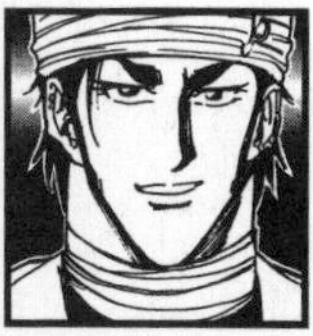

●COCO

ONE OF THE FOUR KINGS, THOUGH HE IS ALSO A FORTUNETELLER. SPECIAL ABILITY: POISON FLOWS IN HIS VEINS.

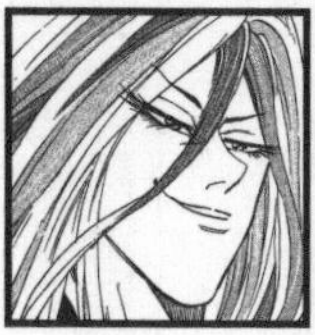

●SUNNY

ONE OF THE FOUR KINGS. SENSORS IN HIS LONG HAIR ENABLE HIM TO "TASTE" THE WORLD. OBSESSED WITH ALL THAT IS BEAUTIFUL.

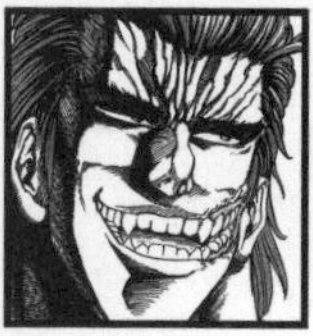

●ZEBRA

ONE OF THE FOUR KINGS. A DANGEROUS INDIVIDUAL WITH SUPERHUMAN HEARING AND VOCAL POWERS.

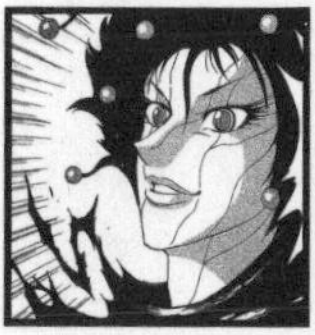

●JOIE

A MYSTERIOUS CHEF WHO BETRAYED GOURMET CORP. NOW ALLIED WITH NEO. SHE LOOKS LIKE FROESE.

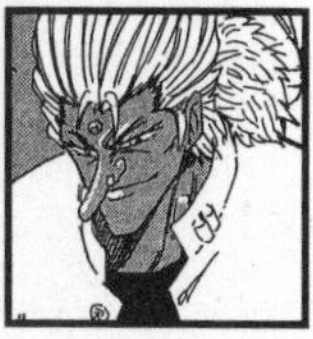

●BRUNCH

A CHEF FROM HEX FOOD WORLD. HE LOOKS LIKE A LONG-NOSED GOBLIN. HERO CHEF AT LEGENDARY "TENGU CASTLE."

WHAT'S FOR DINNER

IN THE AGE OF GOURMET, RENOWNED GOURMET HUNTER TORIKO AND TALENTED IGO HOTEL CHEF KOMATSU MEET AND BECOME PARTNERS. TOGETHER THEY TRAIN TO ENTER THE DEADLY GOURMET WORLD. TORIKO MASTERS THE SECRET ART OF "FOOD'S END" AND KOMATSU IS CELEBRATED AS ONE OF THE WORLD'S TOP 100 CHEFS.

HOWEVER, THE ANIMOSITY BETWEEN THE IGO AND RIVAL GOURMET CORP. EXPLODES INTO ALL-OUT WAR OVER GOURMET GOD ACACIA'S FULL-COURSE MEAL AND ITS MAIN COURSE, GOD. DURING THE FIGHTING, TORIKO LOSES TO STARJUN AND KOMATSU IS KIDNAPPED. IGO PRESIDENT ICHIRYU ALSO ENGAGES IN A CLIMACTIC BATTLE AGAINST GOURMET CORP. BOSS MIDORA AND MEETS A HEROIC YET TRAGIC END. THEIR CLASH ENDS WITH A RAIN OF DEADLY SPICE ANNIHILATING THE HUMAN WORLD.

THE AGE OF GOURMET IS DECLARED OVER. IN ORDER TO GET KOMATSU BACK FROM GOURMET CORP., TORIKO VENTURES INTO THE GOURMET WORLD ON HIS OWN! EIGHTEEN MONTHS LATER, THE PAIR RETURNS HOME ALONG WITH A MASSIVE AMOUNT OF PROVISIONS TO FEED THE HUMAN WORLD. UPON THEIR RETURN, THE TWO ARE COMMISSIONED BY THE NEW IGO PRESIDENT, MANSOM, TO SEARCH FOR THE REMAINDER OF ICHIRYU'S FULL-COURSE MEAL. JOINING FORCES WITH THE OTHER FOUR KINGS, COCO, SUNNY AND ZEBRA, THEY SUCCEED IN RETRIEVING THE MIRACLE INGREDIENT THAT WILL SAVE HUMANITY FROM STARVATION: THE BILLION BIRD!

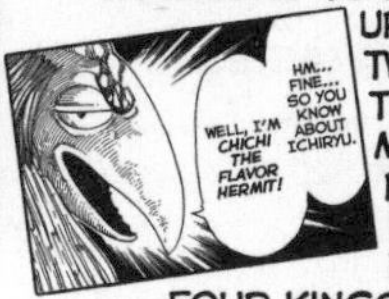
HM... FINE... SO YOU KNOW ABOUT ICHIRYU.
WELL, I'M CHICHI THE FLAVOR HERMIT!

IN ORDER TO REVIVE THE AGE OF GOURMET, THE FIVE MEN TAKE ON AN ENORMOUS ORDER! THEY MUST TRAVEL TO THE GOURMET WORLD AND FIND ACACIA'S FULL COURSE MEAL! ARMED WITH THE INFORMATION AND THE OCTOMELON CAMPER MONSTER GIVEN TO THEM ICHIRYU'S MYSTERIOUS FRIEND CHICHI, THE FIVE MEN SET THEIR SIGHTS ON THE GOURMET WORLD!

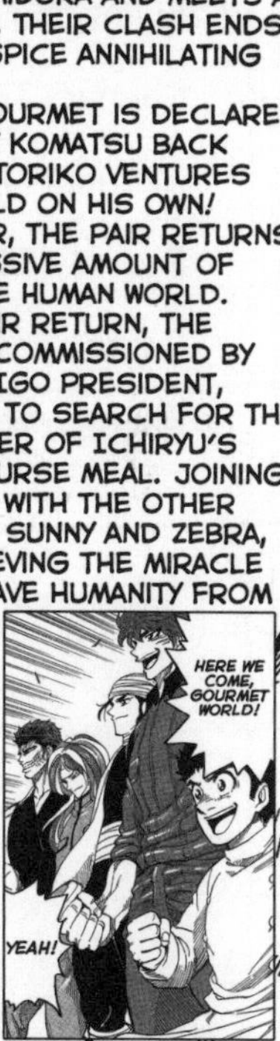
HERE WE COME, GOURMET WORLD!
YEAH!

Contents

TORIKO

GOURMET 273: BAY OF EVIL SPIRITS!!

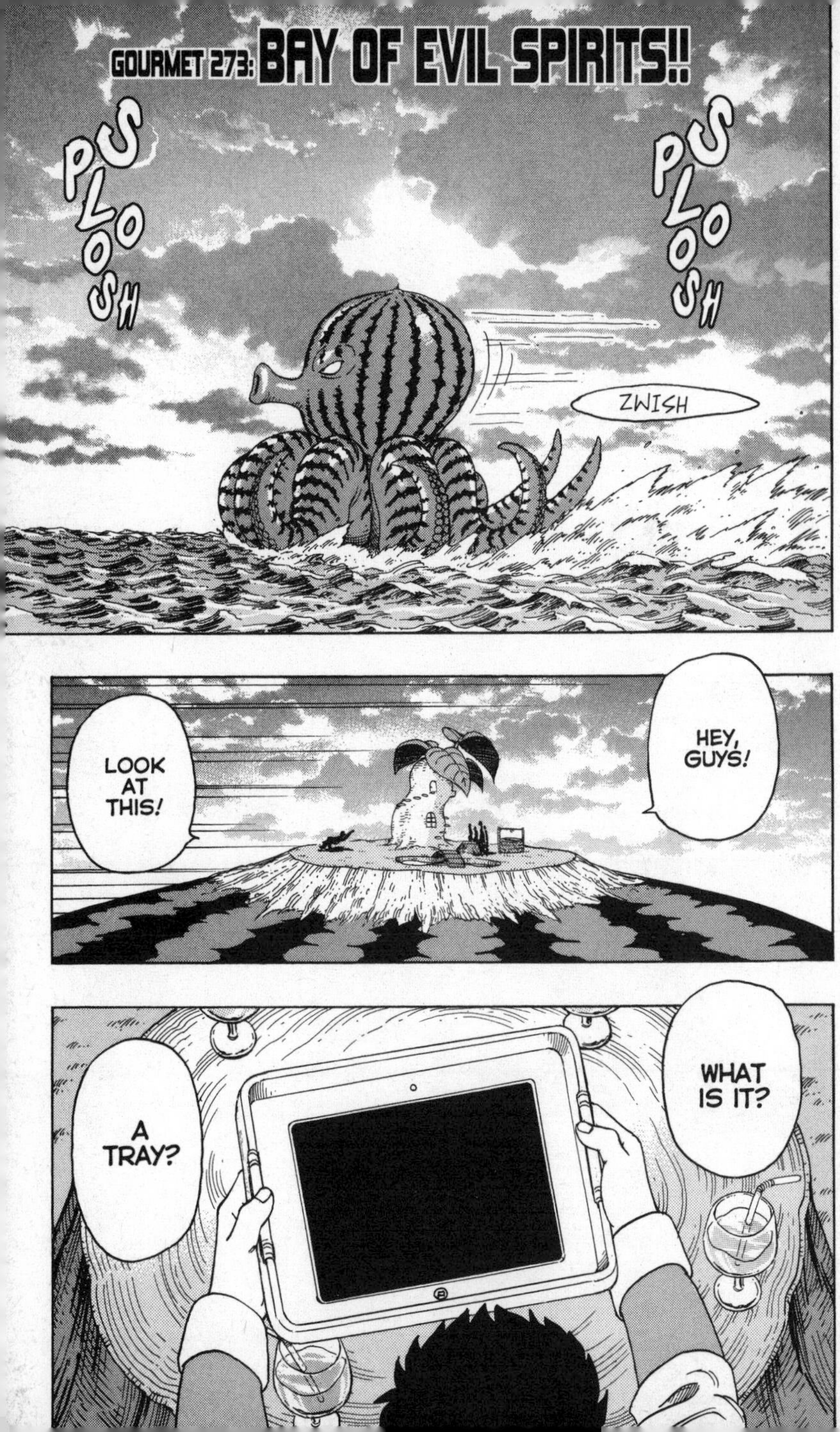
PLOOSH
PLOOSH
ZWISH
HEY, GUYS!
LOOK AT THIS!
WHAT IS IT?
A TRAY?

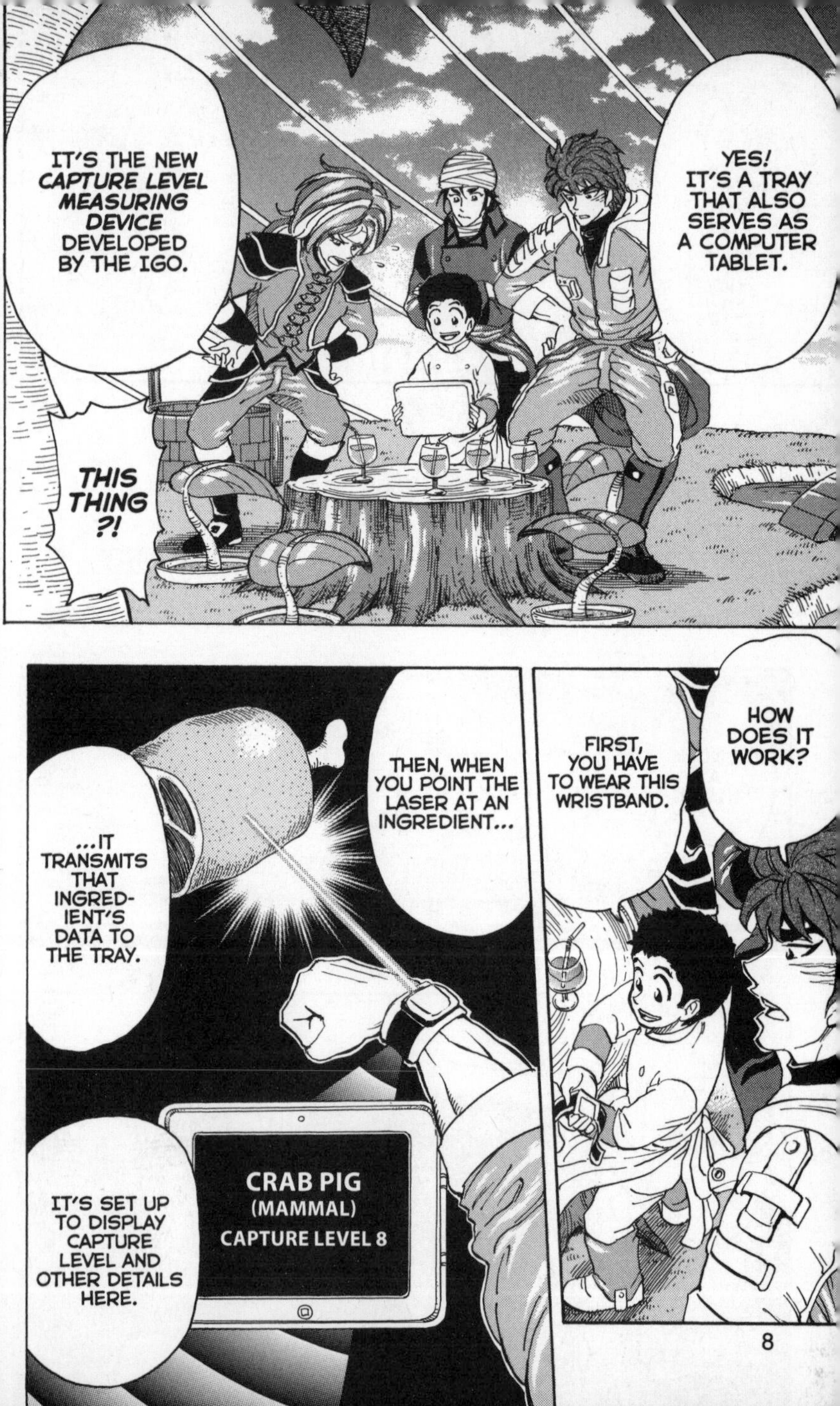
YES! IT'S A TRAY THAT ALSO SERVES AS A COMPUTER TABLET.
IT'S THE NEW *CAPTURE LEVEL MEASURING DEVICE* DEVELOPED BY THE IGO.
THIS THING?!
HOW DOES IT WORK?
FIRST, YOU HAVE TO WEAR THIS WRISTBAND.
THEN, WHEN YOU POINT THE LASER AT AN INGREDIENT...
...IT TRANSMITS THAT INGREDIENT'S DATA TO THE TRAY.
CRAB PIG
(MAMMAL)
CAPTURE LEVEL 8
IT'S SET UP TO DISPLAY CAPTURE LEVEL AND OTHER DETAILS HERE.

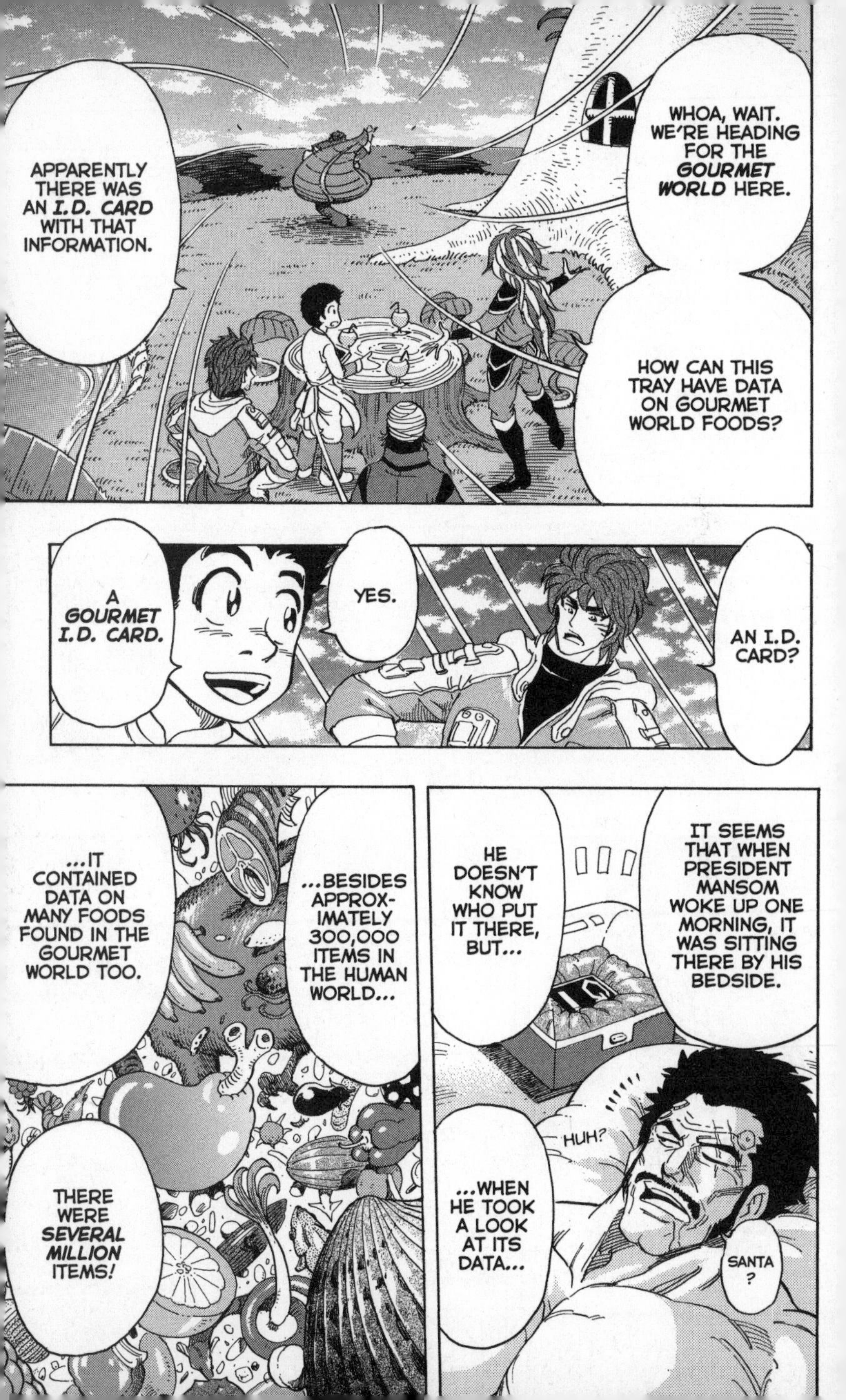
WHOA, WAIT. WE'RE HEADING FOR THE GOURMET WORLD HERE.
HOW CAN THIS TRAY HAVE DATA ON GOURMET WORLD FOODS?
APPARENTLY THERE WAS AN I.D. CARD WITH THAT INFORMATION.
AN I.D. CARD?
YES.
A GOURMET I.D. CARD.
IT SEEMS THAT WHEN PRESIDENT MANSOM WOKE UP ONE MORNING, IT WAS SITTING THERE BY HIS BEDSIDE.
HE DOESN'T KNOW WHO PUT IT THERE, BUT...
HUH?
SANTA?
...WHEN HE TOOK A LOOK AT ITS DATA...
...BESIDES APPROX-IMATELY 300,000 ITEMS IN THE HUMAN WORLD...
...IT CONTAINED DATA ON MANY FOODS FOUND IN THE GOURMET WORLD TOO.
THERE WERE SEVERAL MILLION ITEMS!

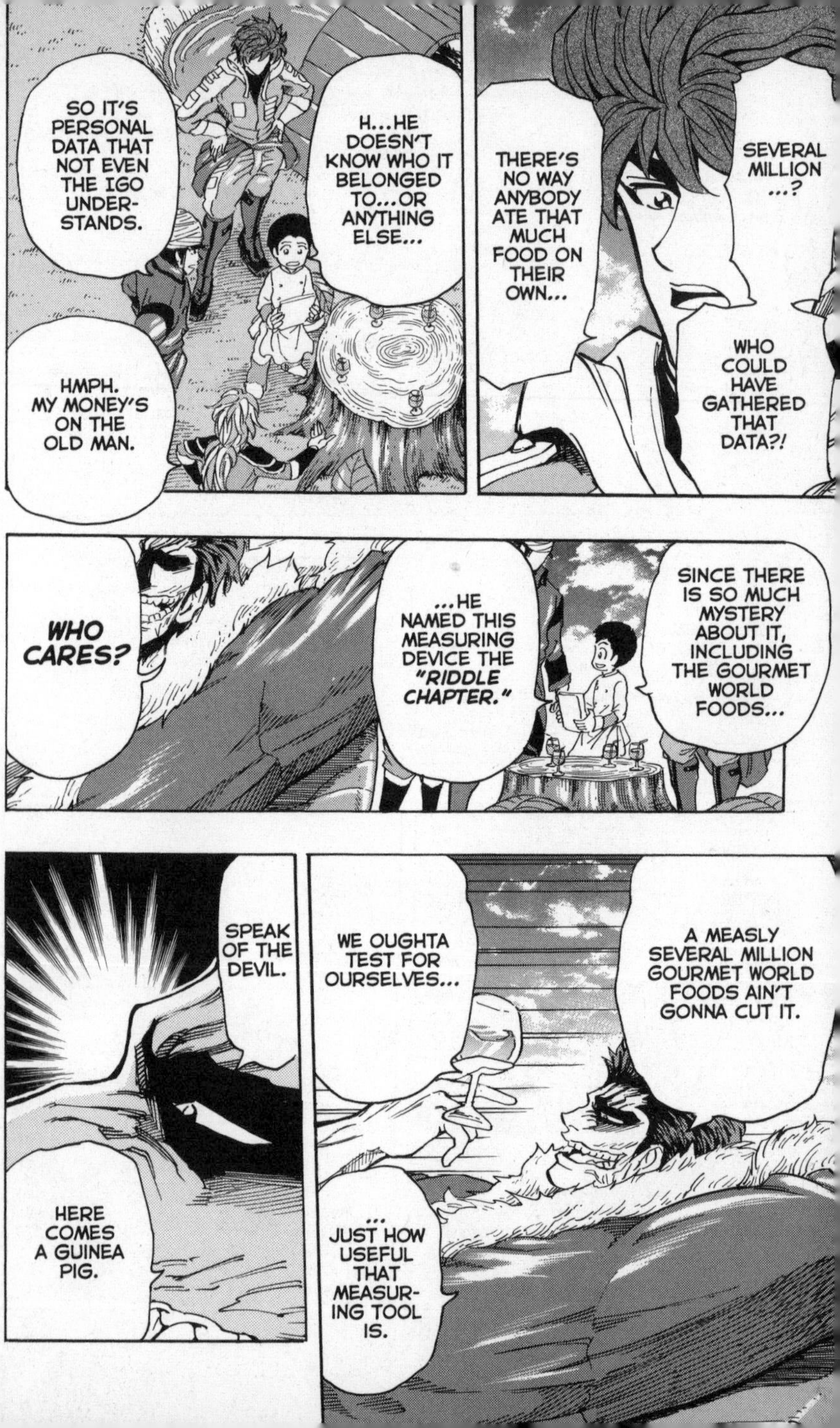
SEVERAL MILLION ...?
THERE'S NO WAY ANYBODY ATE THAT MUCH FOOD ON THEIR OWN...
WHO COULD HAVE GATHERED THAT DATA?!
H...HE DOESN'T KNOW WHO IT BELONGED TO...OR ANYTHING ELSE...
SO IT'S PERSONAL DATA THAT NOT EVEN THE IGO UNDER-STANDS.
HMPH. MY MONEY'S ON THE OLD MAN.
SINCE THERE IS SO MUCH MYSTERY ABOUT IT, INCLUDING THE GOURMET WORLD FOODS...
...HE NAMED THIS MEASURING DEVICE THE "RIDDLE CHAPTER."
WHO CARES?
A MEASLY SEVERAL MILLION GOURMET WORLD FOODS AIN'T GONNA CUT IT.
WE OUGHTA TEST FOR OURSELVES...
... JUST HOW USEFUL THAT MEASUR-ING TOOL IS.
SPEAK OF THE DEVIL.
HERE COMES A GUINEA PIG.

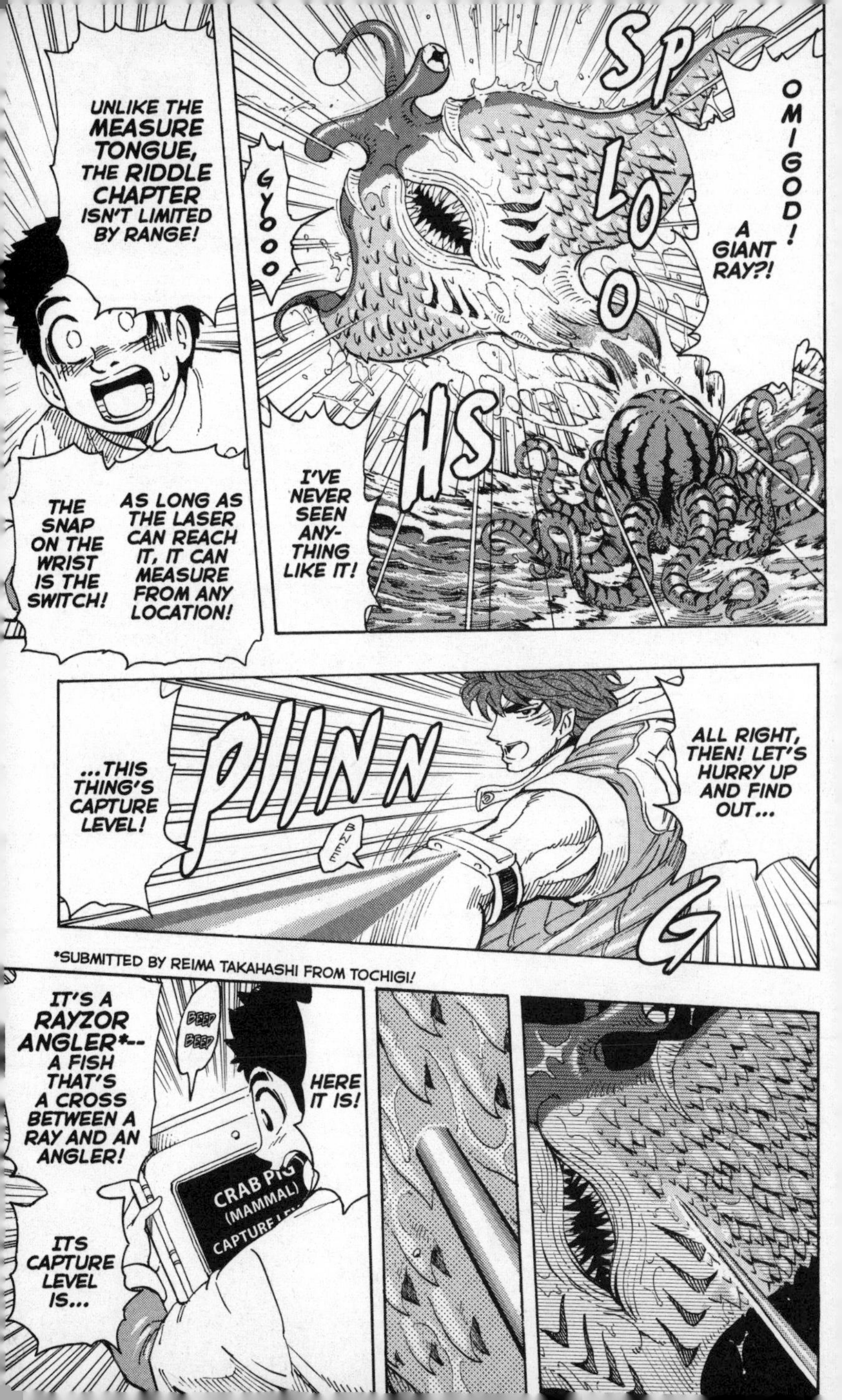
SPLOOSH
OMIGOD!
A GIANT RAY?!
GYOOOO
I'VE NEVER SEEN ANYTHING LIKE IT!
UNLIKE THE MEASURE TONGUE, THE RIDDLE CHAPTER ISN'T LIMITED BY RANGE!
THE SNAP ON THE WRIST IS THE SWITCH! AS LONG AS THE LASER CAN REACH IT, IT CAN MEASURE FROM ANY LOCATION!
ALL RIGHT, THEN! LET'S HURRY UP AND FIND OUT...
PLINNG
BWEE
...THIS THING'S CAPTURE LEVEL!
HERE IT IS!
BEEP BEEP
IT'S A RAYZOR ANGLER*-- A FISH THAT'S A CROSS BETWEEN A RAY AND AN ANGLER!
CRAB PIG
(MAMMAL)
ITS CAPTURE LEVEL IS...

*SUBMITTED BY REIMA TAKAHASHI FROM TOCHIGI!

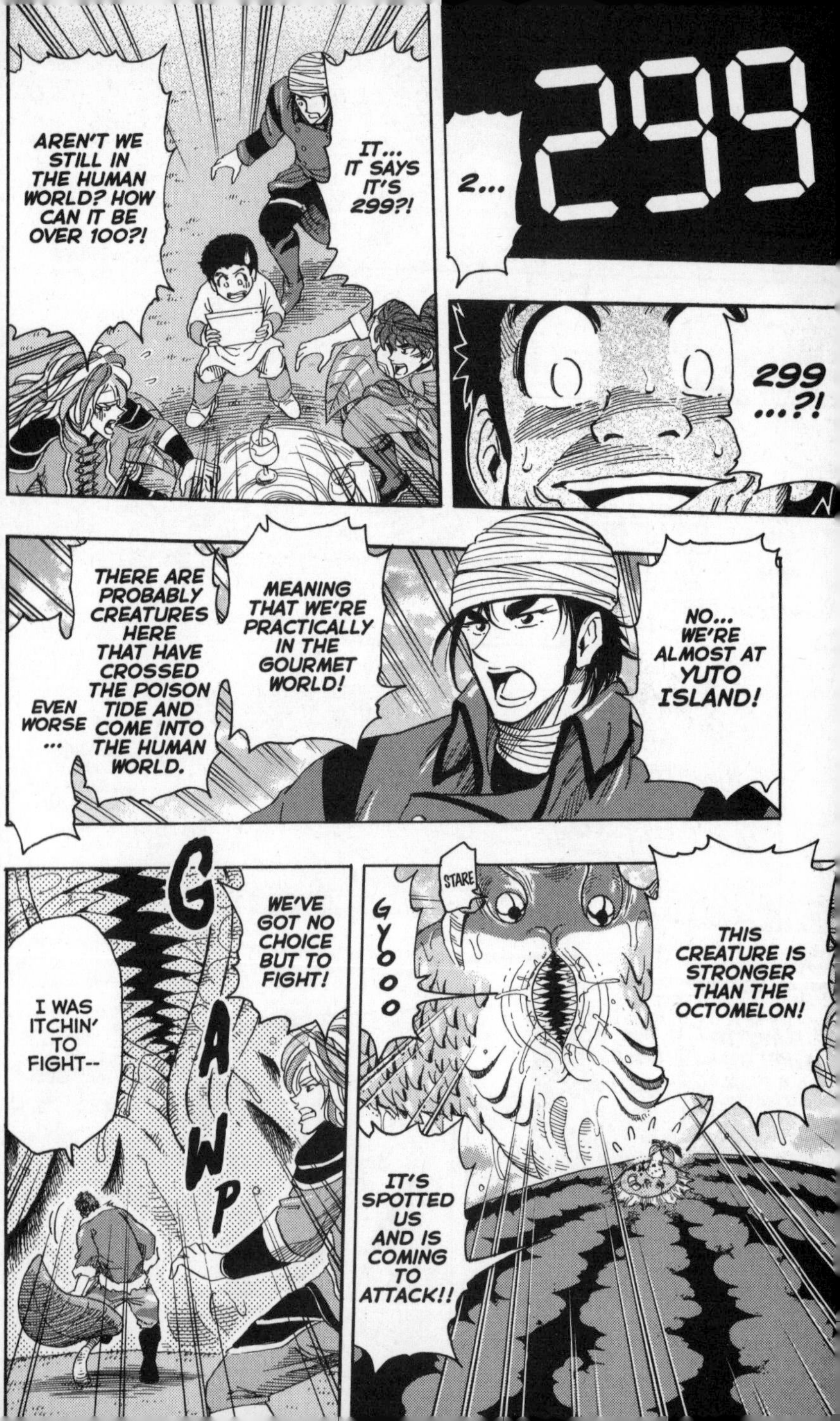
299
2...
299...?!
IT... IT SAYS IT'S 299?!
AREN'T WE STILL IN THE HUMAN WORLD? HOW CAN IT BE OVER 100?!
NO... WE'RE ALMOST AT YUTO ISLAND!
MEANING THAT WE'RE PRACTICALLY IN THE GOURMET WORLD!
EVEN WORSE...
THERE ARE PROBABLY CREATURES HERE THAT HAVE CROSSED THE POISON TIDE AND COME INTO THE HUMAN WORLD.
STARE
THIS CREATURE IS STRONGER THAN THE OCTOMELON!
GYOOO
IT'S SPOTTED US AND IS COMING TO ATTACK!!
WE'VE GOT NO CHOICE BUT TO FIGHT!
GAWP
I WAS ITCHIN' TO FIGHT--

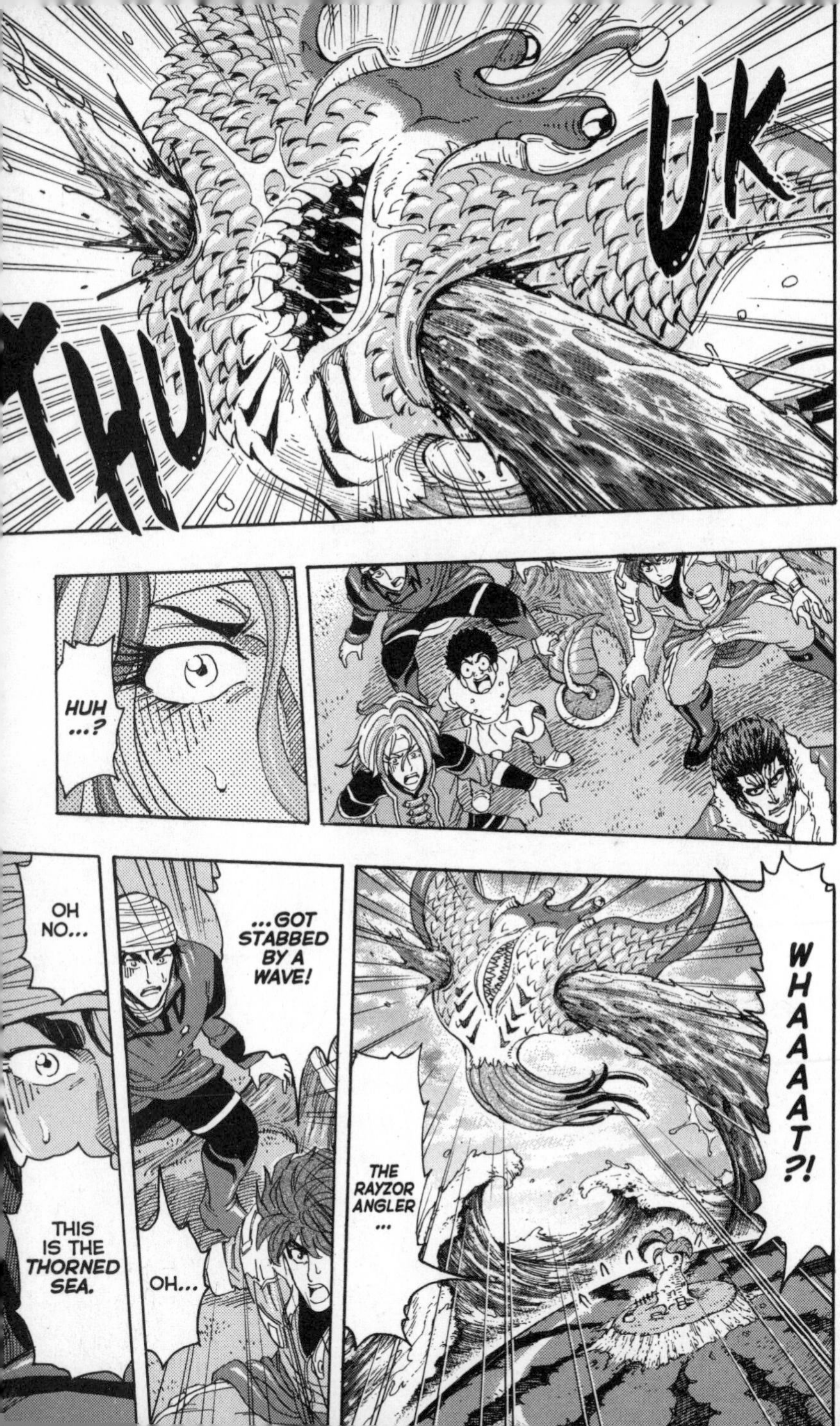
THUUK
HUH ...?
WHAAAAAT?!
THE RAYZOR ANGLER ...
...GOT STABBED BY A WAVE!
OH...
OH NO...
THIS IS THE THORNED SEA.

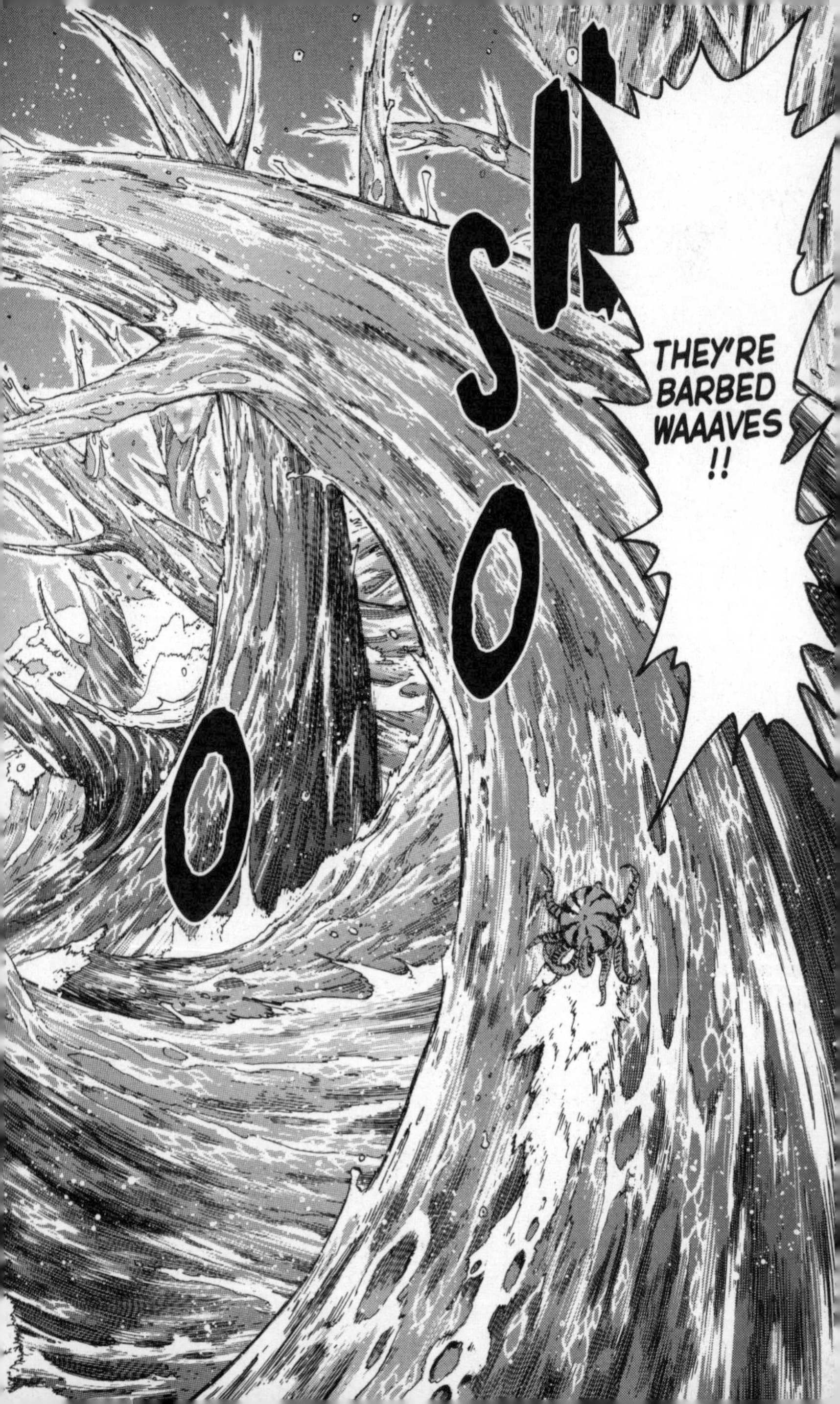
THEY'RE BARBED WAAAVES !!

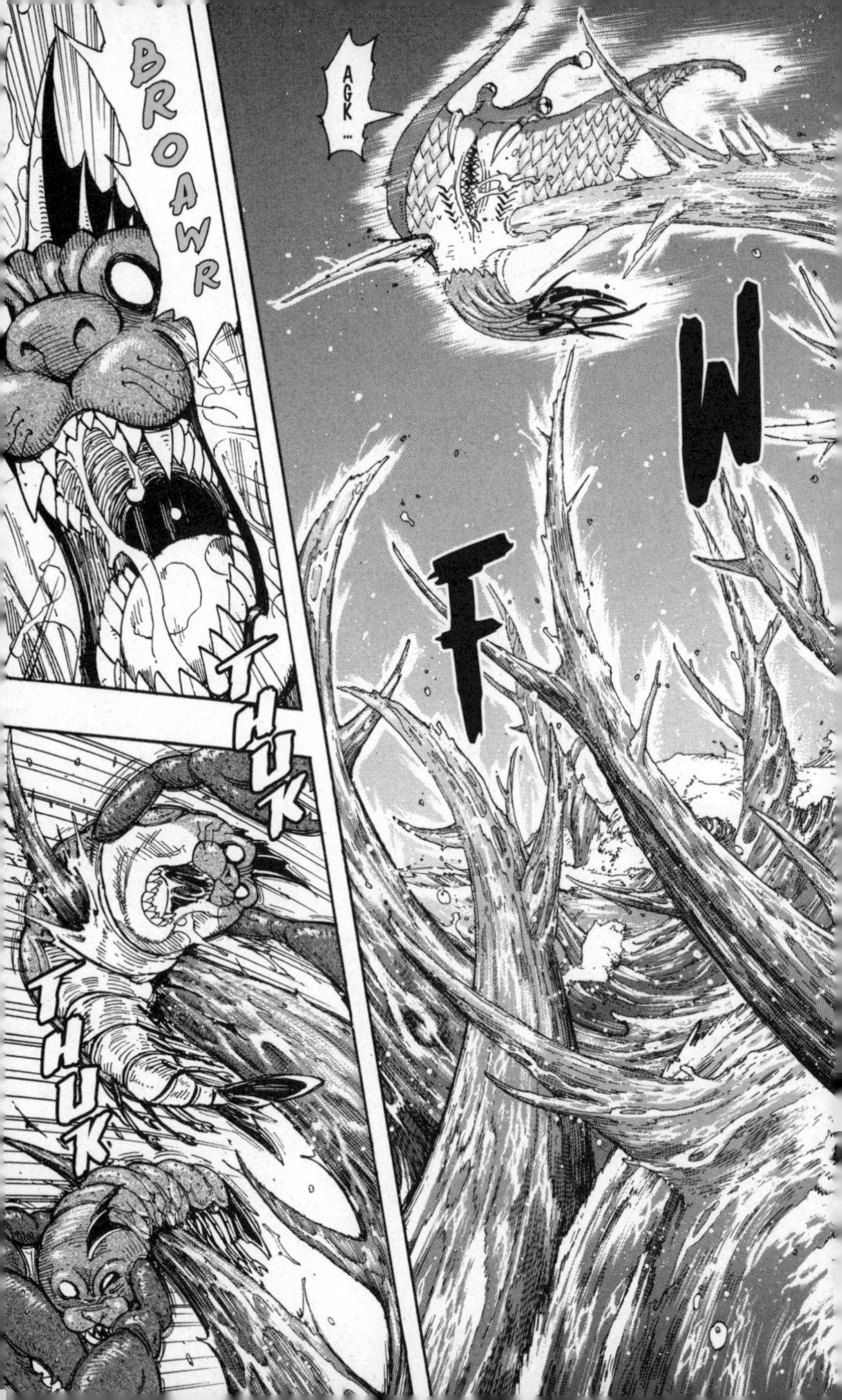

AGK...
W
F
BROAWR
THUK
THUK

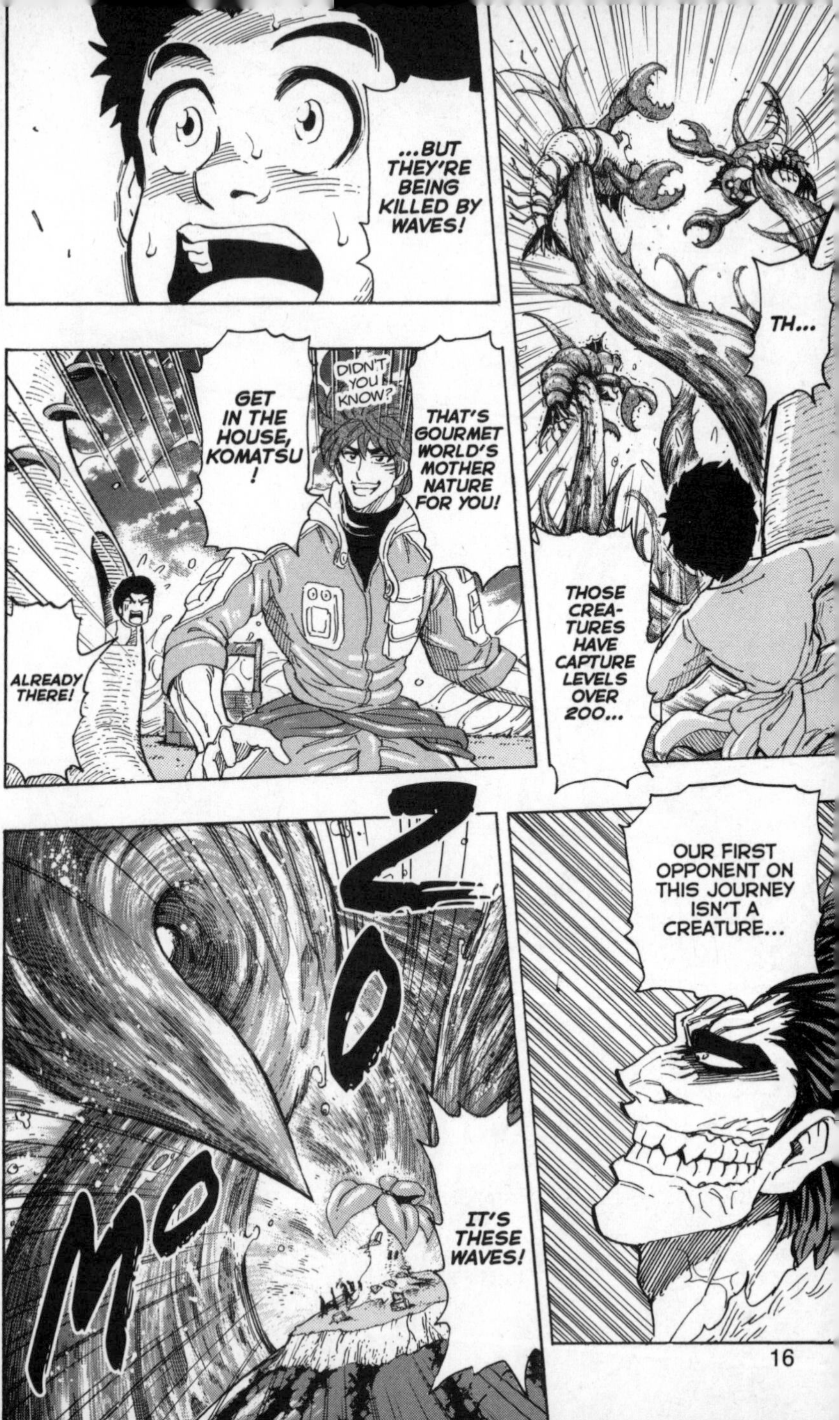
TH...
THOSE CREATURES HAVE CAPTURE LEVELS OVER 200...
...BUT THEY'RE BEING KILLED BY WAVES!
DIDN'T YOU KNOW?
THAT'S GOURMET WORLD'S MOTHER NATURE FOR YOU!
GET IN THE HOUSE, KOMATSU!
ALREADY THERE!
OUR FIRST OPPONENT ON THIS JOURNEY ISN'T A CREATURE...
ZO
MO
IT'S THESE WAVES!

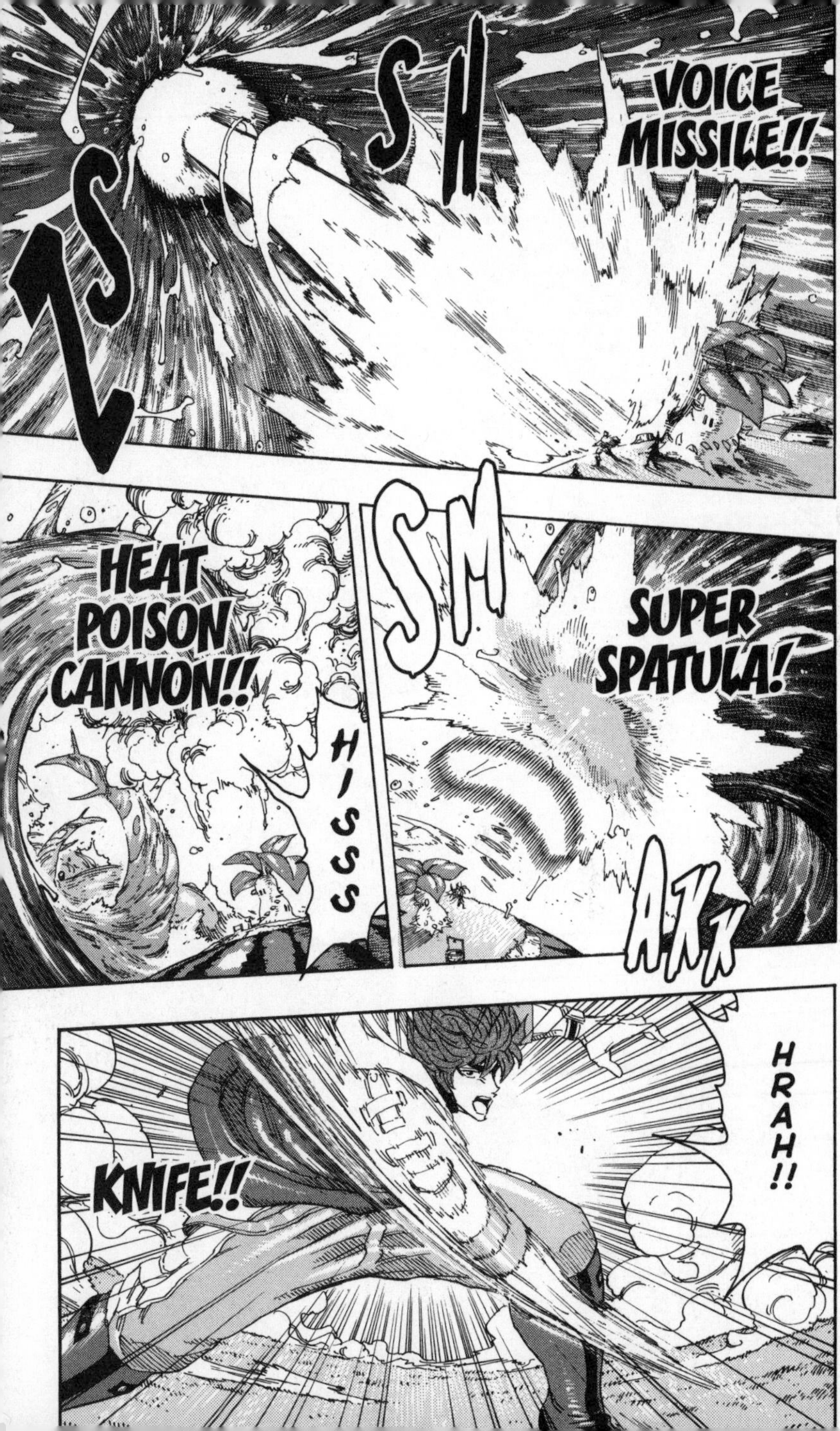

VOICE MISSILE!!
ZS
SH
SM
SUPER SPATULA!
AKK
HEAT POISON CANNON!!
HISSS
HRAH!!
KNIFE!!

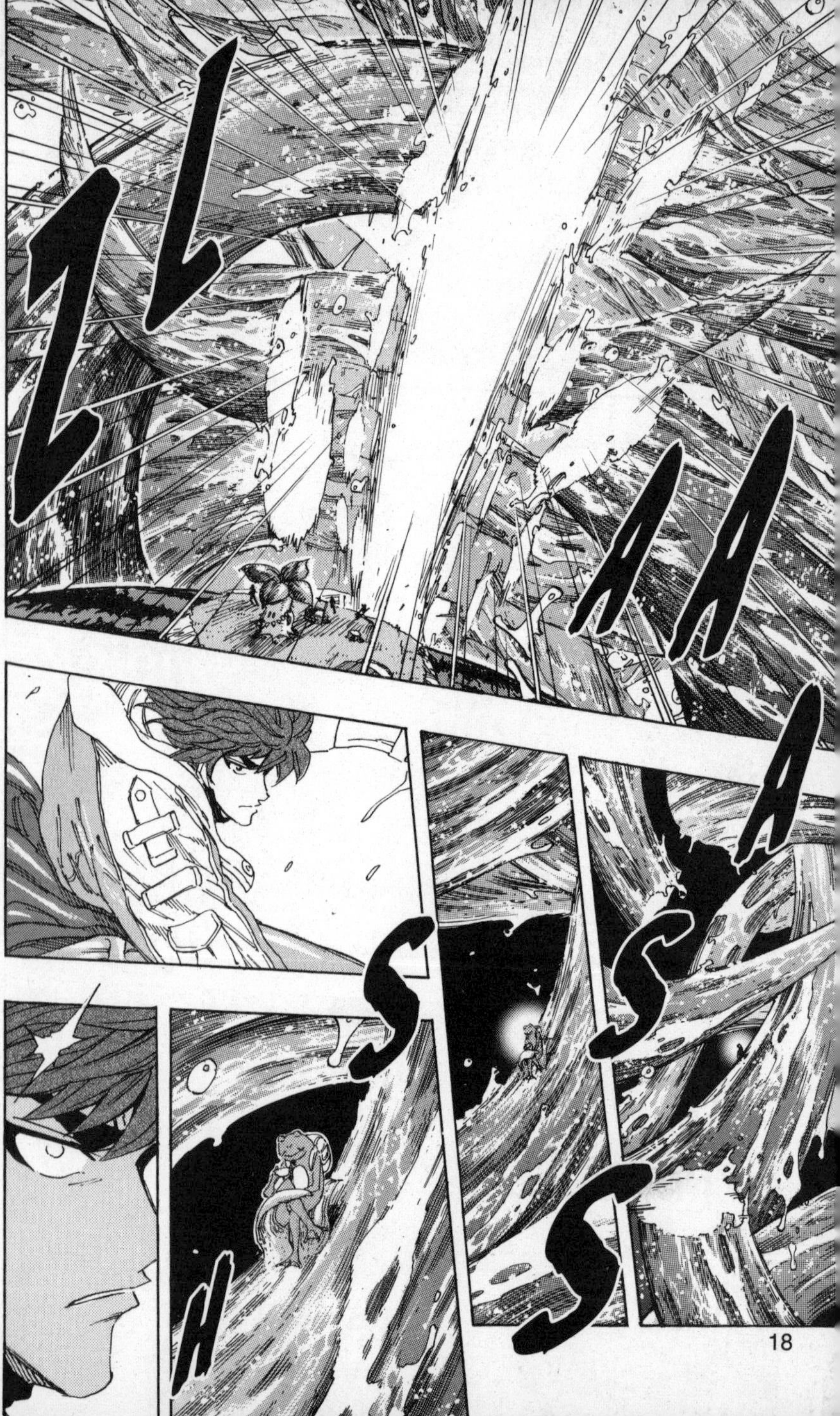
ZZAAAASSSH

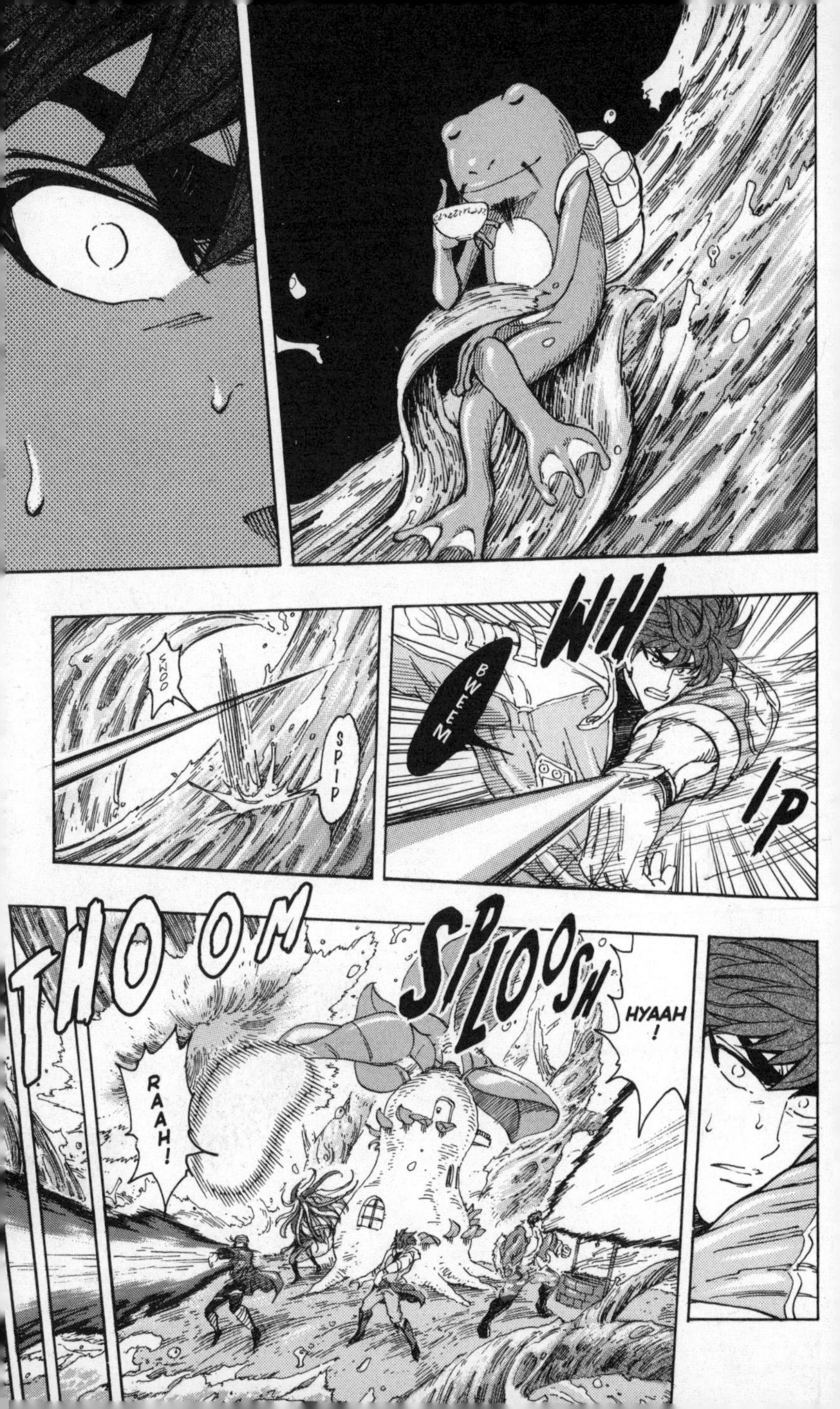
WH
IP
BWEEM
SWOO
SPIP
HYAAH!
SPLOOSH
THOOM
RAAH!

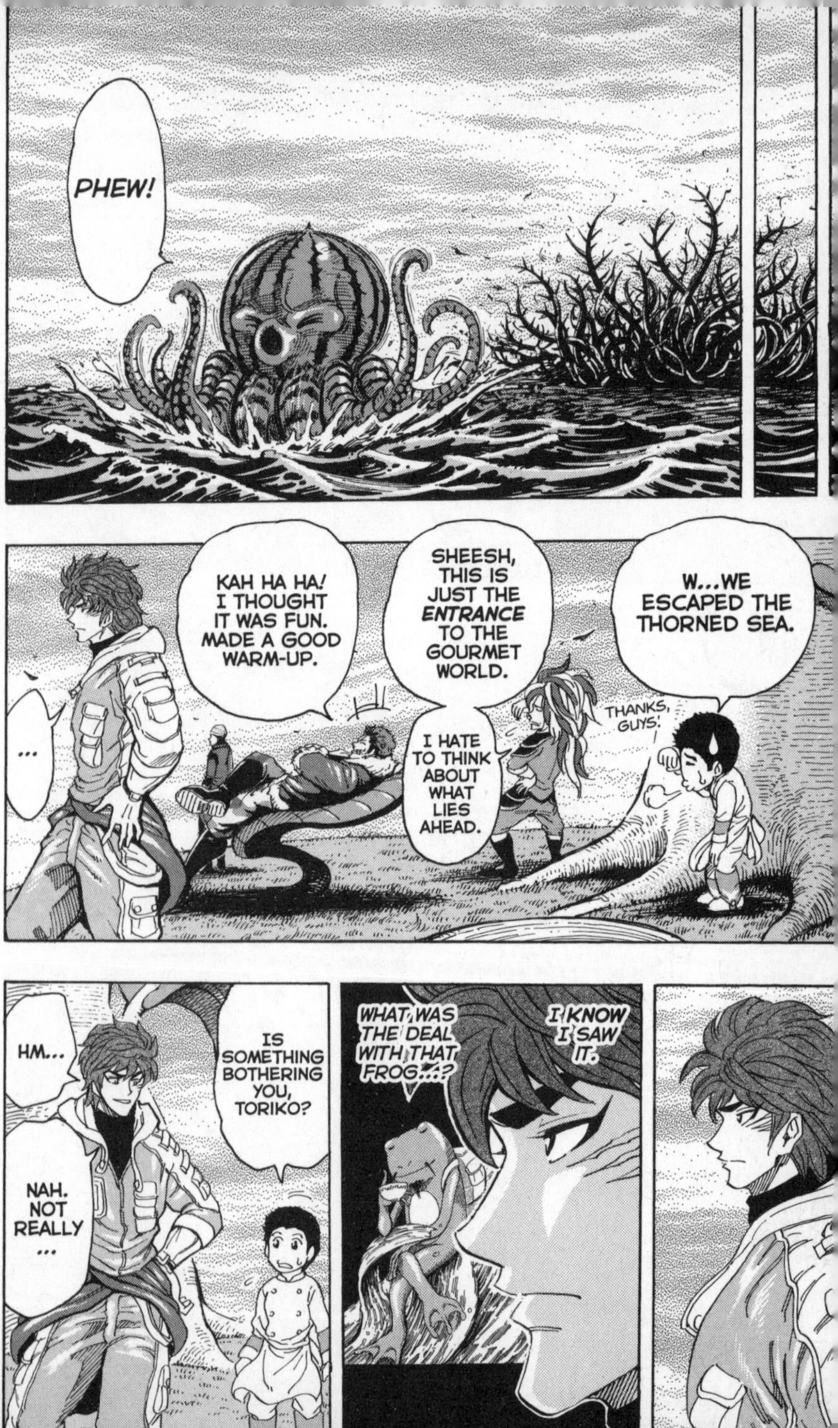
PHEW!
W...WE ESCAPED THE THORNED SEA.
THANKS, GUYS!
SHEESH, THIS IS JUST THE *ENTRANCE* TO THE GOURMET WORLD.
I HATE TO THINK ABOUT WHAT LIES AHEAD.
KAH HA HA! I THOUGHT IT WAS FUN. MADE A GOOD WARM-UP.
...
I KNOW I SAW IT.
WHAT WAS THE DEAL WITH THAT FROG...?
IS SOMETHING BOTHERING YOU, TORIKO?
HM...
NAH. NOT REALLY ...

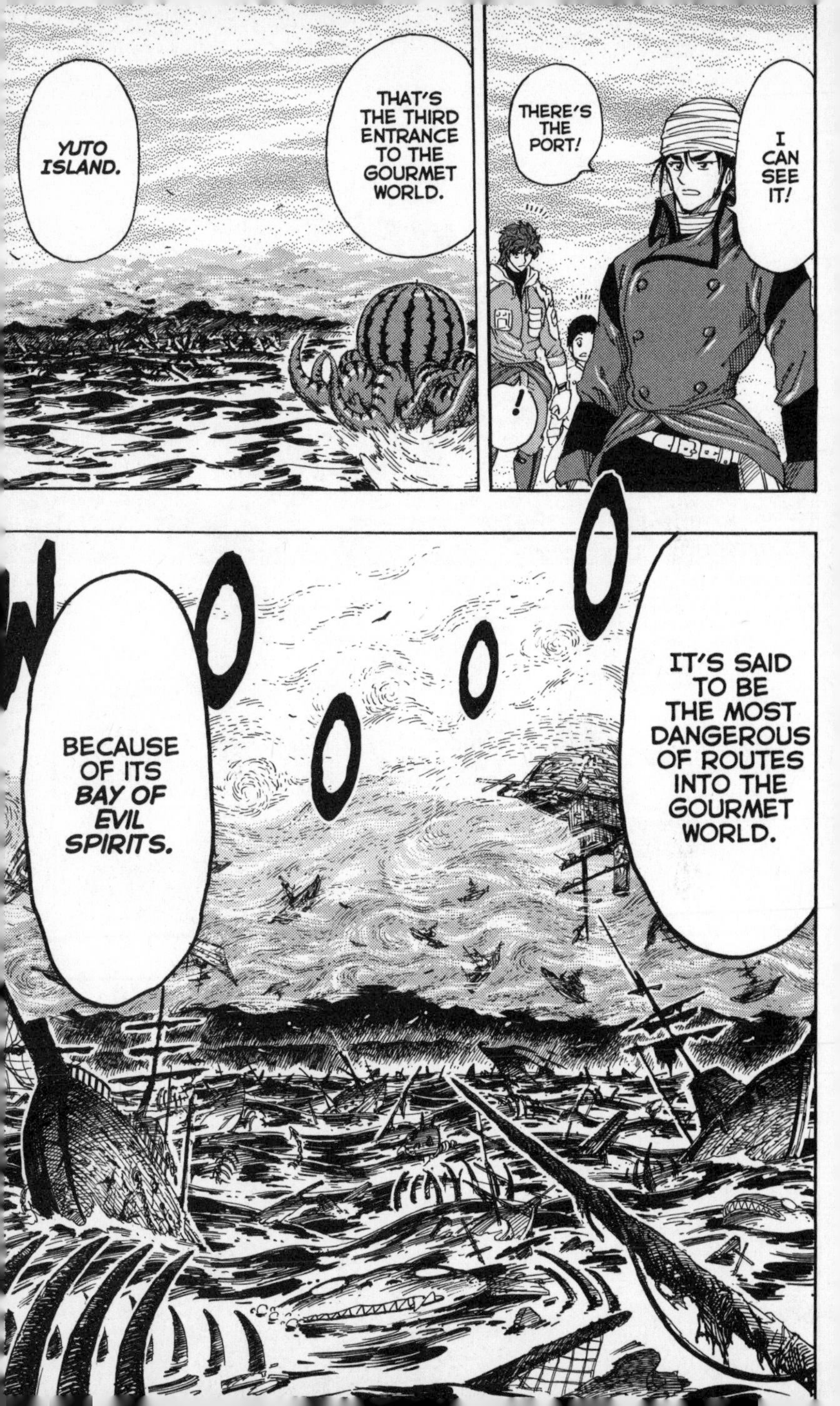
I CAN SEE IT!
THERE'S THE PORT!
!
THAT'S THE THIRD ENTRANCE TO THE GOURMET WORLD.
YUTO ISLAND.
IT'S SAID TO BE THE MOST DANGEROUS OF ROUTES INTO THE GOURMET WORLD.
WOOOO
BECAUSE OF ITS *BAY OF EVIL SPIRITS.*

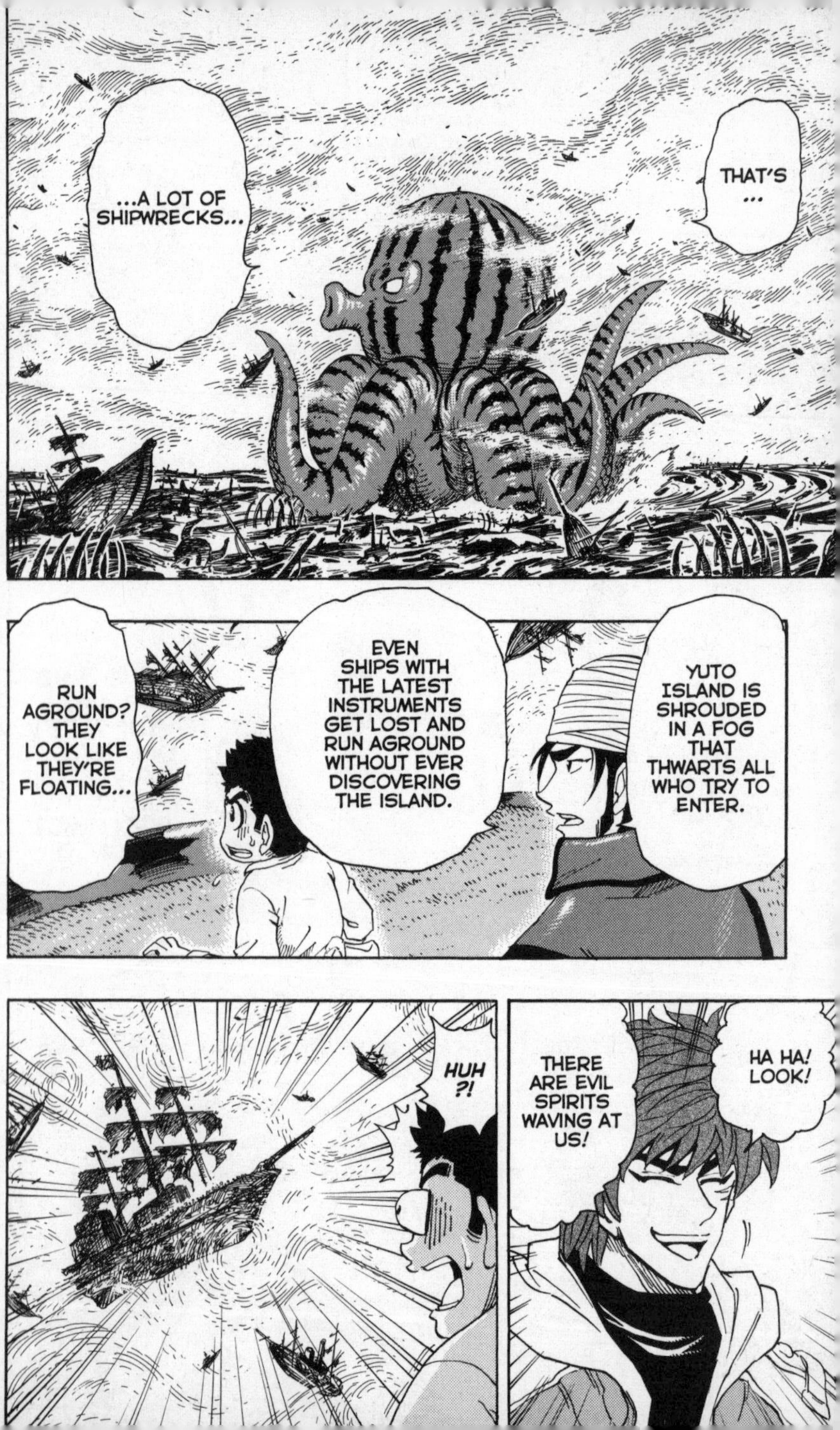
THAT'S ...
...A LOT OF SHIPWRECKS...
YUTO ISLAND IS SHROUDED IN A FOG THAT THWARTS ALL WHO TRY TO ENTER.
EVEN SHIPS WITH THE LATEST INSTRUMENTS GET LOST AND RUN AGROUND WITHOUT EVER DISCOVERING THE ISLAND.
RUN AGROUND? THEY LOOK LIKE THEY'RE FLOATING...
HA HA! LOOK!
THERE ARE EVIL SPIRITS WAVING AT US!
HUH ?!

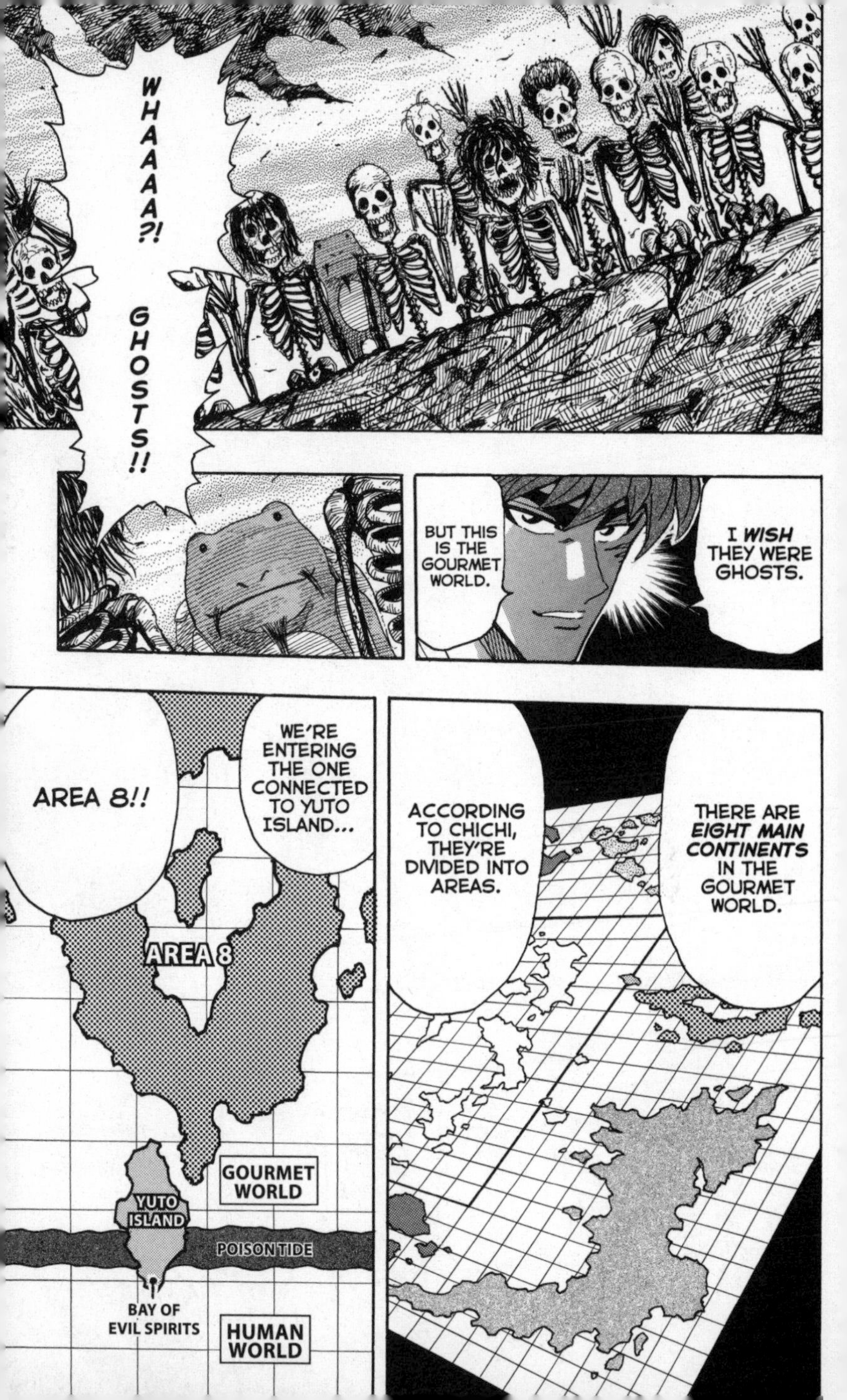
WHAAAAA?!
GHOSTS!!
I *WISH* THEY WERE GHOSTS.
BUT THIS IS THE GOURMET WORLD.
THERE ARE *EIGHT MAIN CONTINENTS* IN THE GOURMET WORLD.
ACCORDING TO CHICHI, THEY'RE DIVIDED INTO AREAS.
WE'RE ENTERING THE ONE CONNECTED TO YUTO ISLAND...
AREA 8!!
AREA 8
GOURMET WORLD
YUTO ISLAND
POISON TIDE
BAY OF EVIL SPIRITS
HUMAN WORLD

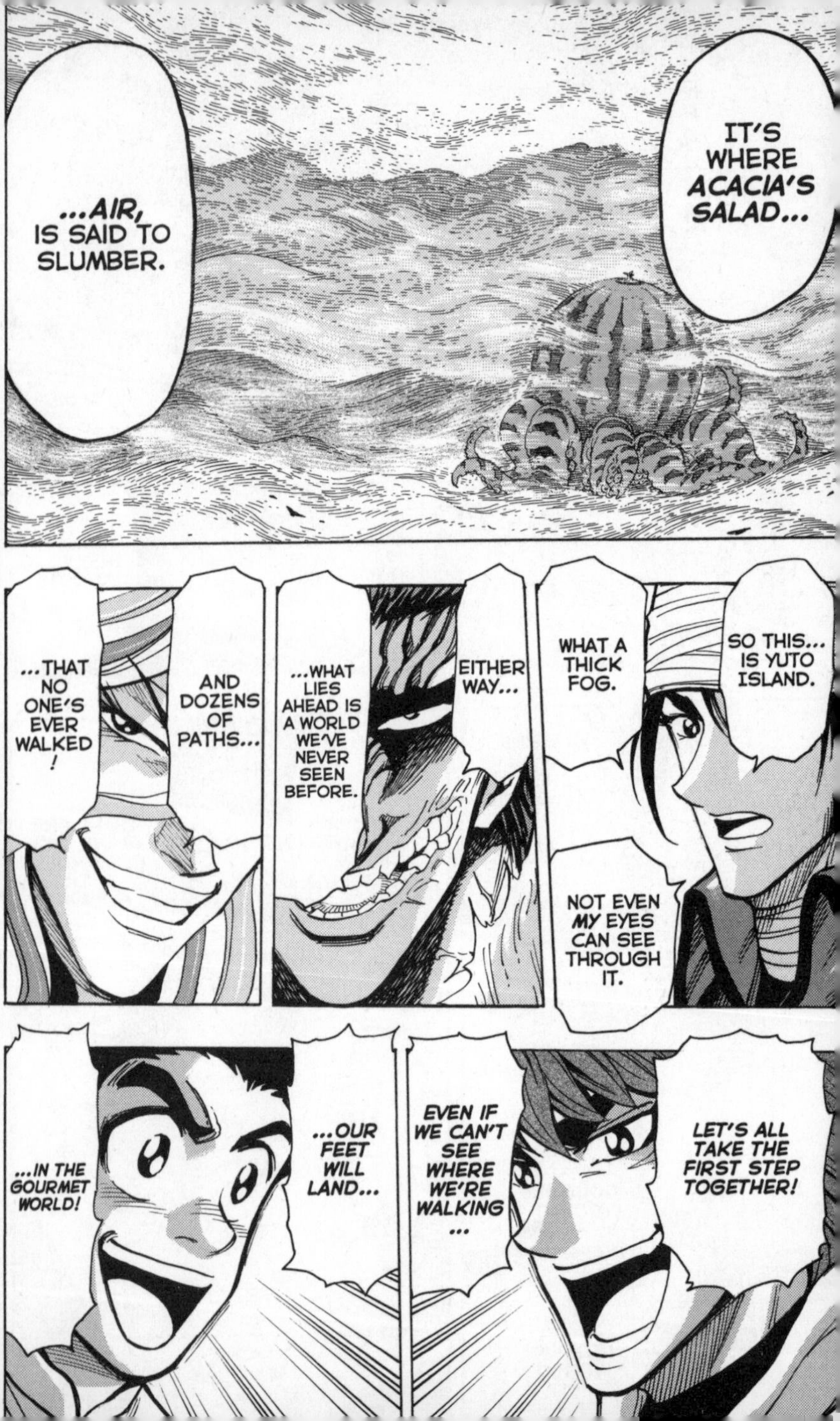
IT'S WHERE ACACIA'S SALAD...
...AIR, IS SAID TO SLUMBER.
SO THIS... IS YUTO ISLAND.
WHAT A THICK FOG.
NOT EVEN MY EYES CAN SEE THROUGH IT.
EITHER WAY...
...WHAT LIES AHEAD IS A WORLD WE'VE NEVER SEEN BEFORE.
AND DOZENS OF PATHS...
...THAT NO ONE'S EVER WALKED!
LET'S ALL TAKE THE FIRST STEP TOGETHER!
EVEN IF WE CAN'T SEE WHERE WE'RE WALKING...
...OUR FEET WILL LAND...
...IN THE GOURMET WORLD!

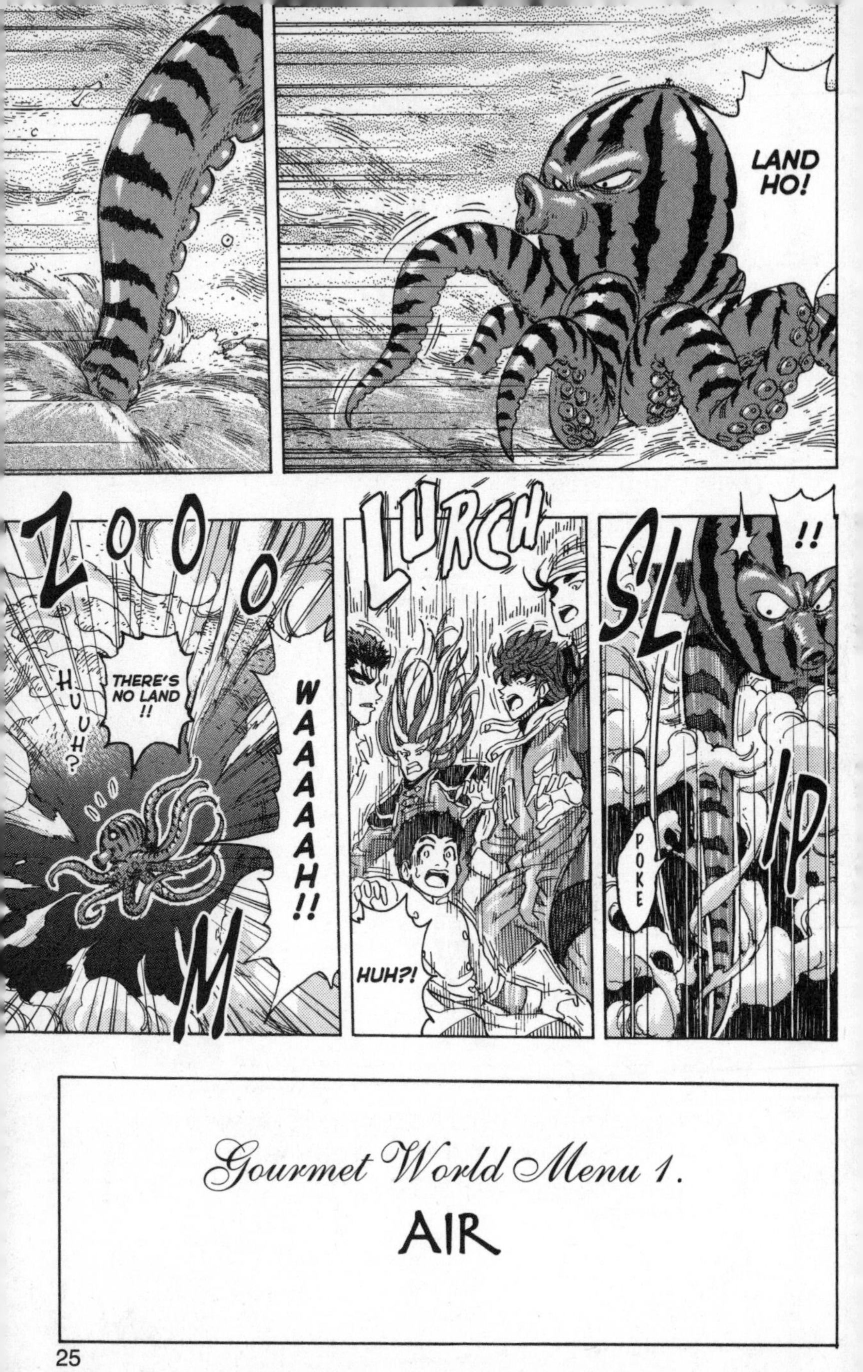
LAND HO!
!!
SLIP
POKE
LURCH
HUH?!
ZOOOM
WAAAAAAAH!!
THERE'S NO LAND !!
HUUUH?

Gourmet World Menu 1.
AIR

TORIKO

GOURMET CHECKLIST

Vol. 297

WEINER EGGPLANT
(VEGETABLE)

CAPTURE LEVEL: LESS THAN 1
HABITAT: WIDESPREAD
SIZE: 30 CM
HEIGHT: ---
WEIGHT: 1.5 KG
PRICE: 700 YEN PER EGGPLANT

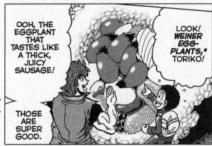

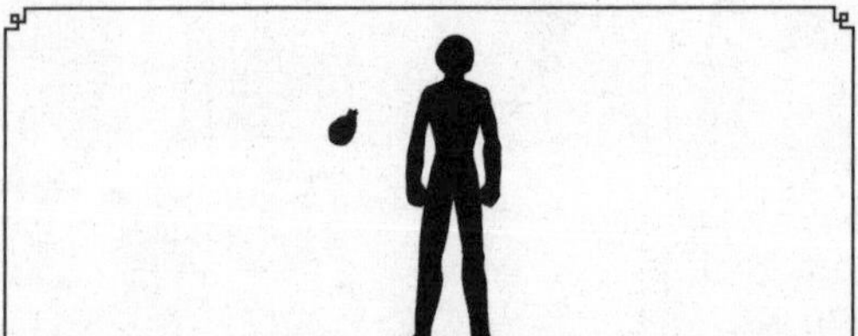

LOOK! WEINER EGG-PLANTS,* TORIKO!
OOH, THE EGGPLANT THAT TASTES LIKE A THICK, JUICY SAUSAGE!
THOSE ARE SUPER GOOD.

SCALE

AN EGGPLANT THAT TASTES JUST LIKE A THICK, JUICY SAUSAGE. WHEN SAUTEED, IT HAS A DELECTABLE CRUNCHY TEXTURE THAT HAS ONE BEGGING FOR MORE. IT IS ONE OF THE INGREDIENTS REQUIRED TO MAKE MONCHY'S FORTUNE ROLL FOR FINDING THE CHOWLIN TEMPLE.

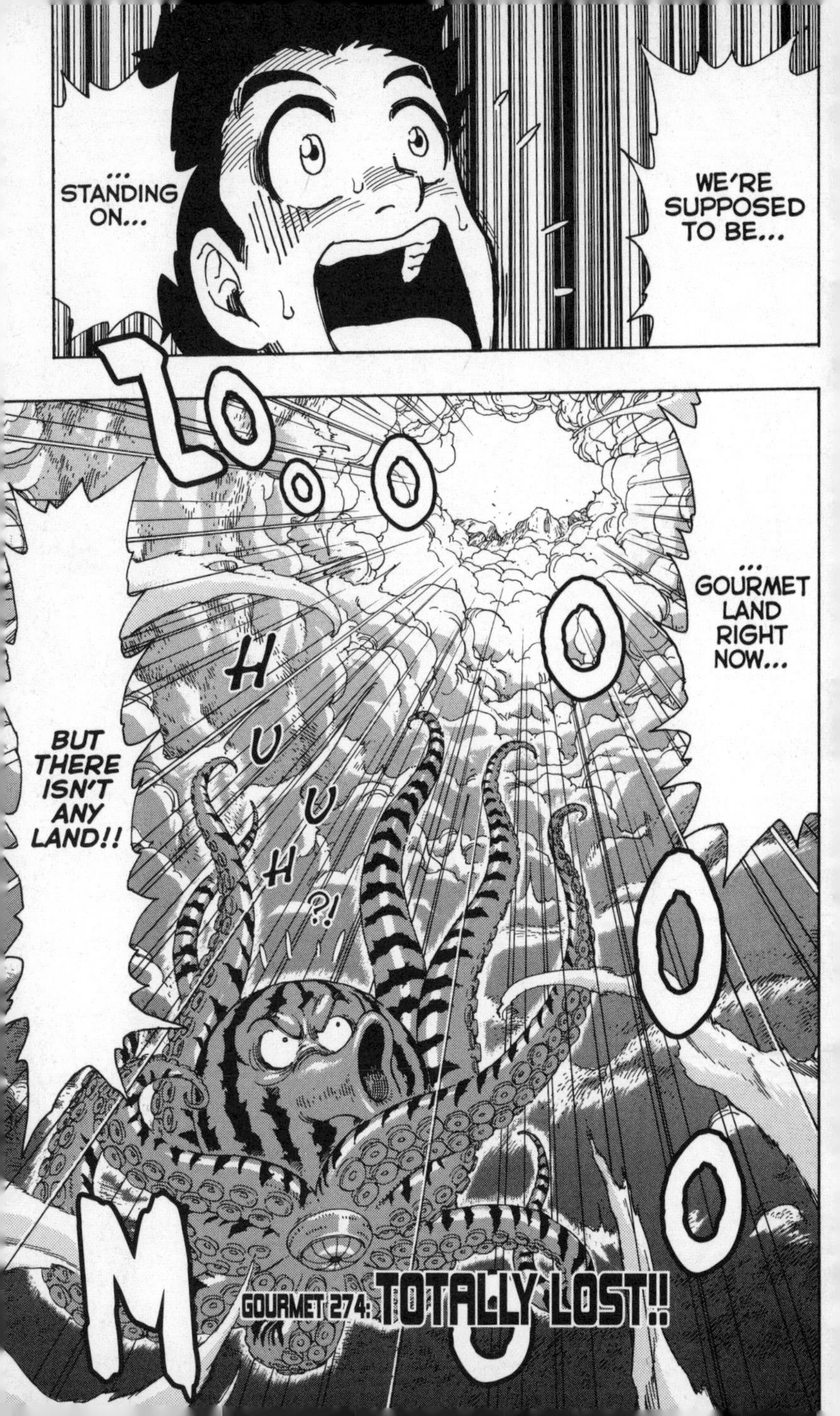
WE'RE SUPPOSED TO BE...
...STANDING ON...
...GOURMET LAND RIGHT NOW...
BUT THERE ISN'T ANY LAND!!
LOOOOOOOM
HUUH?!
GOURMET 274: TOTALLY LOST!!

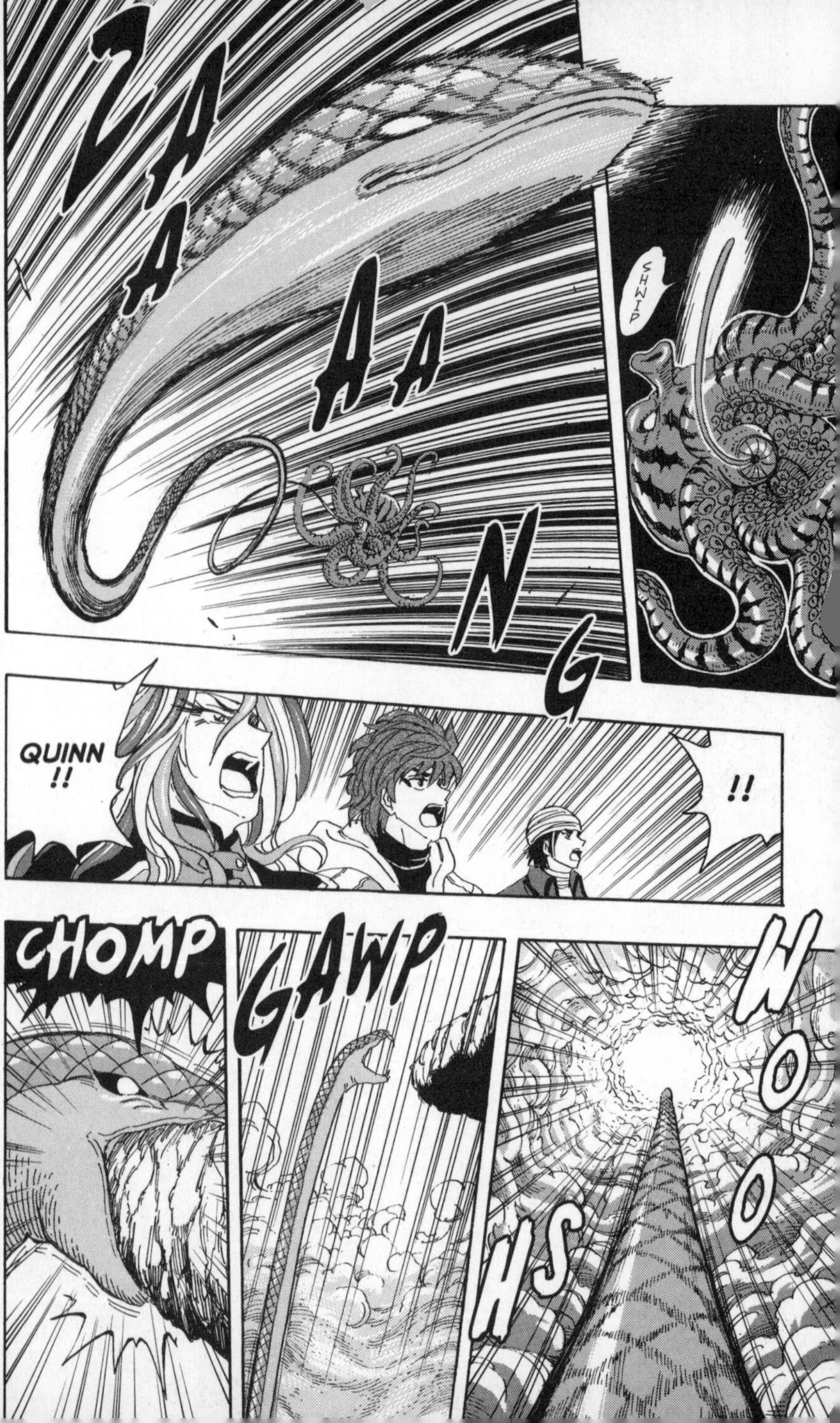
SHWIP
ZAAAAANG
!!
QUINN !!
WOOOSH
GAWP
CHOMP

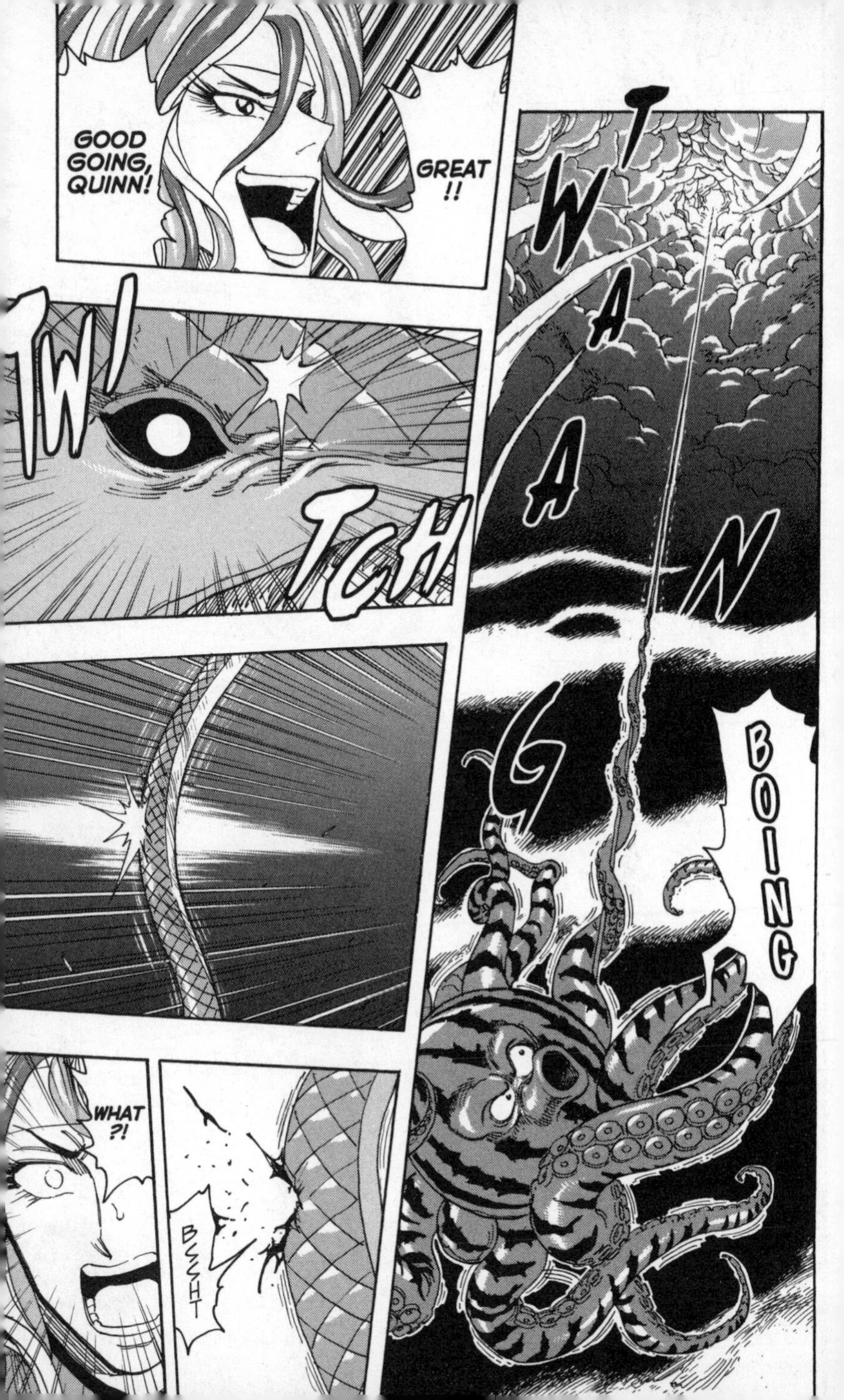
GREAT!!
GOOD GOING, QUINN!
TWANG
BOING
TWITCH
BSSHT
WHAT?!

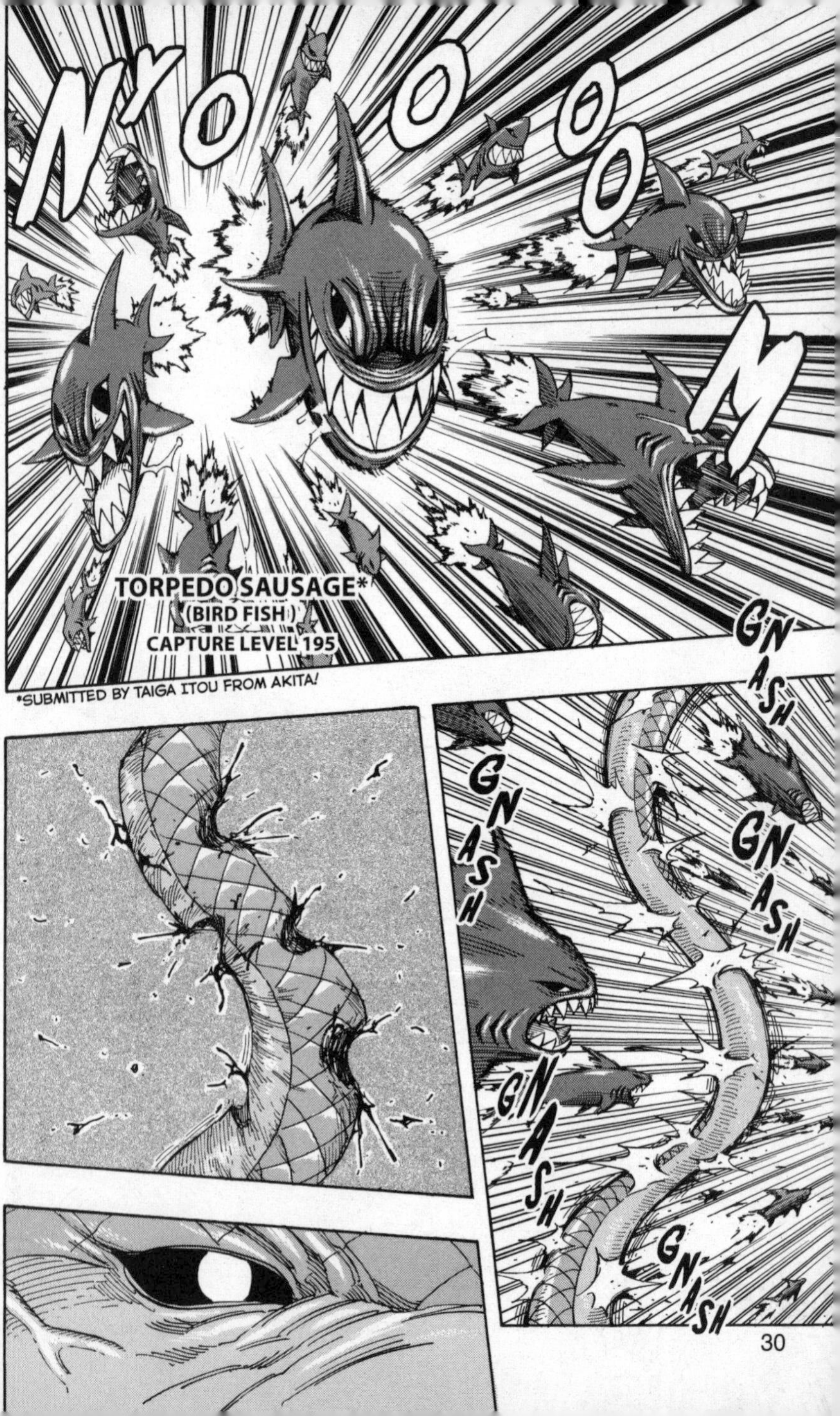
NYOOOOOM
TORPEDO SAUSAGE*
(BIRD FISH)
CAPTURE LEVEL 195
*SUBMITTED BY TAIGA ITOU FROM AKITA!
GNASH
GNASH
GNASH
GNASH
GNASH

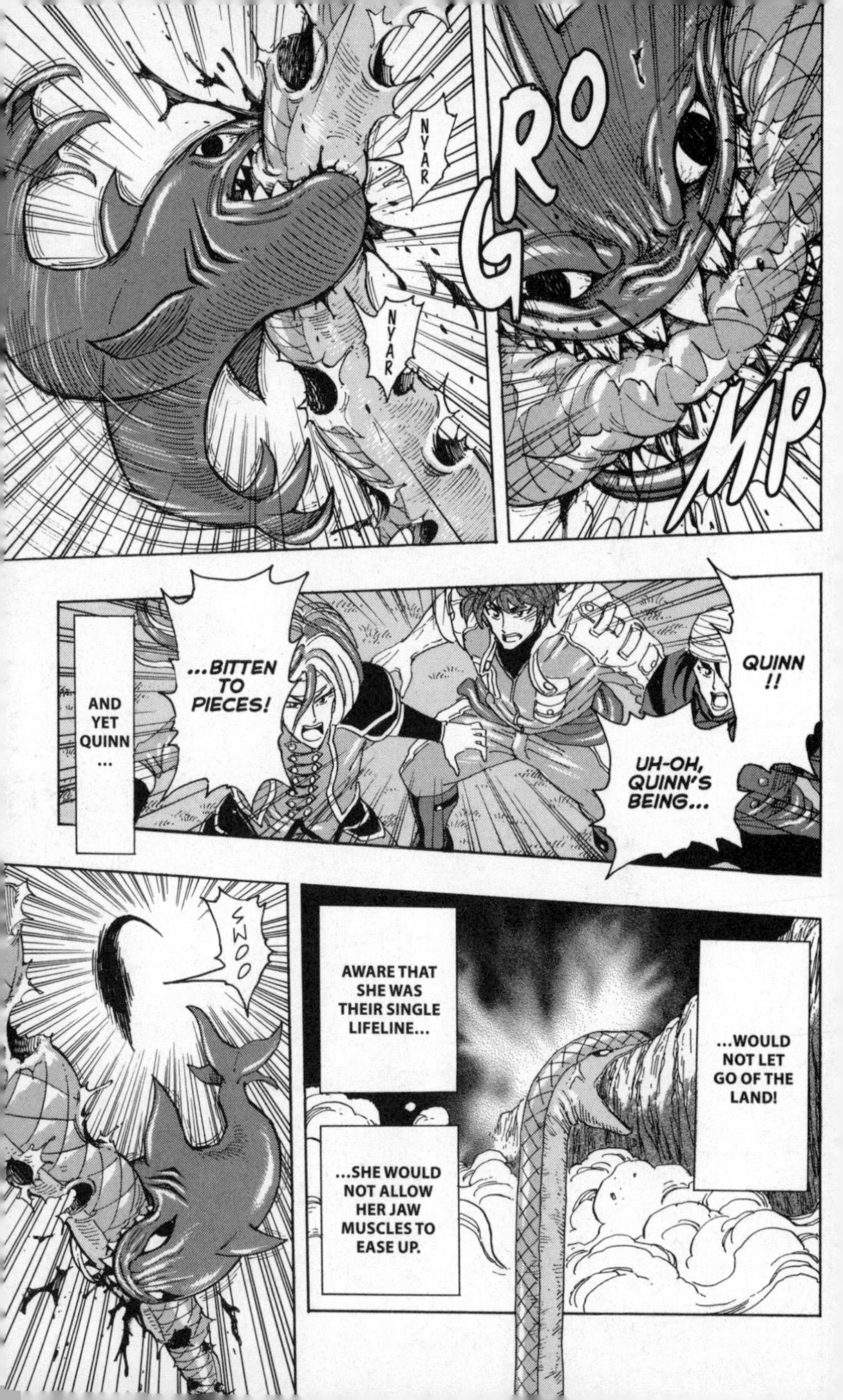
GRO
MP
NYAR
NYAR
QUINN!!
UH-OH, QUINN'S BEING...
...BITTEN TO PIECES!
AND YET QUINN...
...WOULD NOT LET GO OF THE LAND!
AWARE THAT SHE WAS THEIR SINGLE LIFELINE...
...SHE WOULD NOT ALLOW HER JAW MUSCLES TO EASE UP.
SWOO

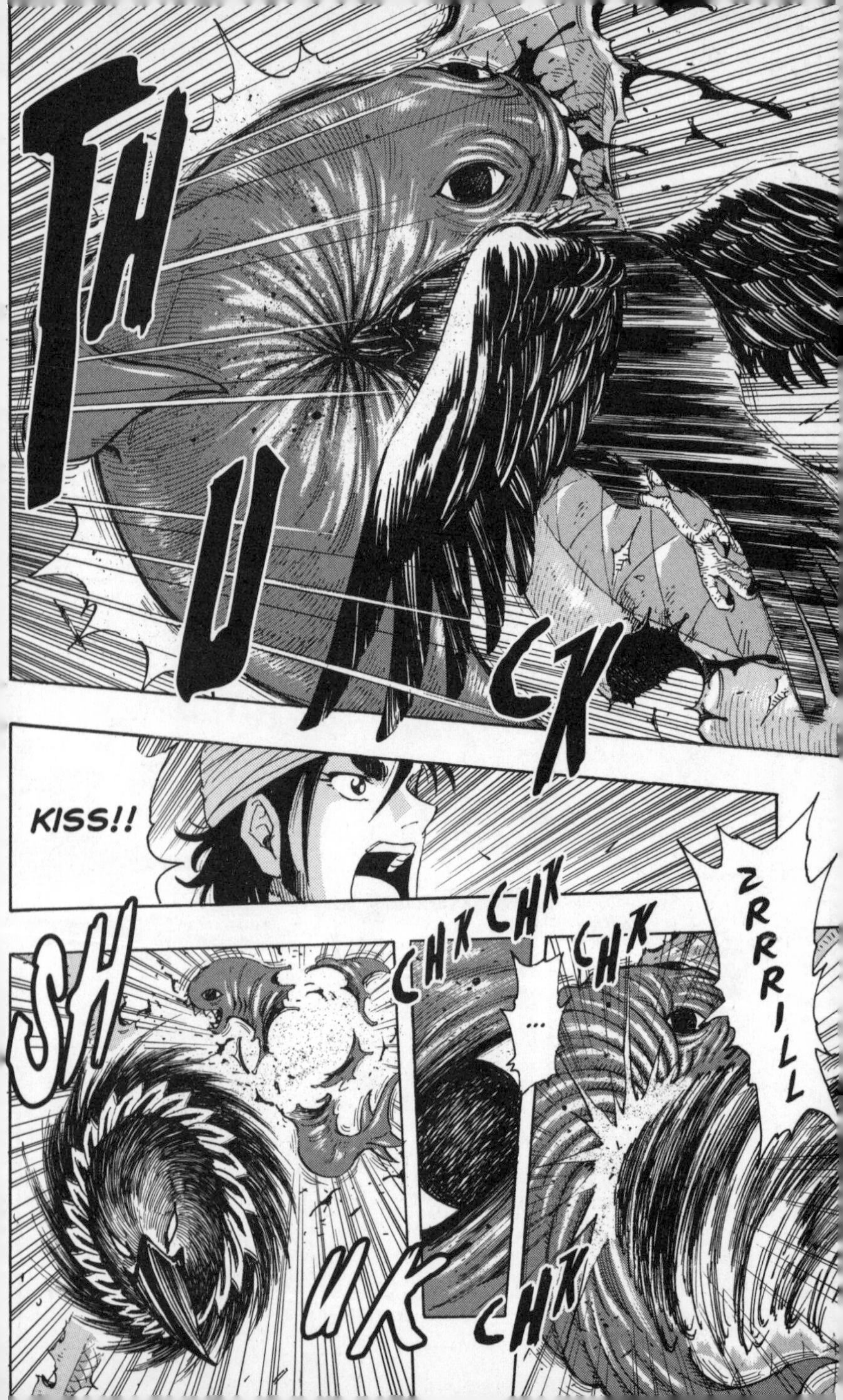
THUNCK
KISS!!
ZRRRILLL
CHK
CHKCHK
...
SHUK
CHK

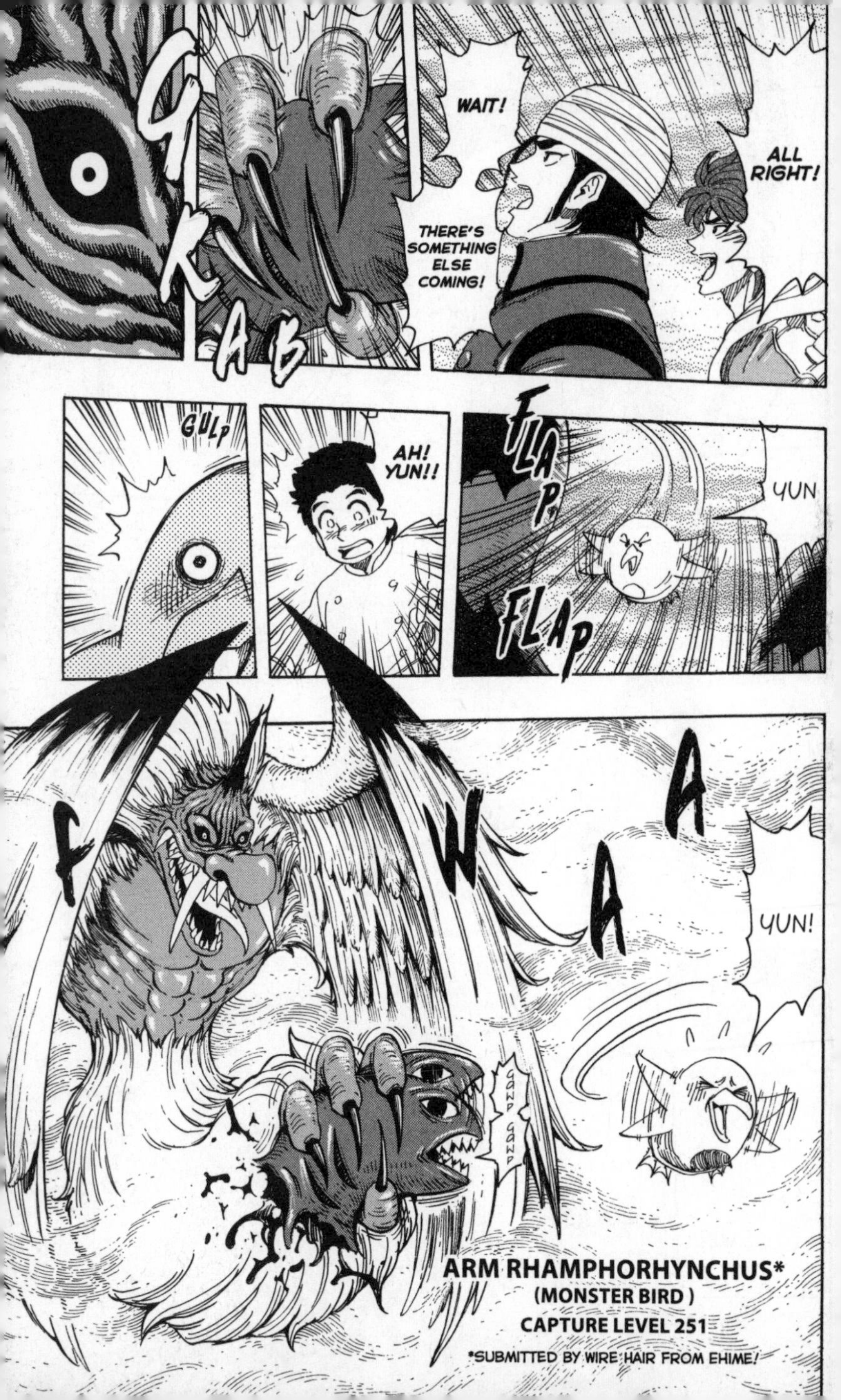

WAIT!
THERE'S SOMETHING ELSE COMING!
ALL RIGHT!
GRAB
YUN
FLAP
FLAP
AH! YUN!!
GULP
YUN!
FWAAA
GONP GONP
ARM RHAMPHORHYNCHUS*
(MONSTER BIRD)
CAPTURE LEVEL 251
*SUBMITTED BY WIRE HAIR FROM EHIME!

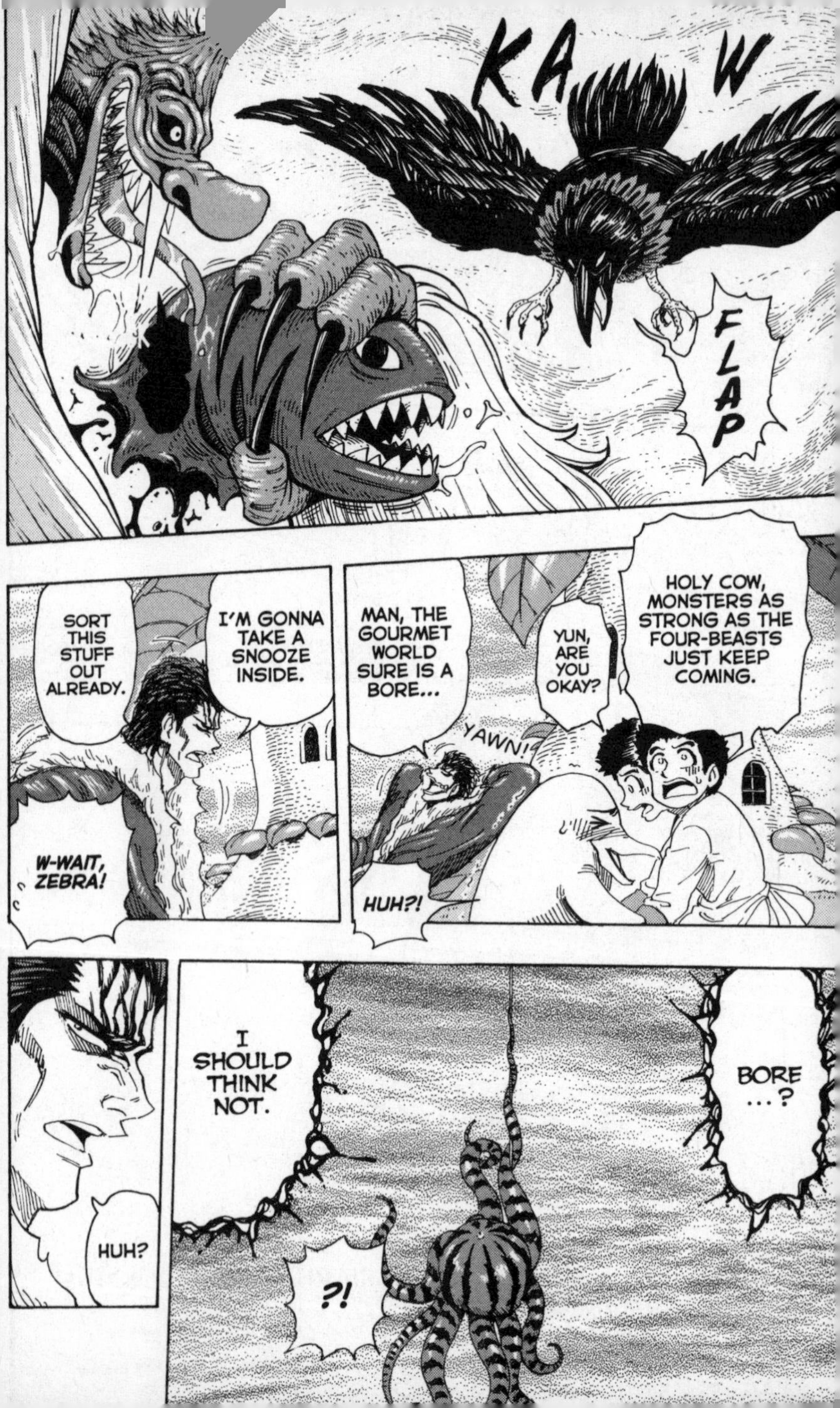
KAW
FLAP
HOLY COW, MONSTERS AS STRONG AS THE FOUR-BEASTS JUST KEEP COMING.
YUN, ARE YOU OKAY?
MAN, THE GOURMET WORLD SURE IS A BORE...
YAWN!
HUH?!
I'M GONNA TAKE A SNOOZE INSIDE.
SORT THIS STUFF OUT ALREADY.
W-WAIT, ZEBRA!
BORE ...?
I SHOULD THINK NOT.
?!
HUH?

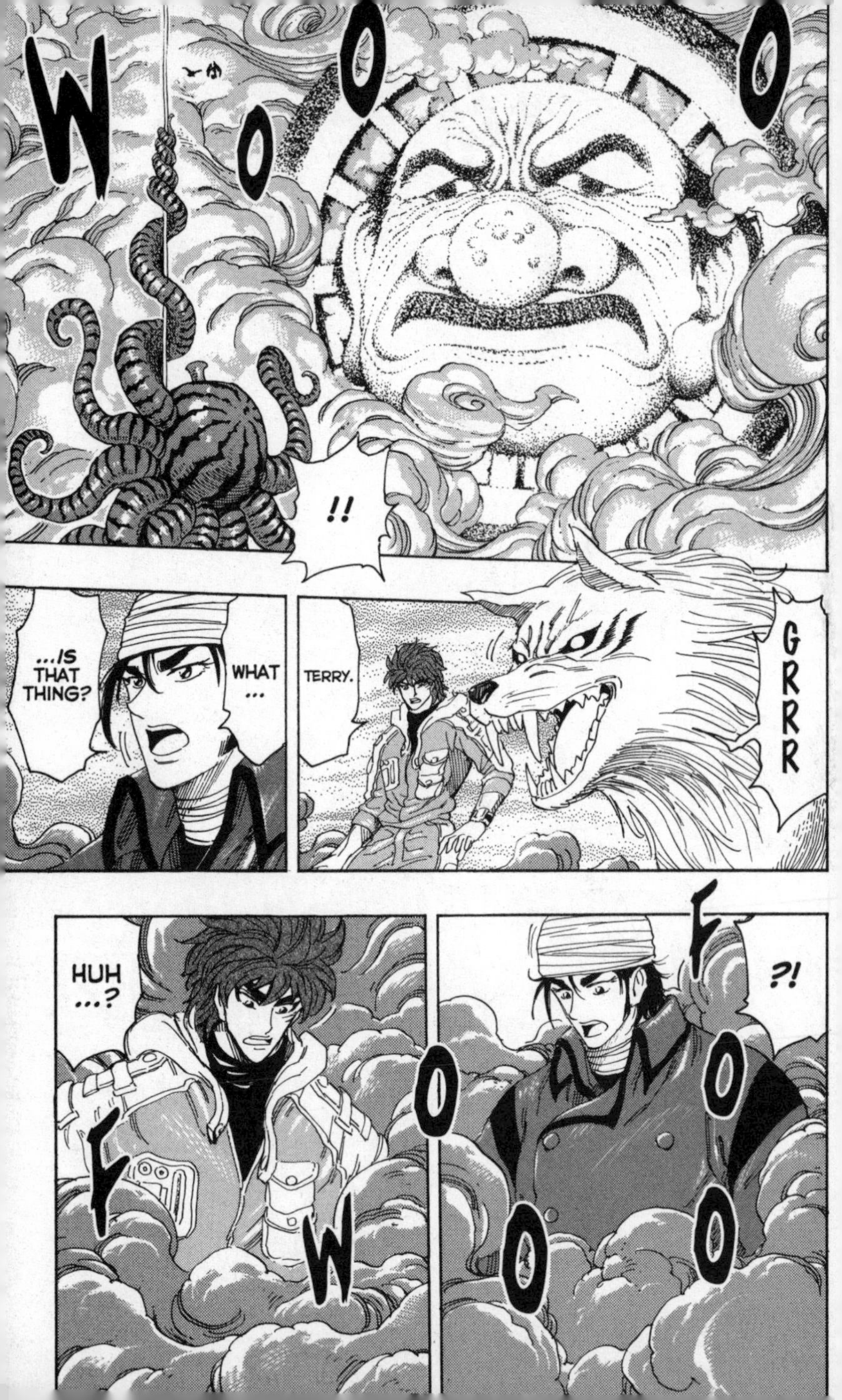
WOOOO
!!
GRRR
TERRY.
WHAT ...
...IS THAT THING?
?!
HUH ...?
FWOOOOF

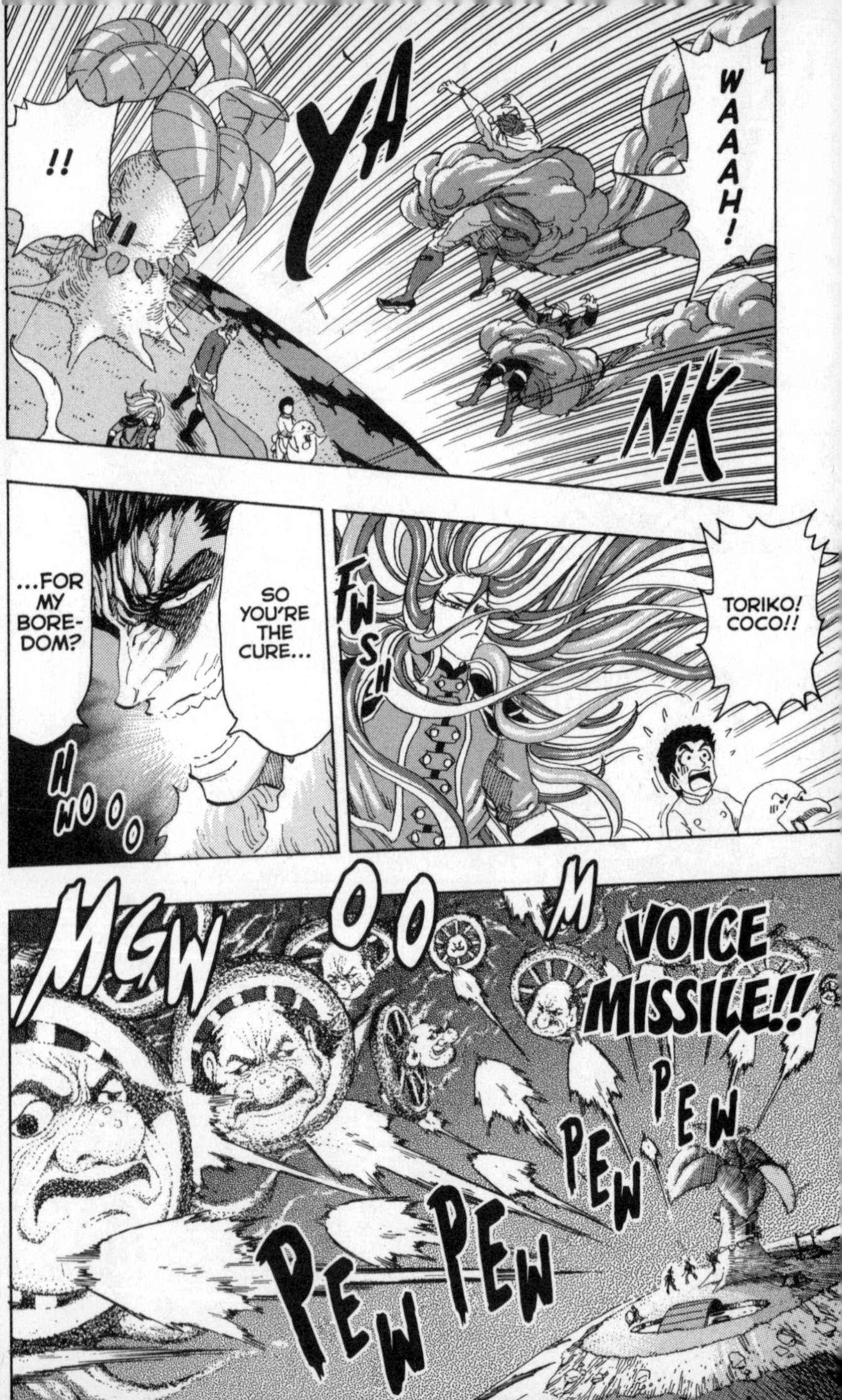
WAAAAH!
YA
NK
!!
TORIKO! COCO!!
FWSSH
SO YOU'RE THE CURE...
...FOR MY BORE-DOM?
HWOOO
MGWOOOM
VOICE MISSILE!!
PEW PEW
PEW PEW
PEW PEW

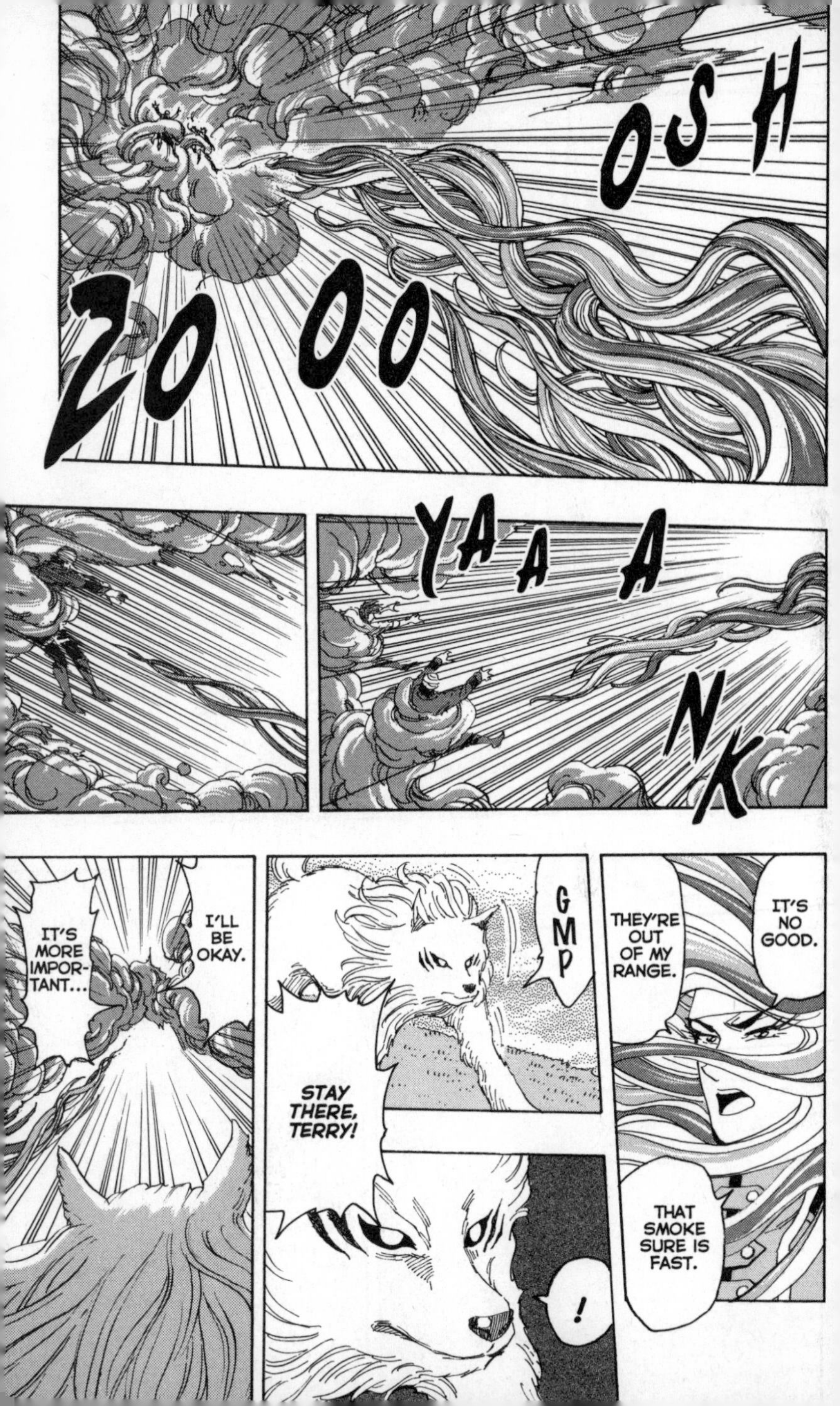
ZOOOOSH
YAAANK
IT'S NO GOOD.
THEY'RE OUT OF MY RANGE.
THAT SMOKE SURE IS FAST.
GMP
STAY THERE, TERRY!
!
I'LL BE OKAY.
IT'S MORE IMPOR-TANT...

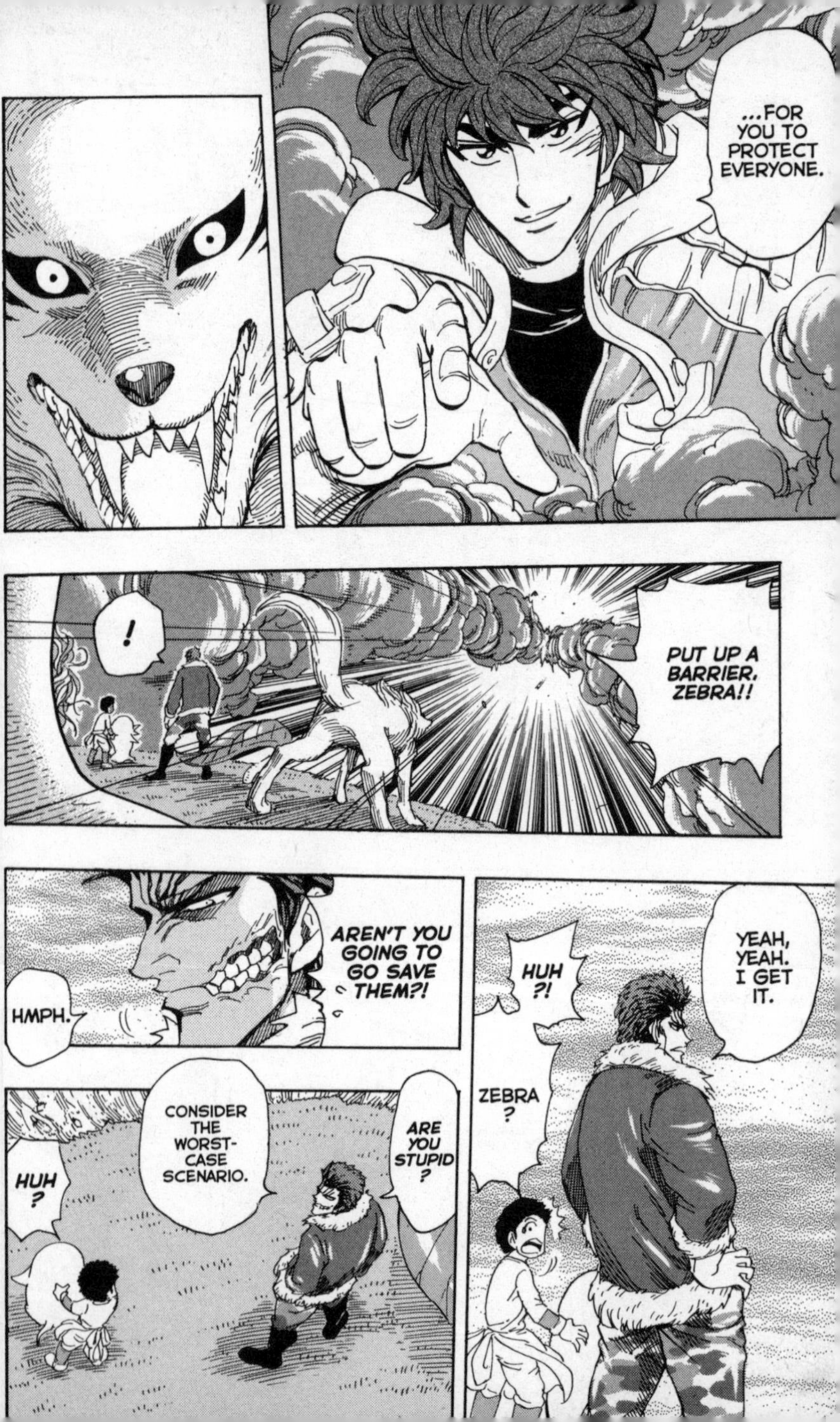
...FOR YOU TO PROTECT EVERYONE.
PUT UP A BARRIER, ZEBRA!!
!
YEAH, YEAH. I GET IT.
HUH ?!
ZEBRA ?
AREN'T YOU GOING TO GO SAVE THEM?!
HMPH.
ARE YOU STUPID ?
CONSIDER THE WORST-CASE SCENARIO.
HUH ?

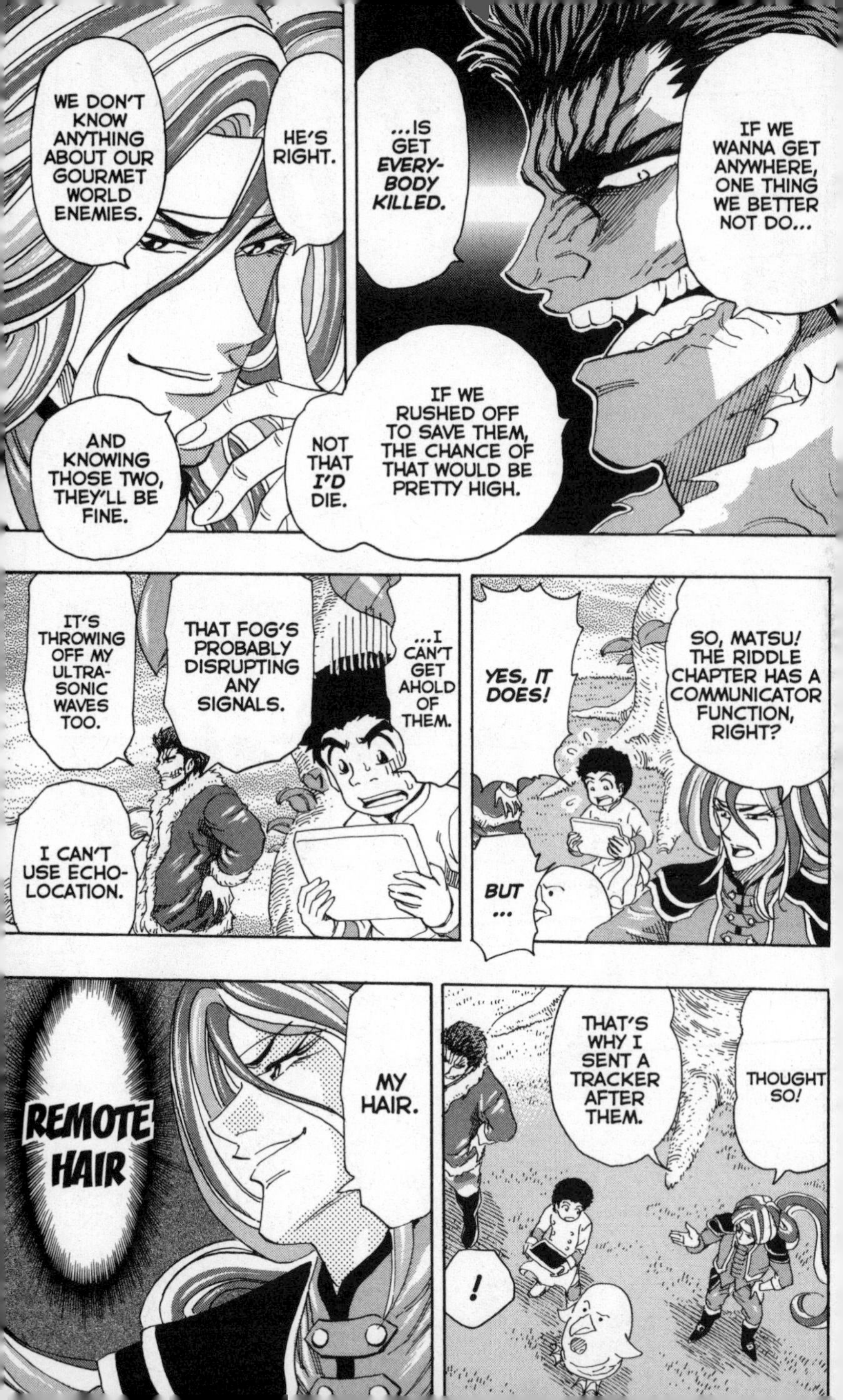
IF WE WANNA GET ANYWHERE, ONE THING WE BETTER NOT DO...
...IS GET *EVERYBODY KILLED.*
IF WE RUSHED OFF TO SAVE THEM, THE CHANCE OF THAT WOULD BE PRETTY HIGH.
NOT THAT *I'D* DIE.
HE'S RIGHT.
WE DON'T KNOW ANYTHING ABOUT OUR GOURMET WORLD ENEMIES.
AND KNOWING THOSE TWO, THEY'LL BE FINE.
SO, MATSU! THE RIDDLE CHAPTER HAS A COMMUNICATOR FUNCTION, RIGHT?
YES, IT DOES!
BUT ...
...I CAN'T GET AHOLD OF THEM.
THAT FOG'S PROBABLY DISRUPTING ANY SIGNALS.
IT'S THROWING OFF MY ULTRA-SONIC WAVES TOO.
I CAN'T USE ECHO-LOCATION.
THOUGHT SO!
THAT'S WHY I SENT A TRACKER AFTER THEM.
!
MY HAIR.
REMOTE HAIR

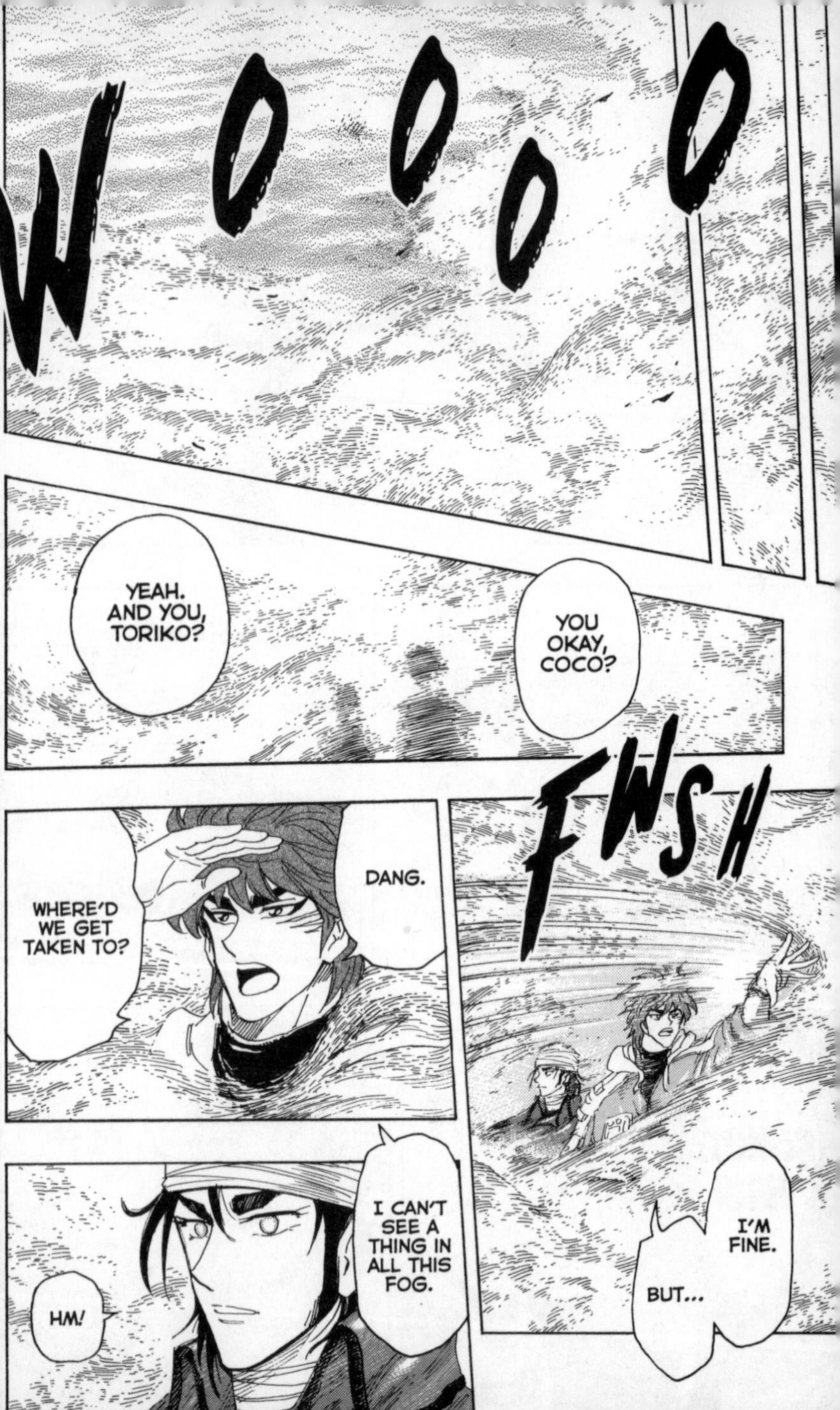
WOOOOO
YOU OKAY, COCO?
YEAH. AND YOU, TORIKO?
FWSH
I'M FINE.
BUT...
DANG.
WHERE'D WE GET TAKEN TO?
I CAN'T SEE A THING IN ALL THIS FOG.
HM!

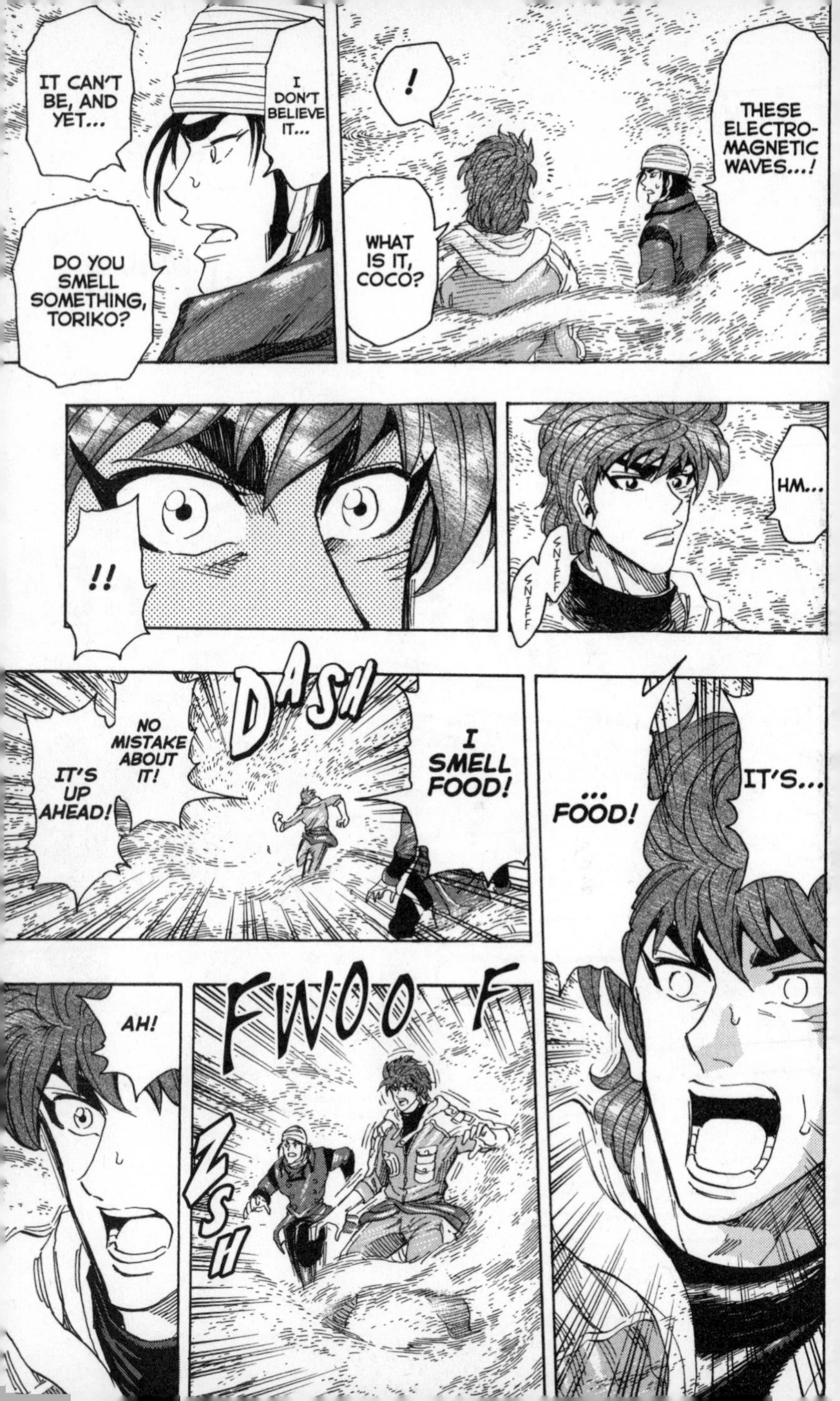
THESE ELECTRO-MAGNETIC WAVES...!
!
WHAT IS IT, COCO?
I DON'T BELIEVE IT...
IT CAN'T BE, AND YET...
DO YOU SMELL SOMETHING, TORIKO?
HM...
SNIFF SNIFF
!!
IT'S...
...FOOD!
I SMELL FOOD!
DASH
NO MISTAKE ABOUT IT!
IT'S UP AHEAD!
FWOOF
WHSH
AH!

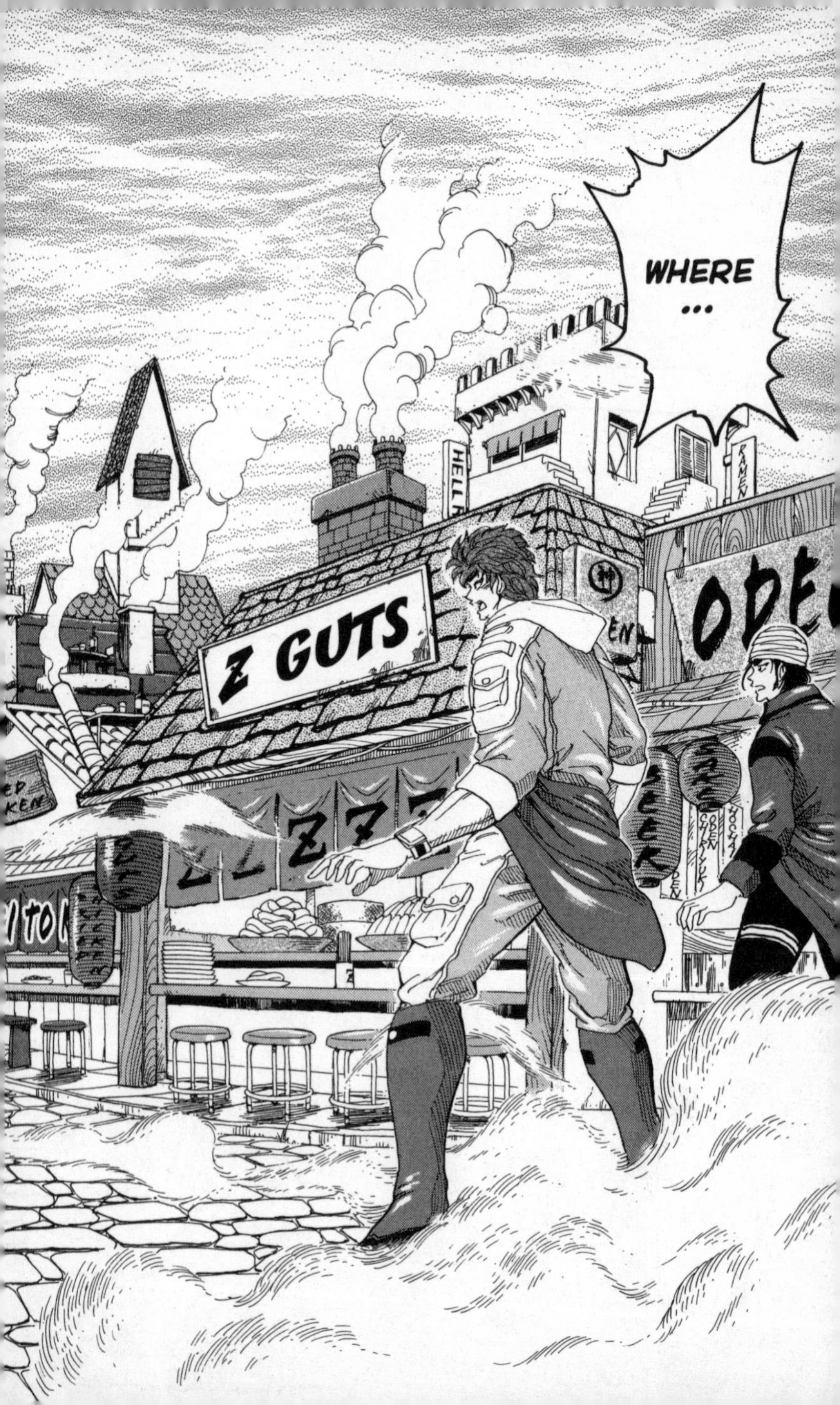
WHERE ...
Z GUTS
ODE
HELL
RAMEN
SAKE
BEER
ODEN
HOCHA
CHIRIYUKI

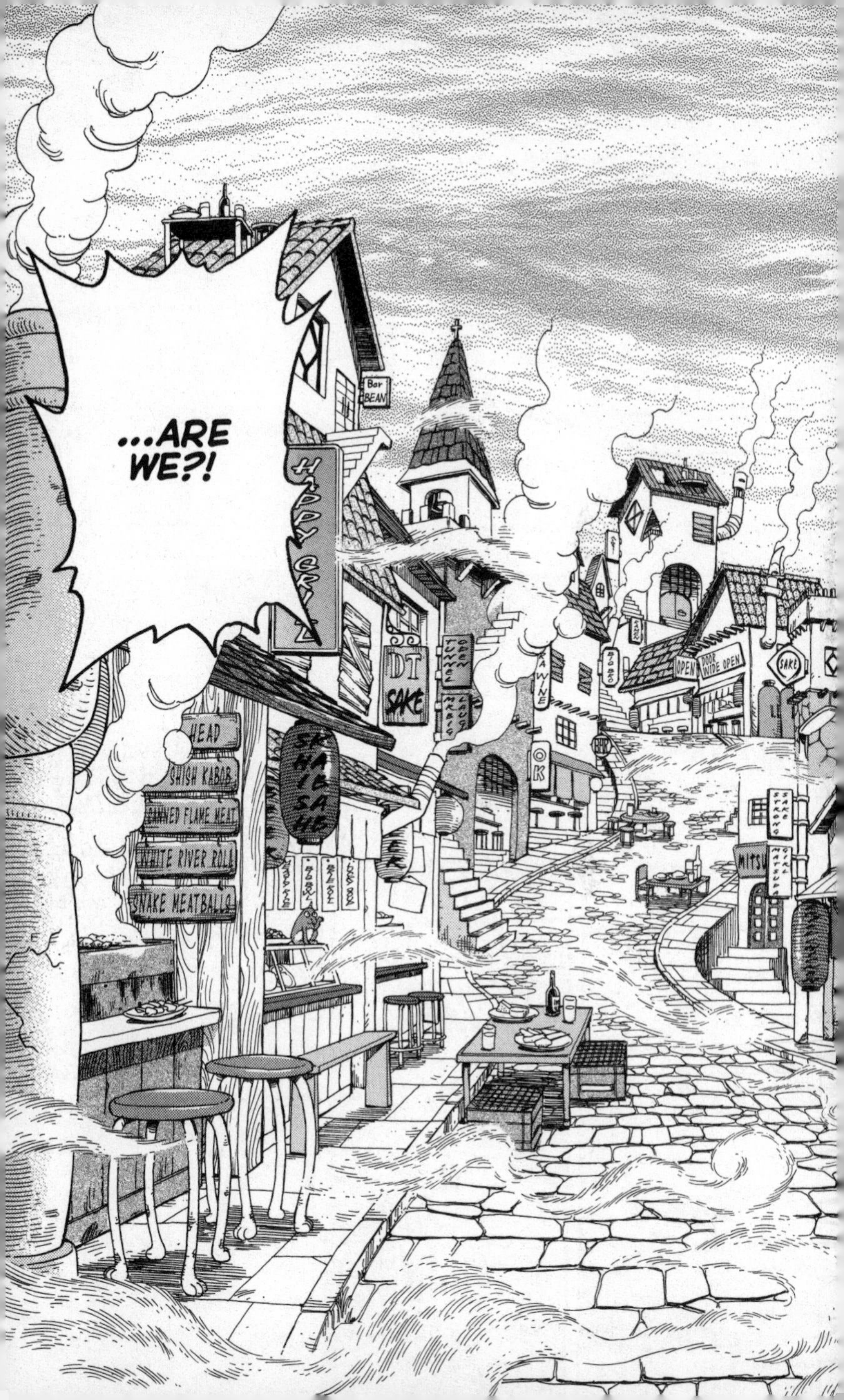
...ARE WE?!
Bar BEAN
DT SAKE
HEAD
SHISH KABOB
OPEN
DOOR WIDE OPEN
SAKE

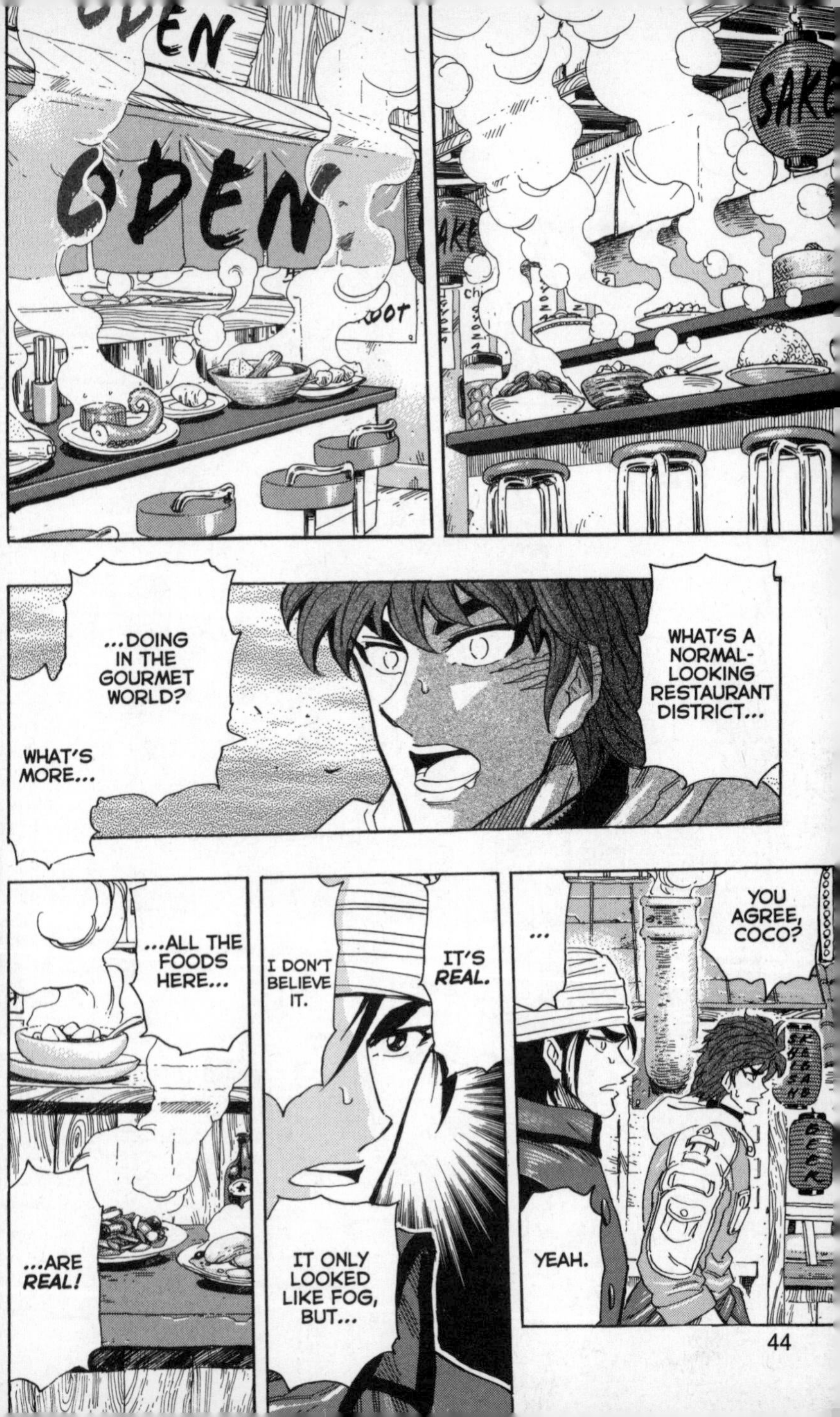
SAKE
SAKE
ODEN
ODEN
WHAT'S A NORMAL-LOOKING RESTAURANT DISTRICT...
...DOING IN THE GOURMET WORLD?
WHAT'S MORE...
YOU AGREE, COCO?
...
YEAH.
IT'S *REAL.*
I DON'T BELIEVE IT.
IT ONLY LOOKED LIKE FOG, BUT...
...ALL THE FOODS HERE...
...ARE *REAL!*

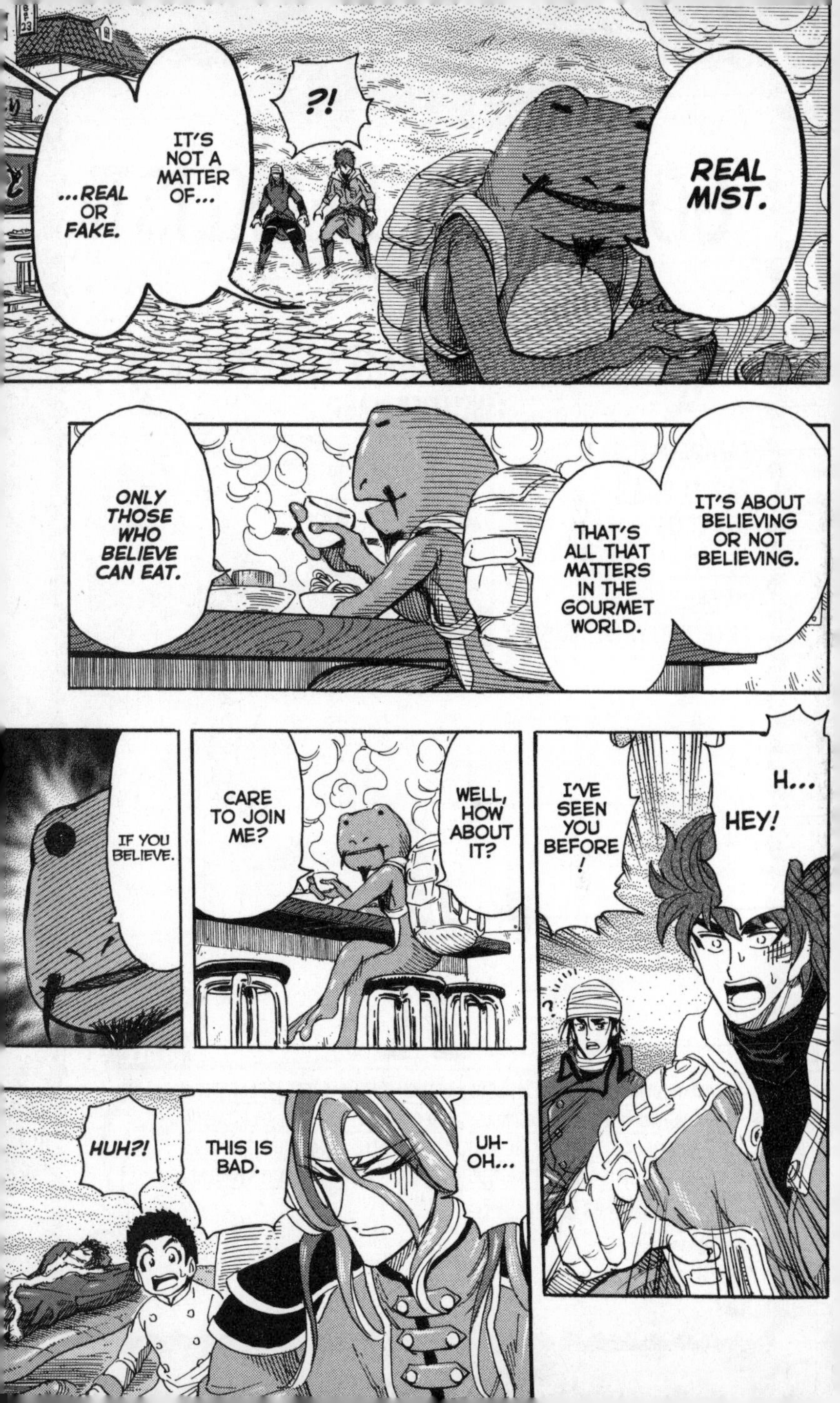
REAL MIST.
?!
IT'S NOT A MATTER OF...
...REAL OR FAKE.
IT'S ABOUT BELIEVING OR NOT BELIEVING.
THAT'S ALL THAT MATTERS IN THE GOURMET WORLD.
ONLY THOSE WHO BELIEVE CAN EAT.
H...
HEY!
I'VE SEEN YOU BEFORE!
WELL, HOW ABOUT IT?
CARE TO JOIN ME?
IF YOU BELIEVE.
UH-OH...
THIS IS BAD.
HUH?!

GOURMET CHECKLIST

Vol. 298

IMITATION CRABMEAT FLOWER
(SHELLFISH PLANT)

CAPTURE LEVEL: 7 – 12

HABITAT: OCEANS

SIZE: 50 CM

HEIGHT: ---

WEIGHT: 3 KG

PRICE: 2,000 YEN PER BLOSSOM

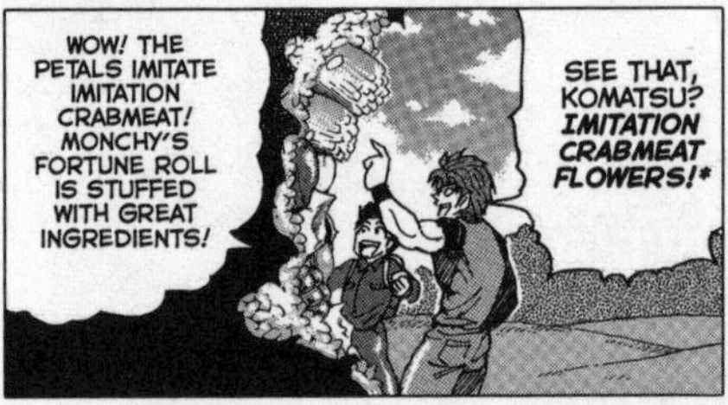
SEE THAT, KOMATSU? *IMITATION CRABMEAT FLOWERS!**
WOW! THE PETALS IMITATE IMITATION CRABMEAT! MONCHY'S FORTUNE ROLL IS STUFFED WITH GREAT INGREDIENTS!

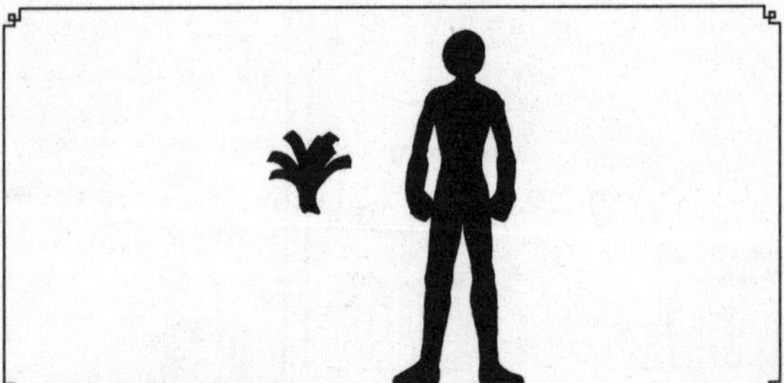

SCALE

A FLOWER THAT BLOOMS INSIDE OF IMITATION CRAB MEAT. THEY ARE EASY TO FIND BUT ARE POTENTIALLY POISONOUS, SO THE CAPTURE LEVEL VARIES. THE PETALS OF THE FLOWER TASTE JUST LIKE THE FANCIEST IMITATION CRABMEAT YOU'LL FIND ON THE MARKET. IT IS ONE OF THE INGREDIENTS REQUIRED TO MAKE MONCHY'S FORTUNE ROLL FOR FINDING THE CHOWLIN TEMPLE.

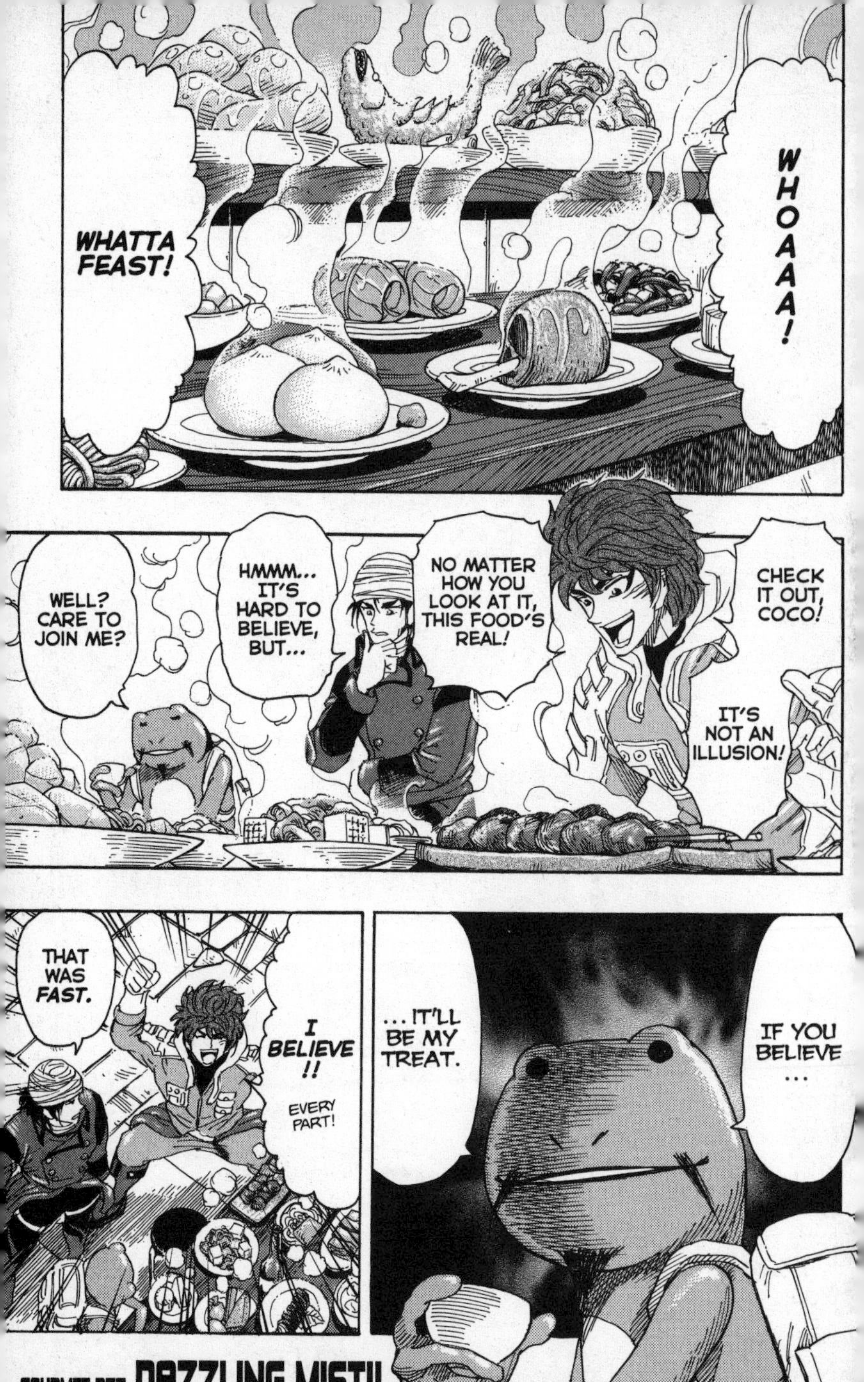
WHOAAAA!
WHATTA FEAST!
CHECK IT OUT, COCO!
IT'S NOT AN ILLUSION!
NO MATTER HOW YOU LOOK AT IT, THIS FOOD'S REAL!
HMMM... IT'S HARD TO BELIEVE, BUT...
WELL? CARE TO JOIN ME?
IF YOU BELIEVE ...
... IT'LL BE MY TREAT.
I BELIEVE !!
EVERY PART!
THAT WAS FAST.

GOURMET 275: DAZZLING MIST!!

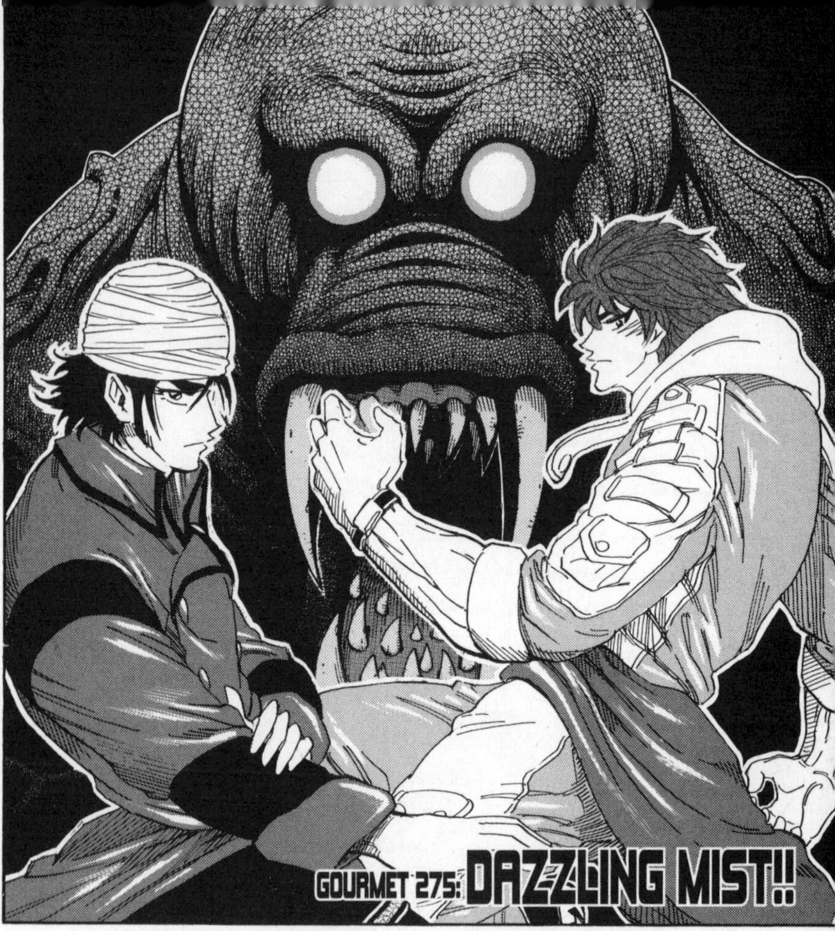
GOURMET 275: DAZZLING MIST!!

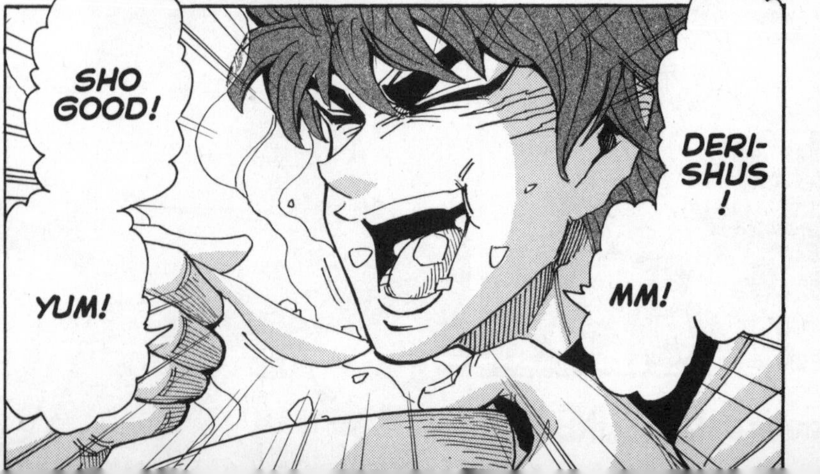
DERI-
SHUS
!
SHO
GOOD!
MM!
YUM!

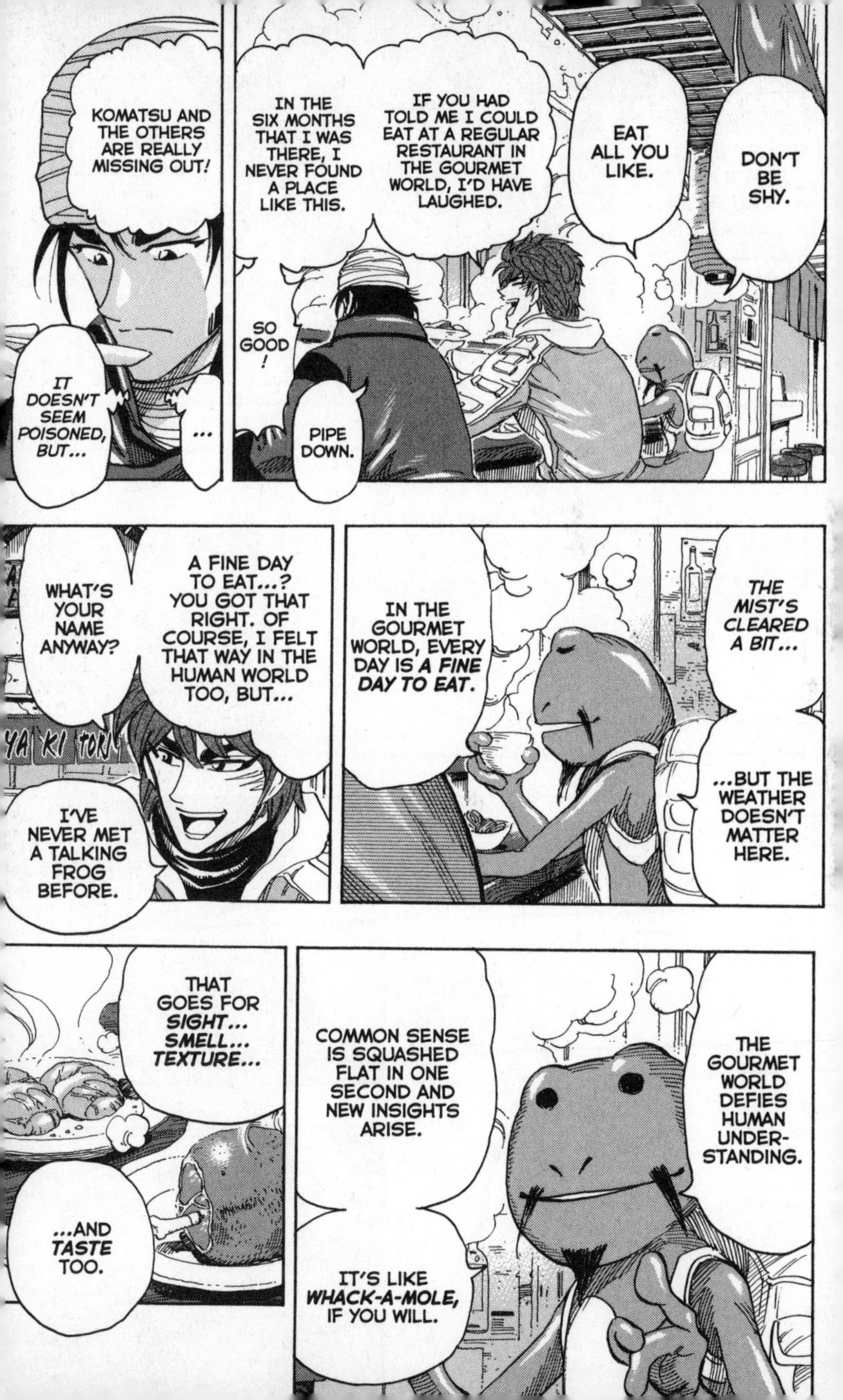
DON'T BE SHY.
EAT ALL YOU LIKE.
IF YOU HAD TOLD ME I COULD EAT AT A REGULAR RESTAURANT IN THE GOURMET WORLD, I'D HAVE LAUGHED.
IN THE SIX MONTHS THAT I WAS THERE, I NEVER FOUND A PLACE LIKE THIS.
SO GOOD!
PIPE DOWN.
KOMATSU AND THE OTHERS ARE REALLY MISSING OUT!
...
IT DOESN'T SEEM POISONED, BUT...
THE MIST'S CLEARED A BIT...
...BUT THE WEATHER DOESN'T MATTER HERE.
IN THE GOURMET WORLD, EVERY DAY IS A FINE DAY TO EAT.
A FINE DAY TO EAT...? YOU GOT THAT RIGHT. OF COURSE, I FELT THAT WAY IN THE HUMAN WORLD TOO, BUT...
WHAT'S YOUR NAME ANYWAY?
YA KI TORI
I'VE NEVER MET A TALKING FROG BEFORE.
THE GOURMET WORLD DEFIES HUMAN UNDER-STANDING.
COMMON SENSE IS SQUASHED FLAT IN ONE SECOND AND NEW INSIGHTS ARISE.
IT'S LIKE WHACK-A-MOLE, IF YOU WILL.
THAT GOES FOR SIGHT... SMELL... TEXTURE...
...AND TASTE TOO.

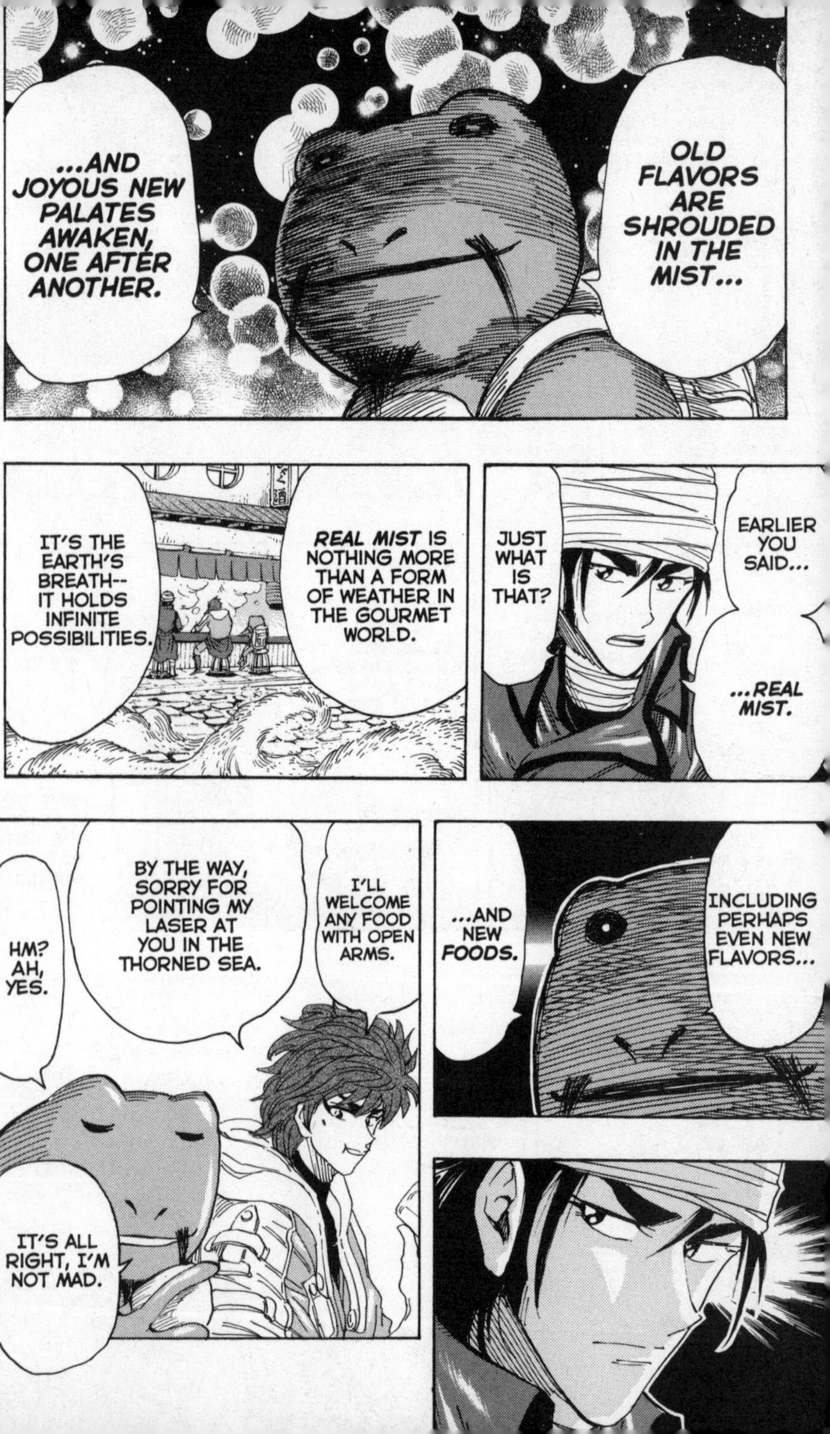
OLD FLAVORS ARE SHROUDED IN THE MIST...
...AND JOYOUS NEW PALATES AWAKEN, ONE AFTER ANOTHER.
EARLIER YOU SAID...
...REAL MIST.
JUST WHAT IS THAT?
REAL MIST IS NOTHING MORE THAN A FORM OF WEATHER IN THE GOURMET WORLD.
IT'S THE EARTH'S BREATH-- IT HOLDS INFINITE POSSIBILITIES.
INCLUDING PERHAPS EVEN NEW FLAVORS...
...AND NEW *FOODS.*
I'LL WELCOME ANY FOOD WITH OPEN ARMS.
BY THE WAY, SORRY FOR POINTING MY LASER AT YOU IN THE THORNED SEA.
HM? AH, YES.
IT'S ALL RIGHT, I'M NOT MAD.

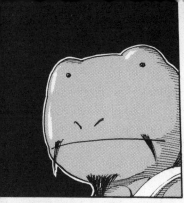

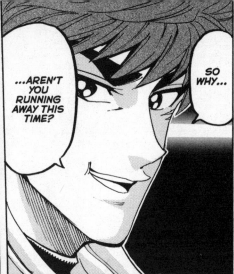

SO WHY...
...AREN'T YOU RUNNING AWAY THIS TIME?
I'M NOT SAYING...
...I DON'T BELIEVE IN *REAL MIST*, BUT...
...ARE YOU GOING TO BECOME ...
... MIST AS WELL?
WHAT ARE YOU?
YOU DON'T SMELL...
...LIKE THE FROG FROM THE OCEAN.

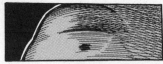

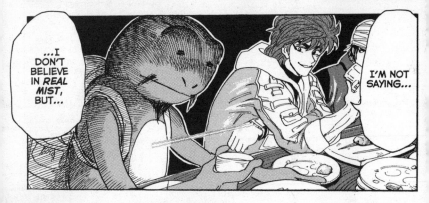

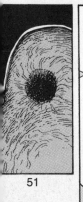

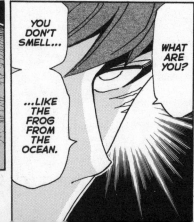

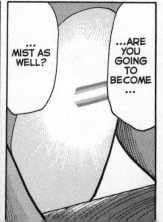

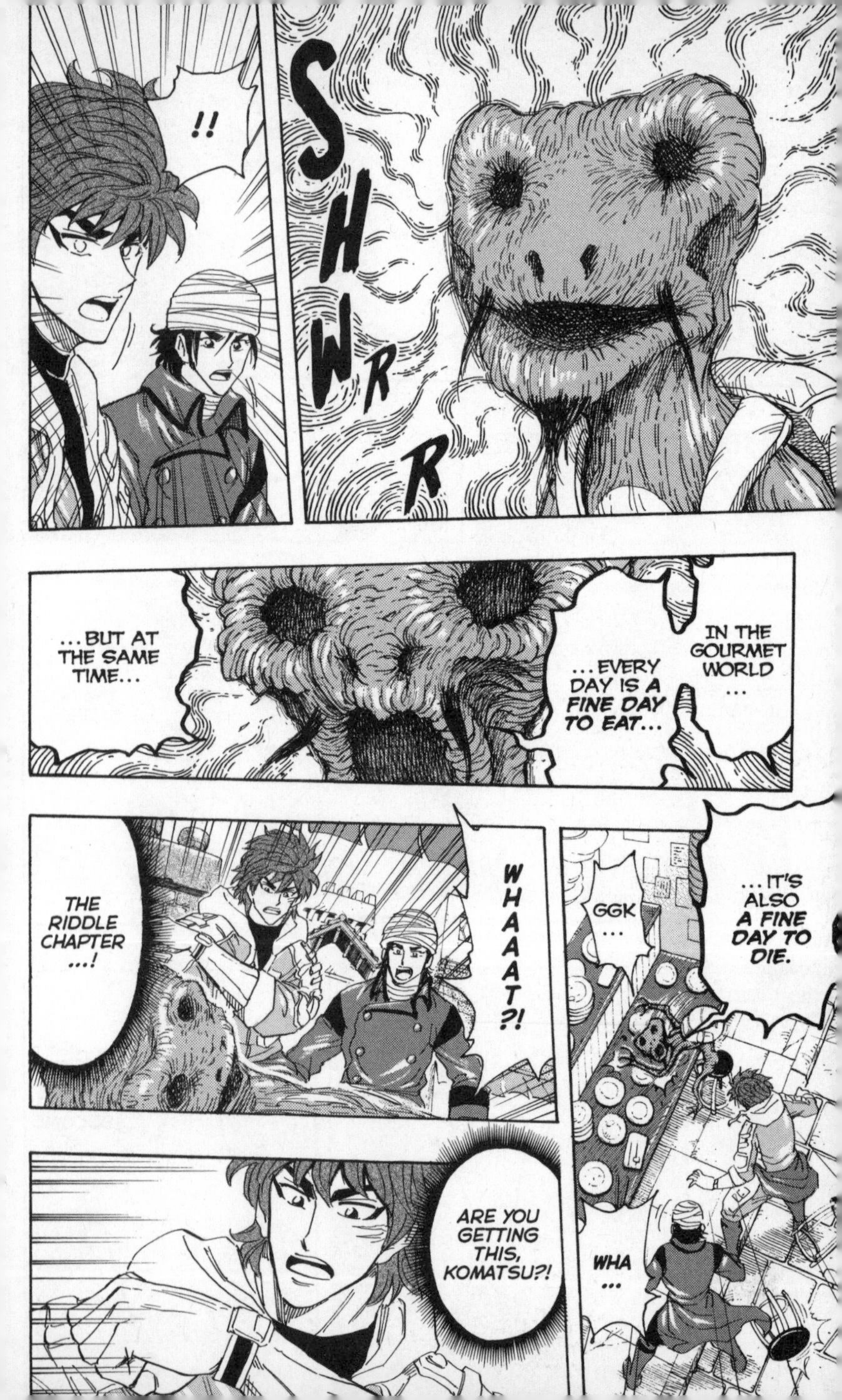
SHWRR
!!
IN THE GOURMET WORLD...
...EVERY DAY IS A FINE DAY TO EAT...
...BUT AT THE SAME TIME...
...IT'S ALSO A FINE DAY TO DIE.
GGK...
WHA...
WHAAAAT?!
THE RIDDLE CHAPTER...!
ARE YOU GETTING THIS, KOMATSU?!

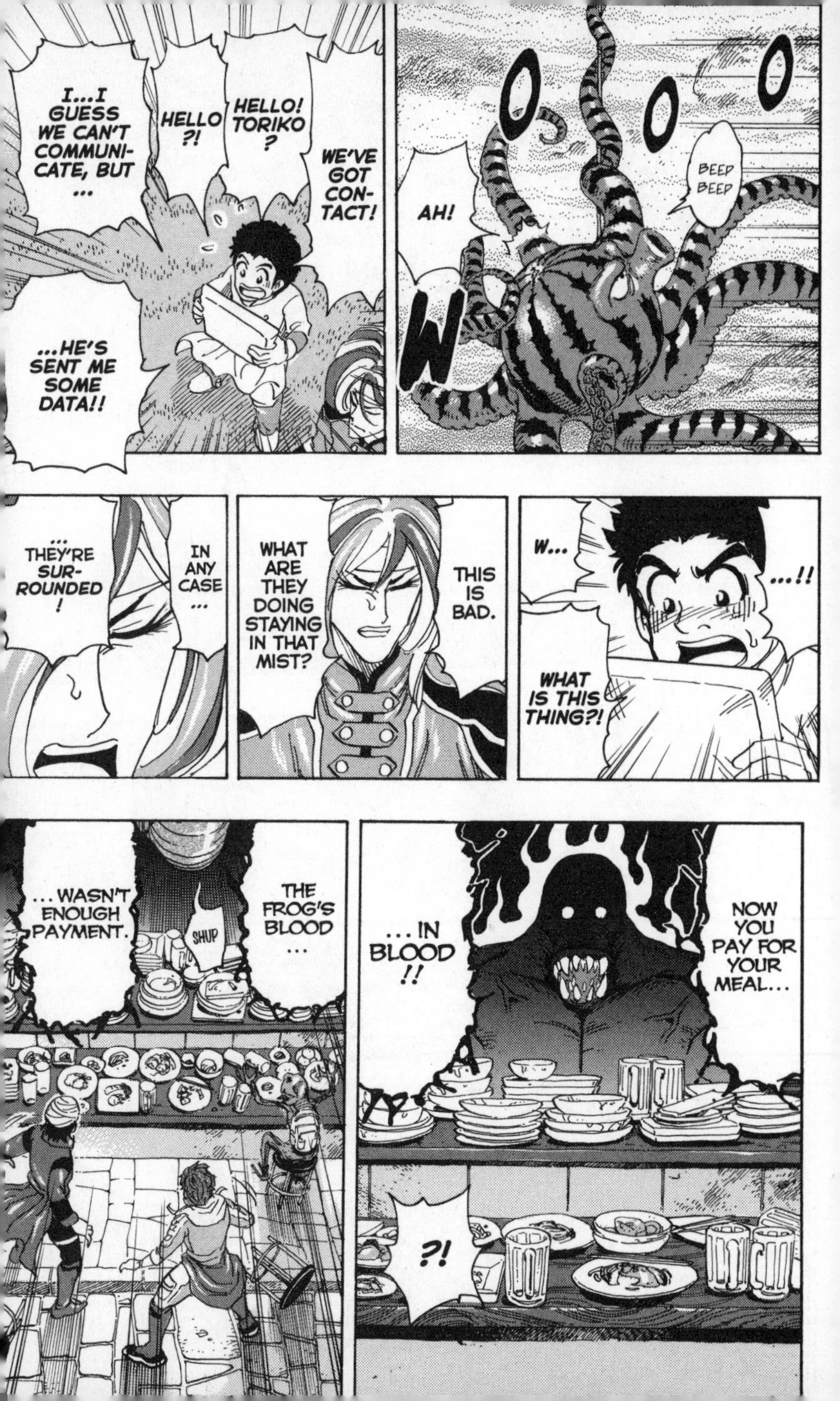
BEEP BEEP
AH!
WOOO
WE'VE GOT CONTACT!
HELLO! TORIKO?
HELLO?!
I...I GUESS WE CAN'T COMMUNICATE, BUT...
...HE'S SENT ME SOME DATA!!
...!!
W...
WHAT IS THIS THING?!
THIS IS BAD.
WHAT ARE THEY DOING STAYING IN THAT MIST?
IN ANY CASE...
...THEY'RE SURROUNDED!
NOW YOU PAY FOR YOUR MEAL...
...IN BLOOD!!
?!
THE FROG'S BLOOD...
SHUP
...WASN'T ENOUGH PAYMENT.

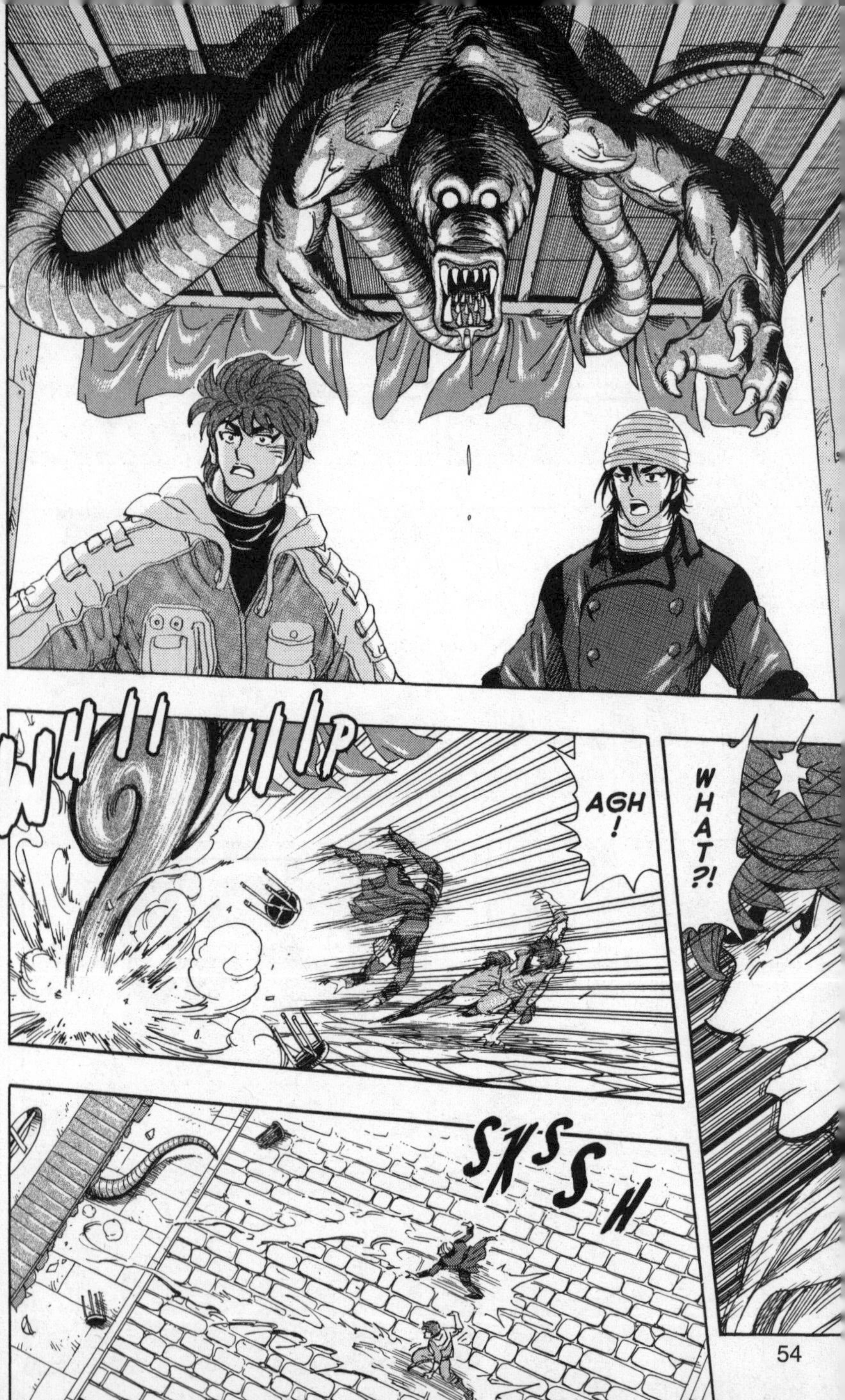
WHAT?!
WHIIIIIP
AGH!
SKSSH

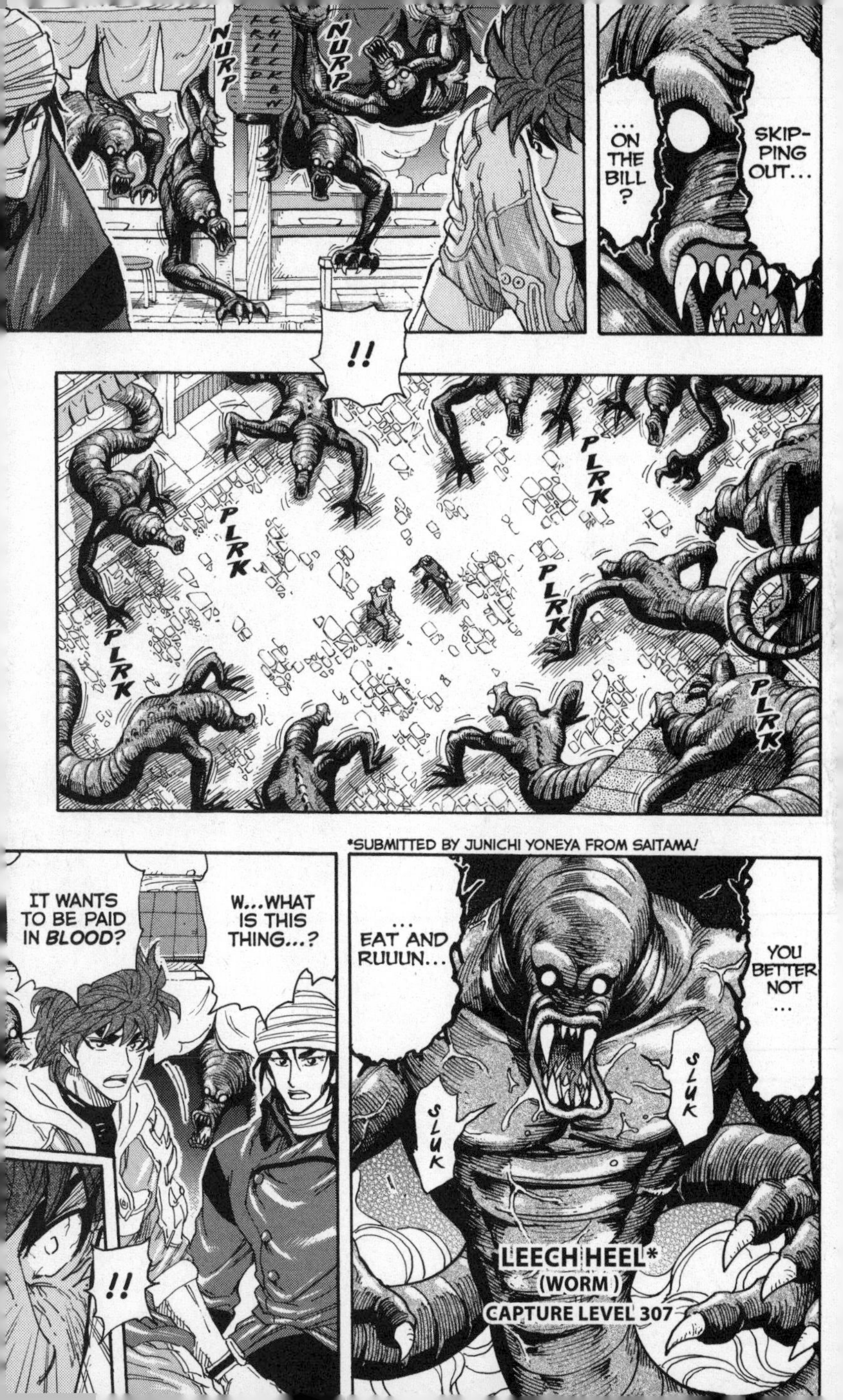
SKIP-PING OUT...
...ON THE BILL?
NURP
NURP
!!
PLRK
PLRK
PLRK
PLRK
PLRK
PLRK
*SUBMITTED BY JUNICHI YONEYA FROM SAITAMA!
YOU BETTER NOT...
...EAT AND RUUUN...
SLUK
SLUK
LEECH HEEL*
(WORM)
CAPTURE LEVEL 307
W...WHAT IS THIS THING...?
IT WANTS TO BE PAID IN *BLOOD*?
!!

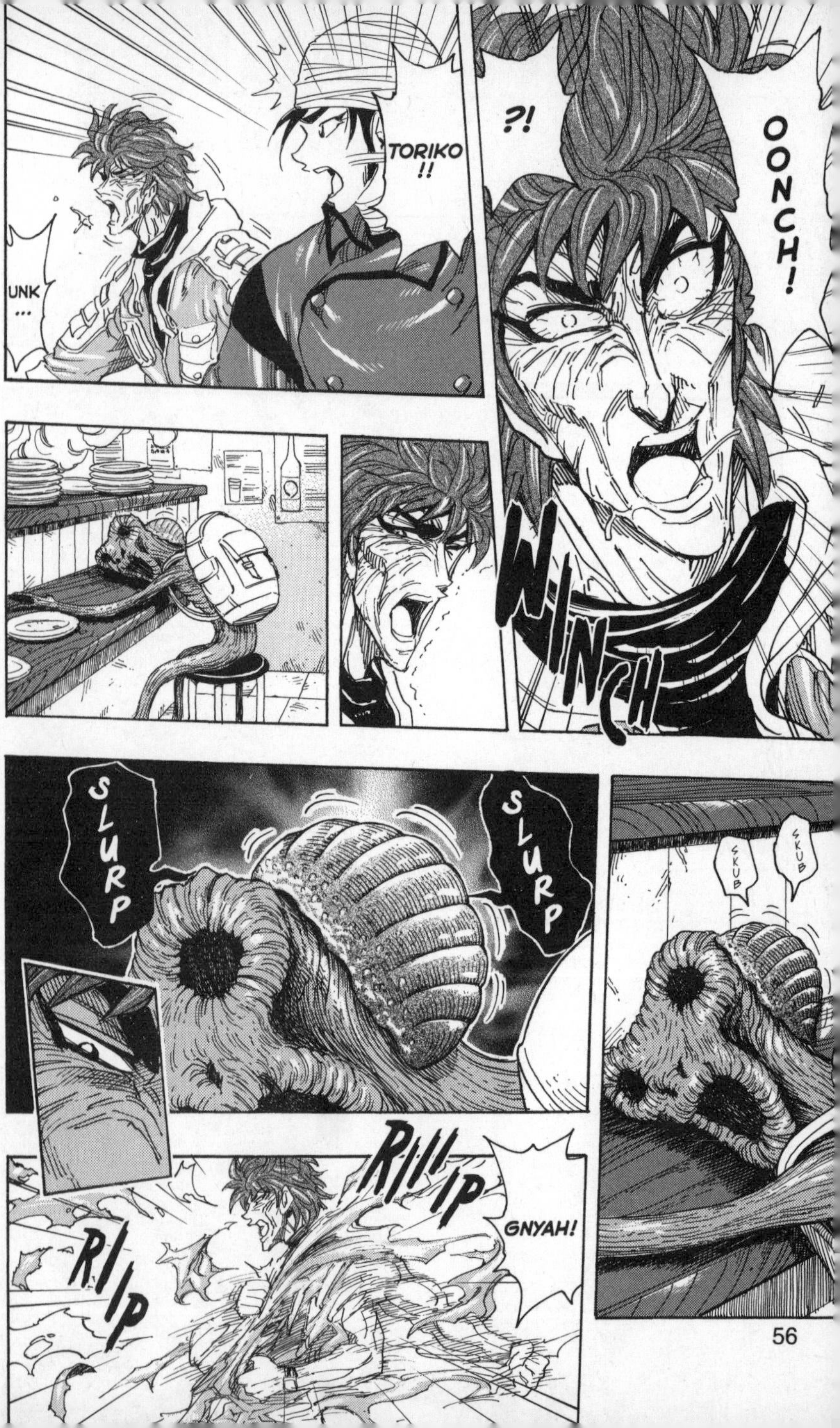
OONCH!
?!
WINCH
TORIKO!!
UNK...
SKUB
SKUB
SLURP
SLURP
RIIIP
GNYAH!
RIIP

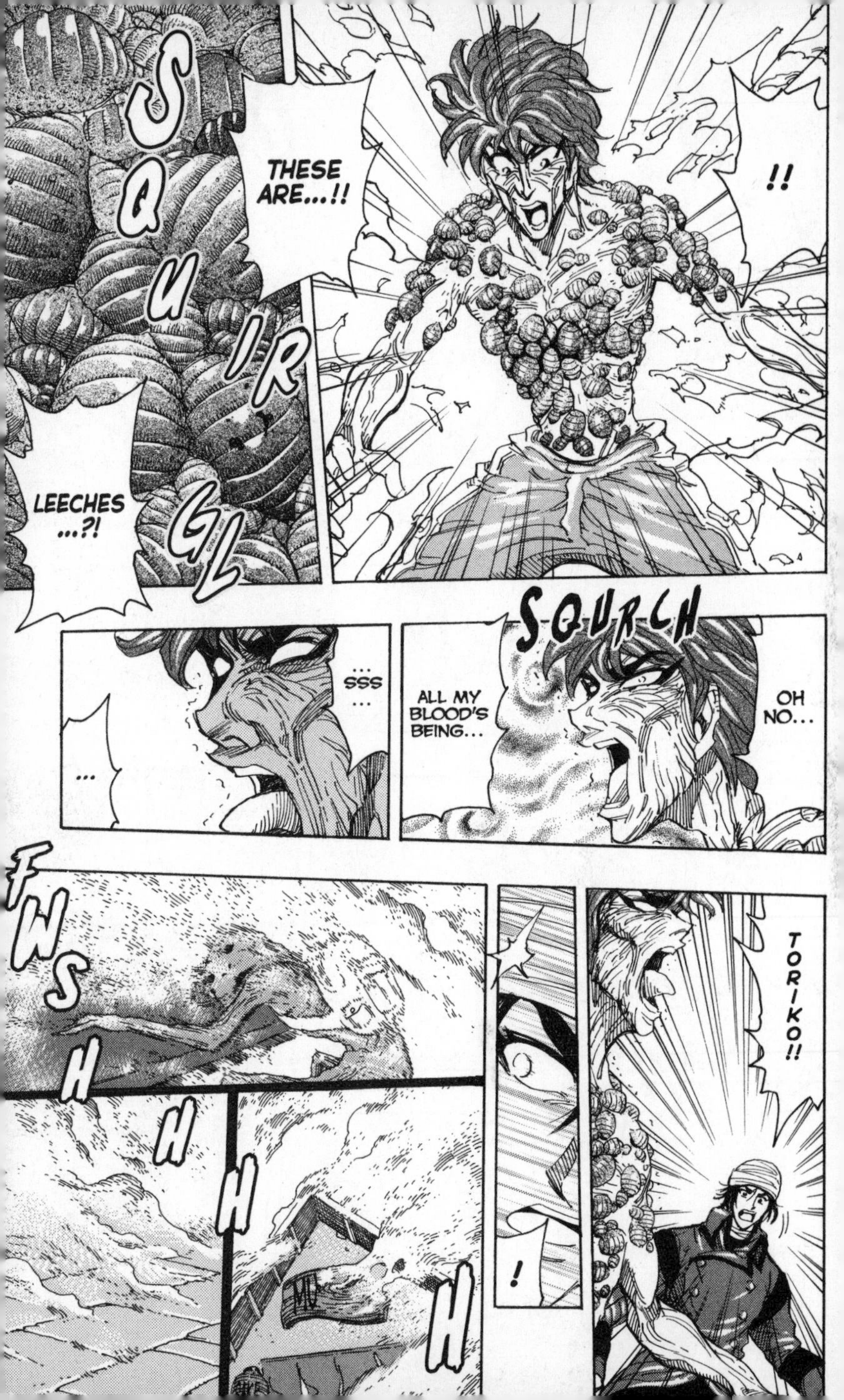

!!
THESE ARE...!!
SQUIRGL
LEECHES ...?!
SQURCH
OH NO...
ALL MY BLOOD'S BEING...
... SSS ...
...
TORIKO!!
!
FWSHHHH

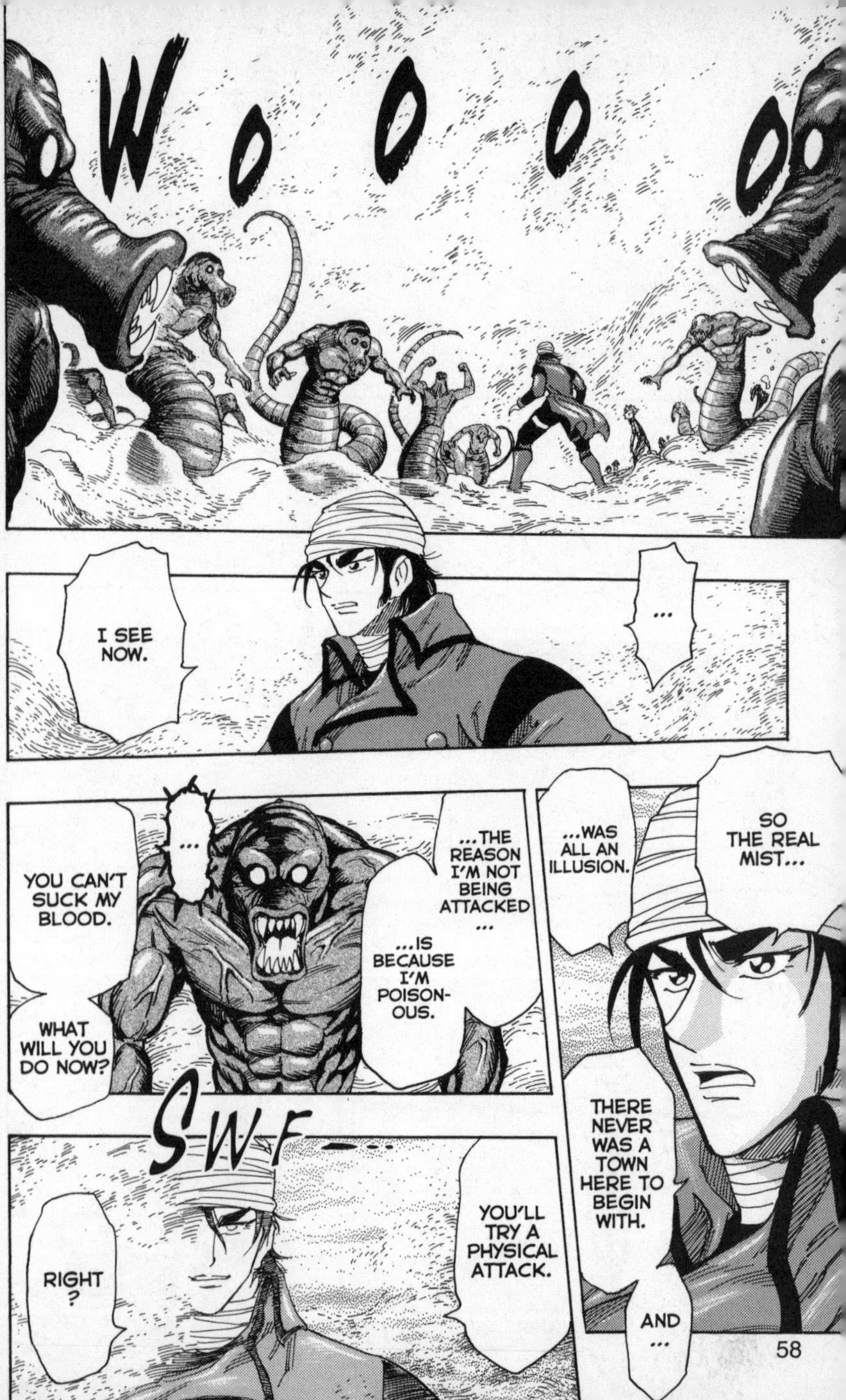
WOOOOOO
...
I SEE NOW.
SO THE REAL MIST...
...WAS ALL AN ILLUSION.
THERE NEVER WAS A TOWN HERE TO BEGIN WITH.
AND ...
...THE REASON I'M NOT BEING ATTACKED ...
...IS BECAUSE I'M POISONOUS.
...
YOU CAN'T SUCK MY BLOOD.
WHAT WILL YOU DO NOW?
SWF
YOU'LL TRY A PHYSICAL ATTACK.
RIGHT?

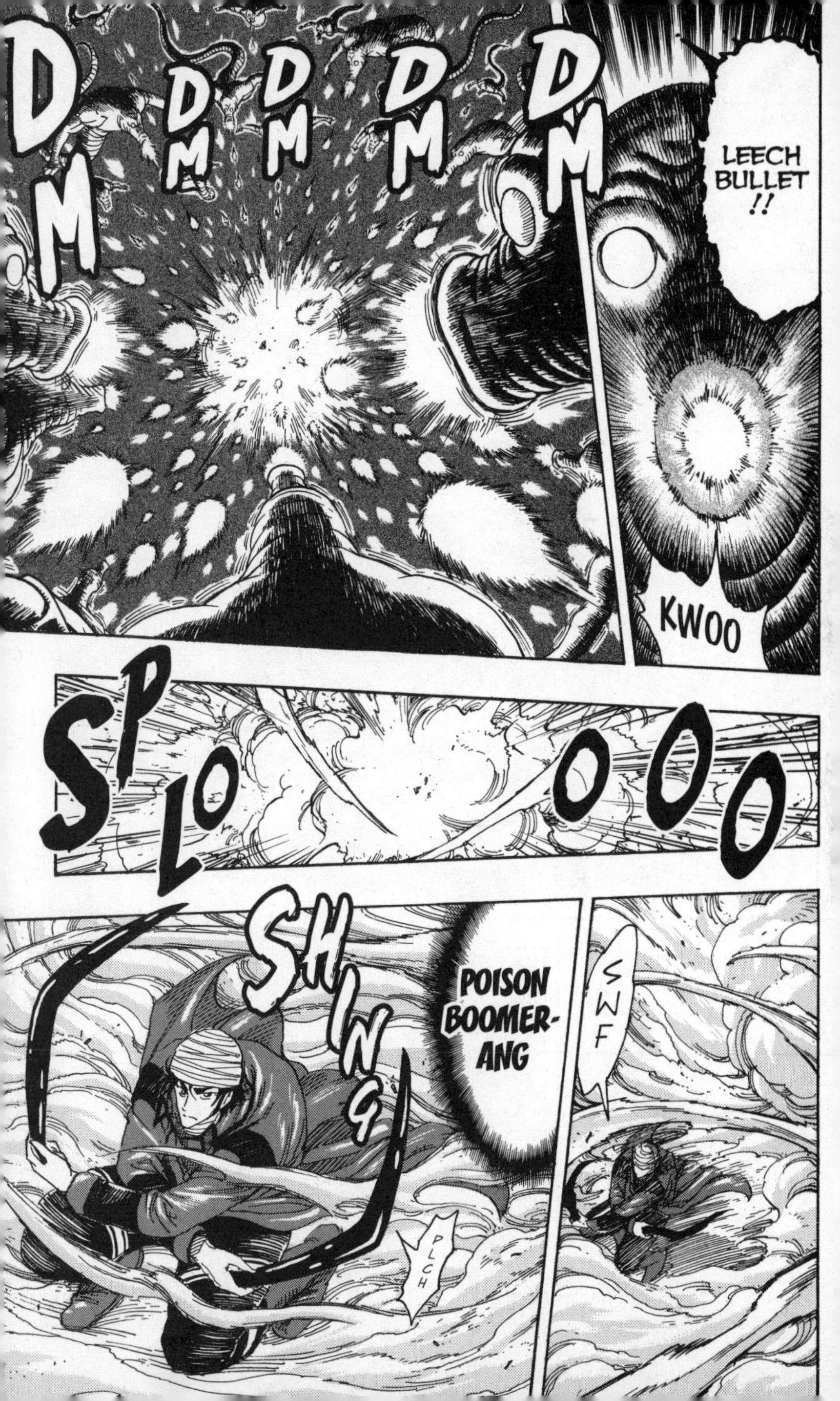

LEECH BULLET!!
KWOO
DM
DM
DM
DM
DM
SPLOOOO
SWF
POISON BOOMER-ANG
SHING
PLCH

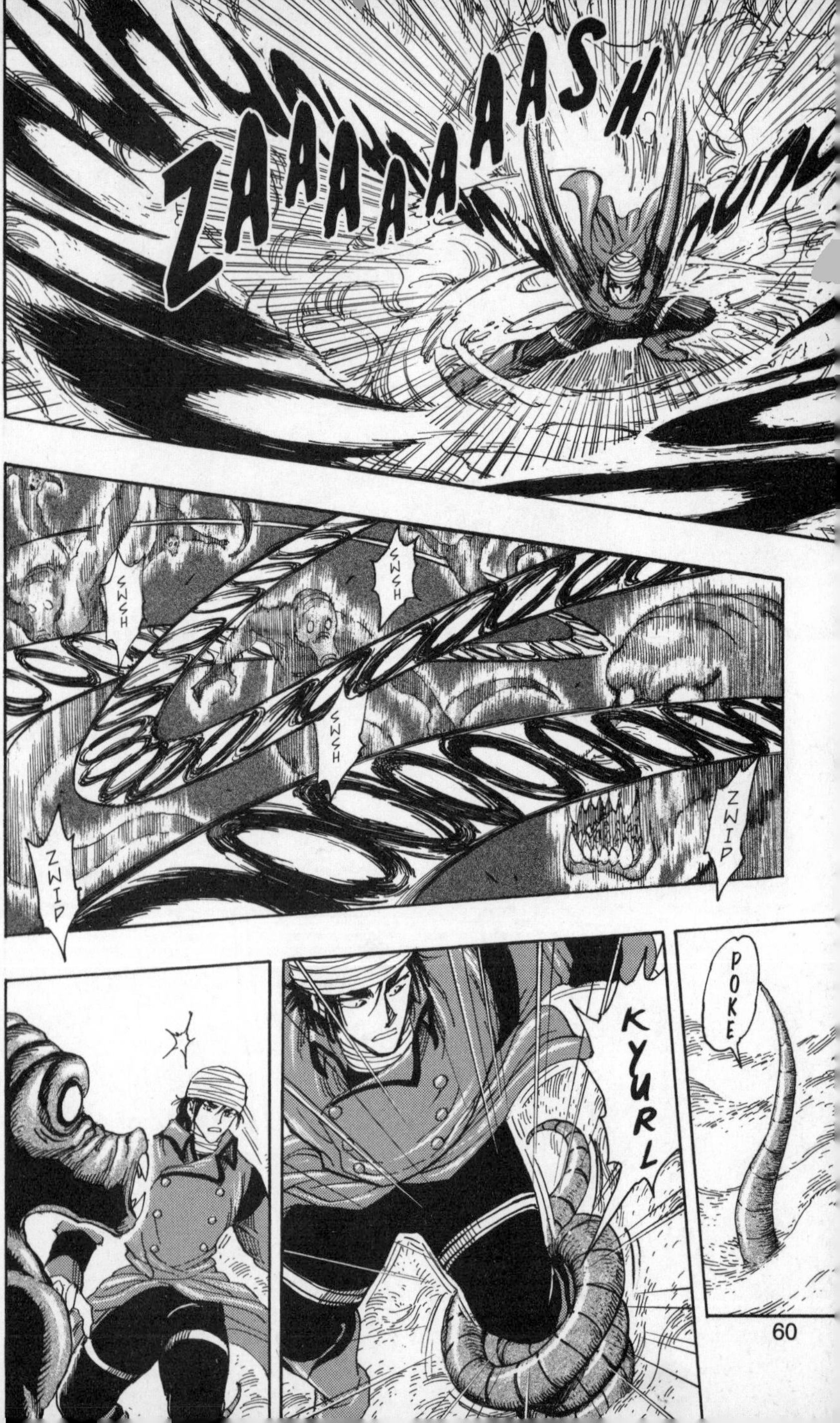
ZAAAAAAASH
SWSH
SWSH
ZWIP
SWSH
ZWIP
POKE
KYURL

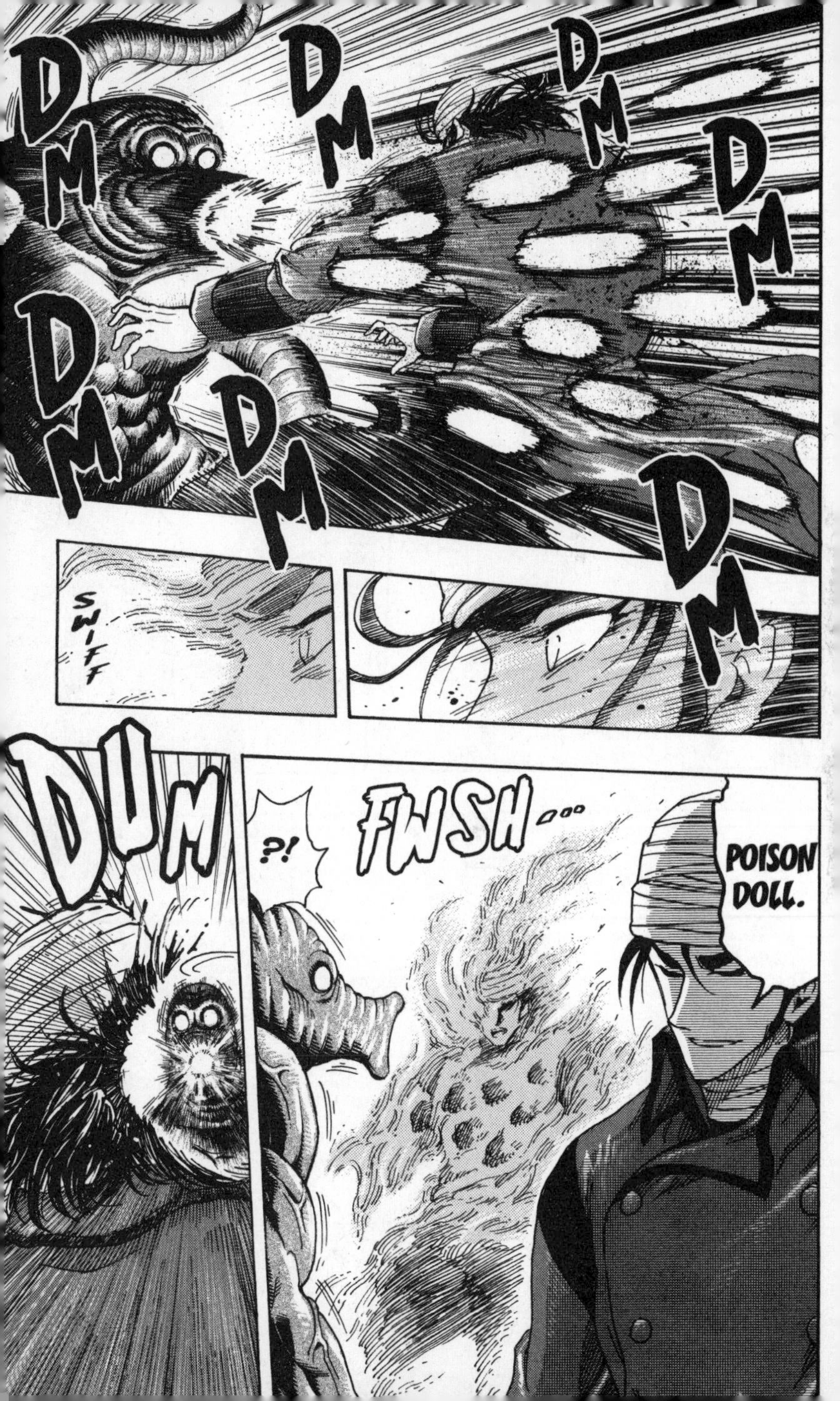

DM
DM
DM
DM
DM
DM
DM
SWIFF
FWSH...
?!
POISON DOLL.
DUM

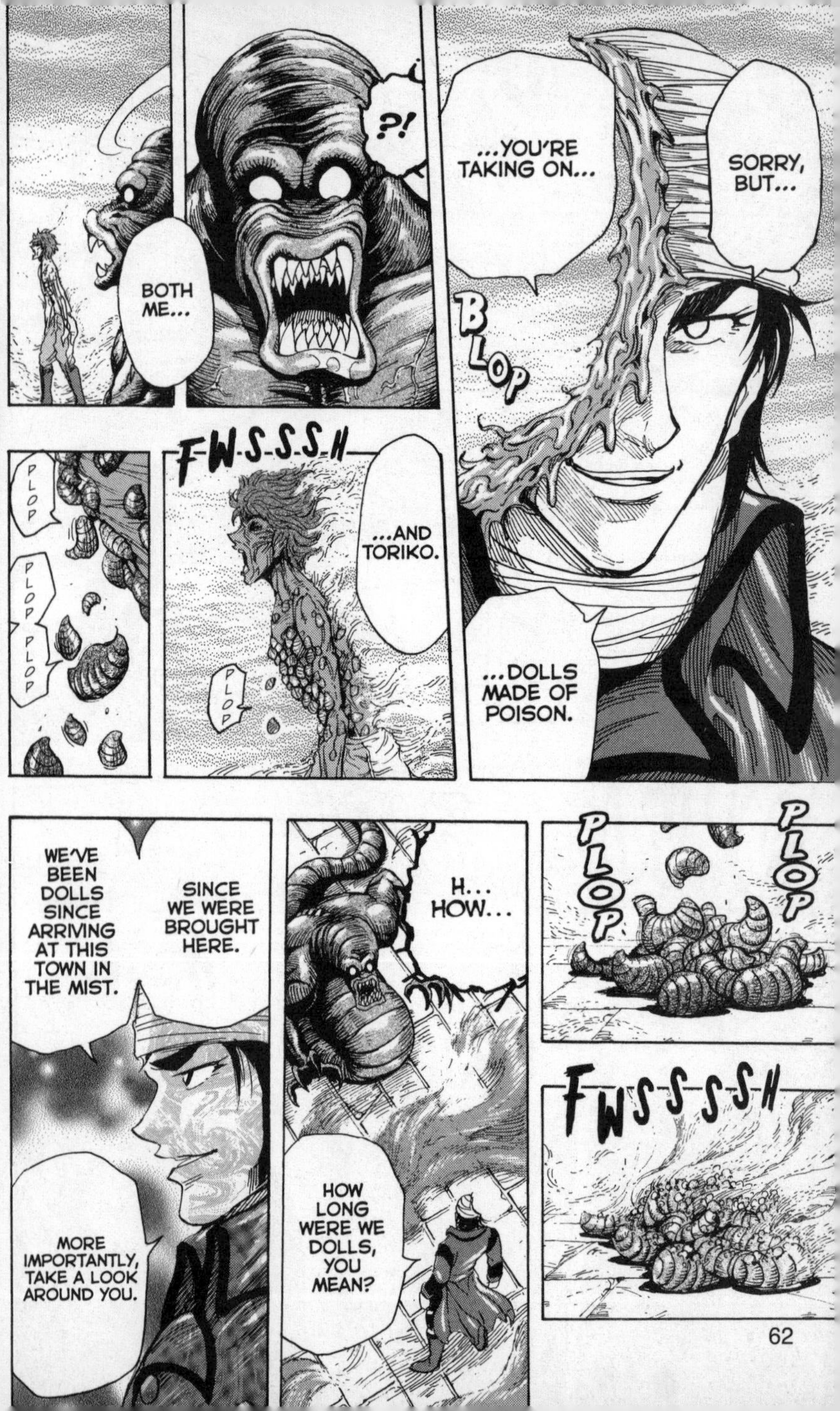
SORRY, BUT...
...YOU'RE TAKING ON...
BLOP
?!
BOTH ME...
FWSSSH
...AND TORIKO.
PLOP
PLOP
PLOP PLOP
PLOP
...DOLLS MADE OF POISON.
PLOP
PLOP
FWSSSSH
H... HOW...
HOW LONG WERE WE DOLLS, YOU MEAN?
SINCE WE WERE BROUGHT HERE.
WE'VE BEEN DOLLS SINCE ARRIVING AT THIS TOWN IN THE MIST.
MORE IMPORTANTLY, TAKE A LOOK AROUND YOU.

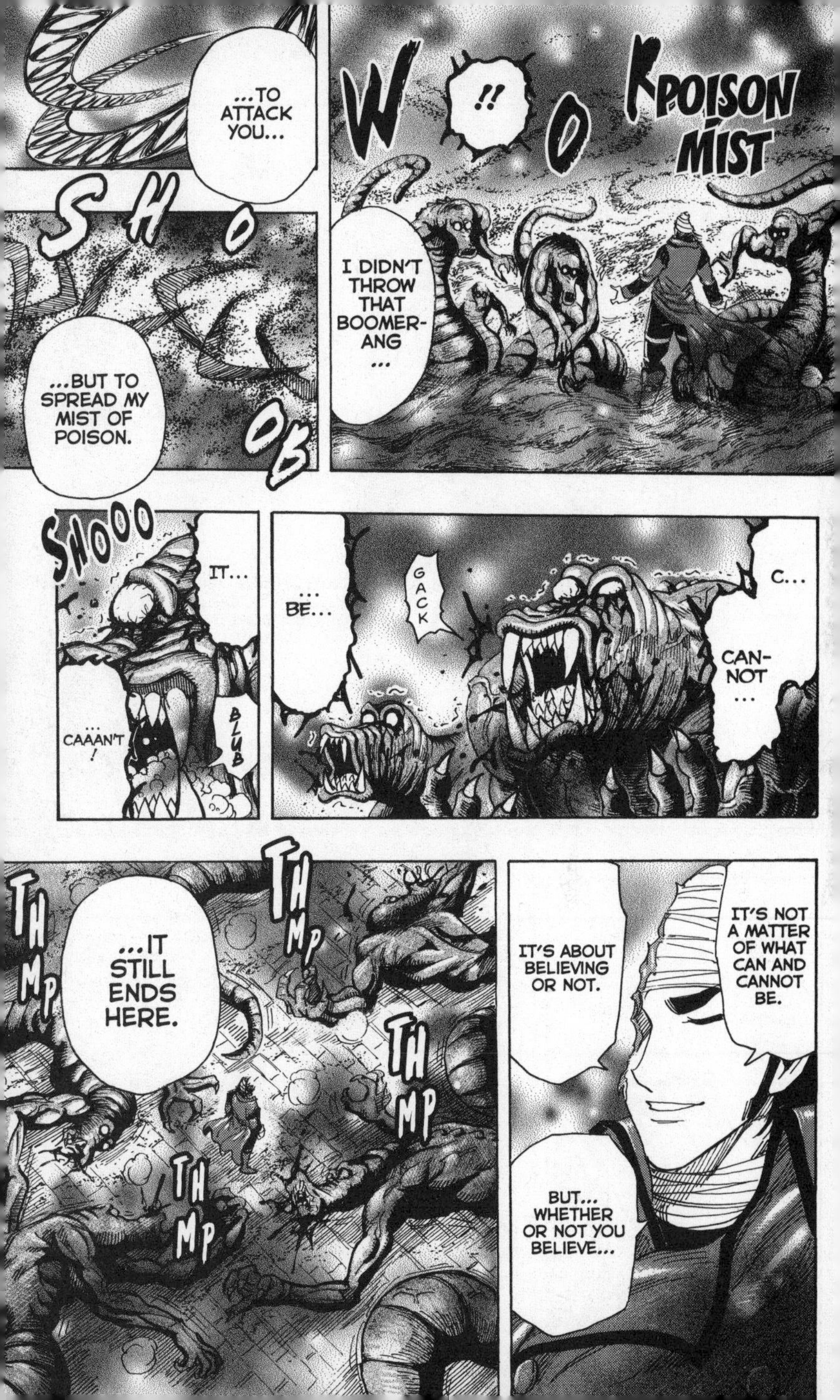
WOO
!!
POISON MIST
I DIDN'T THROW THAT BOOMER-ANG ...
...TO ATTACK YOU...
SHOOOO
...BUT TO SPREAD MY MIST OF POISON.
C...
CAN-NOT ...
GACK
... BE...
SHOOO
IT...
... CAAAN'T !
BLUB
IT'S NOT A MATTER OF WHAT CAN AND CANNOT BE.
IT'S ABOUT BELIEVING OR NOT.
BUT... WHETHER OR NOT YOU BELIEVE...
THMP
THMP
THMP
THMP
...IT STILL ENDS HERE.

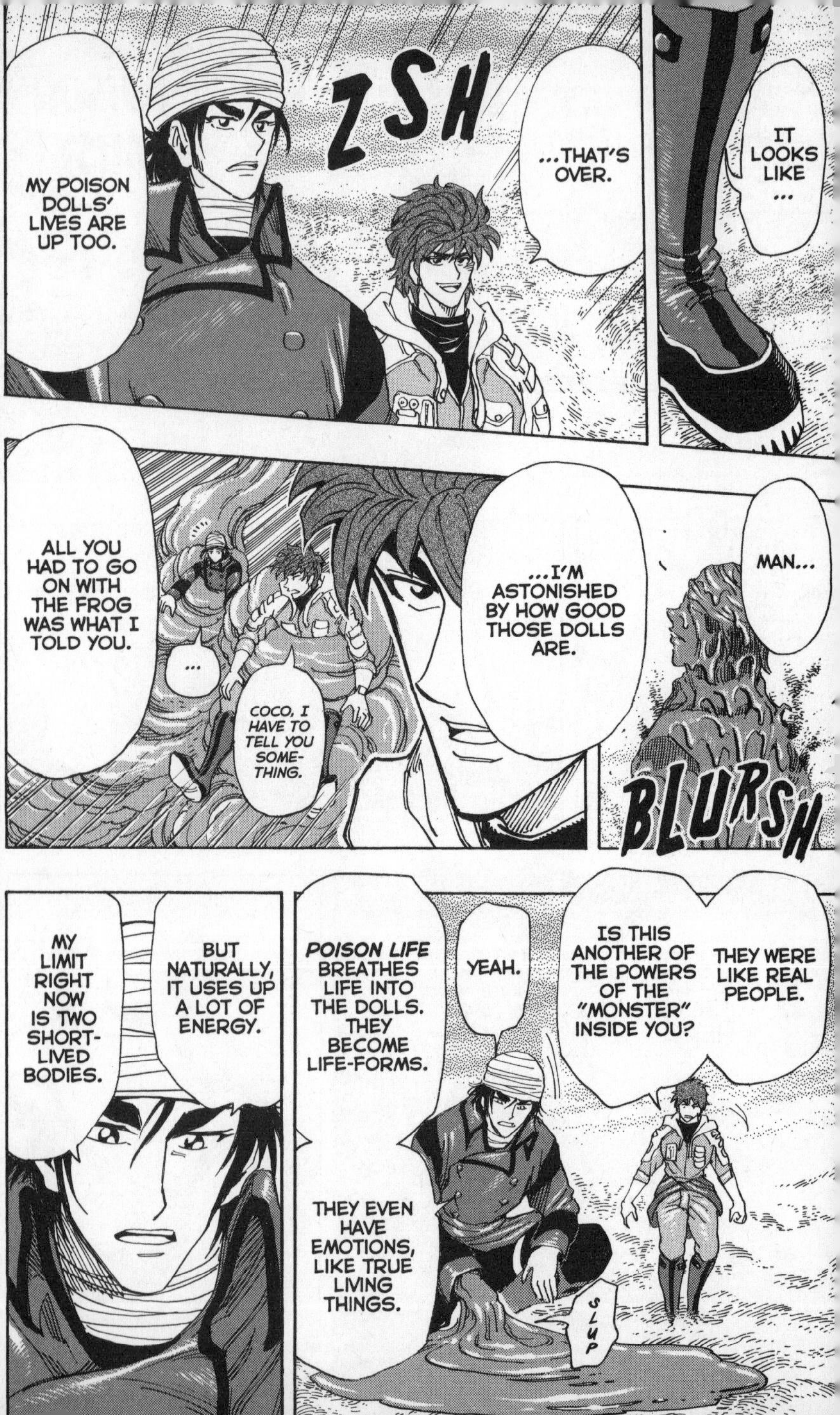
IT LOOKS LIKE ...
...THAT'S OVER.
ZSH
MY POISON DOLLS' LIVES ARE UP TOO.
MAN...
BLURSH
...I'M ASTONISHED BY HOW GOOD THOSE DOLLS ARE.
COCO, I HAVE TO TELL YOU SOMETHING.
...
ALL YOU HAD TO GO ON WITH THE FROG WAS WHAT I TOLD YOU.
THEY WERE LIKE REAL PEOPLE.
IS THIS ANOTHER OF THE POWERS OF THE "MONSTER" INSIDE YOU?
YEAH.
POISON LIFE BREATHES LIFE INTO THE DOLLS. THEY BECOME LIFE-FORMS.
THEY EVEN HAVE EMOTIONS, LIKE TRUE LIVING THINGS.
SLUP
BUT NATURALLY, IT USES UP A LOT OF ENERGY.
MY LIMIT RIGHT NOW IS TWO SHORT-LIVED BODIES.

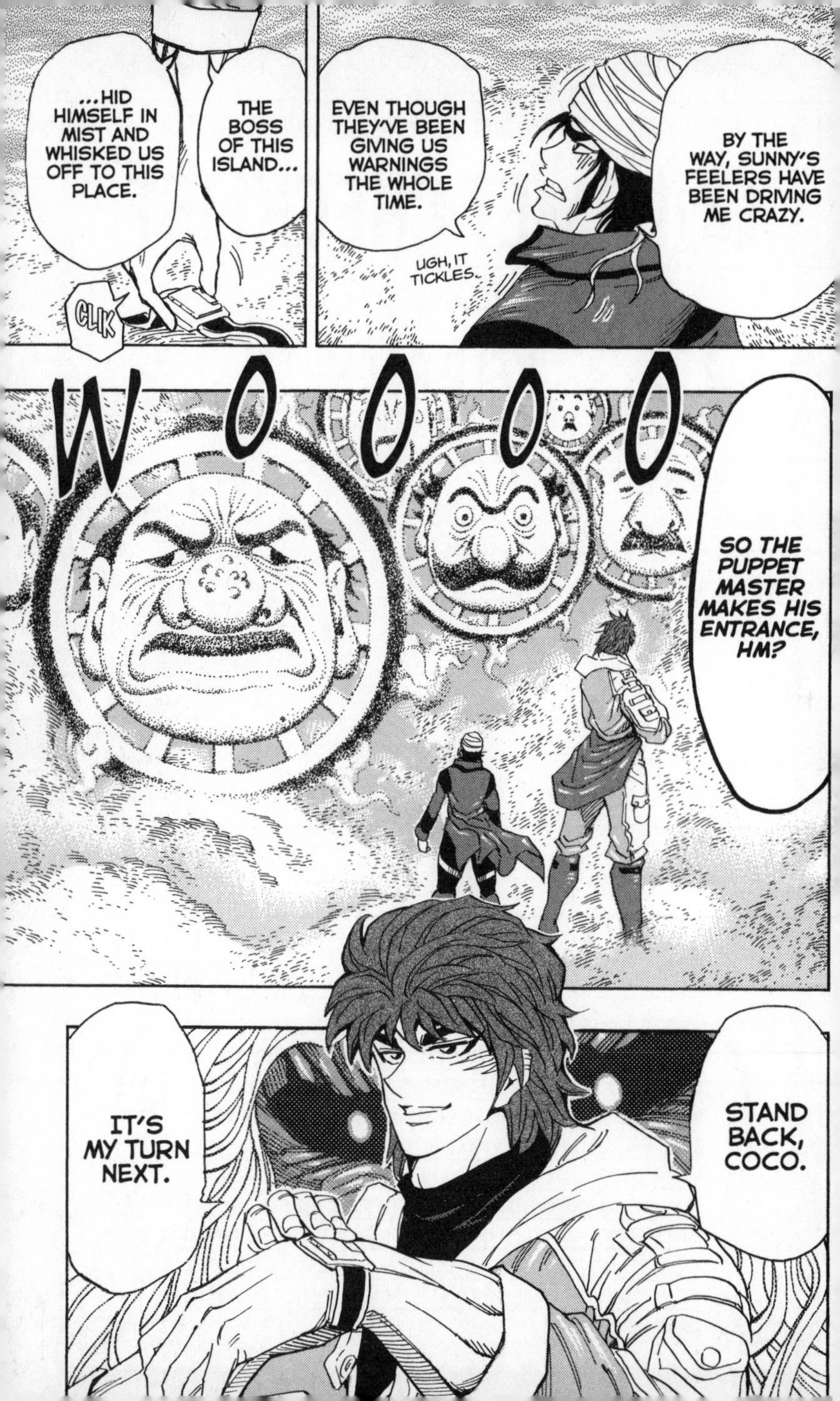
BY THE WAY, SUNNY'S FEELERS HAVE BEEN DRIVING ME CRAZY.
EVEN THOUGH THEY'VE BEEN GIVING US WARNINGS THE WHOLE TIME.
UGH, IT TICKLES.
THE BOSS OF THIS ISLAND...
...HID HIMSELF IN MIST AND WHISKED US OFF TO THIS PLACE.
CLIK
SO THE PUPPET MASTER MAKES HIS ENTRANCE, HM?
WOOOO
STAND BACK, COCO.
IT'S MY TURN NEXT.

GOURMET CHECKLIST

Vol. 299

KELP ROCK
(MINERAL)

HABITAT: UNDERGOUND CAVES

SIZE: 8 CM

HEIGHT: ---

WEIGHT: 100 G

PRICE: 10,000 YEN PER ROCK

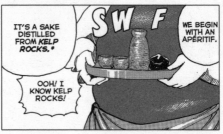

WE BEGIN WITH AN APÉRITIF.
SWF
IT'S A SAKE DISTILLED FROM *KELP ROCKS.**
OOH! I KNOW KELP ROCKS!

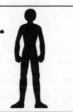

SCALE

A SPECIAL ROCK THAT ABSORBS THE FLAVOR OF KELP AND RELEASES THOSE FLAVORS WHEN BOILED TO BECOME A HIGH-QUALITY KELP STOCK. THE BOILING PROCESS IS EASIER SAID THAN DONE AND IS PAINSTAKINGLY DIFFICULT. FIRST, ONE MUST WARM WATER SO THAT IT REACHES 3 DEGREES CELSIUS AFTER ONE HOUR WHILE SIMULTANEOUSLY LOWERING THE ROCK INTO THE WATER 1 MILLIMETER AT A TIME. IT MUST BE DONE BY HAND, AND IF THE ROCK MOVES EVEN THE SLIGHTEST MILLIMETER TO THE SIDE, THE FLAVORING PROCESS IMMEDIATELY STOPS. IT ALSO DEPENDS ON THE SIZE OF THE ROCK. KELP ROCK IS AN INGREDIENT THAT REQUIRES SPECIAL PREPARATION AND TAKES A FULL FIVE DAYS TO COMPLETELY BREW. THE ALCOHOL DISTILLED FROM THE KELP ROCK MUST ALSO BE DRUNK IN A SPECIFIC MANNER OR ELSE THE TASTE WILL COMPLETELY EVAPORATE.

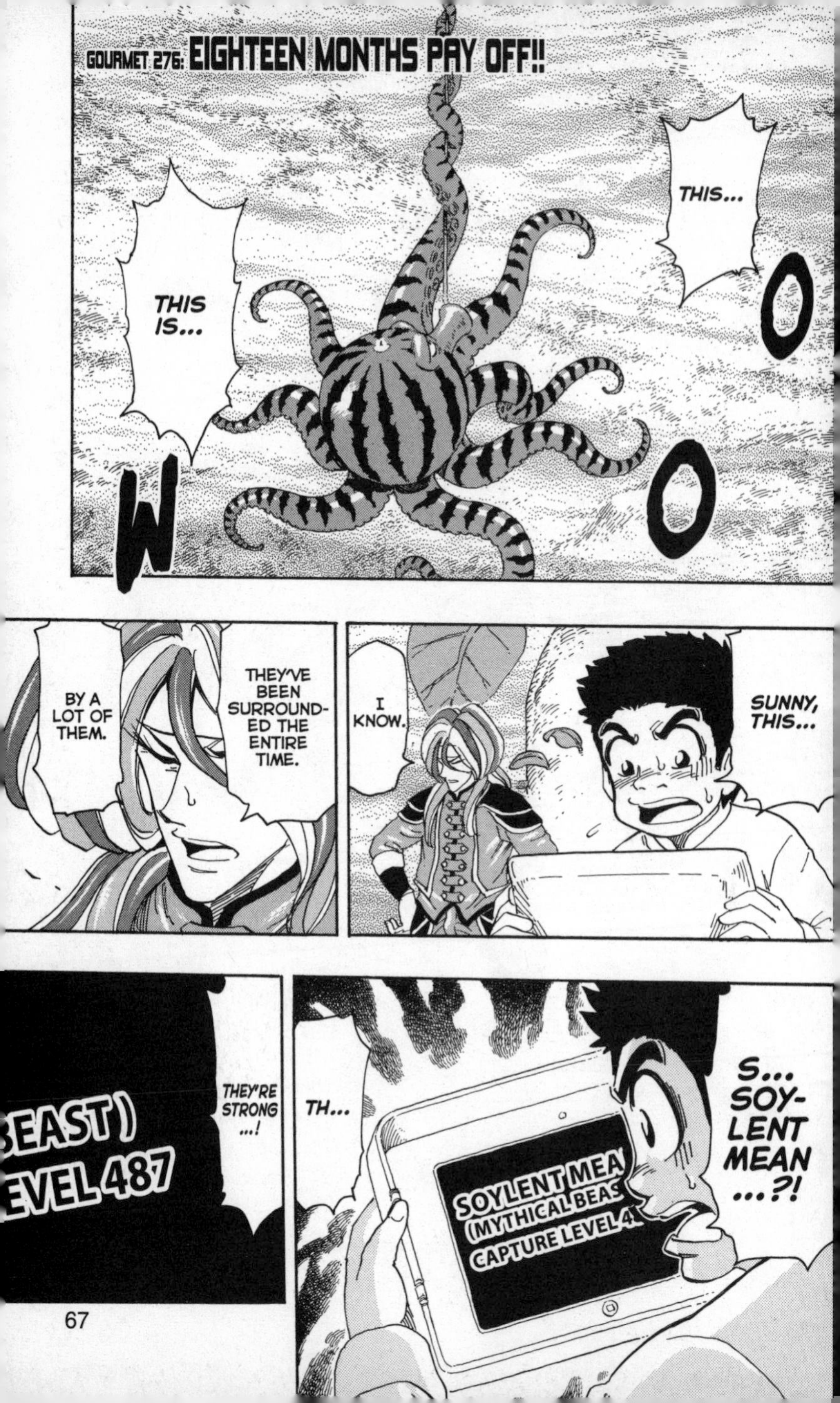
GOURMET 276: EIGHTEEN MONTHS PAY OFF!!
THIS...
THIS IS...
WOO
SUNNY, THIS...
I KNOW.
THEY'VE BEEN SURROUND-ED THE ENTIRE TIME.
BY A LOT OF THEM.
S... SOY-LENT MEAN...?!
SOYLENT MEA
(MYTHICAL BEAS
CAPTURE LEVEL 4
TH...
THEY'RE STRONG...!
BEAST)
EVEL 487

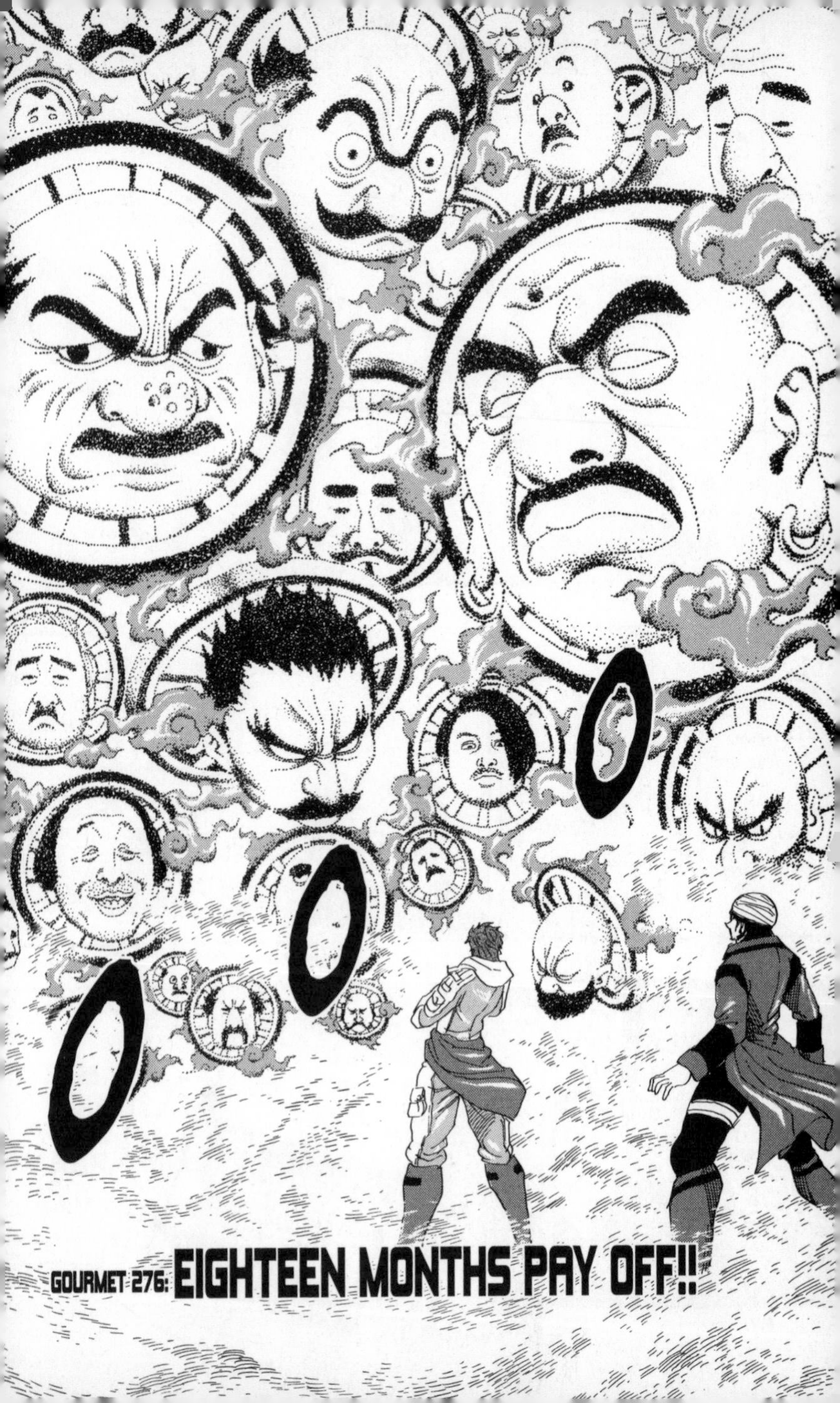
GOURMET 276: EIGHTEEN MONTHS PAY OFF!!

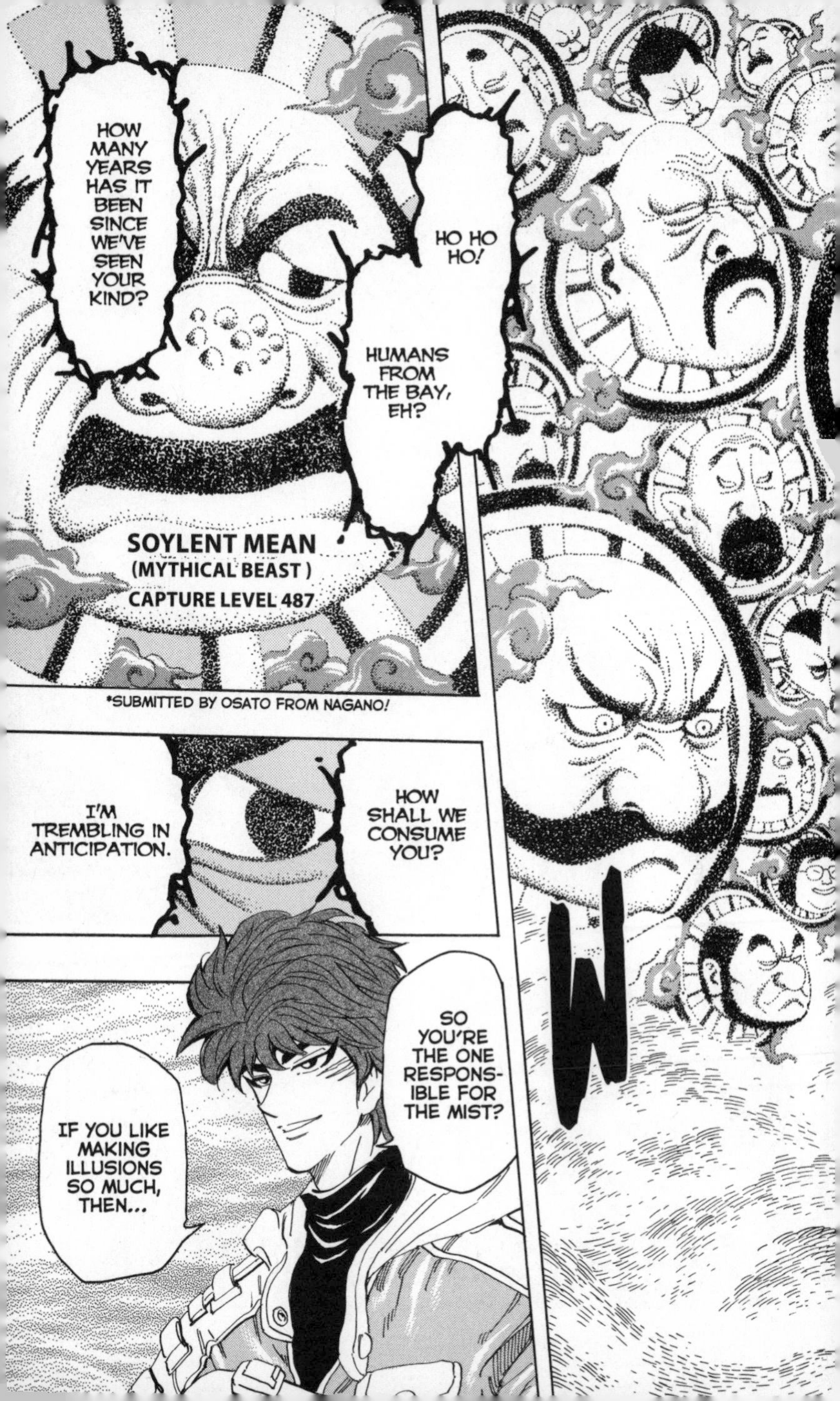
W
HO HO HO!
HUMANS FROM THE BAY, EH?
HOW MANY YEARS HAS IT BEEN SINCE WE'VE SEEN YOUR KIND?
SOYLENT MEAN
(MYTHICAL BEAST)
CAPTURE LEVEL 487
*SUBMITTED BY OSATO FROM NAGANO!
HOW SHALL WE CONSUME YOU?
I'M TREMBLING IN ANTICIPATION.
SO YOU'RE THE ONE RESPONSIBLE FOR THE MIST?
IF YOU LIKE MAKING ILLUSIONS SO MUCH, THEN...

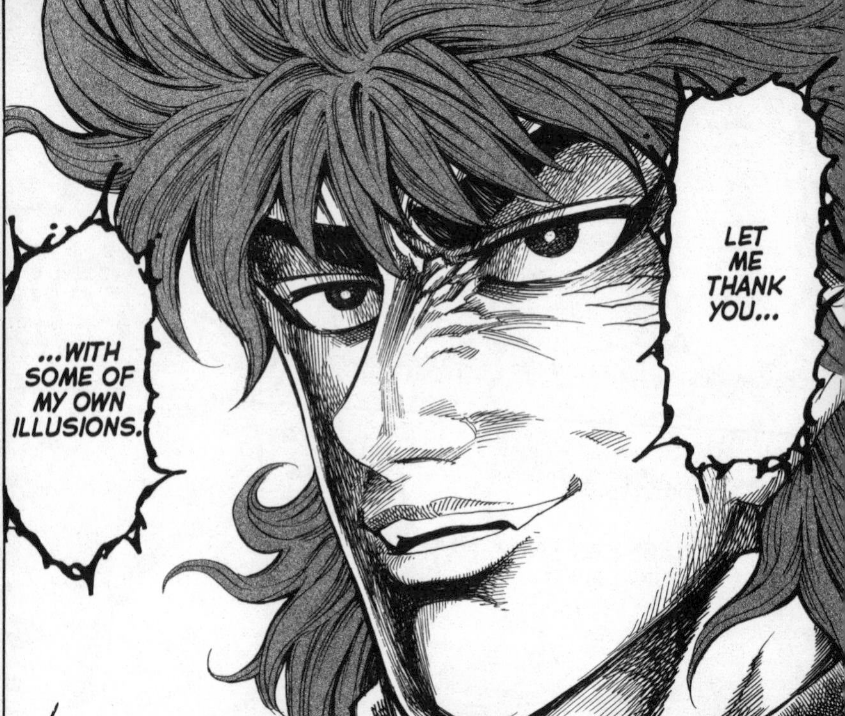
LET ME THANK YOU...
...WITH SOME OF MY OWN ILLUSIONS.

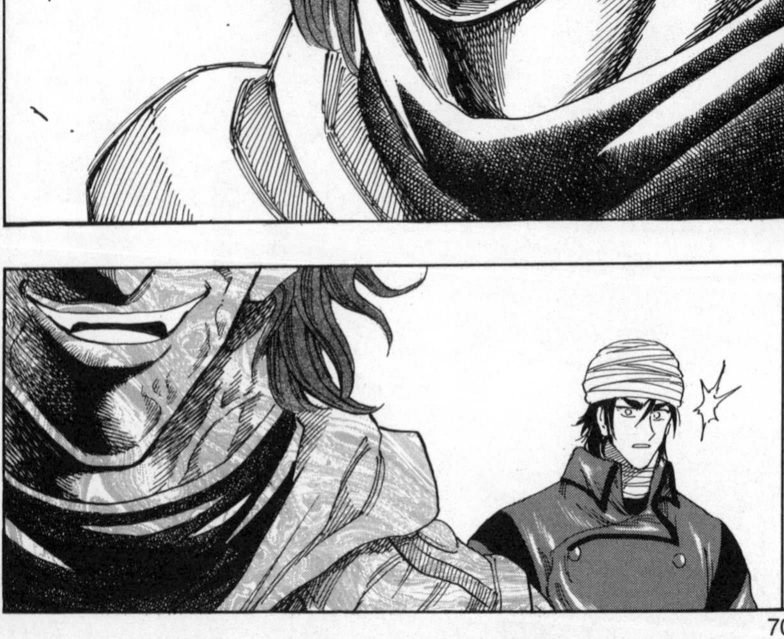

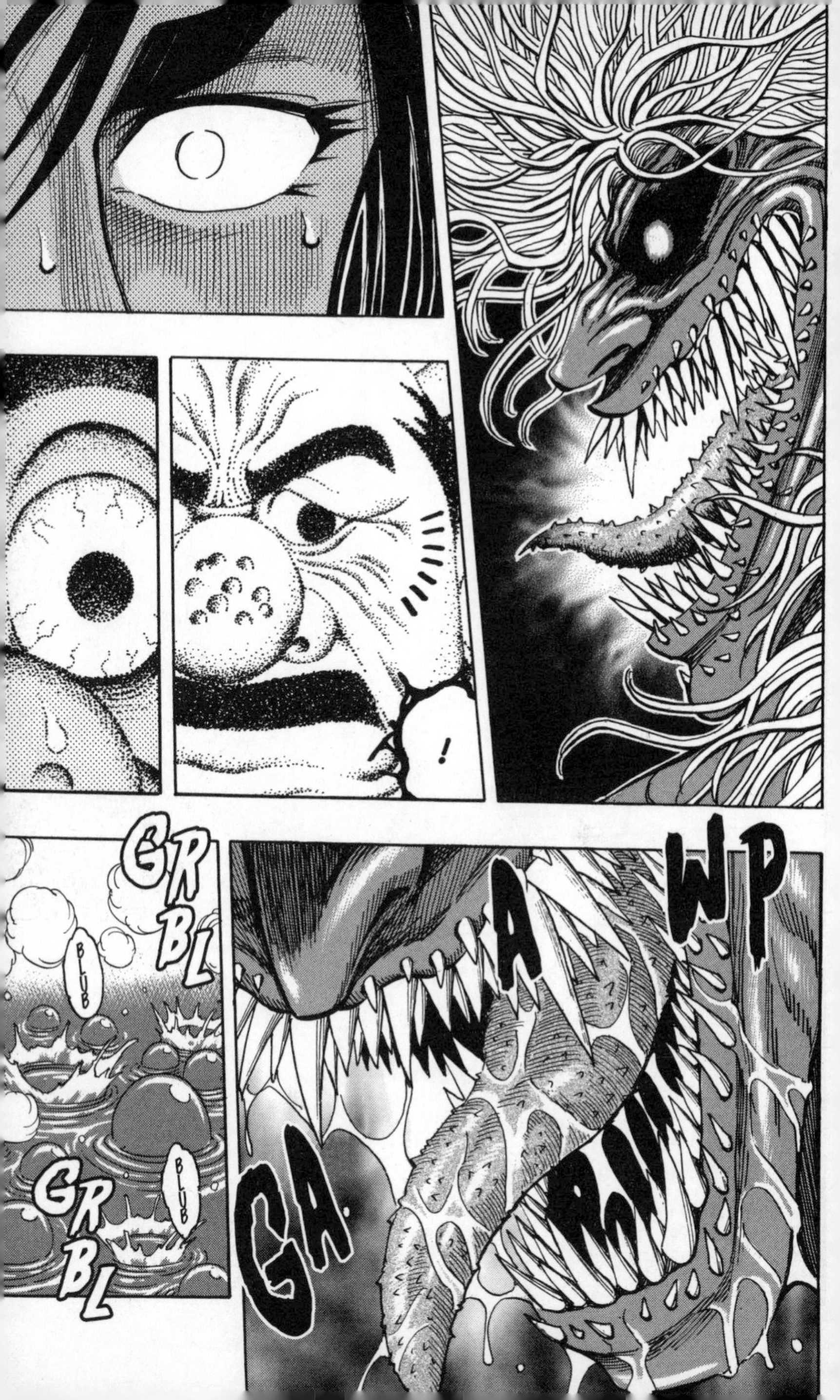
!
GA
A
WP
GRBL
BLUB
GRBL
BLUB

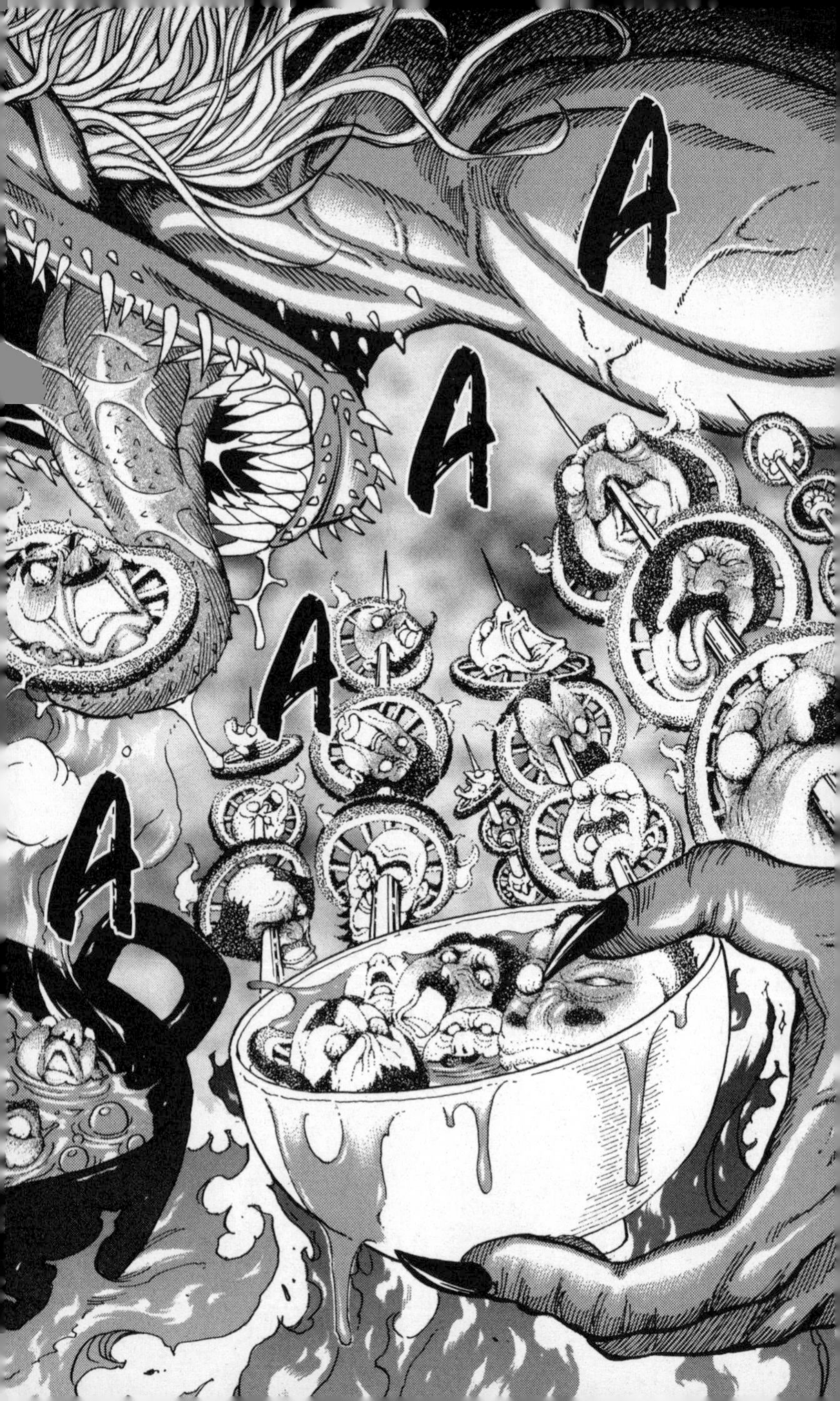
AAAA

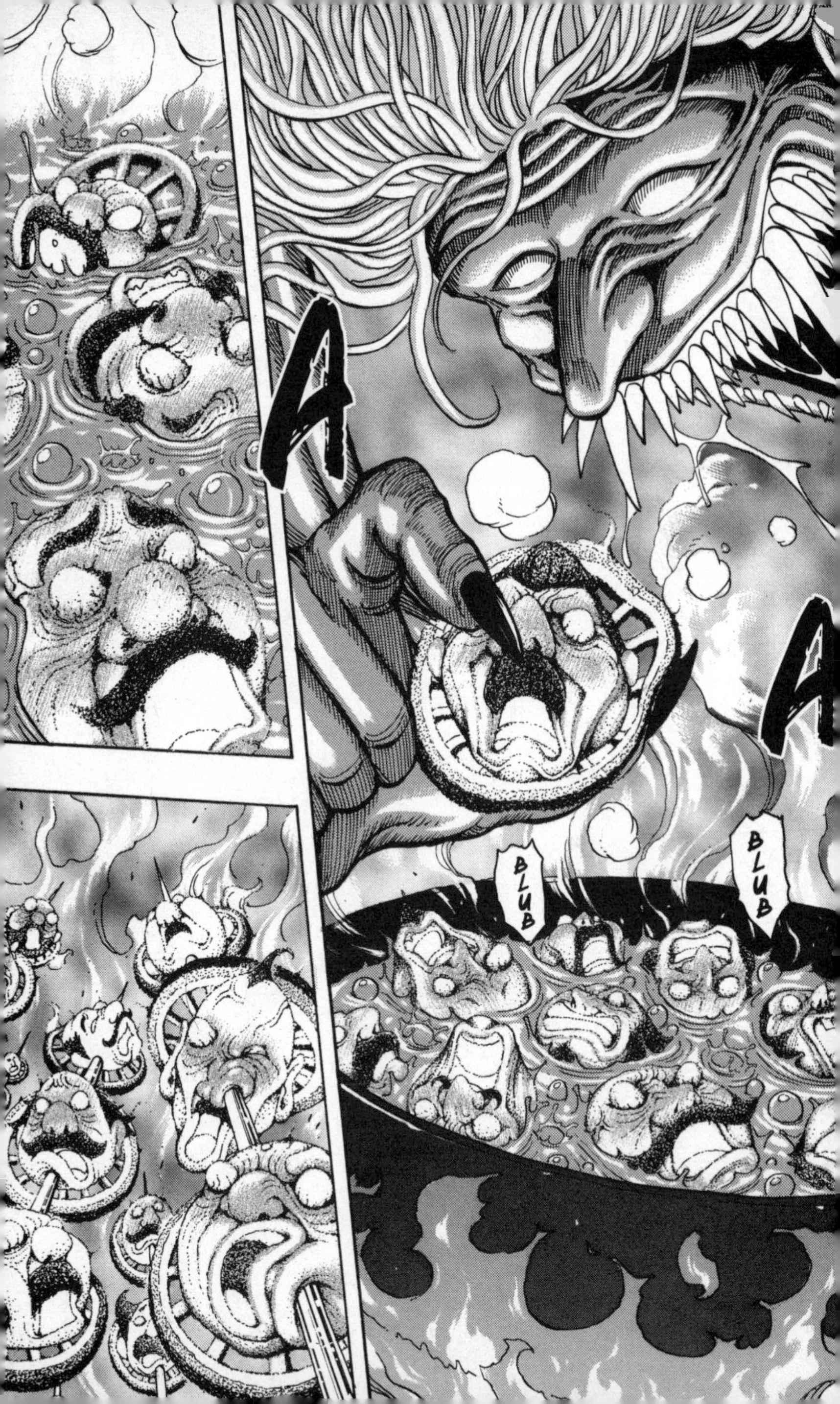
A
A
BLUB
BLUB

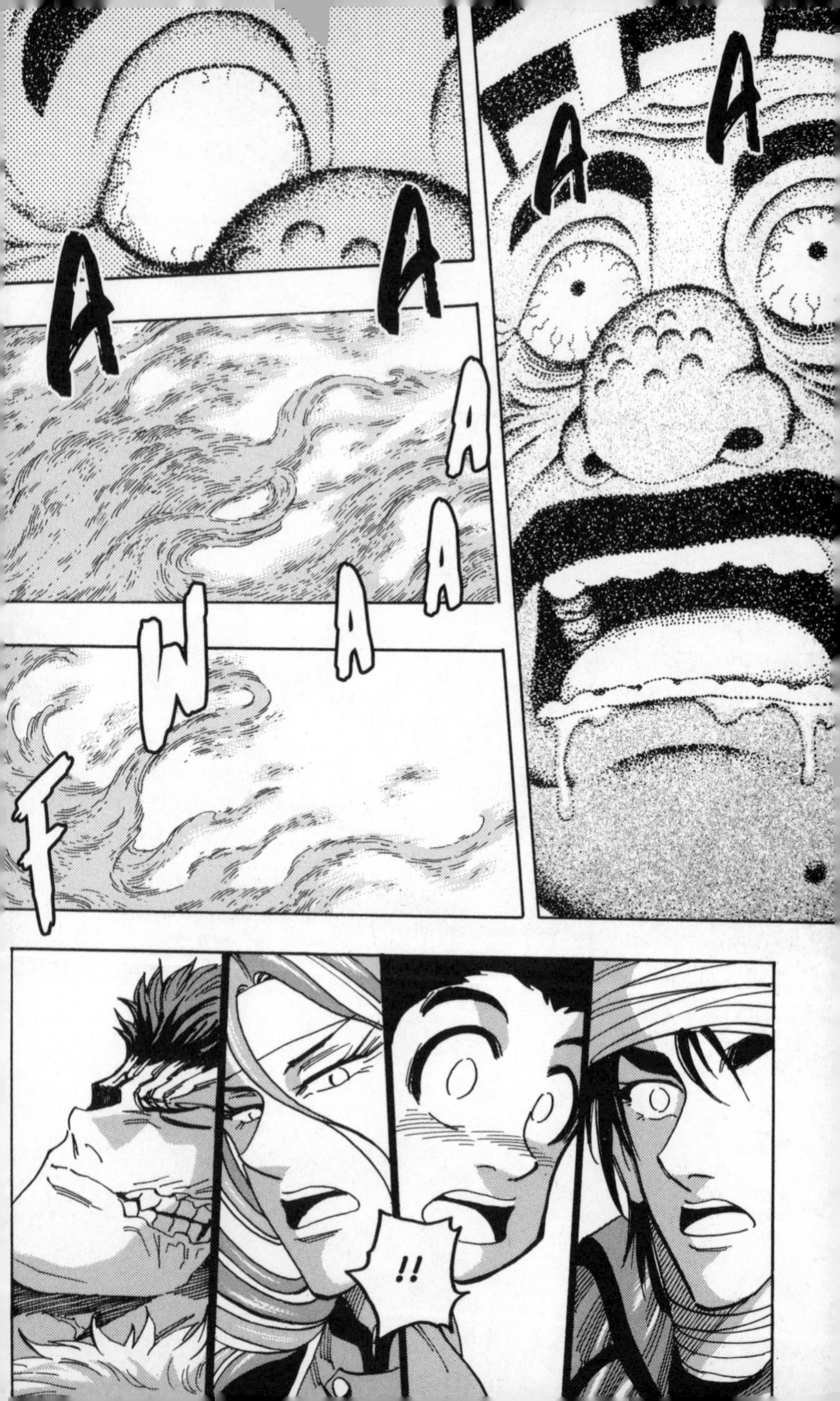
FWAAAAAAA
!!

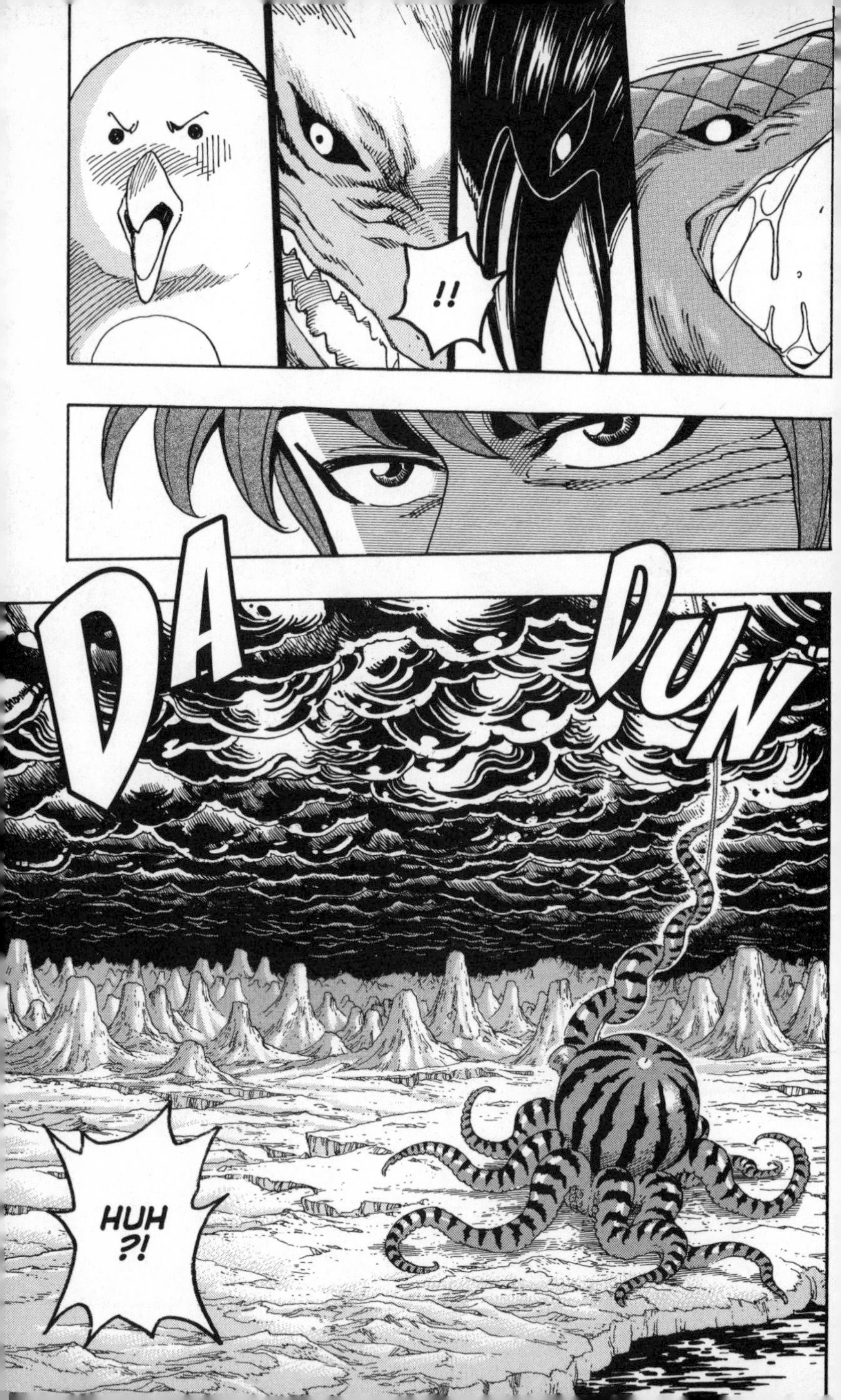
!!
DA DUN
HUH ?!

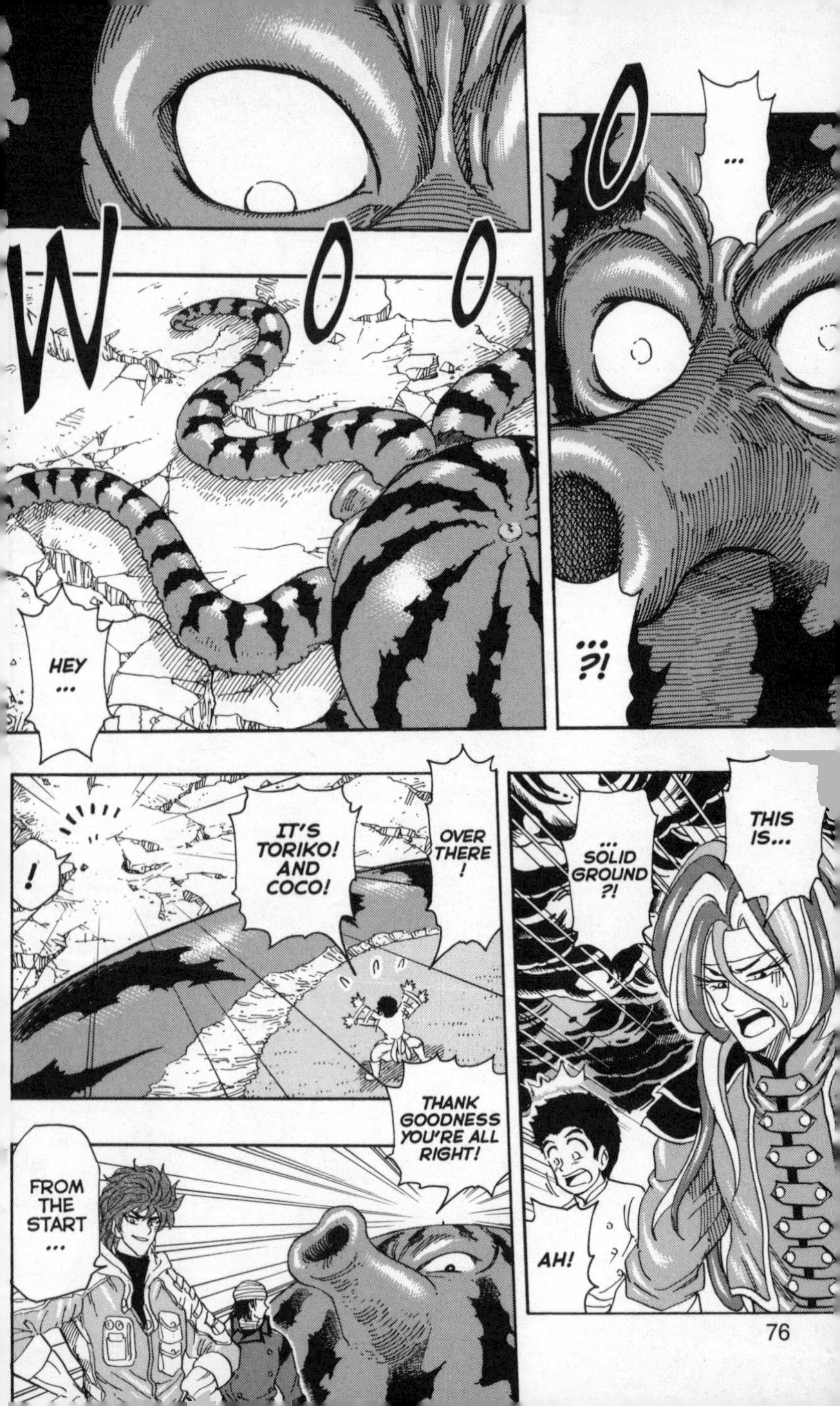
...
...?!
WOOO
HEY...
THIS IS...
...SOLID GROUND?!
AH!
OVER THERE!
IT'S TORIKO! AND COCO!
!
THANK GOODNESS YOU'RE ALL RIGHT!
FROM THE START...

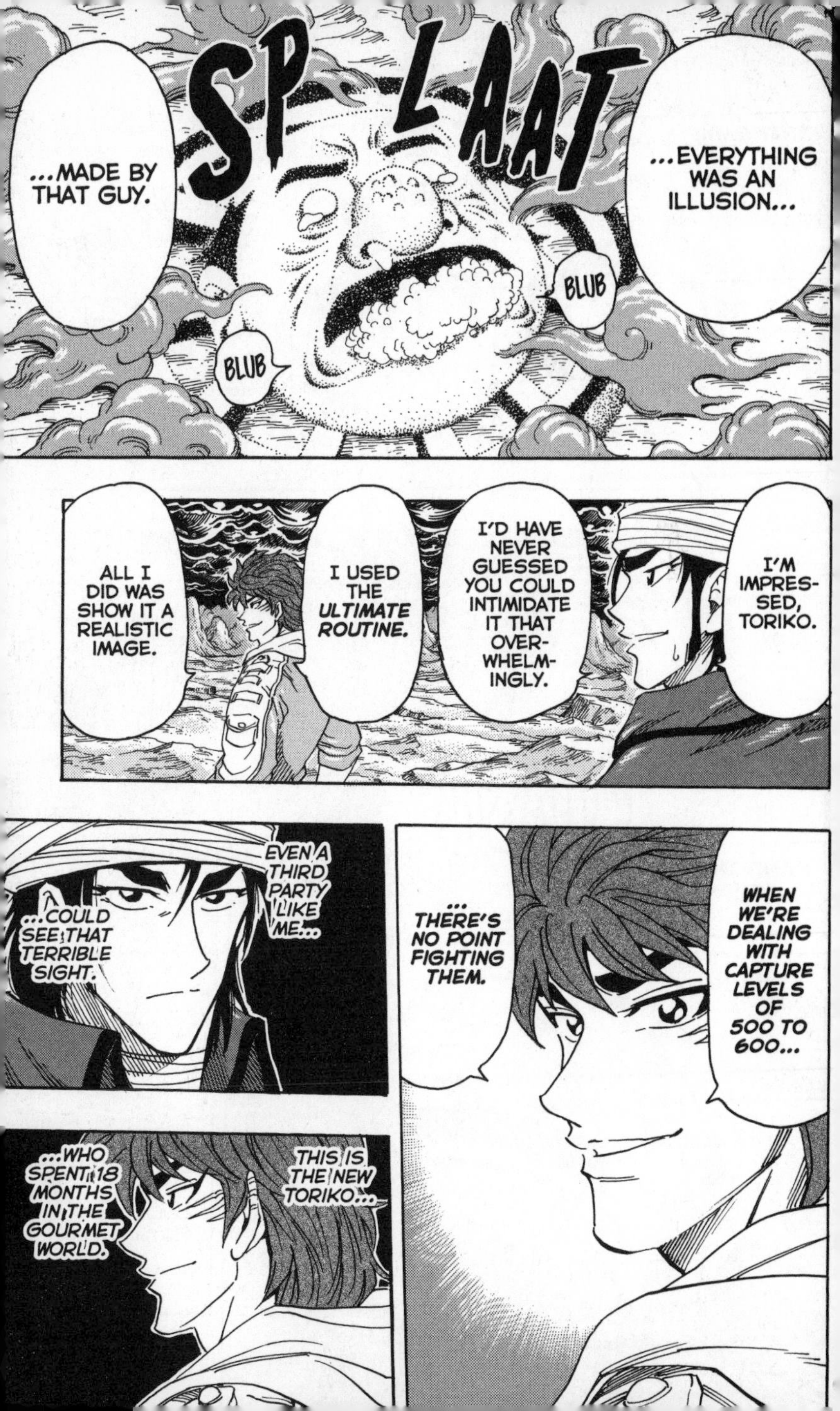

...EVERYTHING WAS AN ILLUSION...
SPLAAT
BLUB
BLUB
...MADE BY THAT GUY.
I'M IMPRESSED, TORIKO.
I'D HAVE NEVER GUESSED YOU COULD INTIMIDATE IT THAT OVERWHELMINGLY.
I USED THE *ULTIMATE ROUTINE.*
ALL I DID WAS SHOW IT A REALISTIC IMAGE.
WHEN WE'RE DEALING WITH CAPTURE LEVELS OF 500 TO 600...
...THERE'S NO POINT FIGHTING THEM.
EVEN A THIRD PARTY LIKE ME...
...COULD SEE THAT TERRIBLE SIGHT.
THIS IS THE NEW TORIKO...
...WHO SPENT 18 MONTHS IN THE GOURMET WORLD.

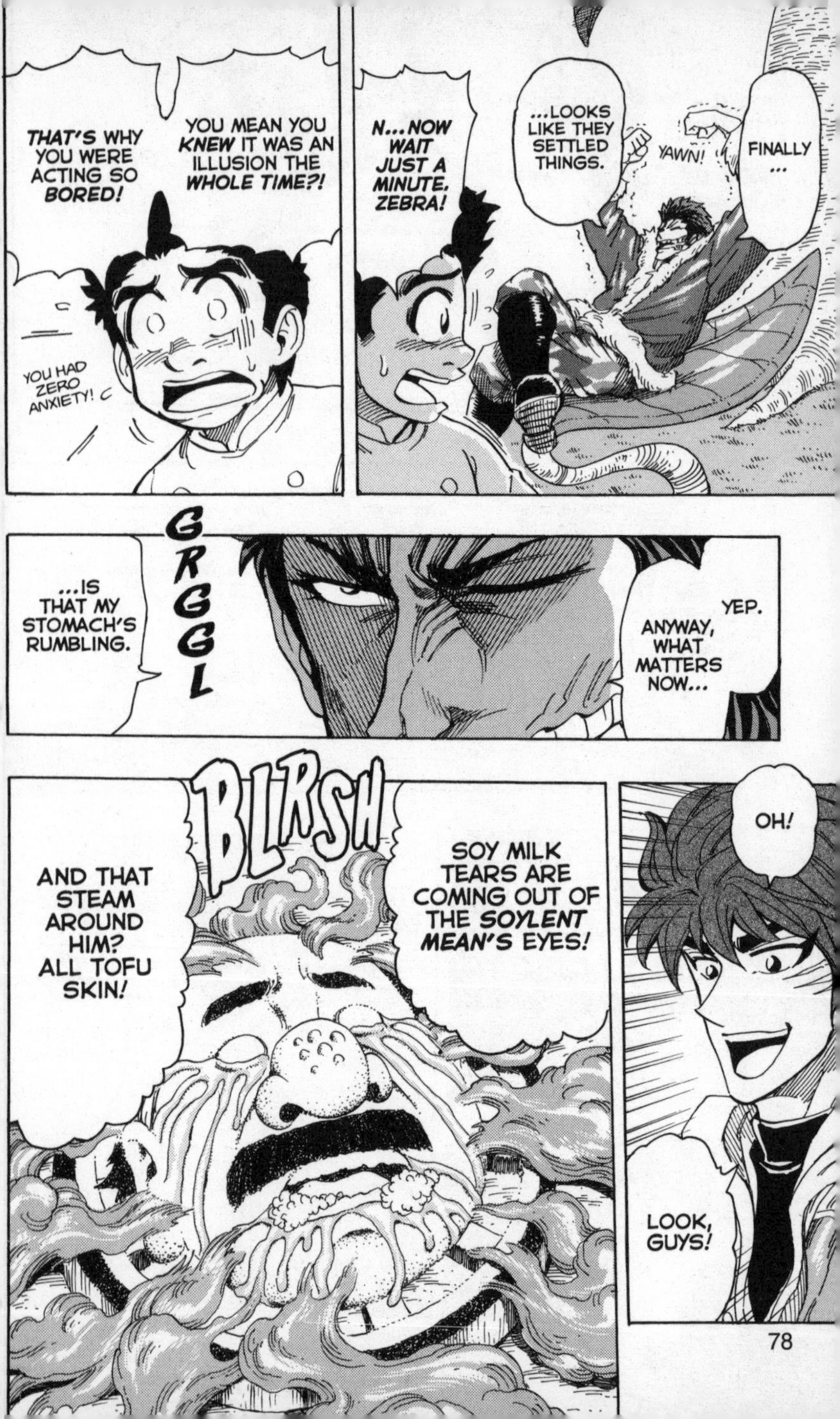
FINALLY ...
YAWN!
...LOOKS LIKE THEY SETTLED THINGS.
N...NOW WAIT JUST A MINUTE, ZEBRA!
YOU MEAN YOU KNEW IT WAS AN ILLUSION THE WHOLE TIME?!
THAT'S WHY YOU WERE ACTING SO BORED!
YOU HAD ZERO ANXIETY!
YEP. ANYWAY, WHAT MATTERS NOW...
GRGGL
...IS THAT MY STOMACH'S RUMBLING.
OH!
LOOK, GUYS!
BLRSH
SOY MILK TEARS ARE COMING OUT OF THE SOYLENT MEAN'S EYES!
AND THAT STEAM AROUND HIM? ALL TOFU SKIN!

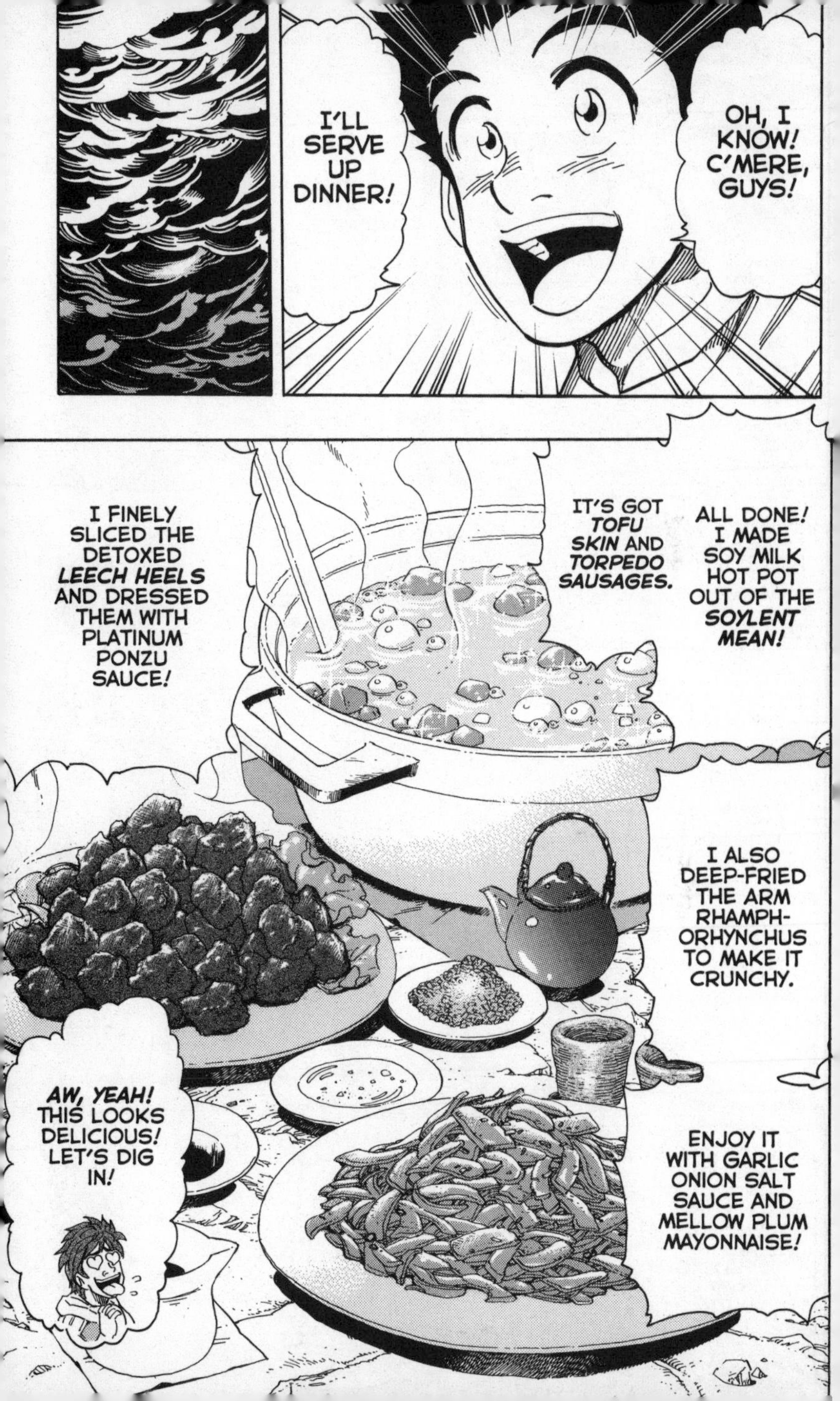
OH, I KNOW! C'MERE, GUYS!
I'LL SERVE UP DINNER!
ALL DONE! I MADE SOY MILK HOT POT OUT OF THE *SOYLENT MEAN!*
IT'S GOT *TOFU SKIN* AND *TORPEDO SAUSAGES.*
I FINELY SLICED THE DETOXED *LEECH HEELS* AND DRESSED THEM WITH PLATINUM PONZU SAUCE!
I ALSO DEEP-FRIED THE ARM RHAMPH-ORHYNCHUS TO MAKE IT CRUNCHY.
ENJOY IT WITH GARLIC ONION SALT SAUCE AND MELLOW PLUM MAYONNAISE!
AW, YEAH! THIS LOOKS DELICIOUS! LET'S DIG IN!

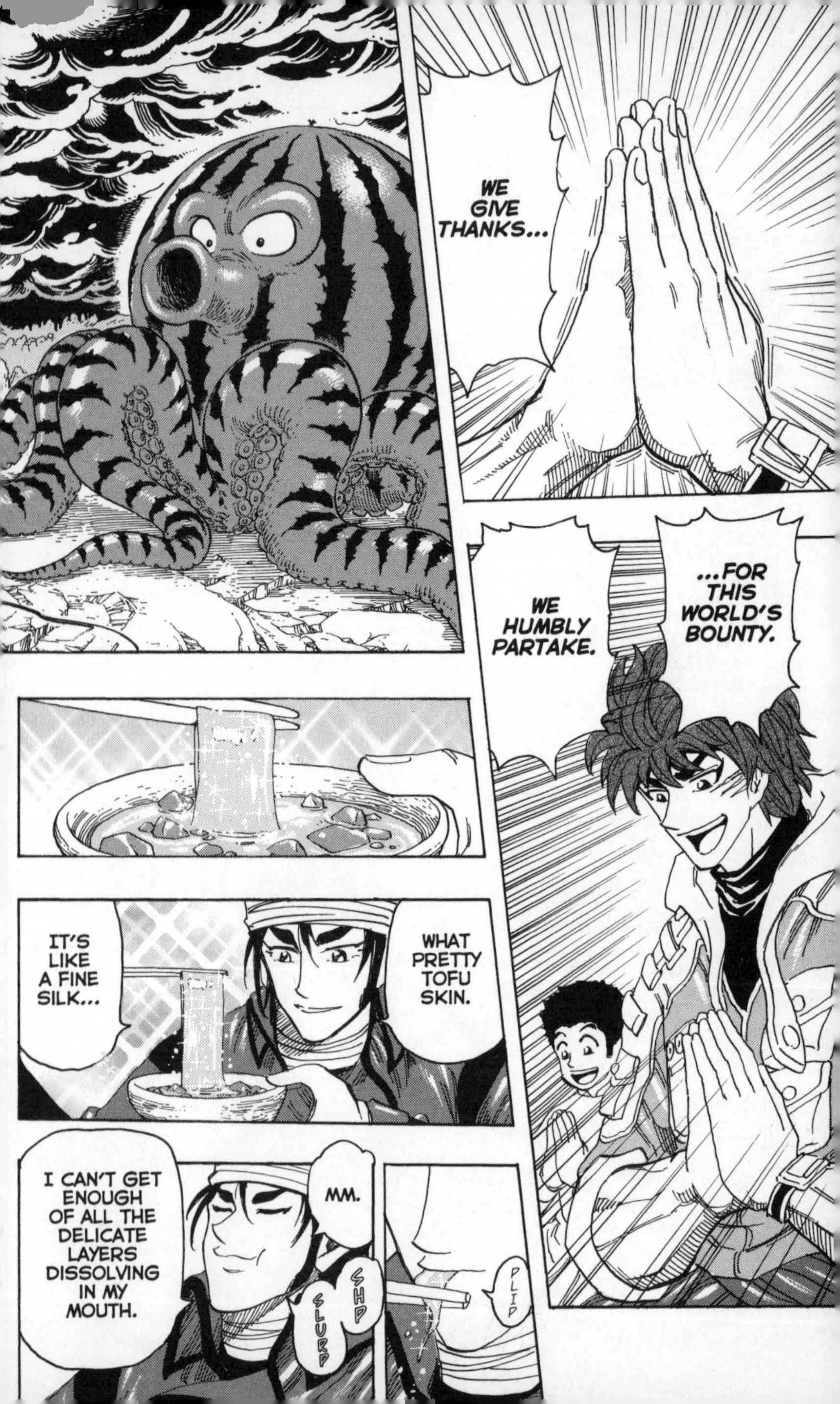
WE GIVE THANKS...
...FOR THIS WORLD'S BOUNTY.
WE HUMBLY PARTAKE.
WHAT PRETTY TOFU SKIN.
IT'S LIKE A FINE SILK...
PLIP
MM.
I CAN'T GET ENOUGH OF ALL THE DELICATE LAYERS DISSOLVING IN MY MOUTH.
SHP
SLURP

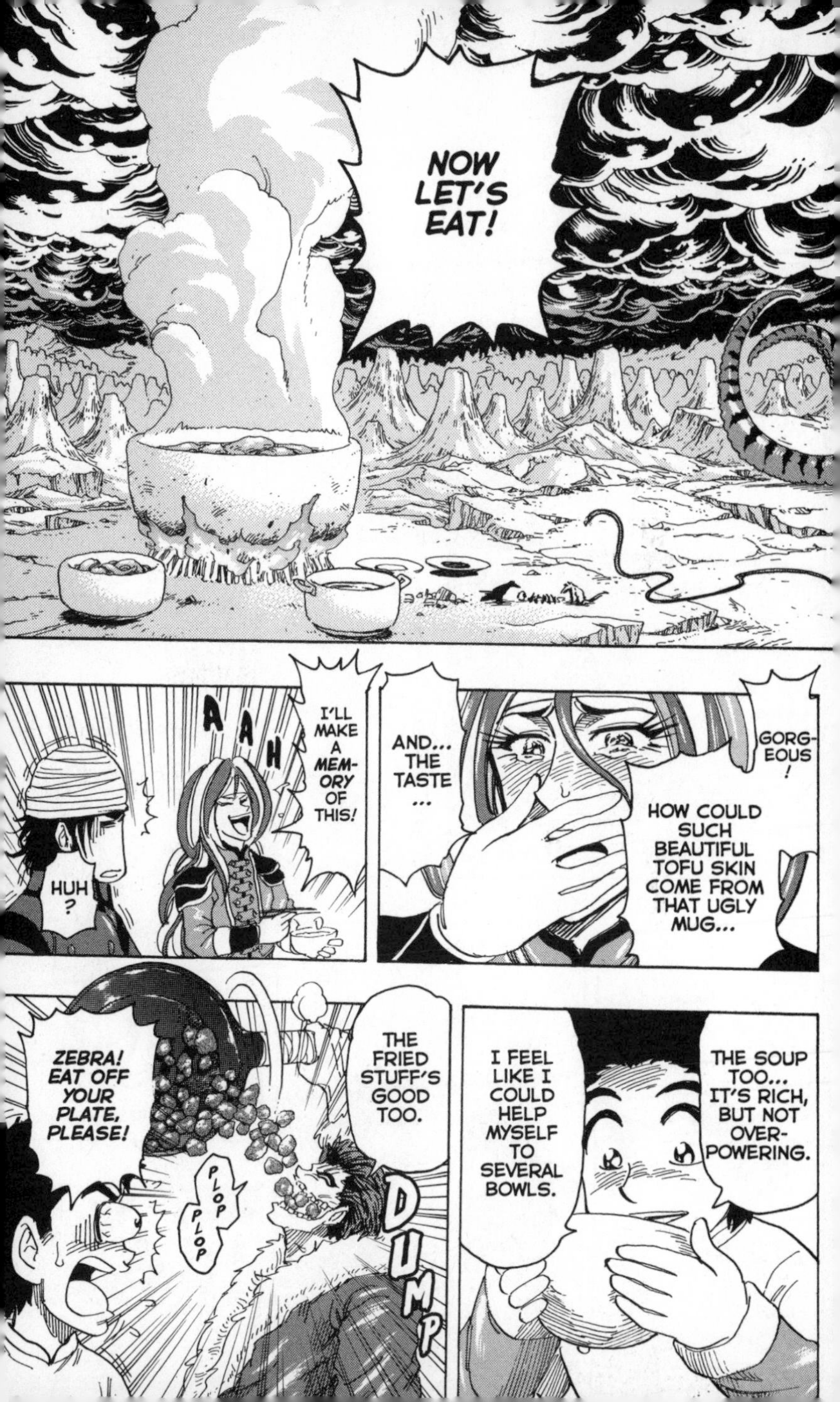
NOW LET'S EAT!
AND... THE TASTE...
GORGEOUS!
HOW COULD SUCH BEAUTIFUL TOFU SKIN COME FROM THAT UGLY MUG...
I'LL MAKE A MEMORY OF THIS!
AAH
HUH?
THE SOUP TOO... IT'S RICH, BUT NOT OVERPOWERING.
I FEEL LIKE I COULD HELP MYSELF TO SEVERAL BOWLS.
THE FRIED STUFF'S GOOD TOO.
DUMP
PLOP PLOP
ZEBRA! EAT OFF YOUR PLATE, PLEASE!

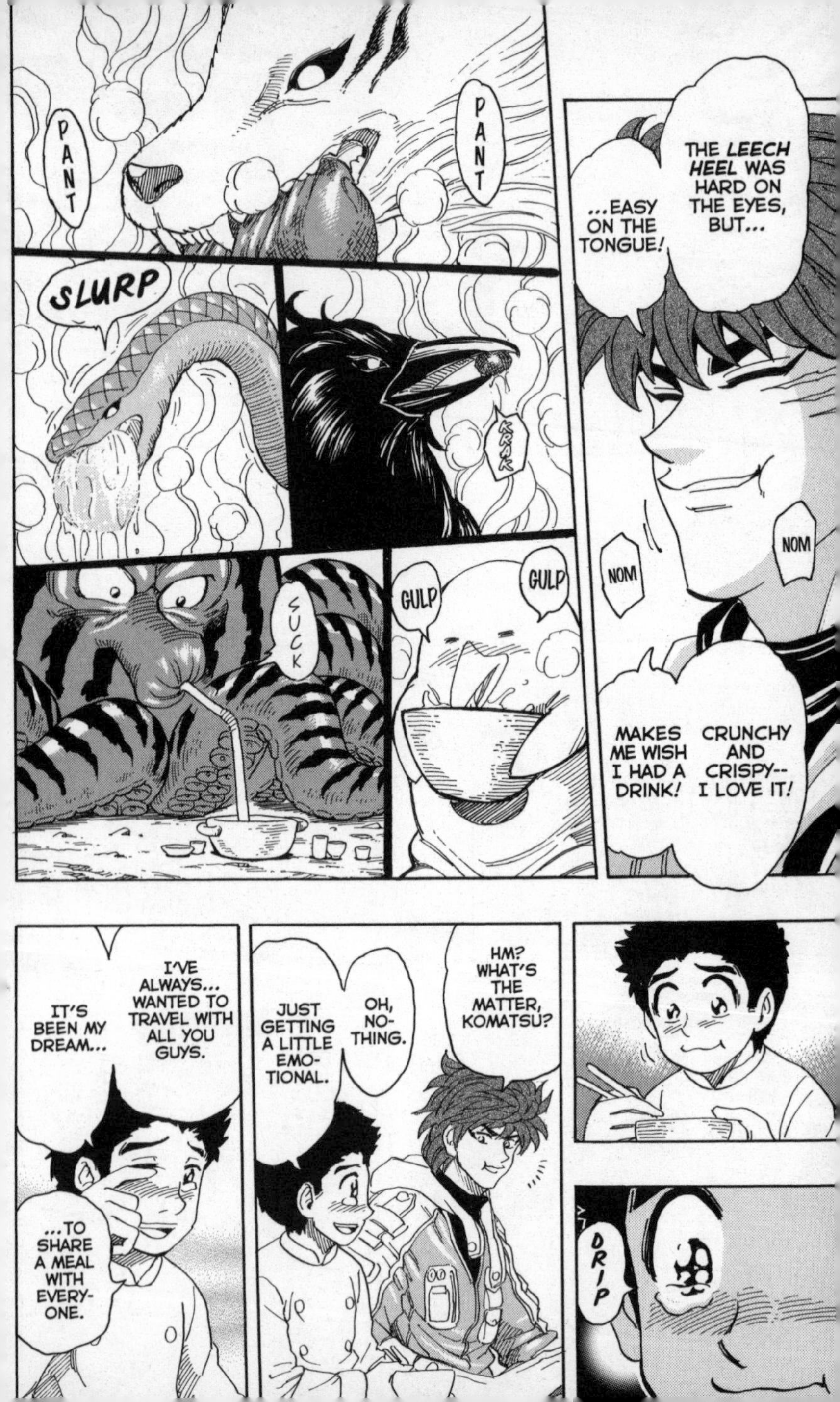
THE *LEECH HEEL* WAS HARD ON THE EYES, BUT...
...EASY ON THE TONGUE!
NOM
NOM
CRUNCHY AND CRISPY-- I LOVE IT!
MAKES ME WISH I HAD A DRINK!
PANT
PANT
KRAK
SLURP
GULP
GULP
SUCK
DRIP
HM? WHAT'S THE MATTER, KOMATSU?
OH, NO-THING.
JUST GETTING A LITTLE EMO-TIONAL.
I'VE ALWAYS... WANTED TO TRAVEL WITH ALL YOU GUYS.
IT'S BEEN MY DREAM...
...TO SHARE A MEAL WITH EVERY-ONE.

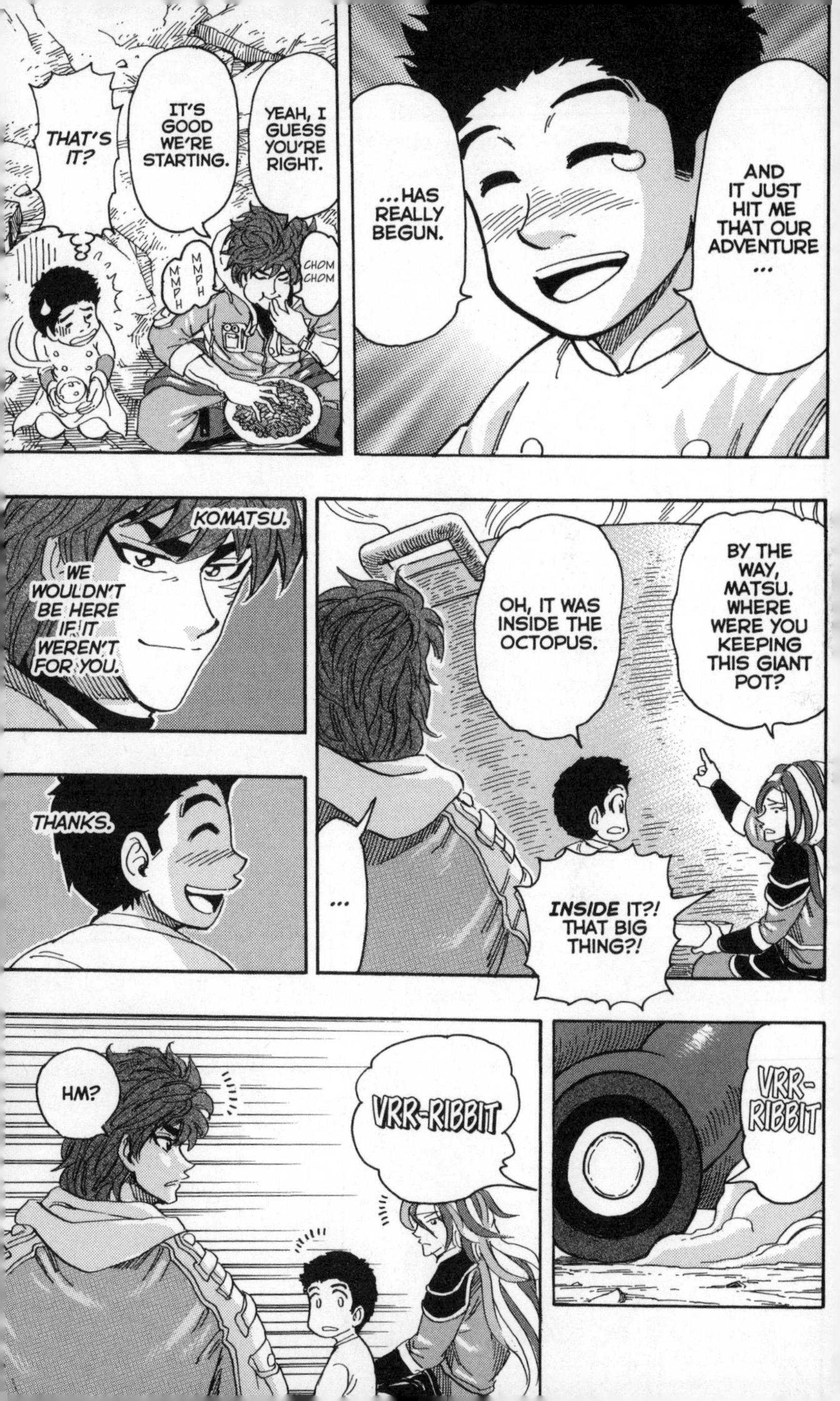
AND IT JUST HIT ME THAT OUR ADVENTURE ...
...HAS REALLY BEGUN.
YEAH, I GUESS YOU'RE RIGHT.
IT'S GOOD WE'RE STARTING.
THAT'S IT?
CHOM CHOM
MMPH MMPH
BY THE WAY, MATSU. WHERE WERE YOU KEEPING THIS GIANT POT?
OH, IT WAS INSIDE THE OCTOPUS.
INSIDE IT?! THAT BIG THING?!
...
KOMATSU.
WE WOULDN'T BE HERE IF IT WEREN'T FOR YOU.
THANKS.
VRR-RIBBIT
VRR-RIBBIT
HM?

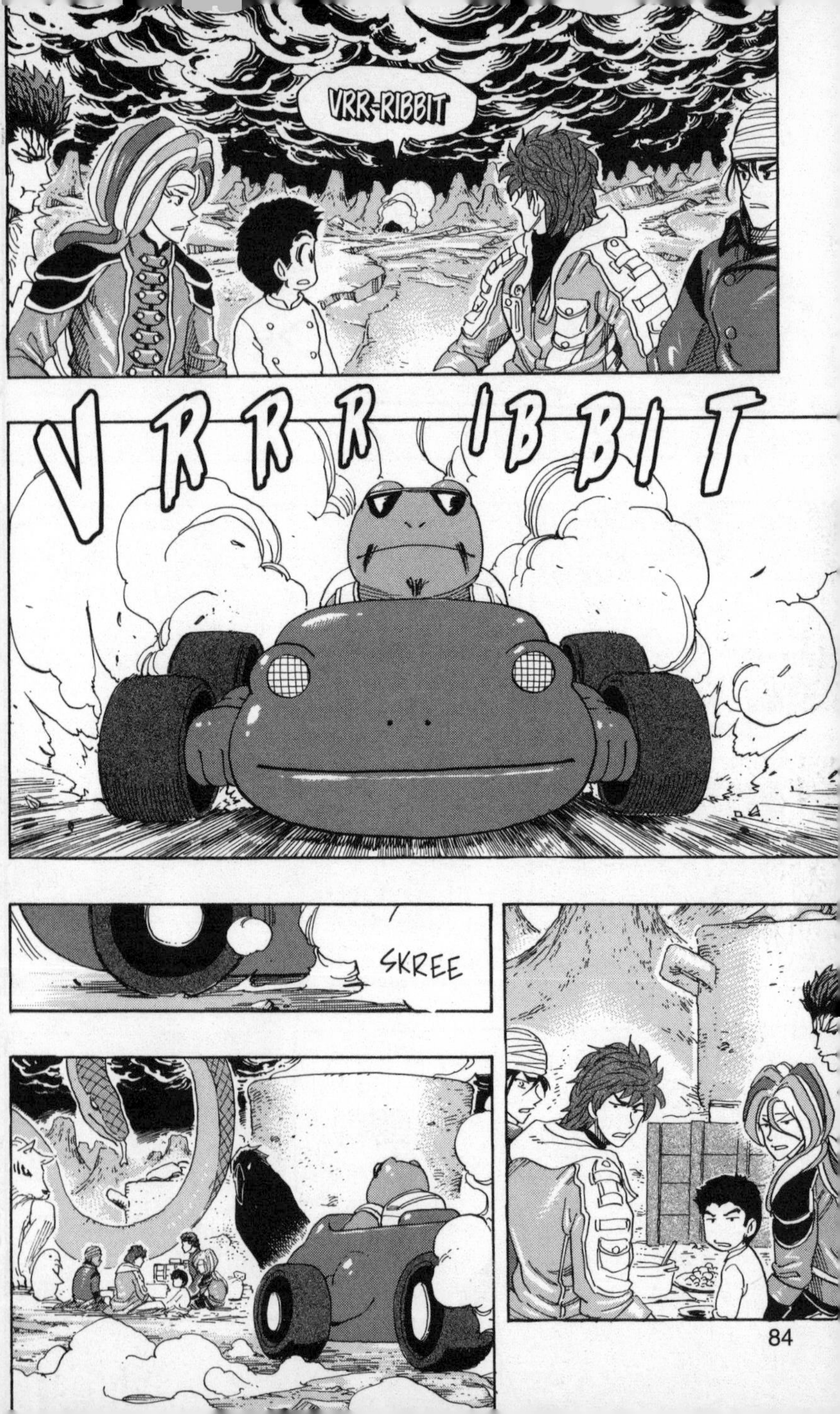
VRR-RIBBIT
VRRRIBBIT
SKREE

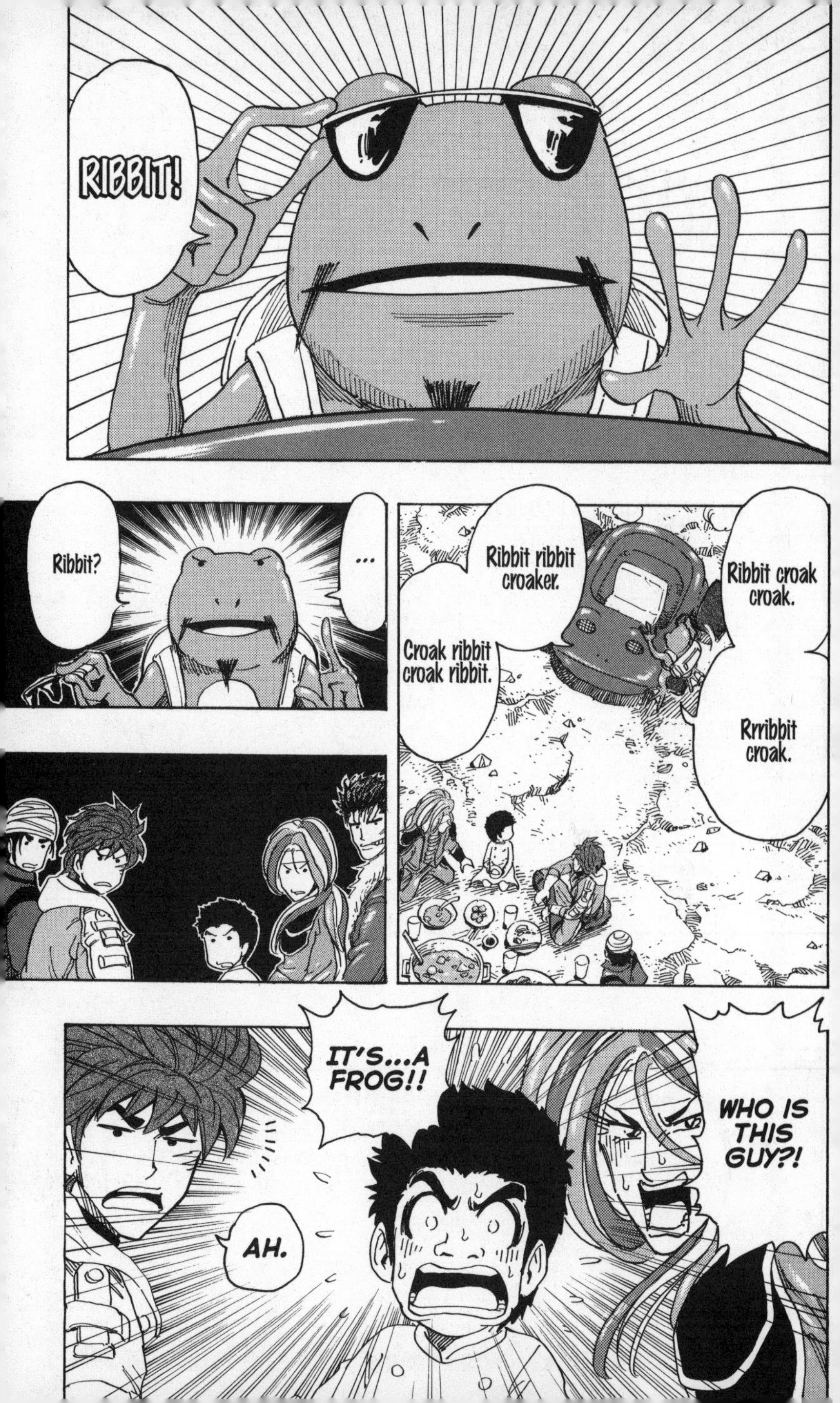
RIBBIT!
Ribbit croak croak.
Rrribbit croak.
Ribbit ribbit croaker.
Croak ribbit croak ribbit.
...
Ribbit?
WHO IS THIS GUY?!
IT'S...A FROG!!
AH.

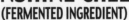

GOURMET CHECKLIST

Vol. 300

SUNSHINE CHEESE
(FERMENTED INGREDIENT)

CAPTURE LEVEL: 3
HABITAT: ARTIFICIALLY PRODUCED BUT ONLY IN SMALL QUANTITIES
SIZE: 10 CM
HEIGHT: ---
WEIGHT: 250 GRAMS
PRICE: 6,000 YEN PER WHEEL

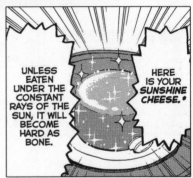

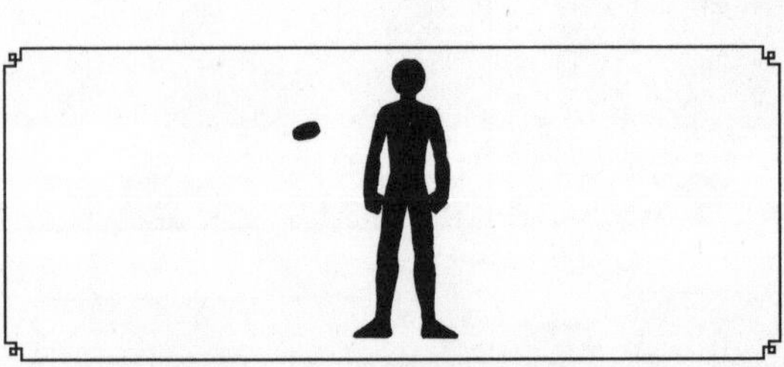

HERE IS YOUR *SUNSHINE CHEESE.**
UNLESS EATEN UNDER THE CONSTANT RAYS OF THE SUN, IT WILL BECOME HARD AS BONE.

SCALE

A UNIQUE AND BEAUTIFUL CHEESE THAT MATURES BY ABSORBING THE GLISTENING RAYS OF THE SUN. IT MUST CONSTANTLY BE SHOWERED IN THE SUN'S RAYS AS IT IS PRODUCED AND EATEN. IF THE CHEESE IS SHROUDED IN DARKNESS, IT WILL HARDEN AND LOSE ITS SIGNATURE SUNSHINE CHEESE FLAVOR, MAKING IT AN INGREDIENT THAT REQUIRES SPECIAL PREPARATION.

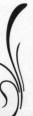

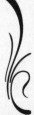

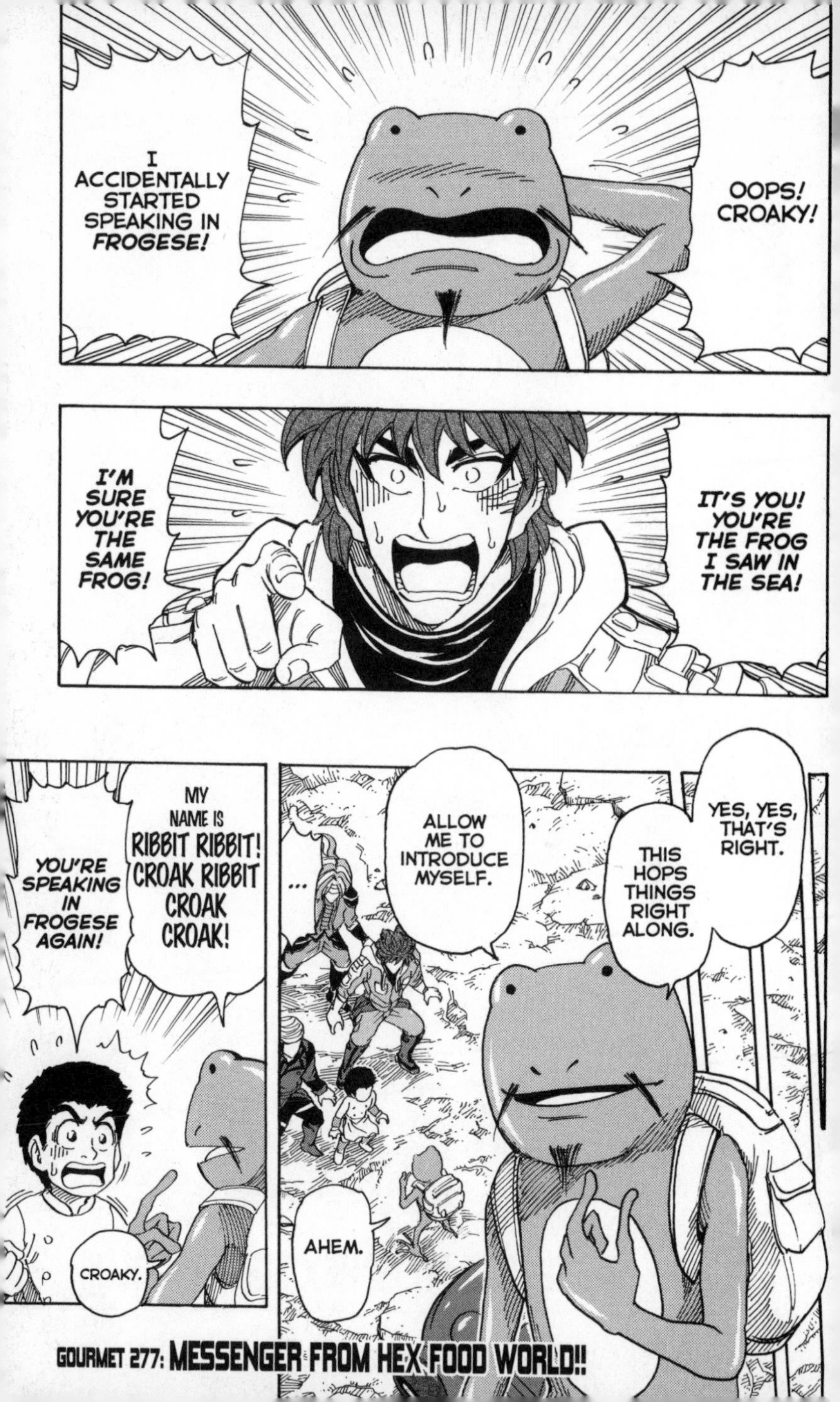
OOPS! CROAKY!
I ACCIDENTALLY STARTED SPEAKING IN FROGESE!
IT'S YOU! YOU'RE THE FROG I SAW IN THE SEA!
I'M SURE YOU'RE THE SAME FROG!
YES, YES, THAT'S RIGHT.
THIS HOPS THINGS RIGHT ALONG.
ALLOW ME TO INTRODUCE MYSELF.
...
AHEM.
MY NAME IS RIBBIT RIBBIT! CROAK RIBBIT CROAK CROAK!
YOU'RE SPEAKING IN FROGESE AGAIN!
CROAKY.
GOURMET 277: MESSENGER FROM HEX FOOD WORLD!!

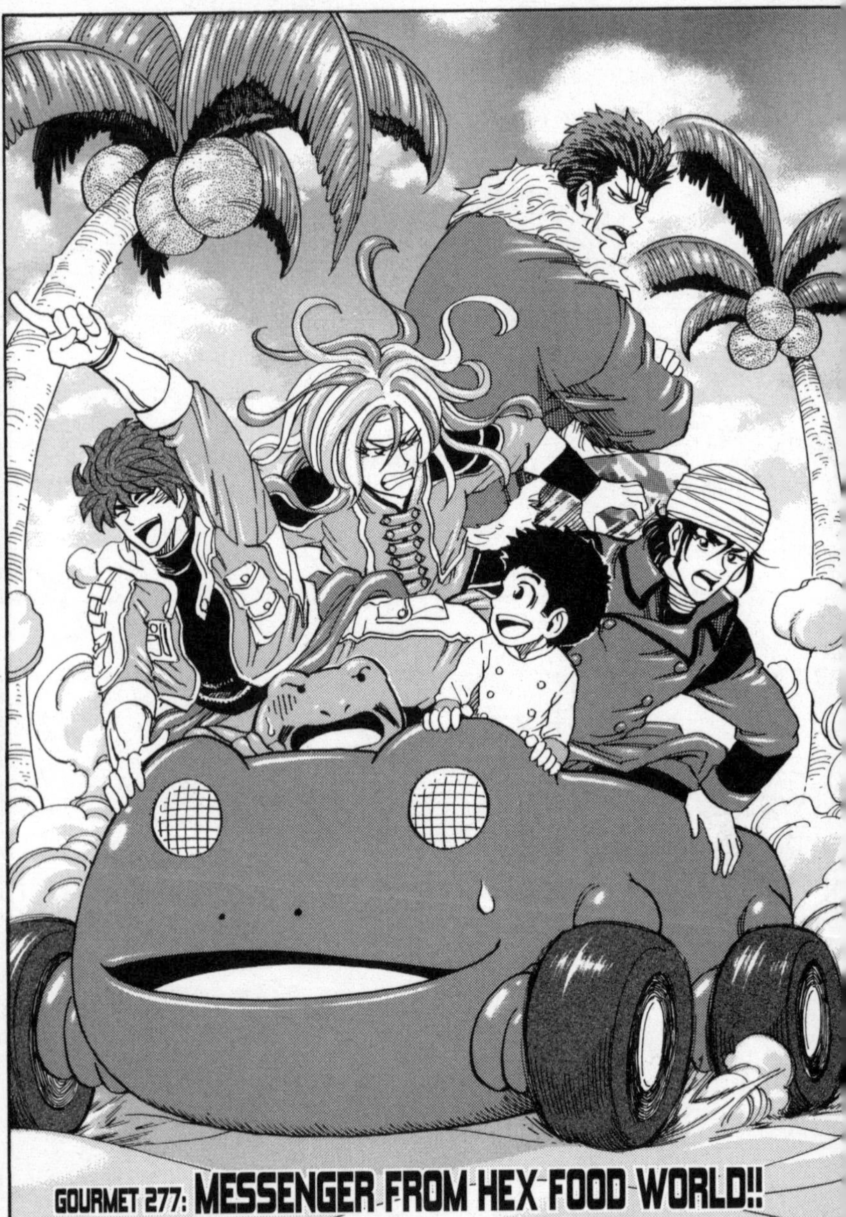
GOURMET 277: MESSENGER FROM HEX FOOD WORLD!!

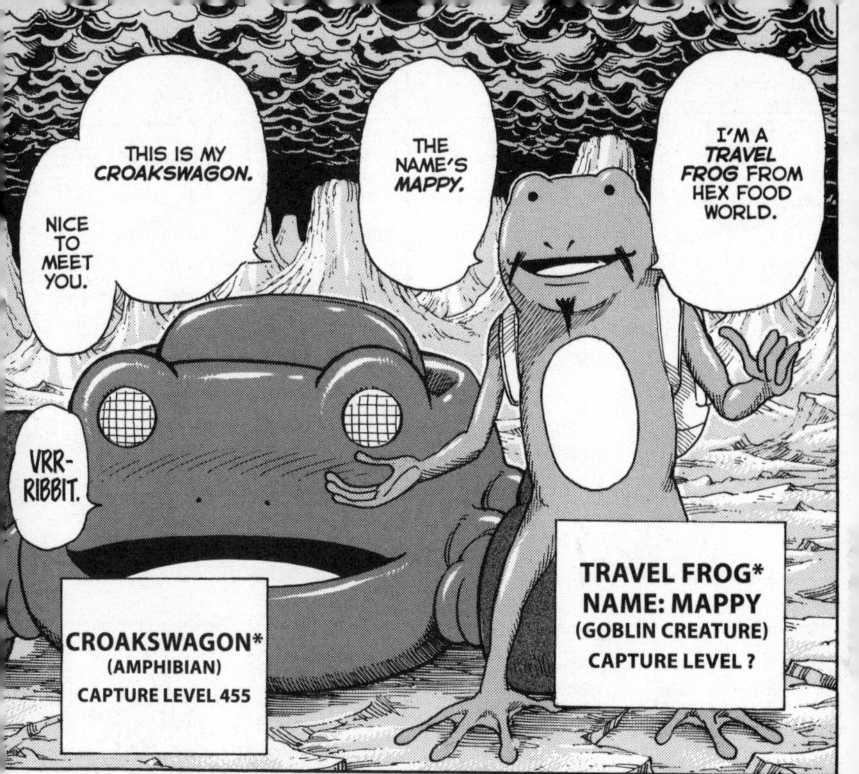
I'M A TRAVEL FROG FROM HEX FOOD WORLD.
THE NAME'S MAPPY.
THIS IS MY CROAKSWAGON.
NICE TO MEET YOU.
VRR-RIBBIT.
TRAVEL FROG* NAME: MAPPY (GOBLIN CREATURE) CAPTURE LEVEL ?
CROAKSWAGON* (AMPHIBIAN) CAPTURE LEVEL 455

*TRAVEL FROG SUBMITTED BY KEITA YOSHIIE FROM NAGANO!

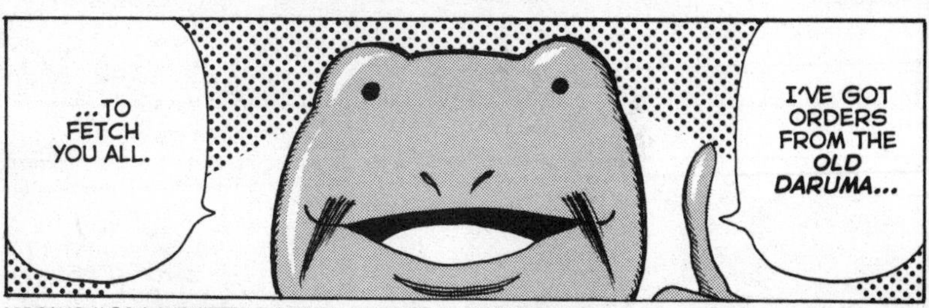
I'VE GOT ORDERS FROM THE OLD DARUMA...
...TO FETCH YOU ALL.

*CROAKSWAGON SUBMITTED BY IZURU INUBUSE FROM OSAKA!

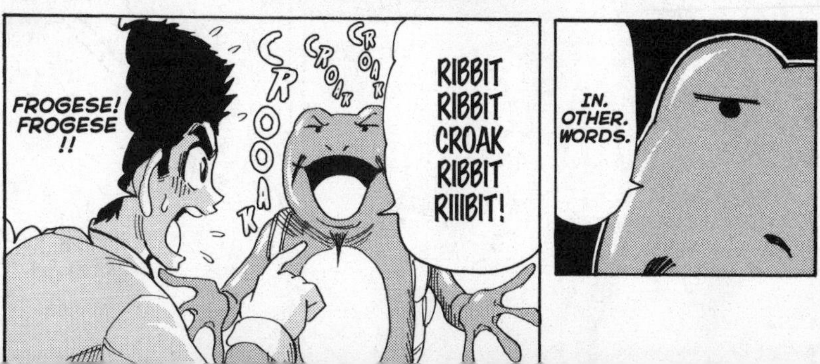
IN. OTHER. WORDS.
RIBBIT RIBBIT CROAK RIBBIT RIIIBIT!
CROAK
CROAK
CROOOAK
FROGESE! FROGESE !!

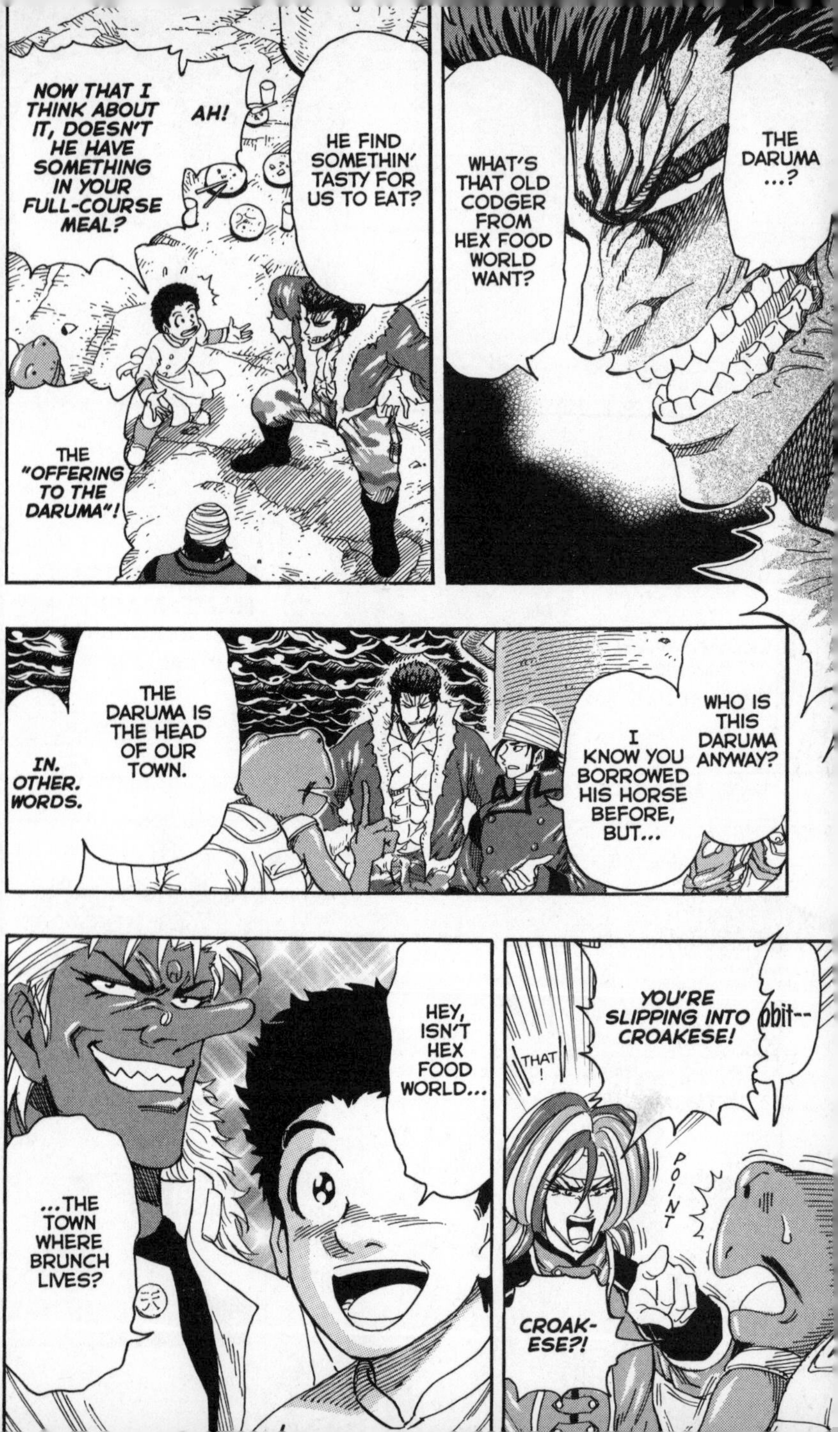
THE DARUMA ...?
WHAT'S THAT OLD CODGER FROM HEX FOOD WORLD WANT?
HE FIND SOMETHIN' TASTY FOR US TO EAT?
AH!
NOW THAT I THINK ABOUT IT, DOESN'T HE HAVE SOMETHING IN YOUR FULL-COURSE MEAL?
THE "OFFERING TO THE DARUMA"!
WHO IS THIS DARUMA ANYWAY?
I KNOW YOU BORROWED HIS HORSE BEFORE, BUT...
THE DARUMA IS THE HEAD OF OUR TOWN.
IN. OTHER. WORDS.
obit--
YOU'RE SLIPPING INTO CROAKESE!
THAT!
POINT
CROAK-ESE?!
HEY, ISN'T HEX FOOD WORLD...
...THE TOWN WHERE BRUNCH LIVES?

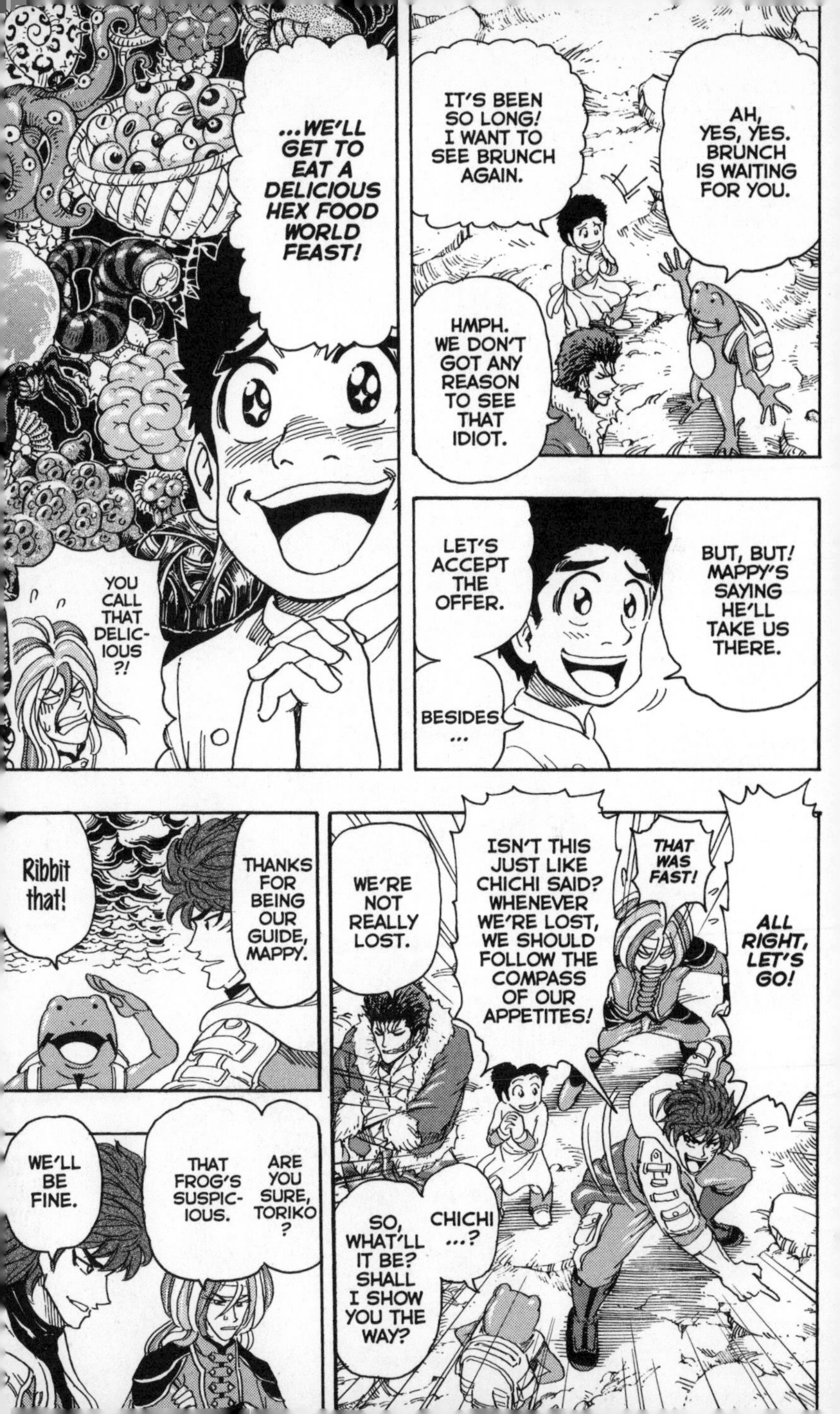
AH, YES, YES. BRUNCH IS WAITING FOR YOU.
IT'S BEEN SO LONG! I WANT TO SEE BRUNCH AGAIN.
HMPH. WE DON'T GOT ANY REASON TO SEE THAT IDIOT.
BUT, BUT! MAPPY'S SAYING HE'LL TAKE US THERE.
LET'S ACCEPT THE OFFER.
BESIDES...
...WE'LL GET TO EAT A DELICIOUS HEX FOOD WORLD FEAST!
YOU CALL THAT DELICIOUS?!
ALL RIGHT, LET'S GO!
THAT WAS FAST!
ISN'T THIS JUST LIKE CHICHI SAID? WHENEVER WE'RE LOST, WE SHOULD FOLLOW THE COMPASS OF OUR APPETITES!
WE'RE NOT REALLY LOST.
CHICHI ...?
SO, WHAT'LL IT BE? SHALL I SHOW YOU THE WAY?
THANKS FOR BEING OUR GUIDE, MAPPY.
Ribbit that!
ARE YOU SURE, TORIKO?
THAT FROG'S SUSPICIOUS.
WE'LL BE FINE.

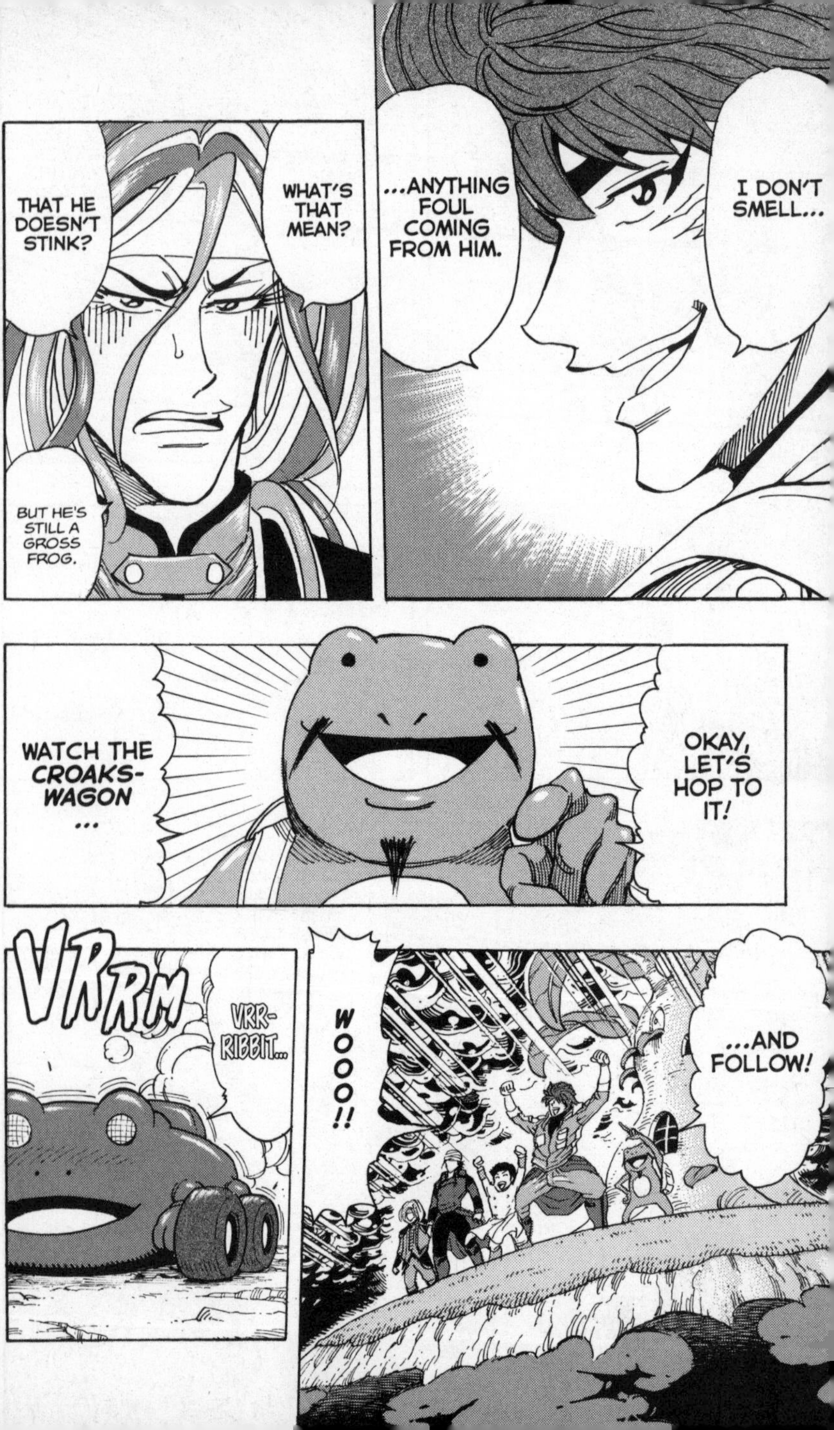
I DON'T SMELL...
...ANYTHING FOUL COMING FROM HIM.
WHAT'S THAT MEAN?
THAT HE DOESN'T STINK?
BUT HE'S STILL A GROSS FROG.
OKAY, LET'S HOP TO IT!
WATCH THE *CROAKS-WAGON* ...
...AND FOLLOW!
WOOOO!!
VRR-RIBBIT...
VRRM

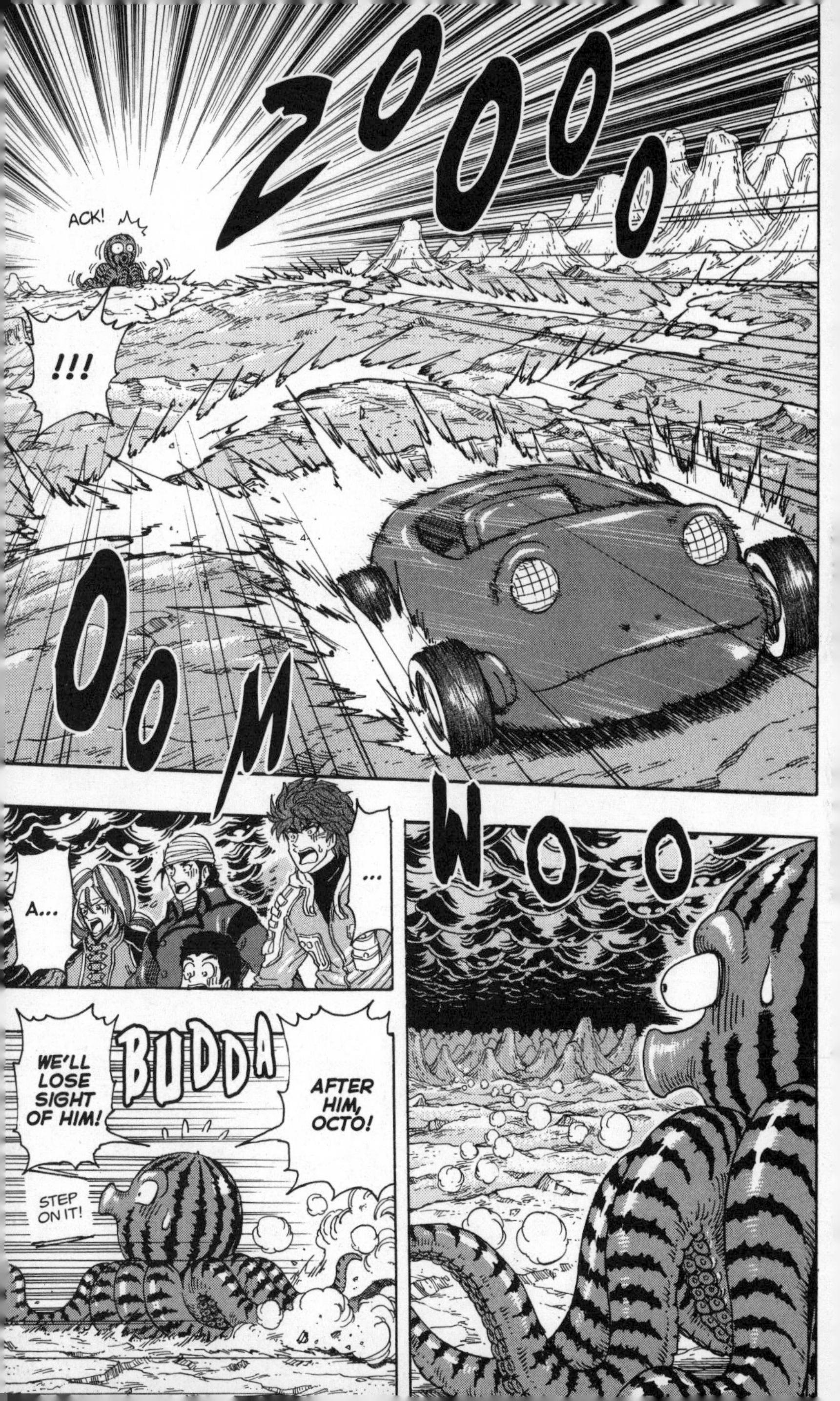
ZOOOOO
ACK!
!!!
OOM
WOOO
...
A...
AFTER HIM, OCTO!
BUDDA
WE'LL LOSE SIGHT OF HIM!
STEP ON IT!

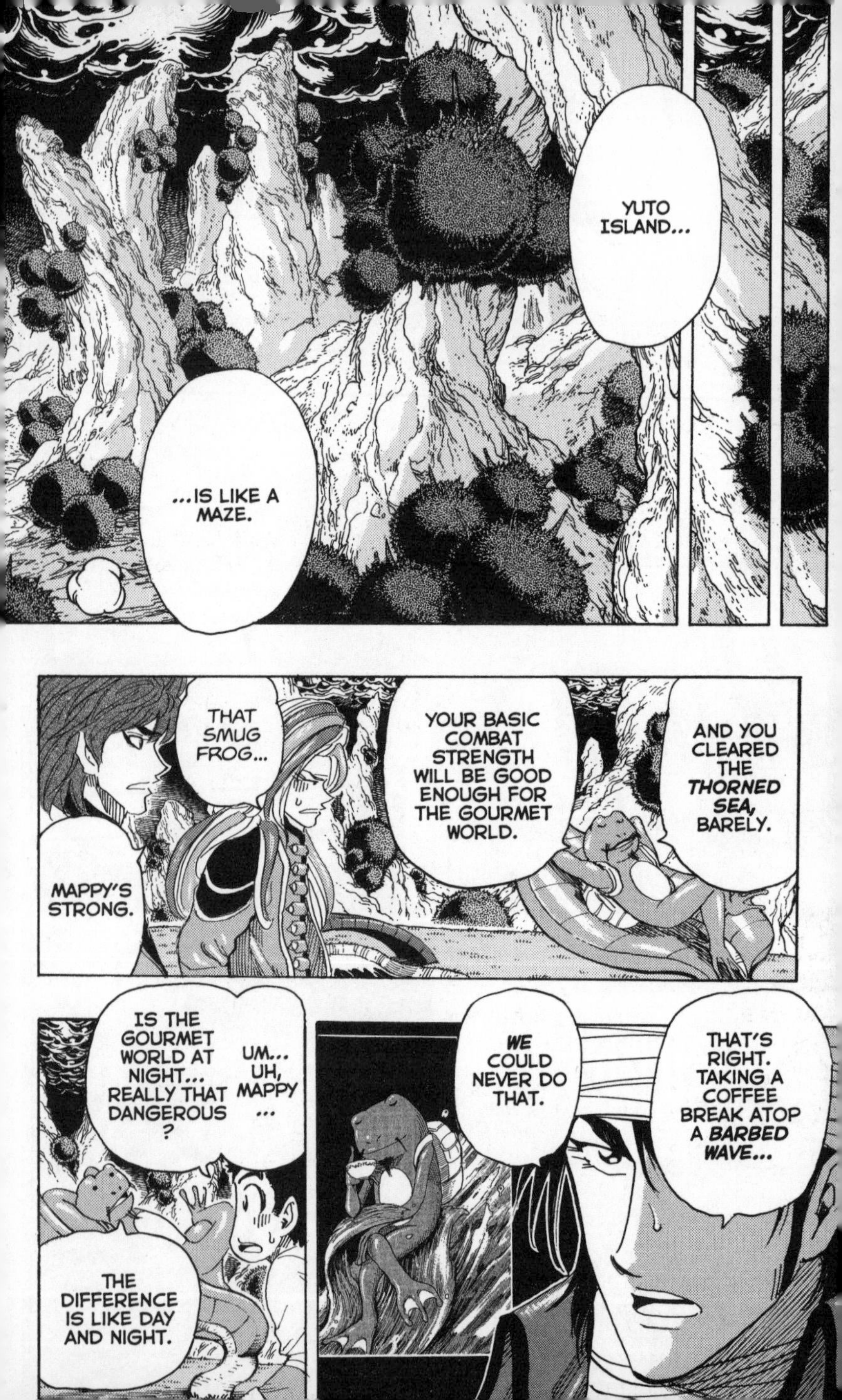
YUTO ISLAND...
...IS LIKE A MAZE.
AND YOU CLEARED THE *THORNED SEA,* BARELY.
YOUR BASIC COMBAT STRENGTH WILL BE GOOD ENOUGH FOR THE GOURMET WORLD.
THAT SMUG FROG...
MAPPY'S STRONG.
THAT'S RIGHT. TAKING A COFFEE BREAK ATOP A *BARBED WAVE...*
WE COULD NEVER DO THAT.
UM... UH, MAPPY...
IS THE GOURMET WORLD AT NIGHT... REALLY THAT DANGEROUS?
THE DIFFERENCE IS LIKE DAY AND NIGHT.

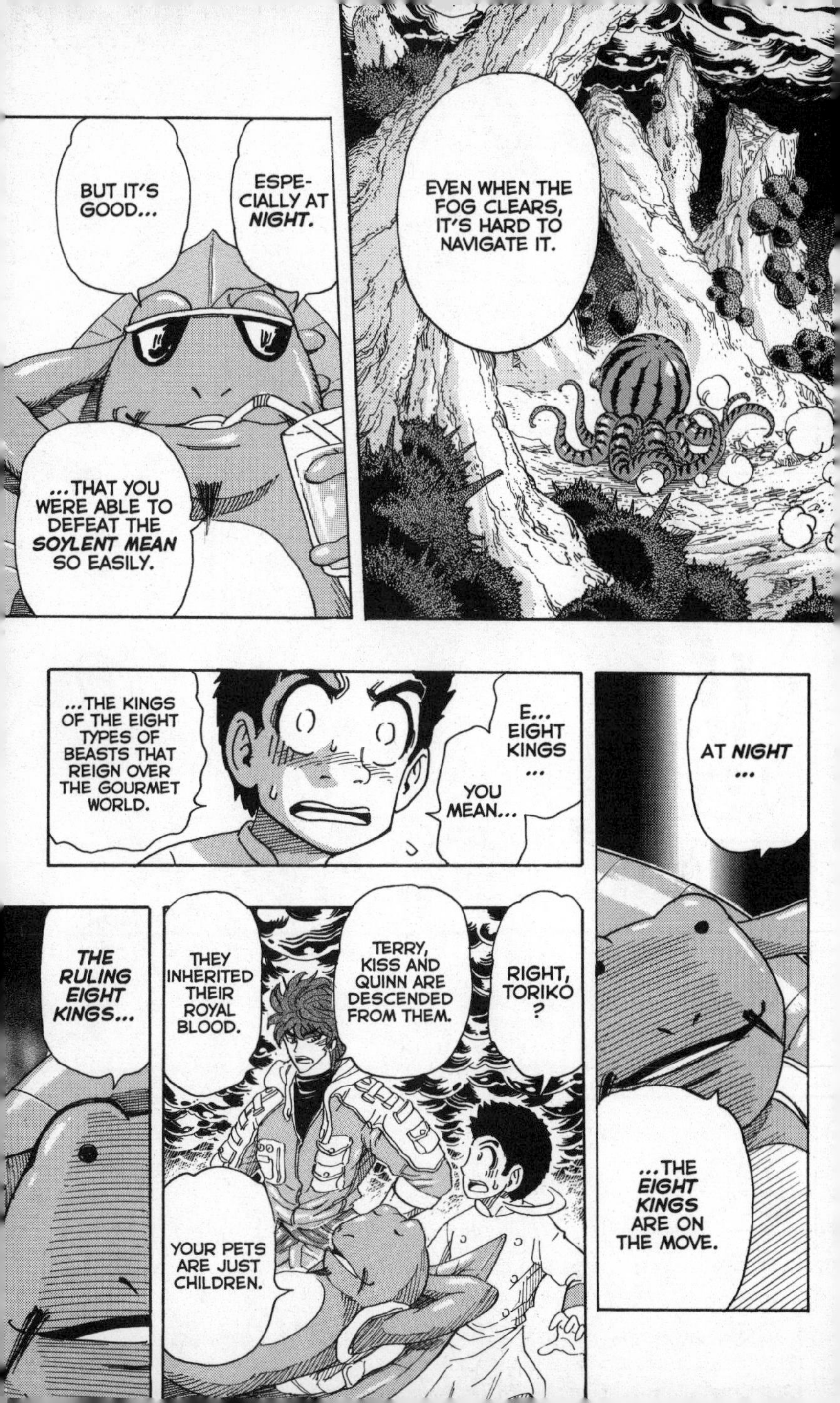
EVEN WHEN THE FOG CLEARS, IT'S HARD TO NAVIGATE IT.
ESPE-CIALLY AT *NIGHT*.
BUT IT'S GOOD...
...THAT YOU WERE ABLE TO DEFEAT THE *SOYLENT MEAN* SO EASILY.
AT *NIGHT*...
...THE *EIGHT KINGS* ARE ON THE MOVE.
E... EIGHT KINGS...
YOU MEAN...
...THE KINGS OF THE EIGHT TYPES OF BEASTS THAT REIGN OVER THE GOURMET WORLD.
RIGHT, TORIKO?
TERRY, KISS AND QUINN ARE DESCENDED FROM THEM.
THEY INHERITED THEIR ROYAL BLOOD.
YOUR PETS ARE JUST CHILDREN.
THE RULING EIGHT KINGS...

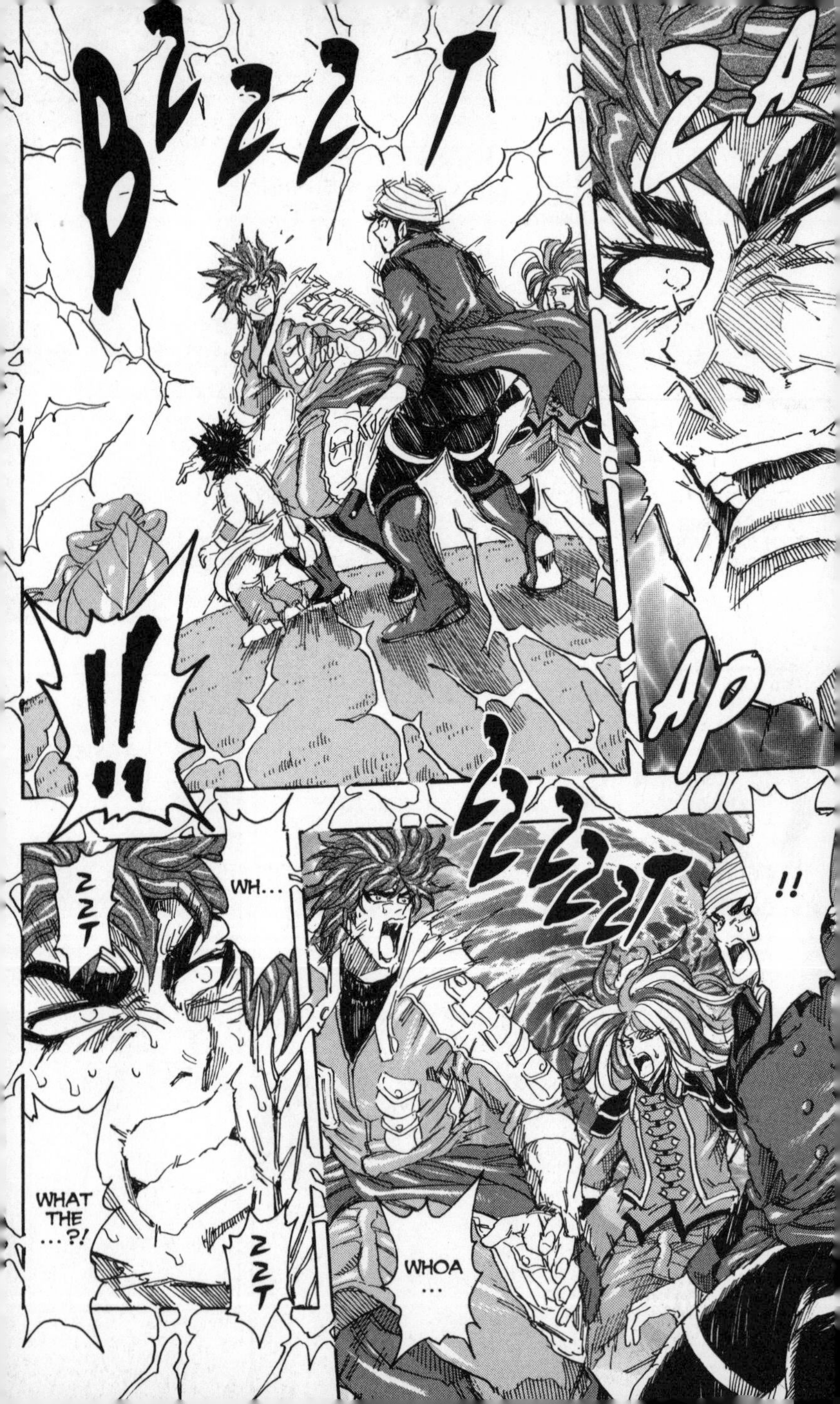
ZA
AP
BZZZT
!!
!!
ZZZZT
WH...
WHOA ...
ZZT
WHAT THE ...?!
ZZT

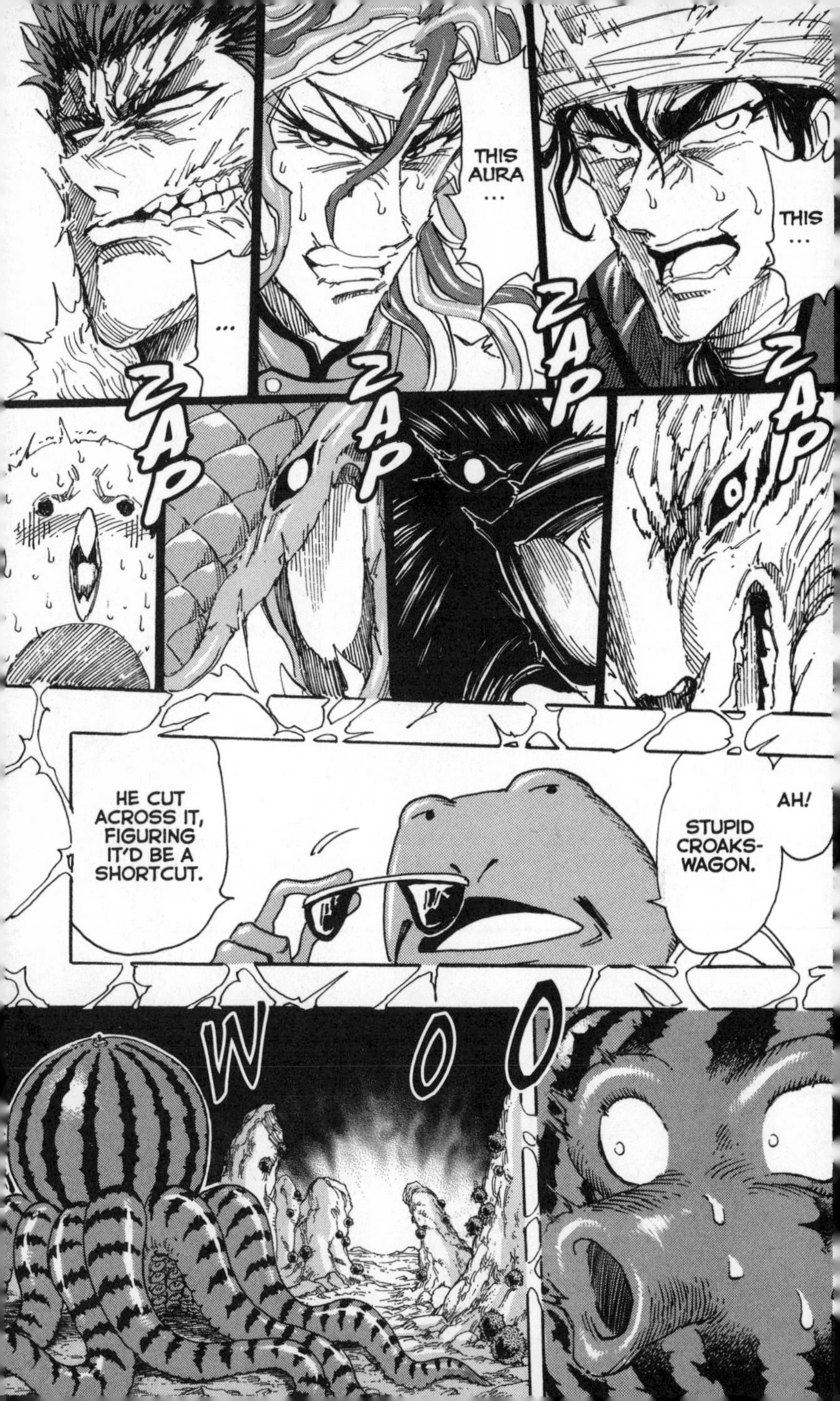
THIS ...
THIS AURA ...
...
ZAP
ZAP
ZAP
ZAP
AH!
STUPID CROAKS-WAGON.
HE CUT ACROSS IT, FIGURING IT'D BE A SHORTCUT.
WOO

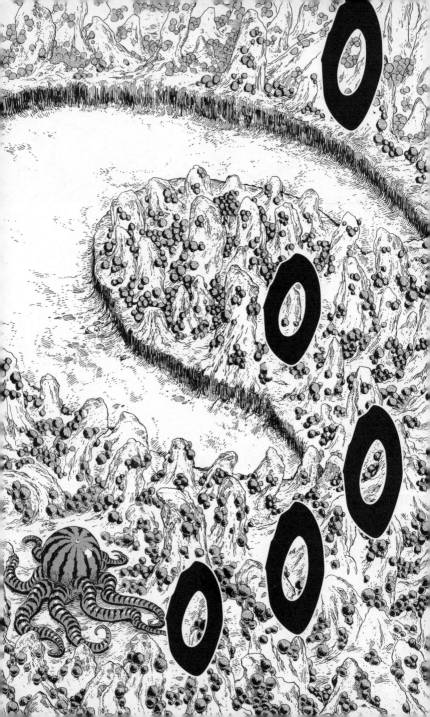

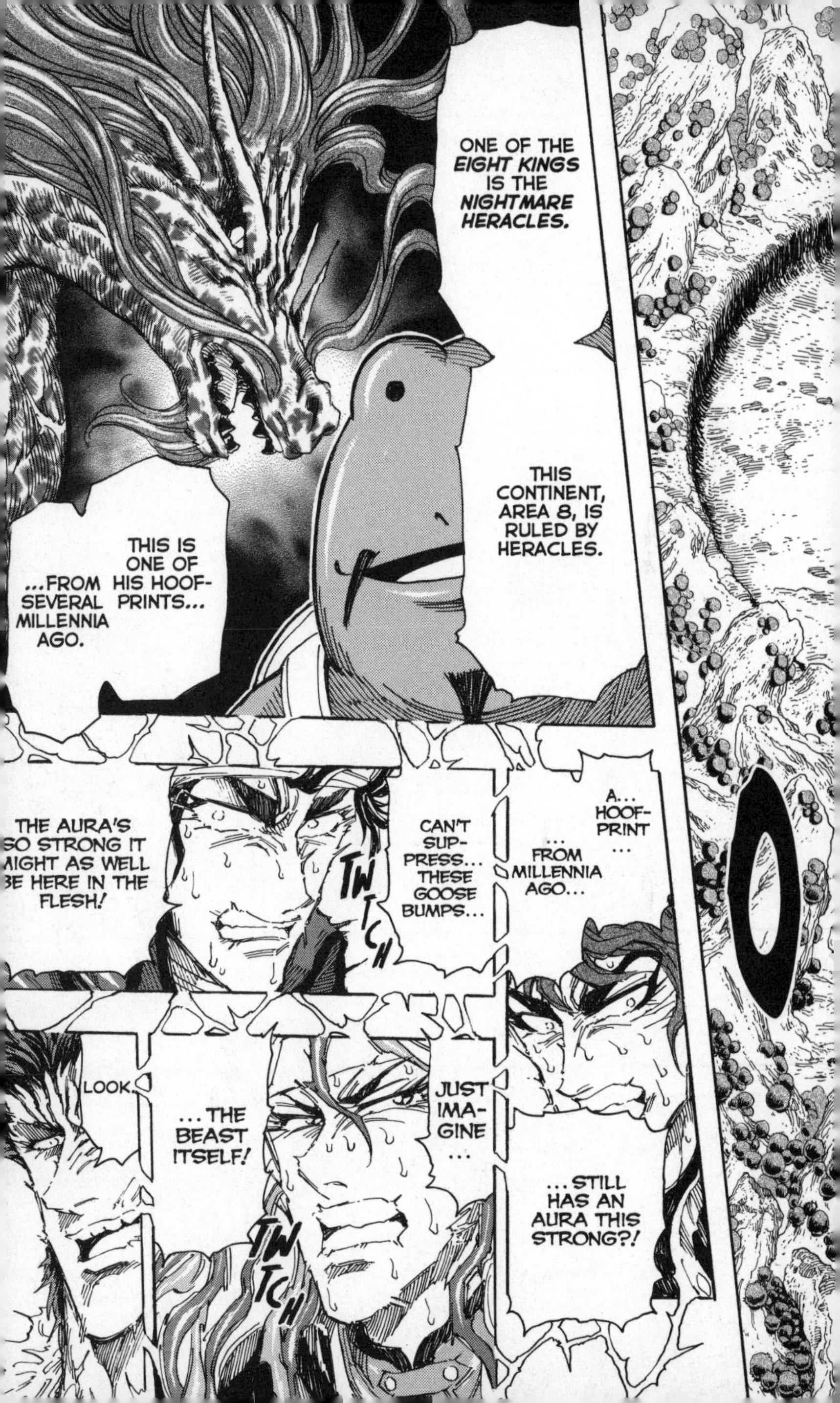

ONE OF THE EIGHT KINGS IS THE NIGHTMARE HERACLES.
THIS CONTINENT, AREA 8, IS RULED BY HERACLES.
THIS IS ONE OF HIS HOOF-PRINTS...
...FROM SEVERAL MILLENNIA AGO.
A... HOOF-PRINT ...
... FROM MILLENNIA AGO...
CAN'T SUP-PRESS... THESE GOOSE BUMPS...
TWITCH
THE AURA'S SO STRONG IT MIGHT AS WELL BE HERE IN THE FLESH!
JUST IMA-GINE ...
...STILL HAS AN AURA THIS STRONG?!
... THE BEAST ITSELF!
TWITCH
LOOK.

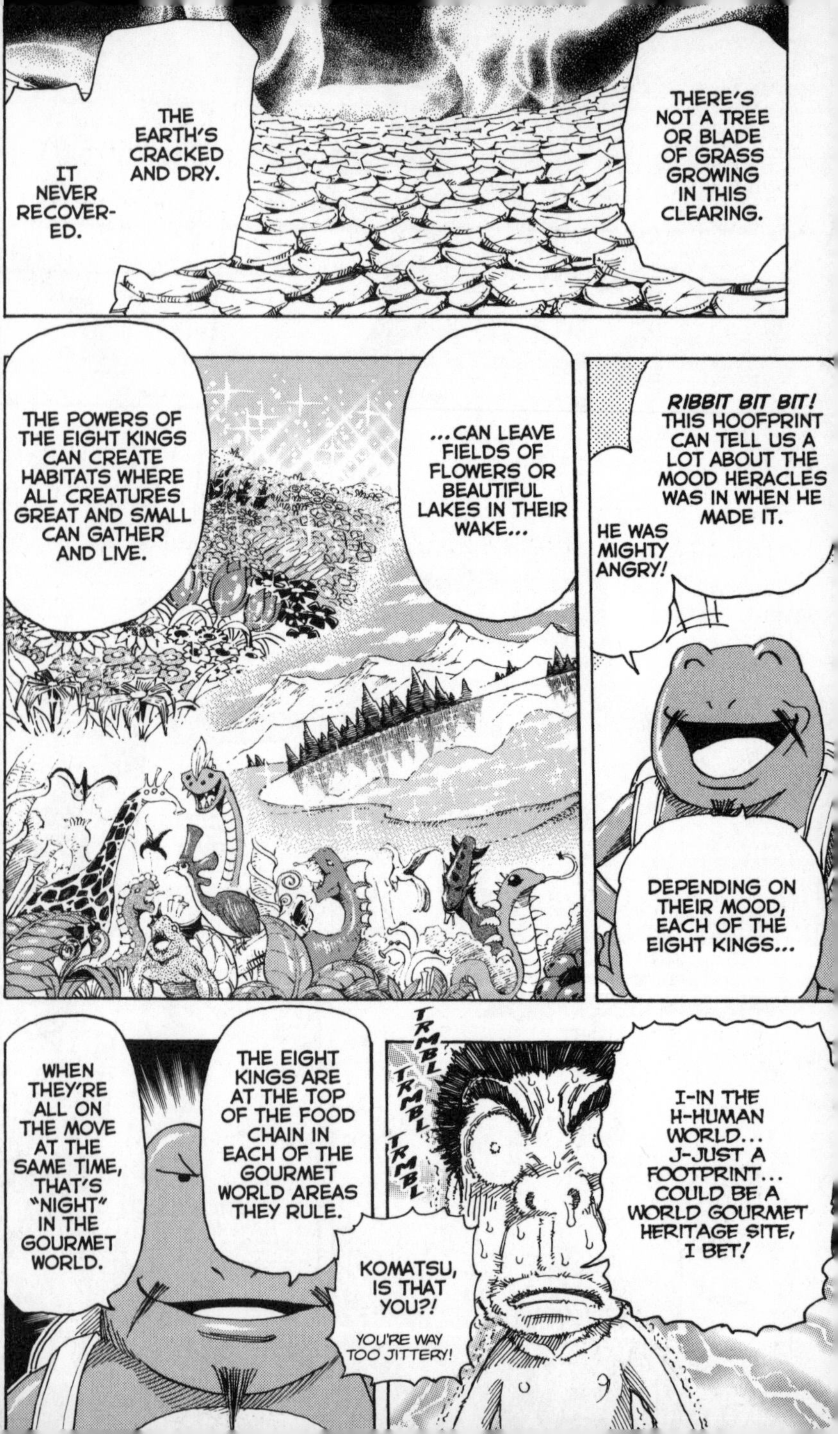
THERE'S NOT A TREE OR BLADE OF GRASS GROWING IN THIS CLEARING.
THE EARTH'S CRACKED AND DRY.
IT NEVER RECOVER-ED.
RIBBIT BIT BIT! THIS HOOFPRINT CAN TELL US A LOT ABOUT THE MOOD HERACLES WAS IN WHEN HE MADE IT.
HE WAS MIGHTY ANGRY!
DEPENDING ON THEIR MOOD, EACH OF THE EIGHT KINGS...
...CAN LEAVE FIELDS OF FLOWERS OR BEAUTIFUL LAKES IN THEIR WAKE...
THE POWERS OF THE EIGHT KINGS CAN CREATE HABITATS WHERE ALL CREATURES GREAT AND SMALL CAN GATHER AND LIVE.
TRMBL TRMBL TRMBL
I-IN THE H-HUMAN WORLD... J-JUST A FOOTPRINT... COULD BE A WORLD GOURMET HERITAGE SITE, I BET!
KOMATSU, IS THAT YOU?!
YOU'RE WAY TOO JITTERY!
THE EIGHT KINGS ARE AT THE TOP OF THE FOOD CHAIN IN EACH OF THE GOURMET WORLD AREAS THEY RULE.
WHEN THEY'RE ALL ON THE MOVE AT THE SAME TIME, THAT'S "NIGHT" IN THE GOURMET WORLD.

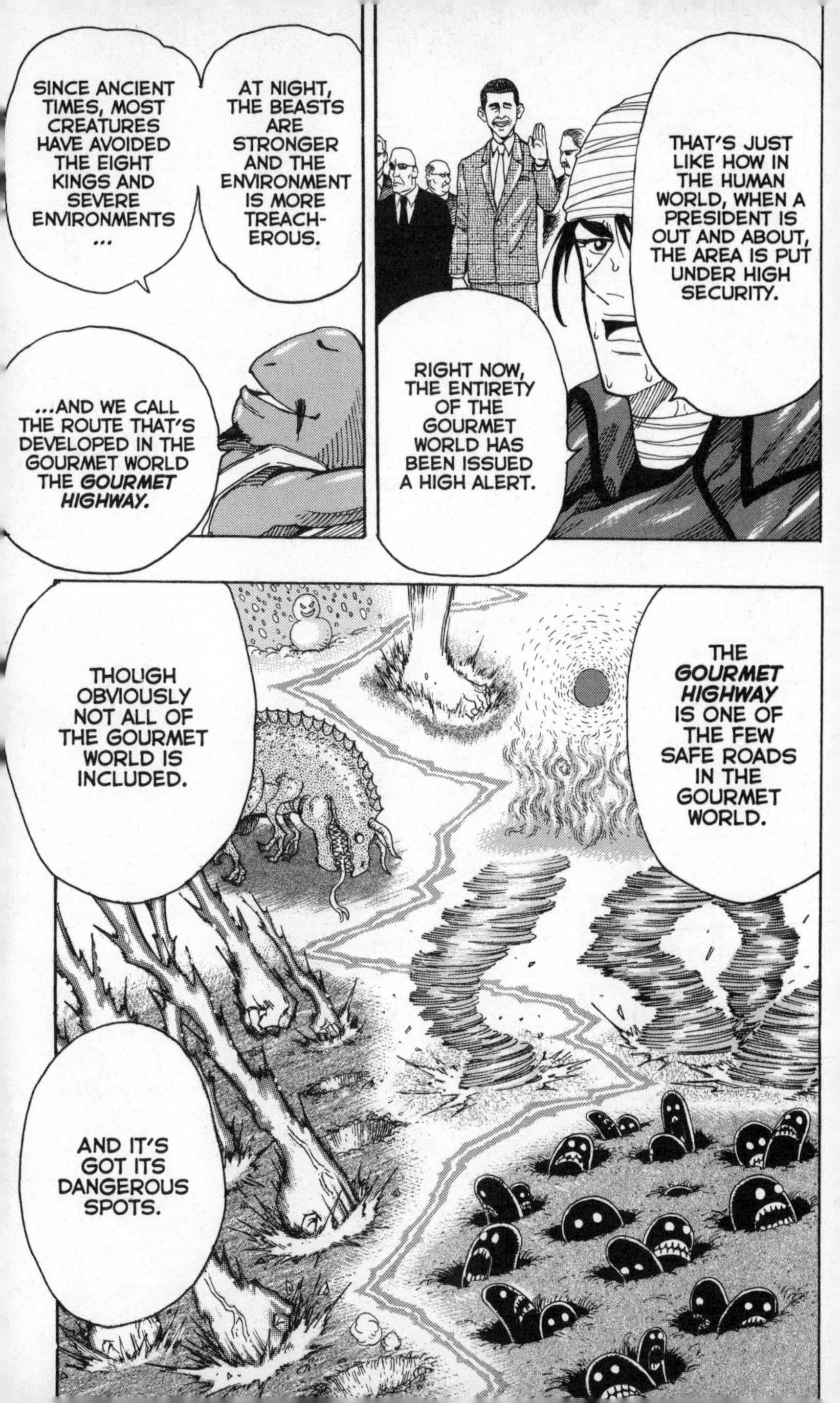

THAT'S JUST LIKE HOW IN THE HUMAN WORLD, WHEN A PRESIDENT IS OUT AND ABOUT, THE AREA IS PUT UNDER HIGH SECURITY.
RIGHT NOW, THE ENTIRETY OF THE GOURMET WORLD HAS BEEN ISSUED A HIGH ALERT.
AT NIGHT, THE BEASTS ARE STRONGER AND THE ENVIRONMENT IS MORE TREACH-EROUS.
SINCE ANCIENT TIMES, MOST CREATURES HAVE AVOIDED THE EIGHT KINGS AND SEVERE ENVIRONMENTS...
...AND WE CALL THE ROUTE THAT'S DEVELOPED IN THE GOURMET WORLD THE *GOURMET HIGHWAY.*
THE *GOURMET HIGHWAY* IS ONE OF THE FEW SAFE ROADS IN THE GOURMET WORLD.
THOUGH OBVIOUSLY NOT ALL OF THE GOURMET WORLD IS INCLUDED.
AND IT'S GOT ITS DANGEROUS SPOTS.

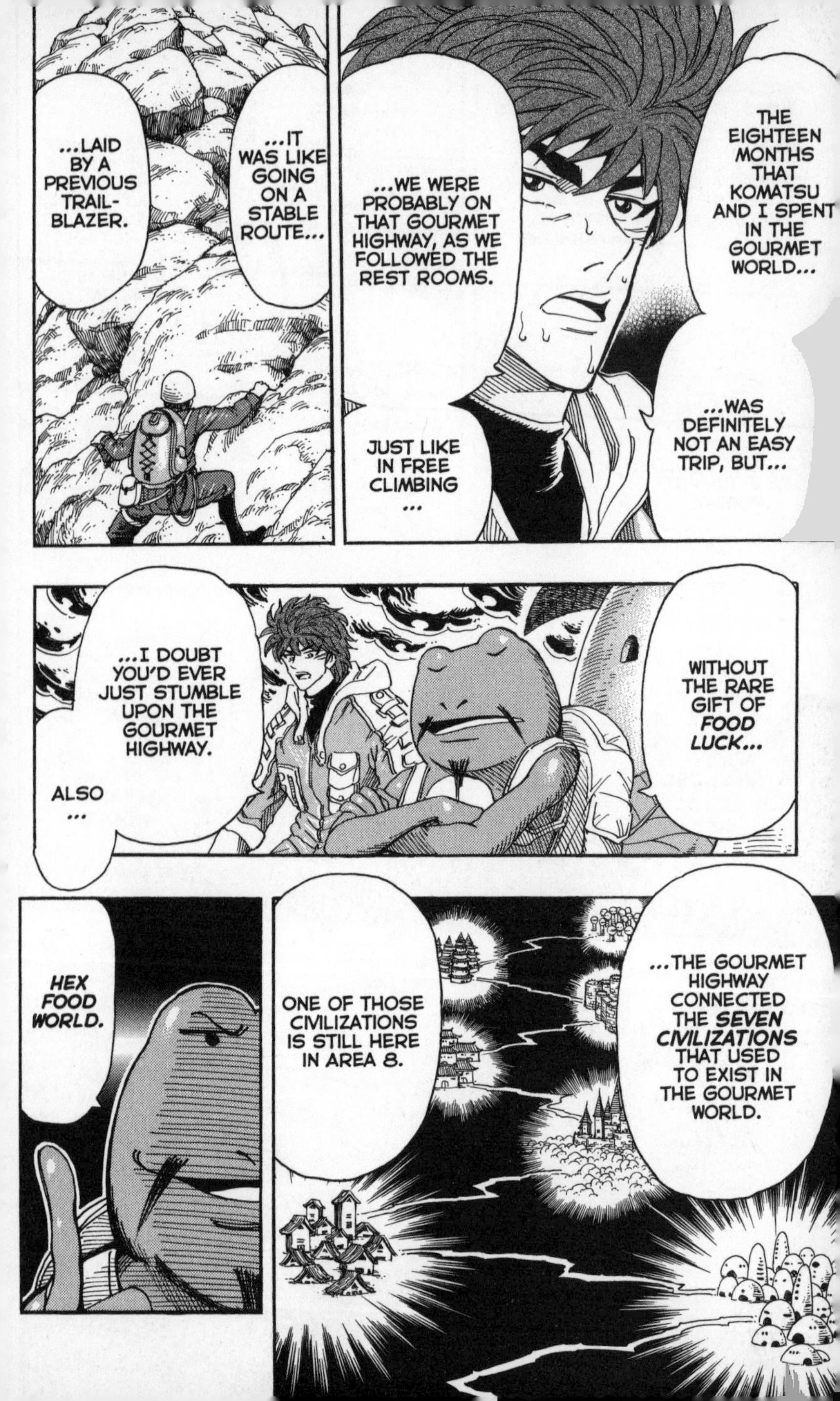
THE EIGHTEEN MONTHS THAT KOMATSU AND I SPENT IN THE GOURMET WORLD...
...WAS DEFINITELY NOT AN EASY TRIP, BUT...
...WE WERE PROBABLY ON THAT GOURMET HIGHWAY, AS WE FOLLOWED THE REST ROOMS.
JUST LIKE IN FREE CLIMBING ...
...IT WAS LIKE GOING ON A STABLE ROUTE...
...LAID BY A PREVIOUS TRAIL-BLAZER.
WITHOUT THE RARE GIFT OF *FOOD LUCK*...
...I DOUBT YOU'D EVER JUST STUMBLE UPON THE GOURMET HIGHWAY.
ALSO ...
...THE GOURMET HIGHWAY CONNECTED THE *SEVEN CIVILIZATIONS* THAT USED TO EXIST IN THE GOURMET WORLD.
ONE OF THOSE CIVILIZATIONS IS STILL HERE IN AREA 8.
HEX FOOD WORLD.

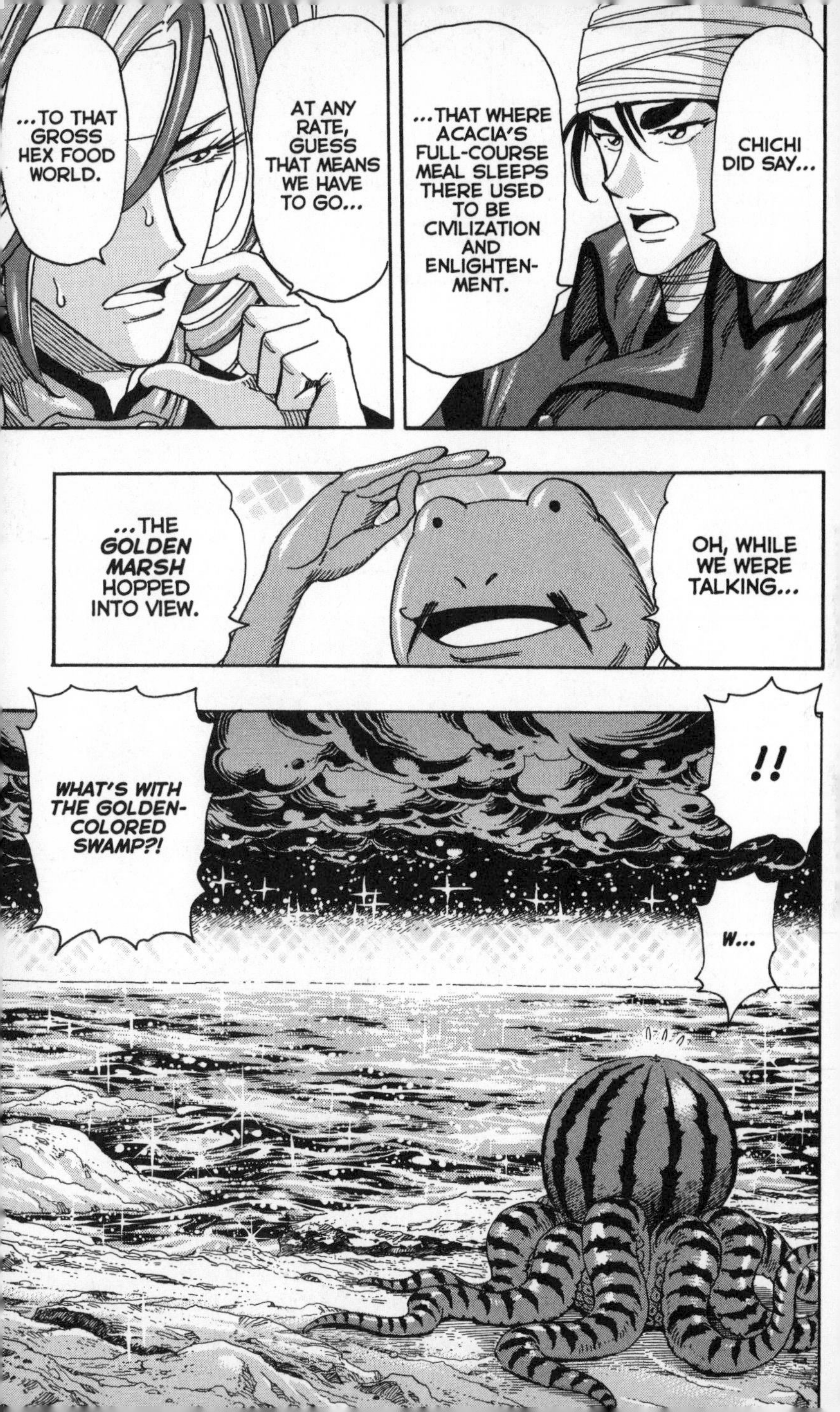
CHICHI DID SAY...
...THAT WHERE ACACIA'S FULL-COURSE MEAL SLEEPS THERE USED TO BE CIVILIZATION AND ENLIGHTEN-MENT.
AT ANY RATE, GUESS THAT MEANS WE HAVE TO GO...
...TO THAT GROSS HEX FOOD WORLD.
OH, WHILE WE WERE TALKING...
...THE *GOLDEN MARSH* HOPPED INTO VIEW.
!!
W...
WHAT'S WITH THE GOLDEN-COLORED SWAMP?!

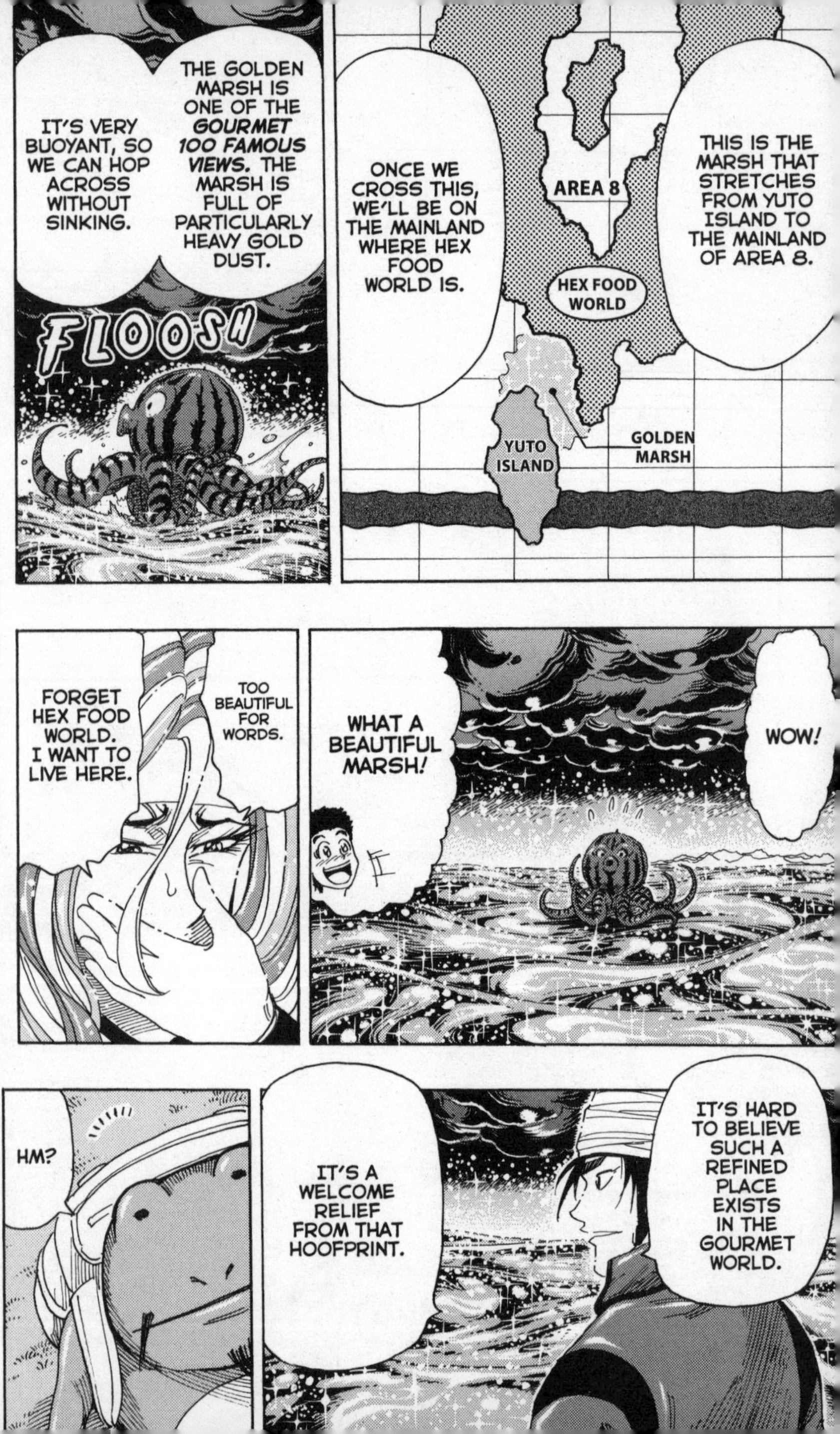
THIS IS THE MARSH THAT STRETCHES FROM YUTO ISLAND TO THE MAINLAND OF AREA 8.
AREA 8
HEX FOOD WORLD
GOLDEN MARSH
YUTO ISLAND
ONCE WE CROSS THIS, WE'LL BE ON THE MAINLAND WHERE HEX FOOD WORLD IS.
THE GOLDEN MARSH IS ONE OF THE *GOURMET 100 FAMOUS VIEWS.* THE MARSH IS FULL OF PARTICULARLY HEAVY GOLD DUST.
IT'S VERY BUOYANT, SO WE CAN HOP ACROSS WITHOUT SINKING.
FLOOSH
WOW!
WHAT A BEAUTIFUL MARSH!
TOO BEAUTIFUL FOR WORDS.
FORGET HEX FOOD WORLD. I WANT TO LIVE HERE.
IT'S HARD TO BELIEVE SUCH A REFINED PLACE EXISTS IN THE GOURMET WORLD.
IT'S A WELCOME RELIEF FROM THAT HOOFPRINT.
HM?

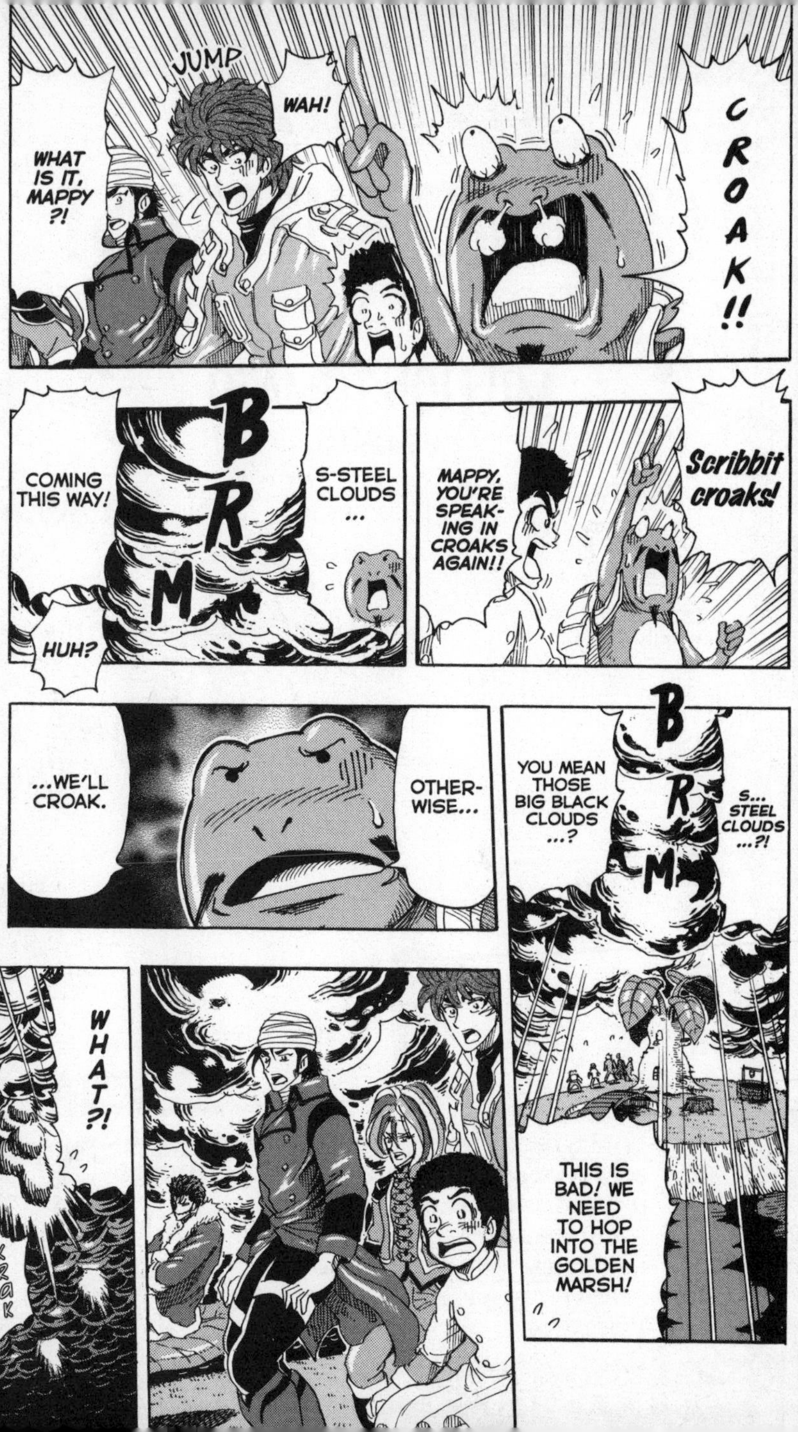
CROAK!!
WAH!
JUMP
WHAT IS IT, MAPPY?!
Scribbit croaks!
MAPPY, YOU'RE SPEAK-ING IN CROAKS AGAIN!!
S-STEEL CLOUDS...
BRM
COMING THIS WAY!
HUH?
S... STEEL CLOUDS...?!
BRM
YOU MEAN THOSE BIG BLACK CLOUDS...?
THIS IS BAD! WE NEED TO HOP INTO THE GOLDEN MARSH!
OTHER-WISE...
...WE'LL CROAK.
WHAT?!
KRAK

GOURMET CHECKLIST

Vol. 301

MILLION TOMATO
(VEGETABLE)

CAPTURE LEVEL: 11
HABITAT: FERTILE SOIL
SIZE: 12 CM
HEIGHT: ---
WEIGHT: 80 GRAMS
PRICE: 7,000 YEN PER TOMATO

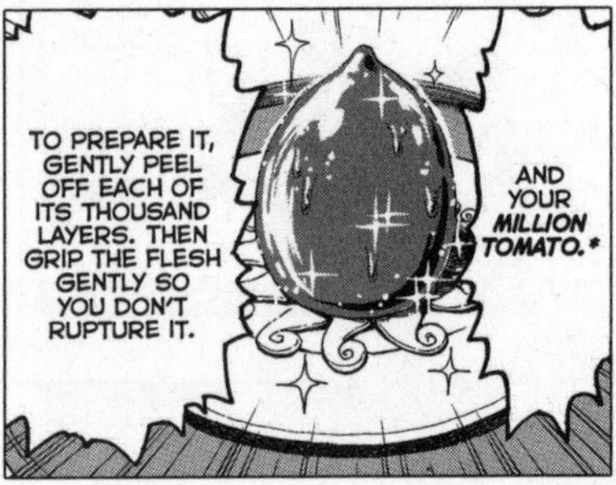
AND YOUR MILLION TOMATO.*
TO PREPARE IT, GENTLY PEEL OFF EACH OF ITS THOUSAND LAYERS. THEN GRIP THE FLESH GENTLY SO YOU DON'T RUPTURE IT.

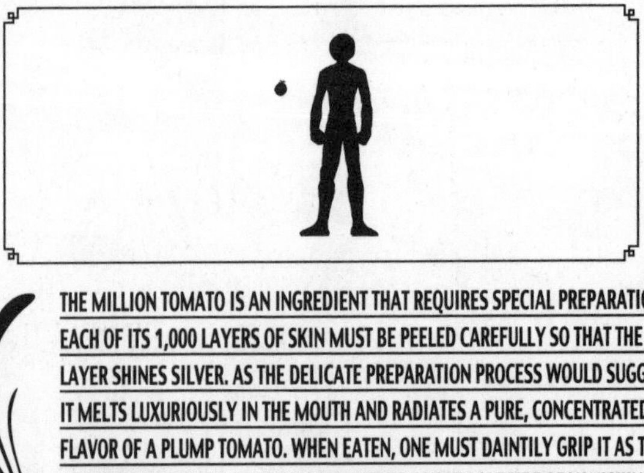
SCALE

THE MILLION TOMATO IS AN INGREDIENT THAT REQUIRES SPECIAL PREPARATION AS EACH OF ITS 1,000 LAYERS OF SKIN MUST BE PEELED CAREFULLY SO THAT THE FINAL LAYER SHINES SILVER. AS THE DELICATE PREPARATION PROCESS WOULD SUGGEST, IT MELTS LUXURIOUSLY IN THE MOUTH AND RADIATES A PURE, CONCENTRATED FLAVOR OF A PLUMP TOMATO. WHEN EATEN, ONE MUST DAINTILY GRIP IT AS TO NOT BREAK THE FLESH. THIS FOOD HAS YET TO BE SEEN OUTSIDE OF VANISHING JAPANESE CUISINE.

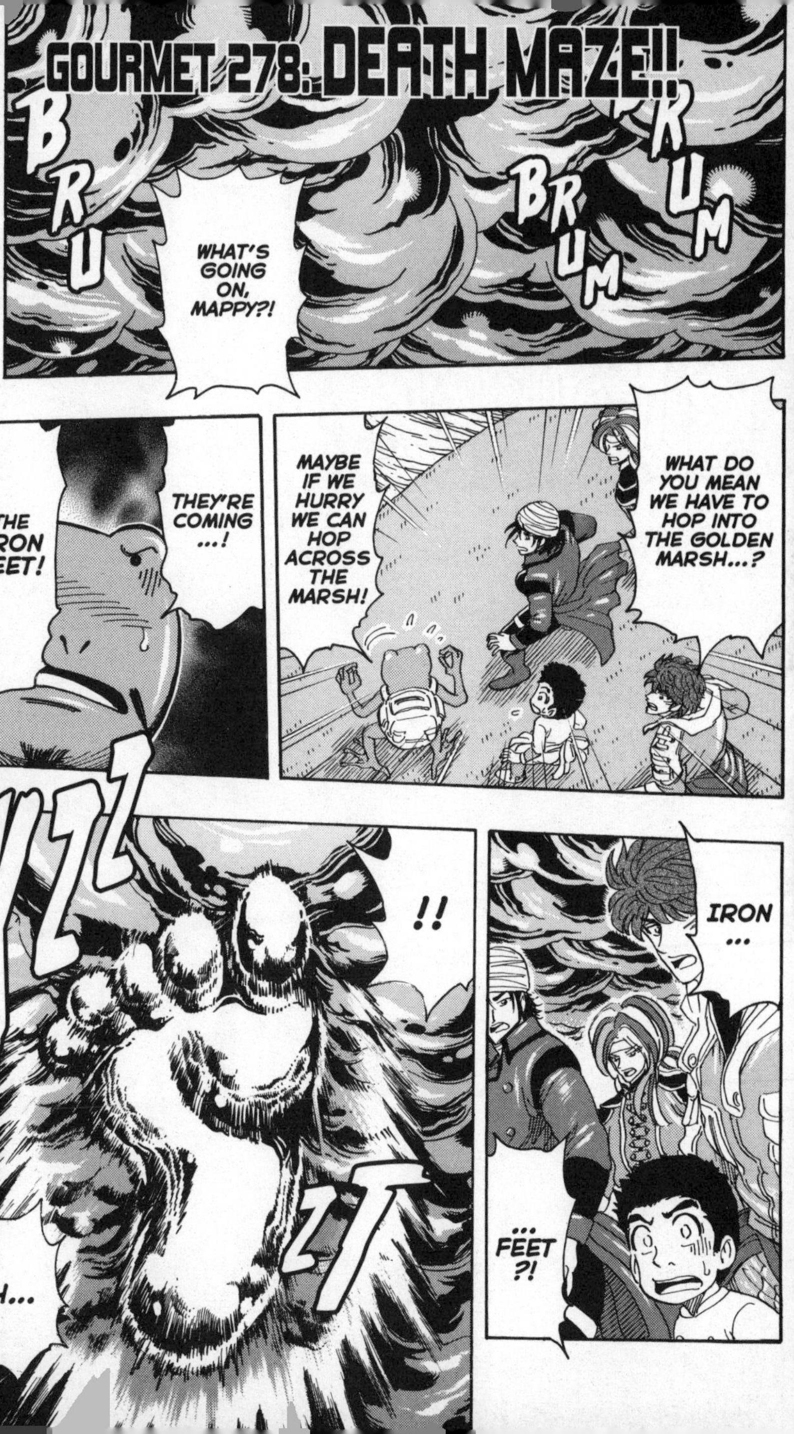
GOURMET 278: DEATH MAZE!!
BRU
WHAT'S GOING ON, MAPPY?!
BRUM
WHAT DO YOU MEAN WE HAVE TO HOP INTO THE GOLDEN MARSH...?
MAYBE IF WE HURRY WE CAN HOP ACROSS THE MARSH!
THEY'RE COMING ...!
THE IRON FEET!
IRON ...
... FEET ?!
!!
KZZZT
H...

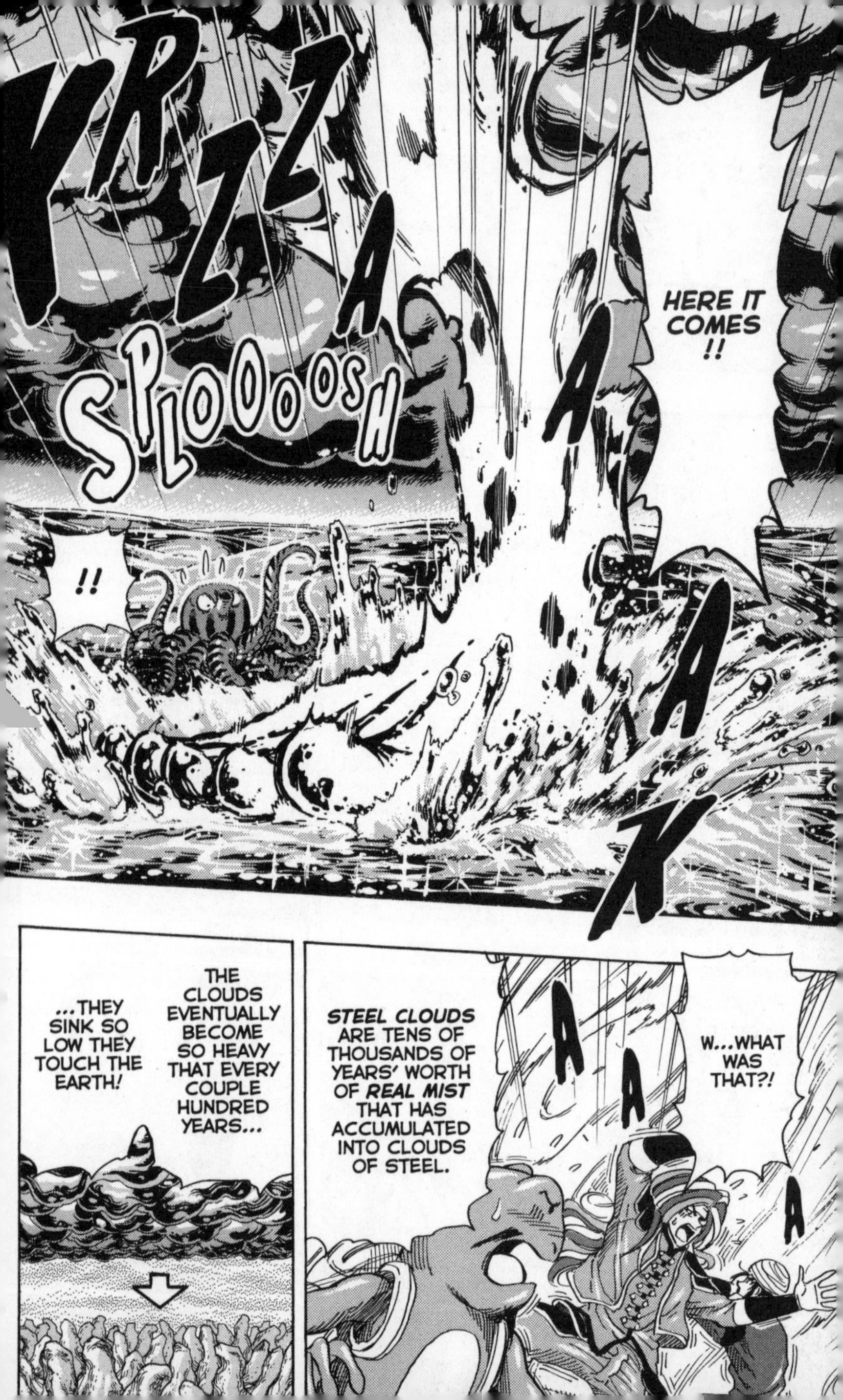
HERE IT COMES !!
VRZZAAAK
SPLOOOOSH
!!
AAA
W...WHAT WAS THAT?!
STEEL CLOUDS ARE TENS OF THOUSANDS OF YEARS' WORTH OF **REAL MIST** THAT HAS ACCUMULATED INTO CLOUDS OF STEEL.
THE CLOUDS EVENTUALLY BECOME SO HEAVY THAT EVERY COUPLE HUNDRED YEARS...
...THEY SINK SO LOW THEY TOUCH THE EARTH!

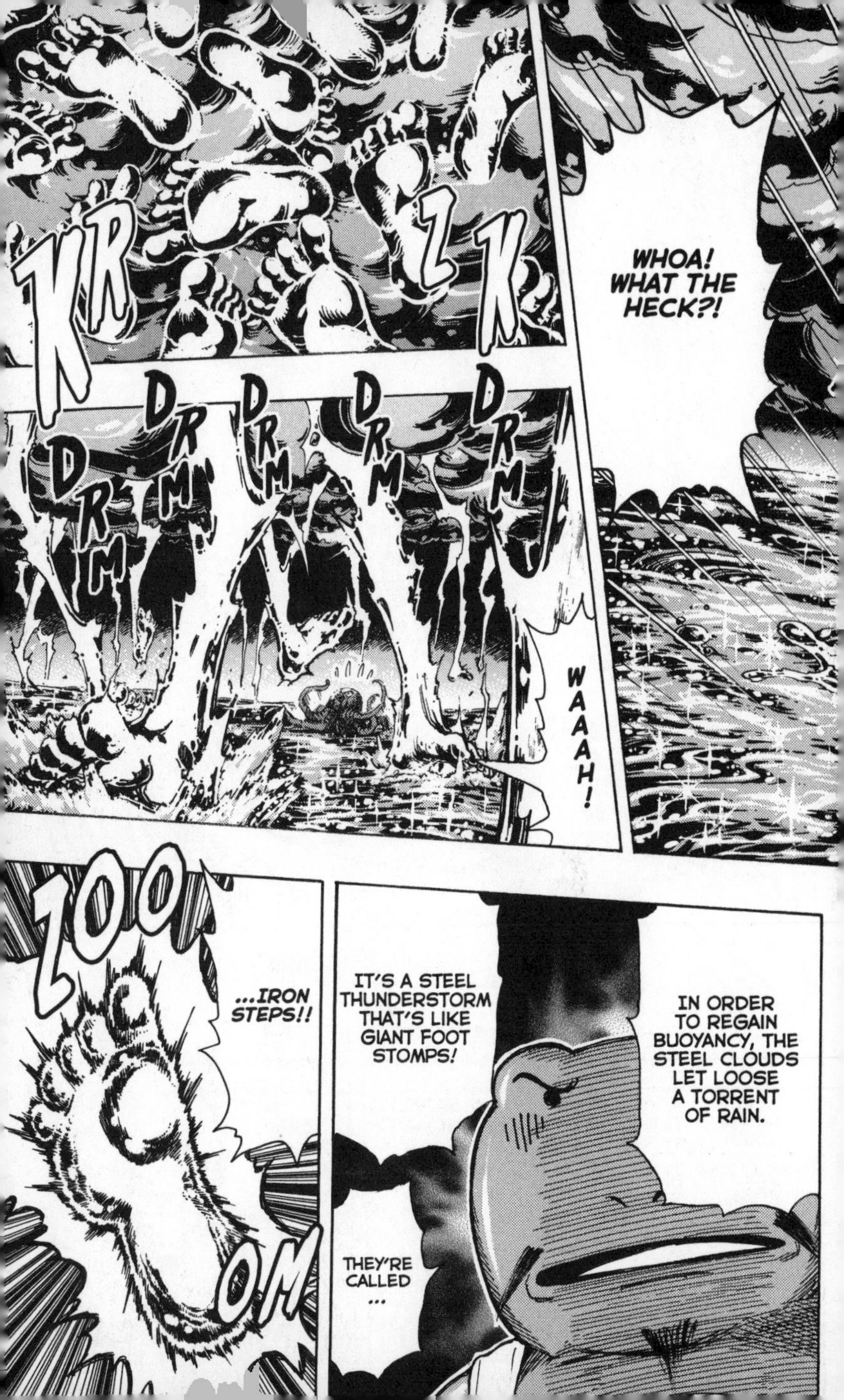
WHOA! WHAT THE HECK?!
KRZK
DRM DRM DRM DRM DRM
WAAAH!
IN ORDER TO REGAIN BUOYANCY, THE STEEL CLOUDS LET LOOSE A TORRENT OF RAIN.
IT'S A STEEL THUNDERSTORM THAT'S LIKE GIANT FOOT STOMPS!
THEY'RE CALLED ...
...IRON STEPS!!
ZOOOM

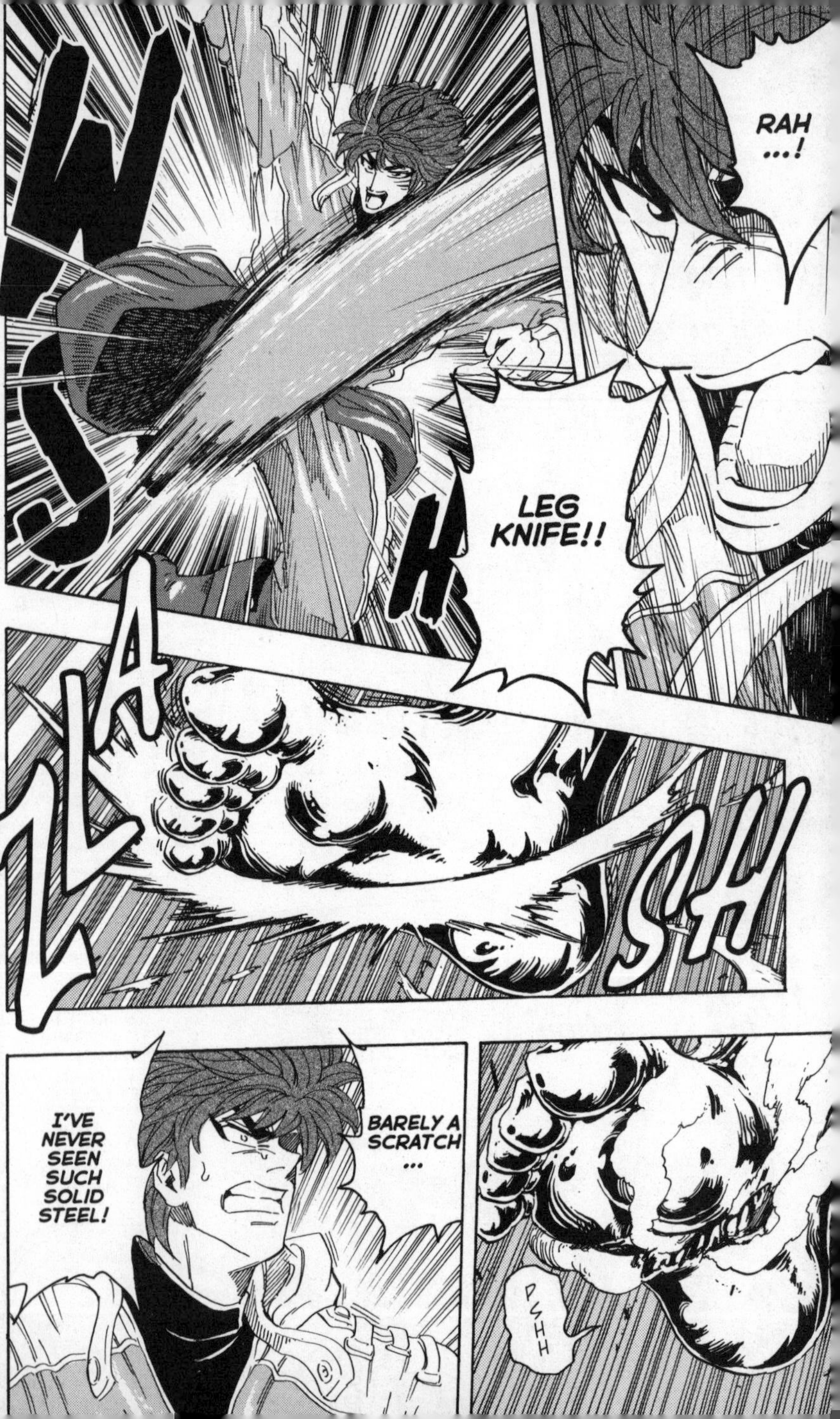
RAH ...!
LEG KNIFE!!
WSH
ZASH
PSHH
BARELY A SCRATCH ...
I'VE NEVER SEEN SUCH SOLID STEEL!

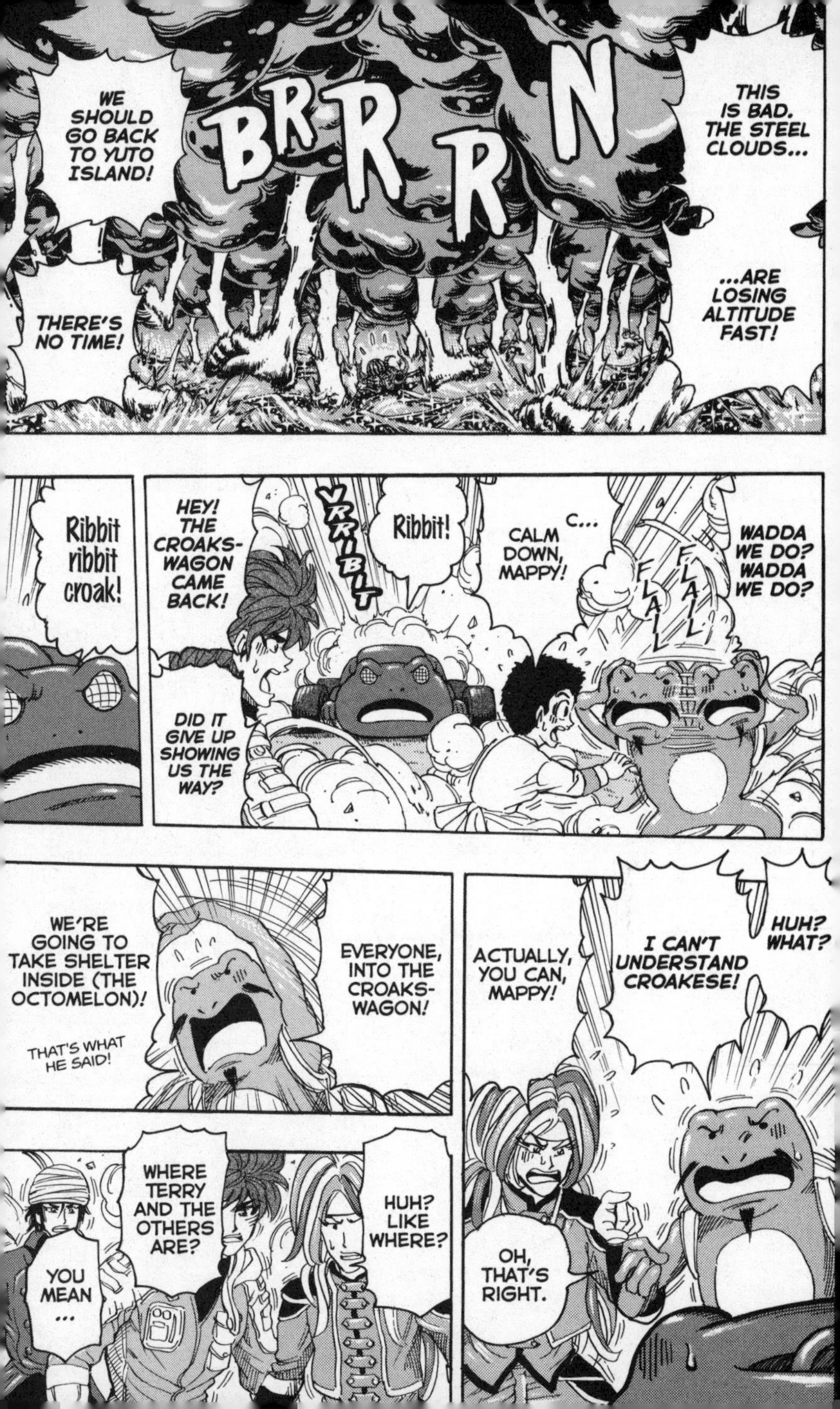
THIS IS BAD. THE STEEL CLOUDS...
...ARE LOSING ALTITUDE FAST!
BRRRN
WE SHOULD GO BACK TO YUTO ISLAND!
THERE'S NO TIME!
WADDA WE DO? WADDA WE DO?
FLALL FLALL
C...
CALM DOWN, MAPPY!
Ribbit!
VRRIBIT
HEY! THE CROAKS-WAGON CAME BACK!
DID IT GIVE UP SHOWING US THE WAY?
Ribbit ribbit croak!
HUH? WHAT?
I CAN'T UNDERSTAND CROAKESE!
ACTUALLY, YOU CAN, MAPPY!
OH, THAT'S RIGHT.
EVERYONE, INTO THE CROAKS-WAGON!
WE'RE GOING TO TAKE SHELTER INSIDE (THE OCTOMELON)!
THAT'S WHAT HE SAID!
HUH? LIKE WHERE?
WHERE TERRY AND THE OTHERS ARE?
YOU MEAN ...

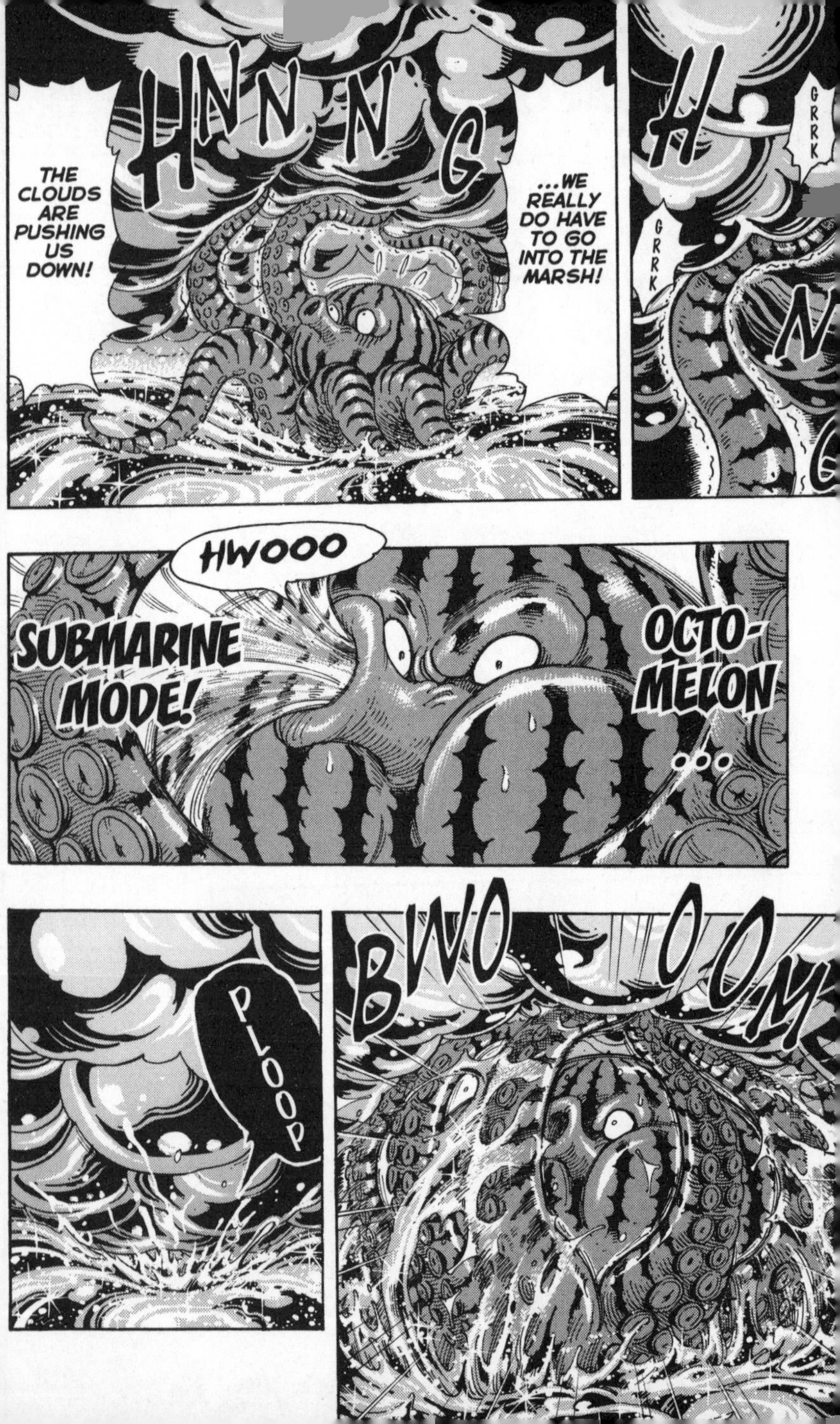

HNG
GRRK
GRRK
HNNNG
...WE REALLY DO HAVE TO GO INTO THE MARSH!
THE CLOUDS ARE PUSHING US DOWN!
HWOOO
OCTO-MELON...
SUBMARINE MODE!
BWOOOM
PLOOP

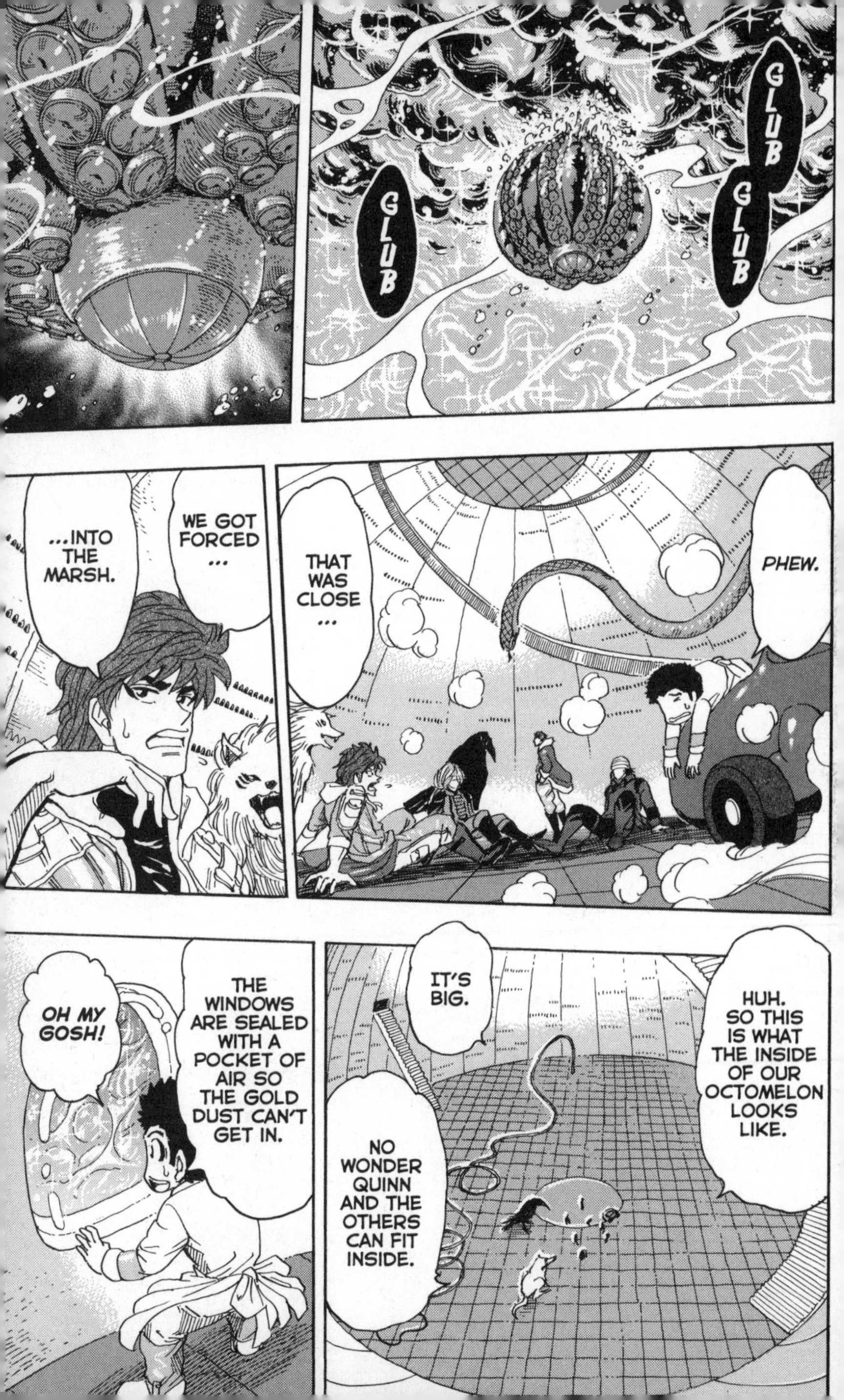
GLUB
GLUB
GLUB
PHEW.
THAT WAS CLOSE...
WE GOT FORCED...
...INTO THE MARSH.
HUH. SO THIS IS WHAT THE INSIDE OF OUR OCTOMELON LOOKS LIKE.
IT'S BIG.
NO WONDER QUINN AND THE OTHERS CAN FIT INSIDE.
THE WINDOWS ARE SEALED WITH A POCKET OF AIR SO THE GOLD DUST CAN'T GET IN.
OH MY GOSH!

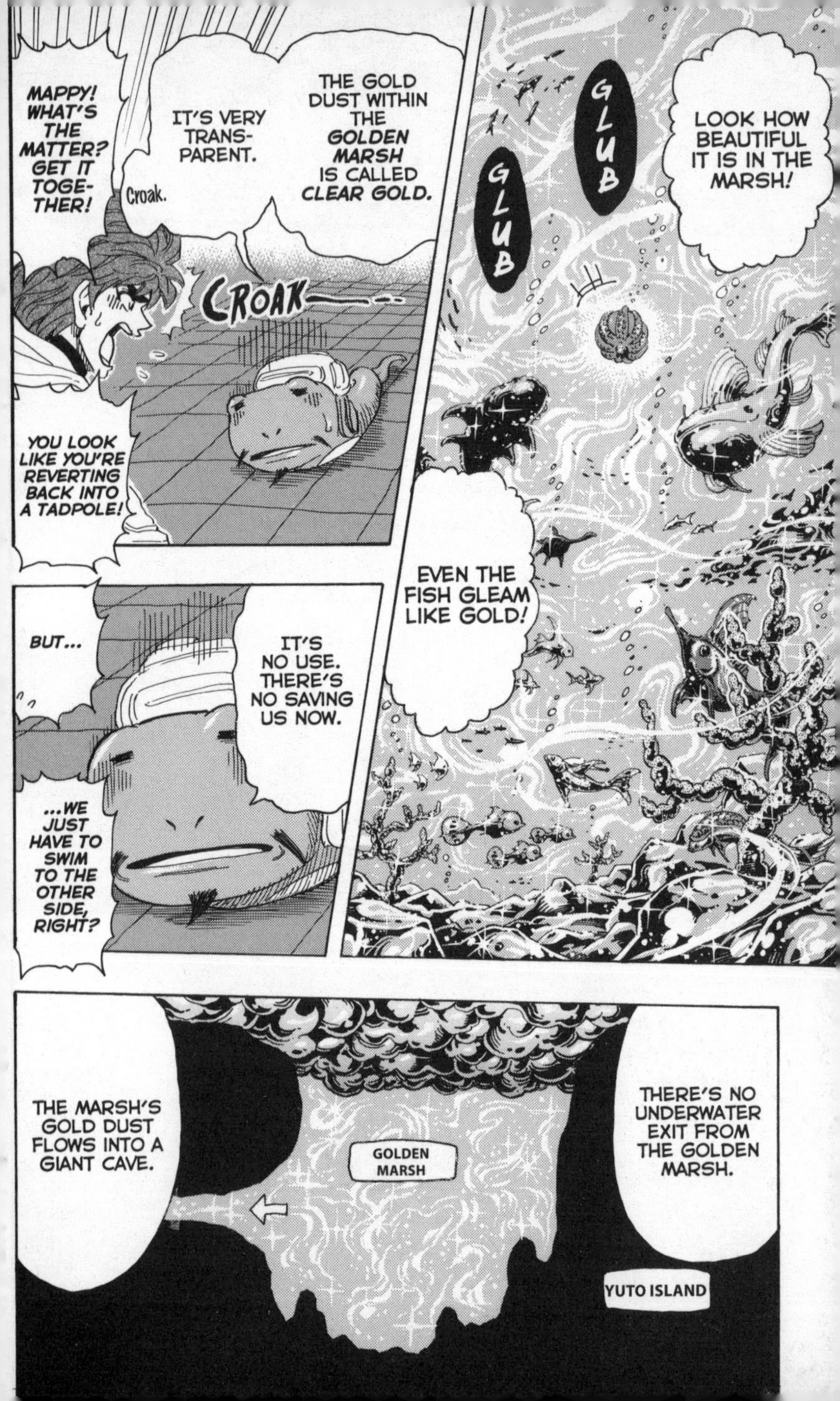

LOOK HOW BEAUTIFUL IT IS IN THE MARSH!
GLUB
GLUB
EVEN THE FISH GLEAM LIKE GOLD!
THE GOLD DUST WITHIN THE GOLDEN MARSH IS CALLED CLEAR GOLD.
IT'S VERY TRANS-PARENT.
Croak.
MAPPY! WHAT'S THE MATTER? GET IT TOGE-THER!
CROAK—
YOU LOOK LIKE YOU'RE REVERTING BACK INTO A TADPOLE!
IT'S NO USE. THERE'S NO SAVING US NOW.
BUT...
...WE JUST HAVE TO SWIM TO THE OTHER SIDE, RIGHT?
THERE'S NO UNDERWATER EXIT FROM THE GOLDEN MARSH.
GOLDEN MARSH
THE MARSH'S GOLD DUST FLOWS INTO A GIANT CAVE.
YUTO ISLAND

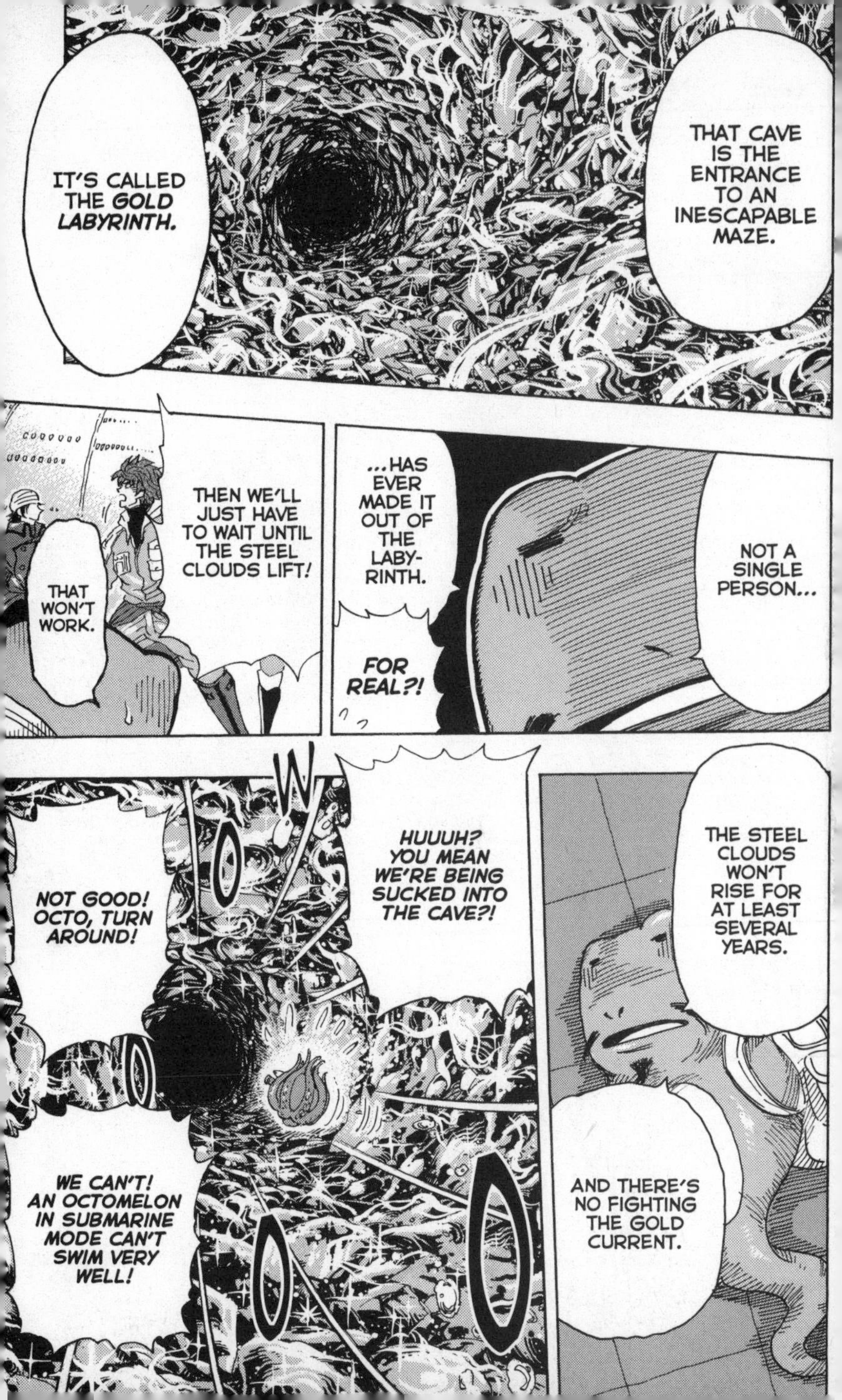
THAT CAVE IS THE ENTRANCE TO AN INESCAPABLE MAZE.
IT'S CALLED THE *GOLD LABYRINTH*.
NOT A SINGLE PERSON...
...HAS EVER MADE IT OUT OF THE LABY-RINTH.
FOR REAL?!
THEN WE'LL JUST HAVE TO WAIT UNTIL THE STEEL CLOUDS LIFT!
THAT WON'T WORK.
THE STEEL CLOUDS WON'T RISE FOR AT LEAST SEVERAL YEARS.
AND THERE'S NO FIGHTING THE GOLD CURRENT.
HUUUH? YOU MEAN WE'RE BEING SUCKED INTO THE CAVE?!
NOT GOOD! OCTO, TURN AROUND!
WE CAN'T! AN OCTOMELON IN SUBMARINE MODE CAN'T SWIM VERY WELL!

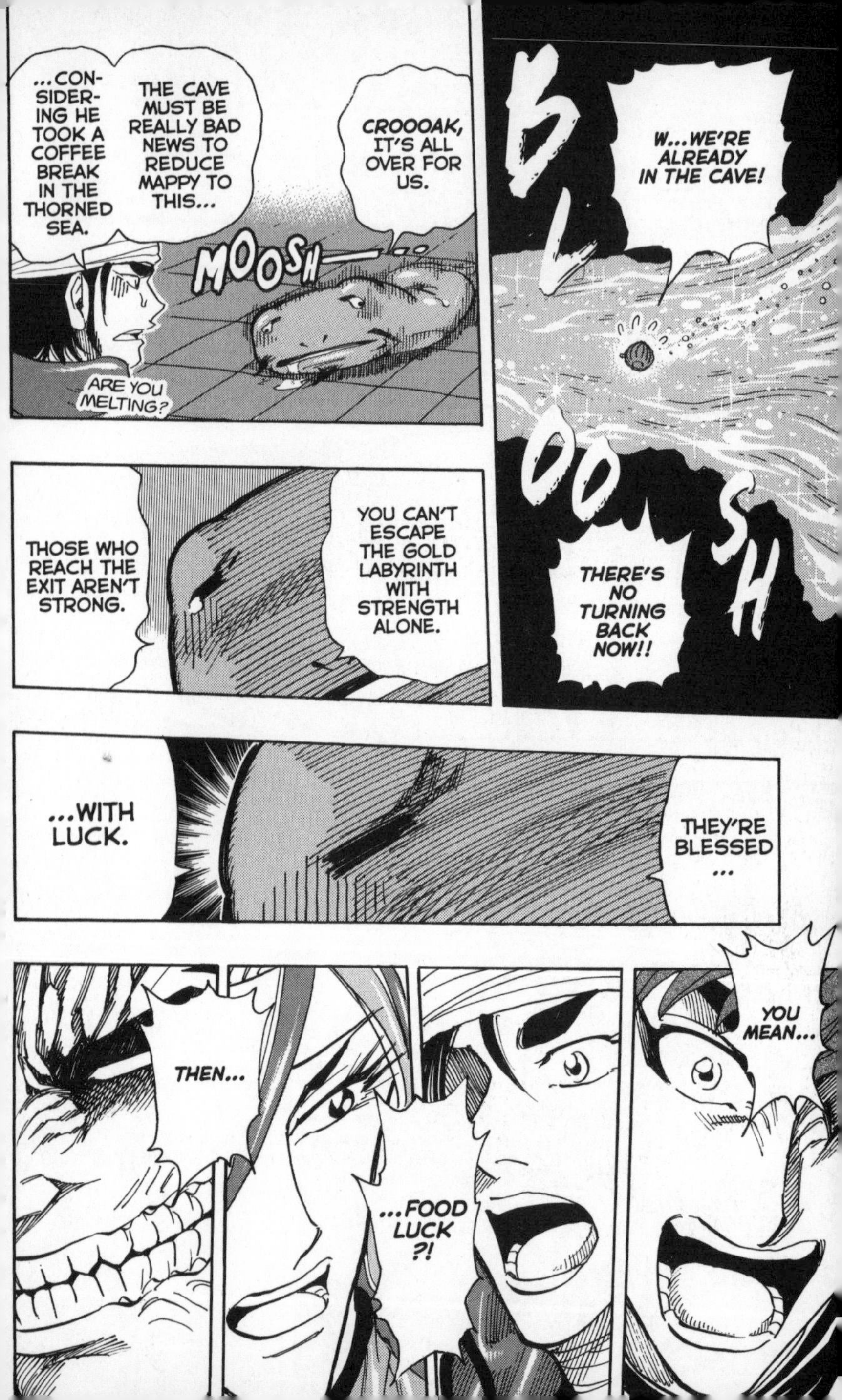

BLOOSH
W...WE'RE ALREADY IN THE CAVE!
THERE'S NO TURNING BACK NOW!!
CROOOAK, IT'S ALL OVER FOR US.
MOOSH
THE CAVE MUST BE REALLY BAD NEWS TO REDUCE MAPPY TO THIS...
...CONSIDERING HE TOOK A COFFEE BREAK IN THE THORNED SEA.
ARE YOU MELTING?
YOU CAN'T ESCAPE THE GOLD LABYRINTH WITH STRENGTH ALONE.
THOSE WHO REACH THE EXIT AREN'T STRONG.
THEY'RE BLESSED...
...WITH LUCK.
YOU MEAN...
THEN...
...FOOD LUCK?!

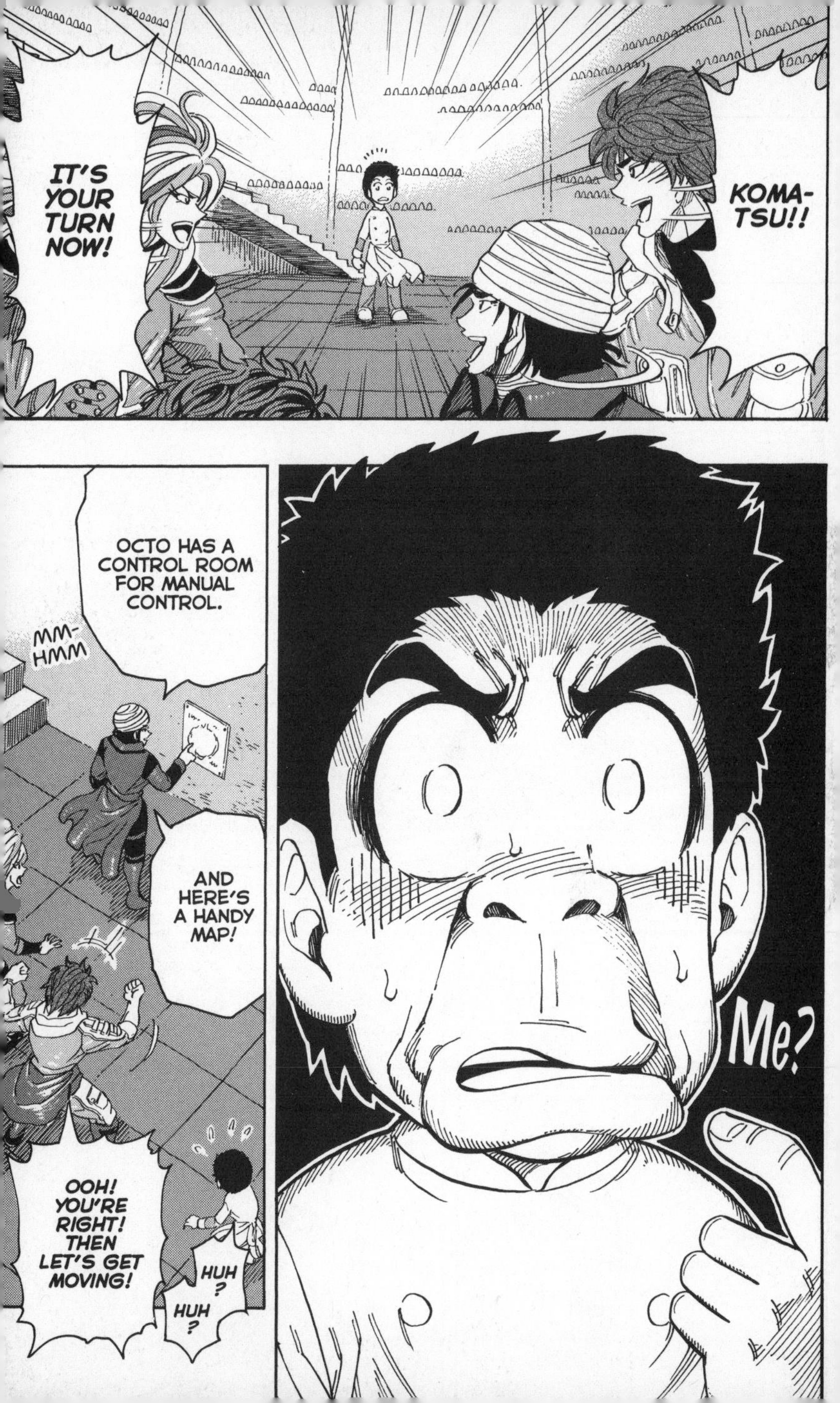
KOMATSU!!
IT'S YOUR TURN NOW!
Me?
OCTO HAS A CONTROL ROOM FOR MANUAL CONTROL.
MM-HMM
AND HERE'S A HANDY MAP!
HUH?
OOH! YOU'RE RIGHT! THEN LET'S GET MOVING!
HUH?

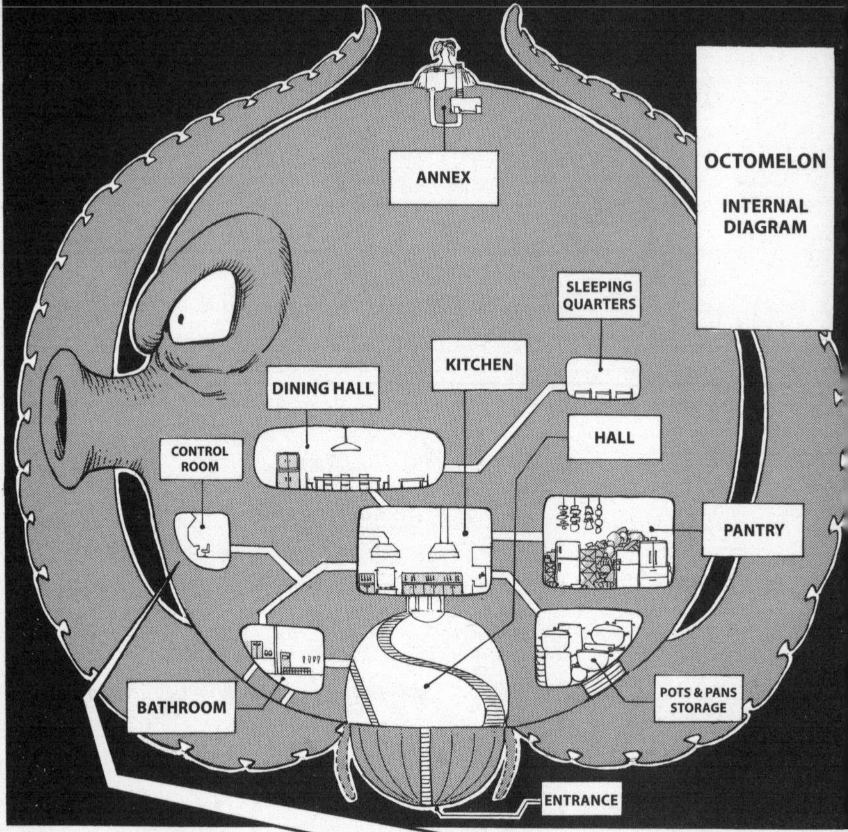
OCTOMELON
INTERNAL DIAGRAM
ANNEX
SLEEPING QUARTERS
KITCHEN
DINING HALL
HALL
CONTROL ROOM
PANTRY
BATHROOM
POTS & PANS STORAGE
ENTRANCE

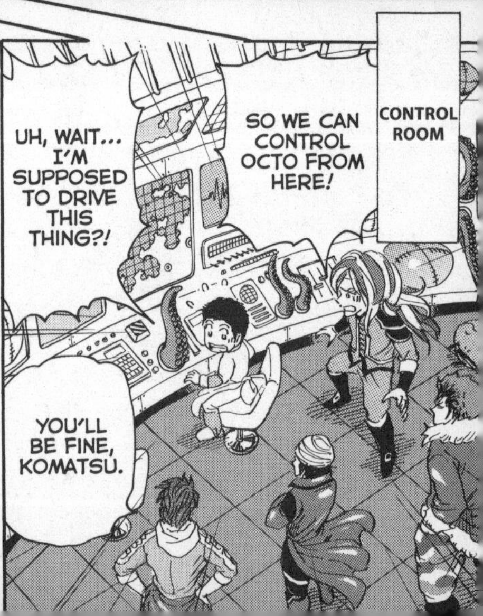
CONTROL ROOM
SO WE CAN CONTROL OCTO FROM HERE!
UH, WAIT... I'M SUPPOSED TO DRIVE THIS THING?!
YOU'LL BE FINE, KOMATSU.

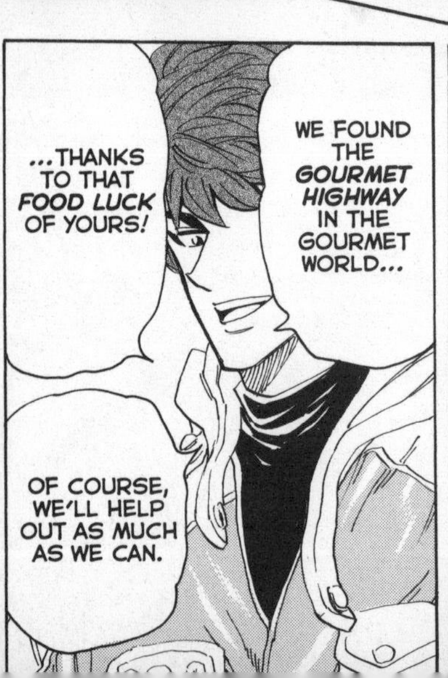
WE FOUND THE GOURMET HIGHWAY IN THE GOURMET WORLD...
...THANKS TO THAT FOOD LUCK OF YOURS!
OF COURSE, WE'LL HELP OUT AS MUCH AS WE CAN.

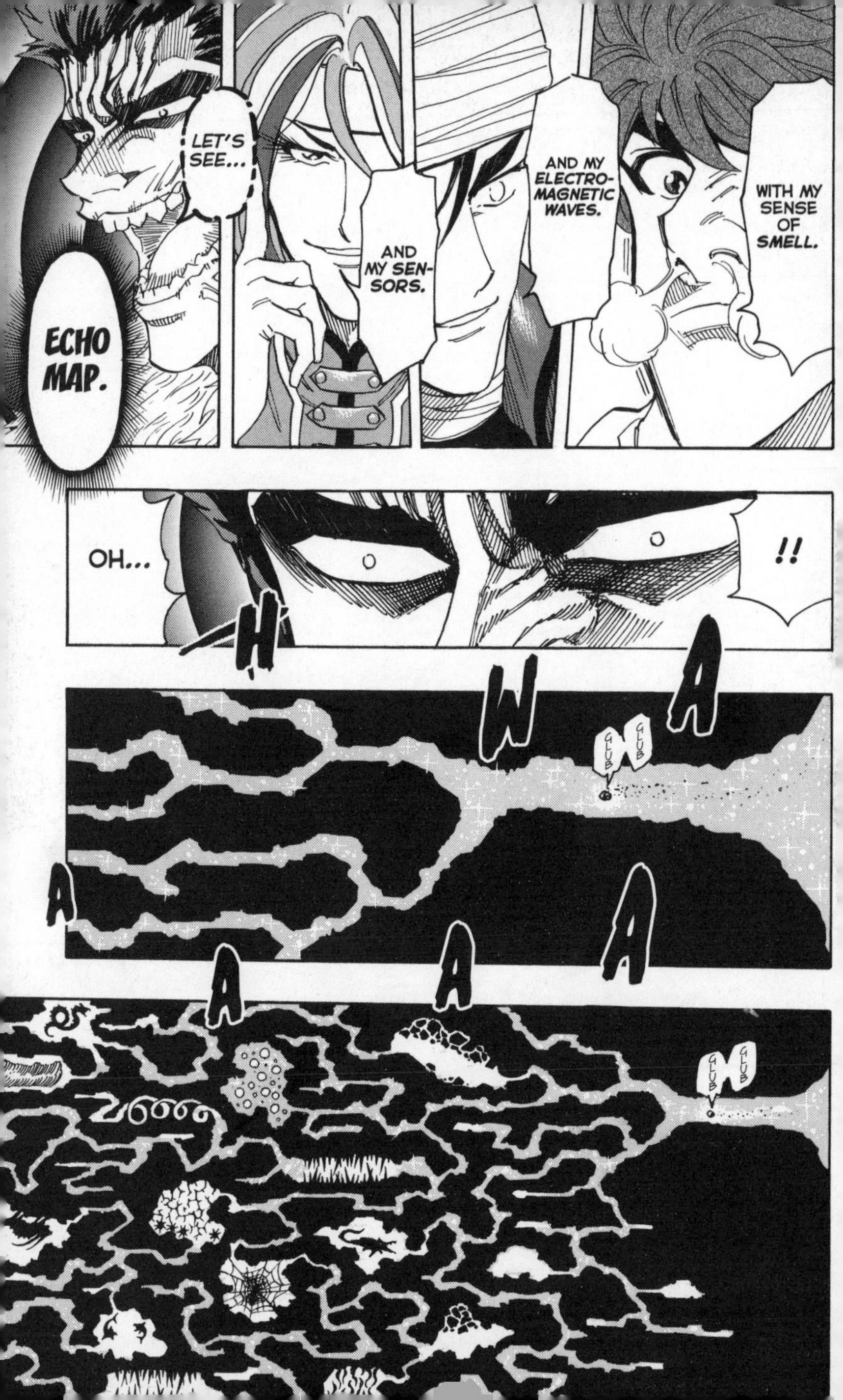
WITH MY SENSE OF SMELL.
AND MY ELECTRO-MAGNETIC WAVES.
AND MY SEN-SORS.
LET'S SEE...
ECHO MAP.
!!
OH...
H
W
A
GLUB
GLUB
A
A
A
A
GLUB
GLUB

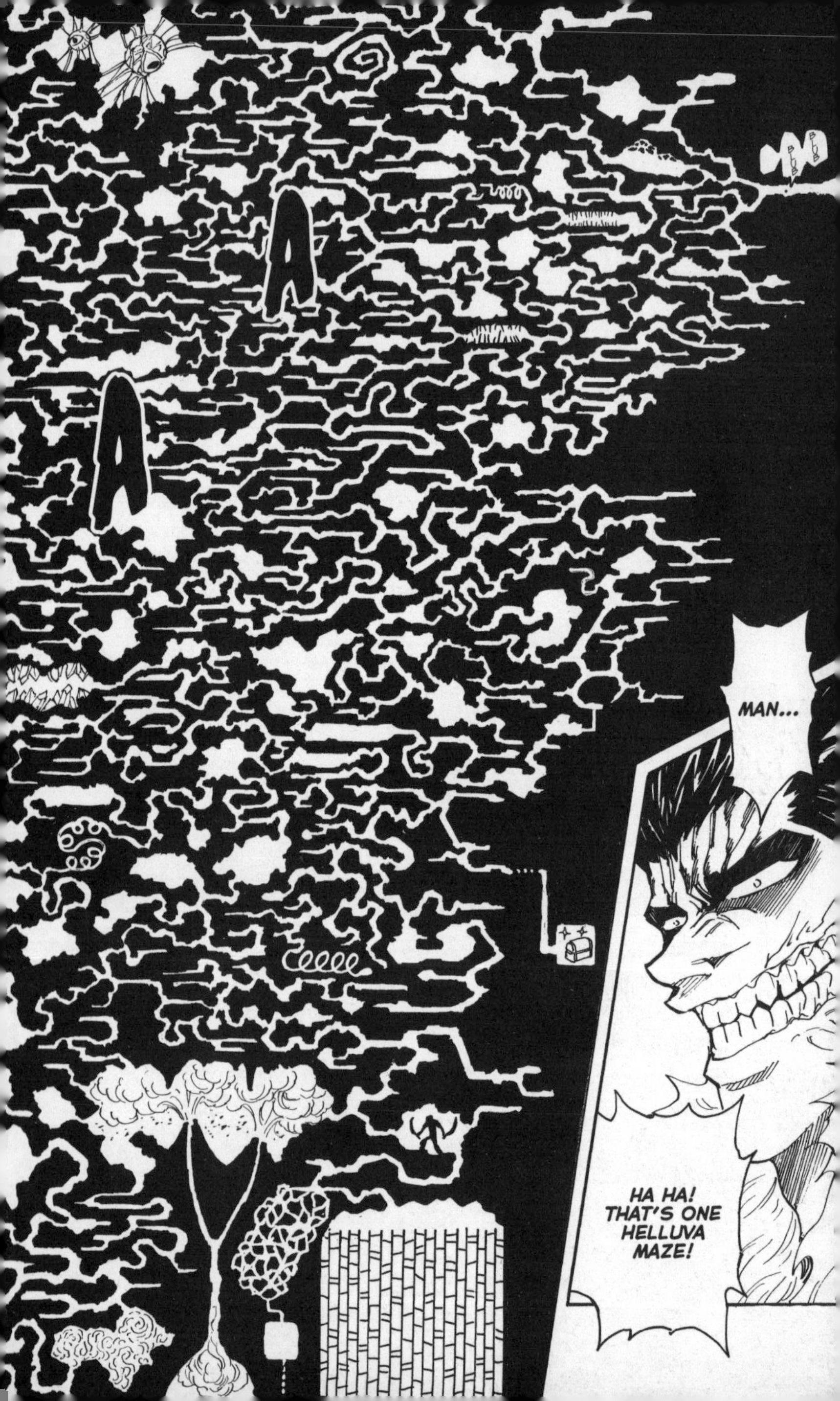
BLUB BLUB
MAN...
HA HA! THAT'S ONE HELLUVA MAZE!

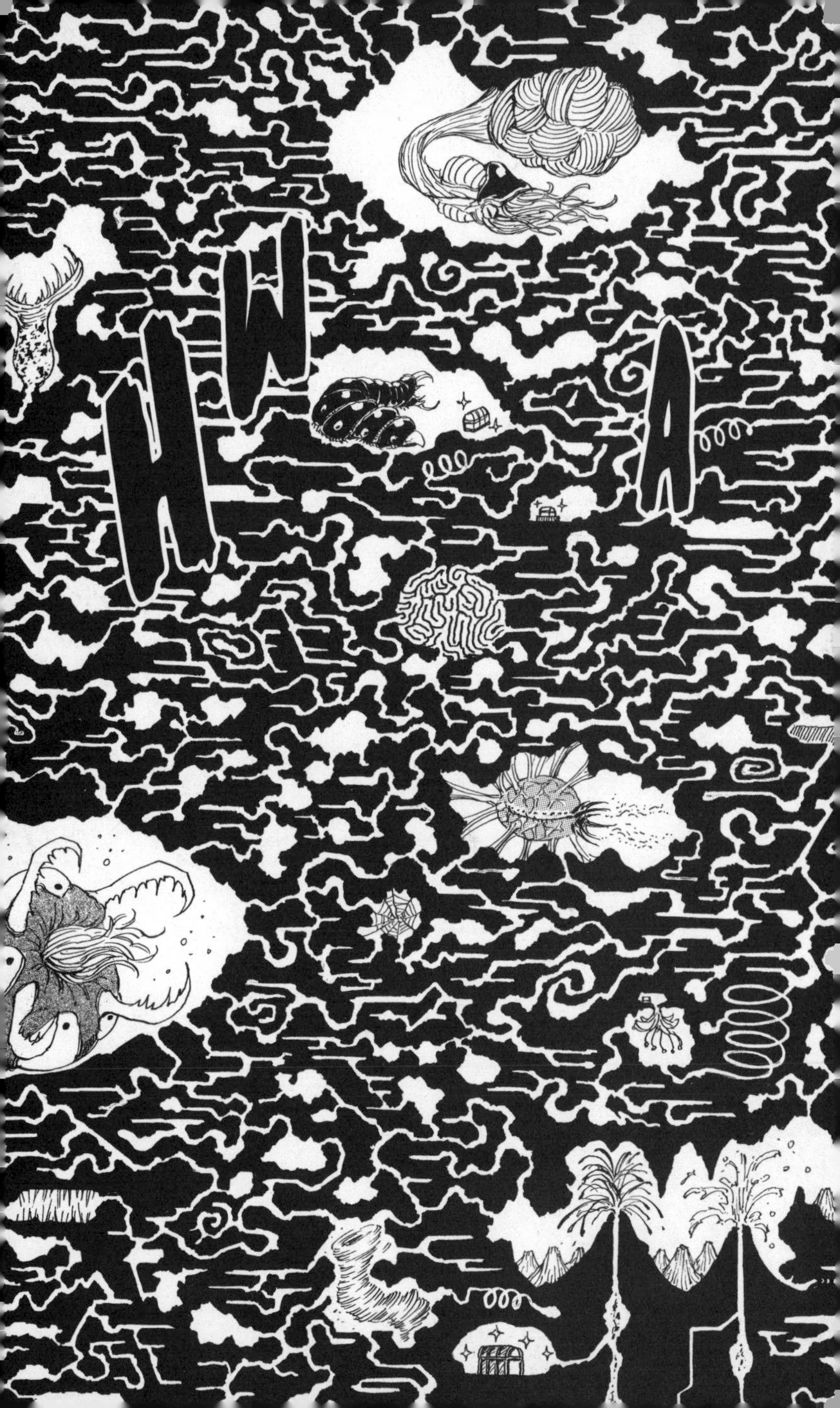
HWA

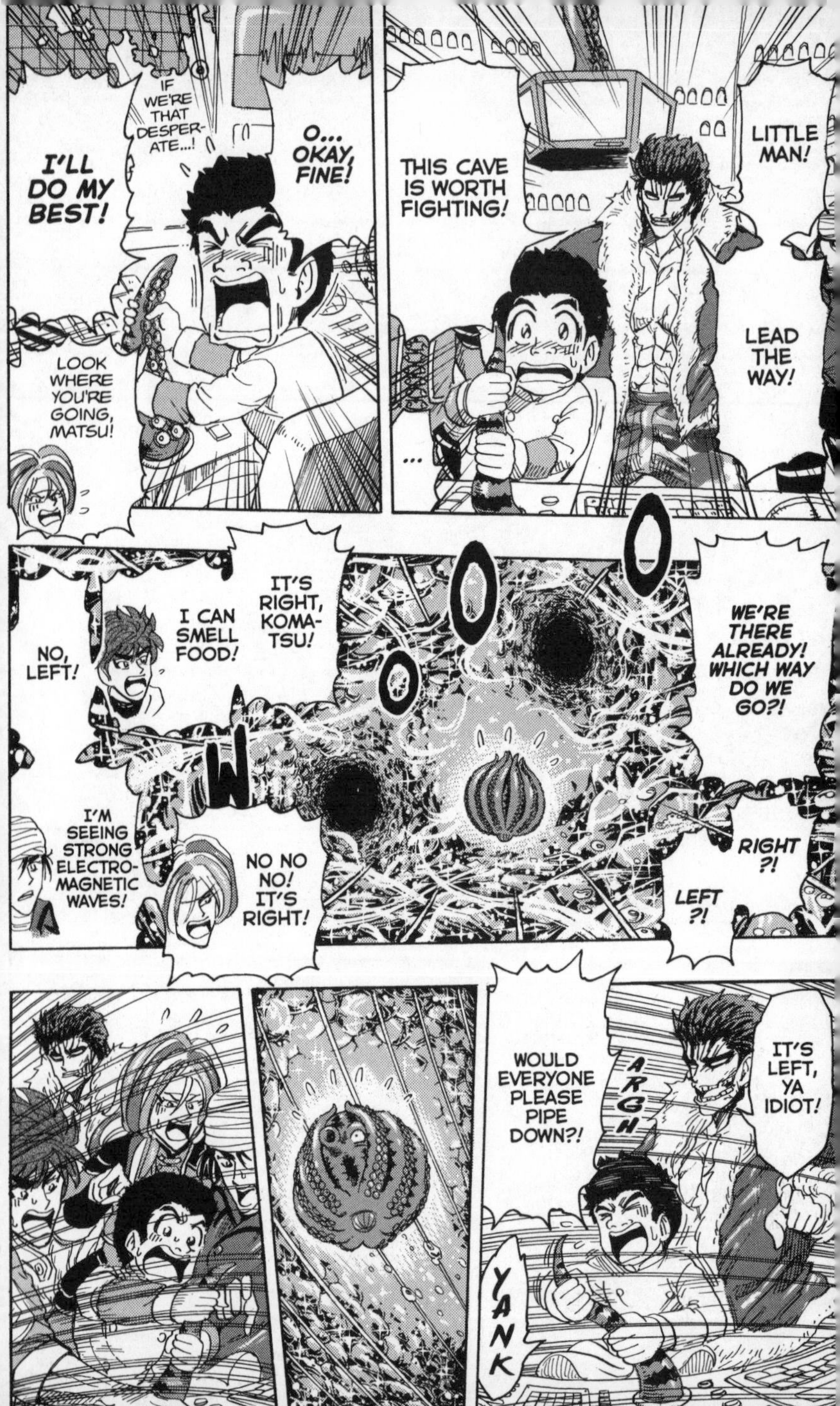
LITTLE MAN!
LEAD THE WAY!
THIS CAVE IS WORTH FIGHTING!
...
O... OKAY, FINE!
IF WE'RE THAT DESPER-ATE...!
I'LL DO MY BEST!
LOOK WHERE YOU'RE GOING, MATSU!
WE'RE THERE ALREADY! WHICH WAY DO WE GO?!
IT'S RIGHT, KOMA-TSU!
I CAN SMELL FOOD!
NO, LEFT!
RIGHT ?!
LEFT ?!
NO NO NO! IT'S RIGHT!
I'M SEEING STRONG ELECTRO-MAGNETIC WAVES!
IT'S LEFT, YA IDIOT!
ARGH
WOULD EVERYONE PLEASE PIPE DOWN?!
YANK

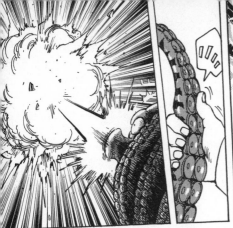

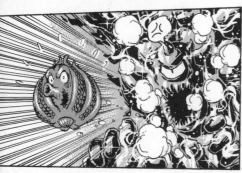

EVEN IN THIS INESCAPABLE MAZE...

W...WHY IS IT...?

...

...

123

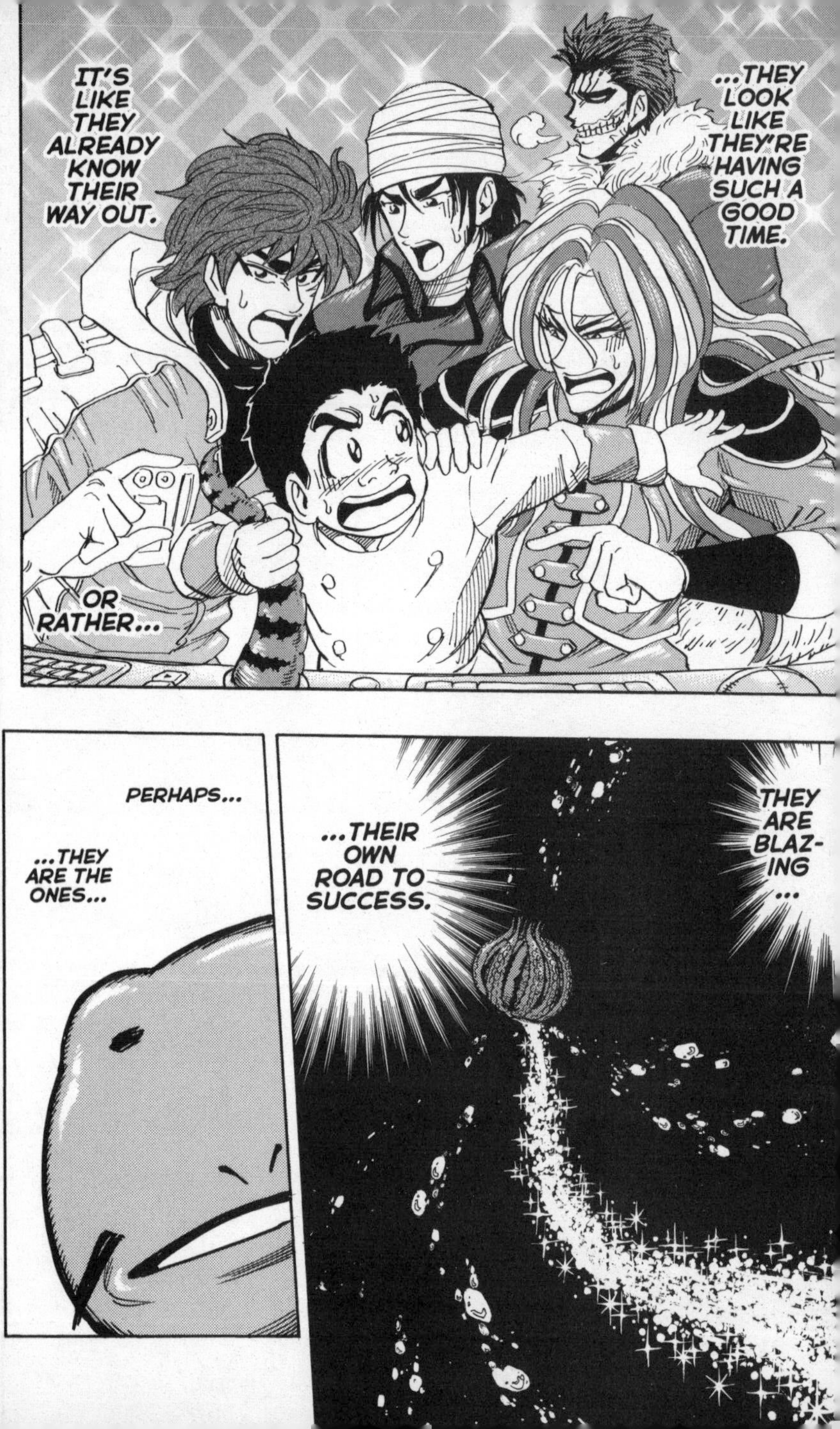
...THEY LOOK LIKE THEY'RE HAVING SUCH A GOOD TIME.
IT'S LIKE THEY ALREADY KNOW THEIR WAY OUT.
OR RATHER...
THEY ARE BLAZ-ING...
...THEIR OWN ROAD TO SUCCESS.
PERHAPS...
...THEY ARE THE ONES...

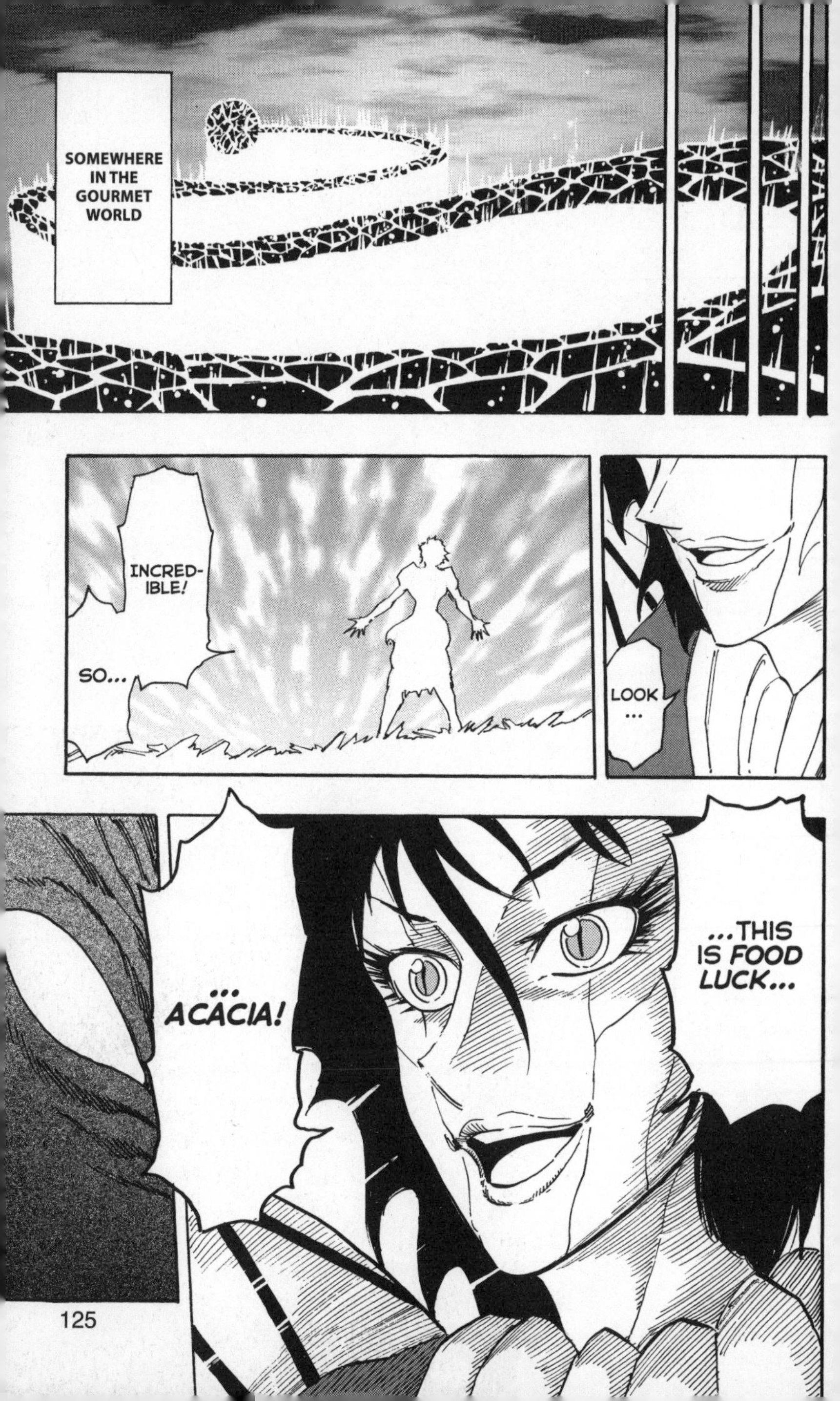
SOMEWHERE IN THE GOURMET WORLD
LOOK...
INCRED-IBLE!
SO...
...THIS IS FOOD LUCK...
...ACACIA!

[redacted]

GOURMET 279: ROAD SIGN!!

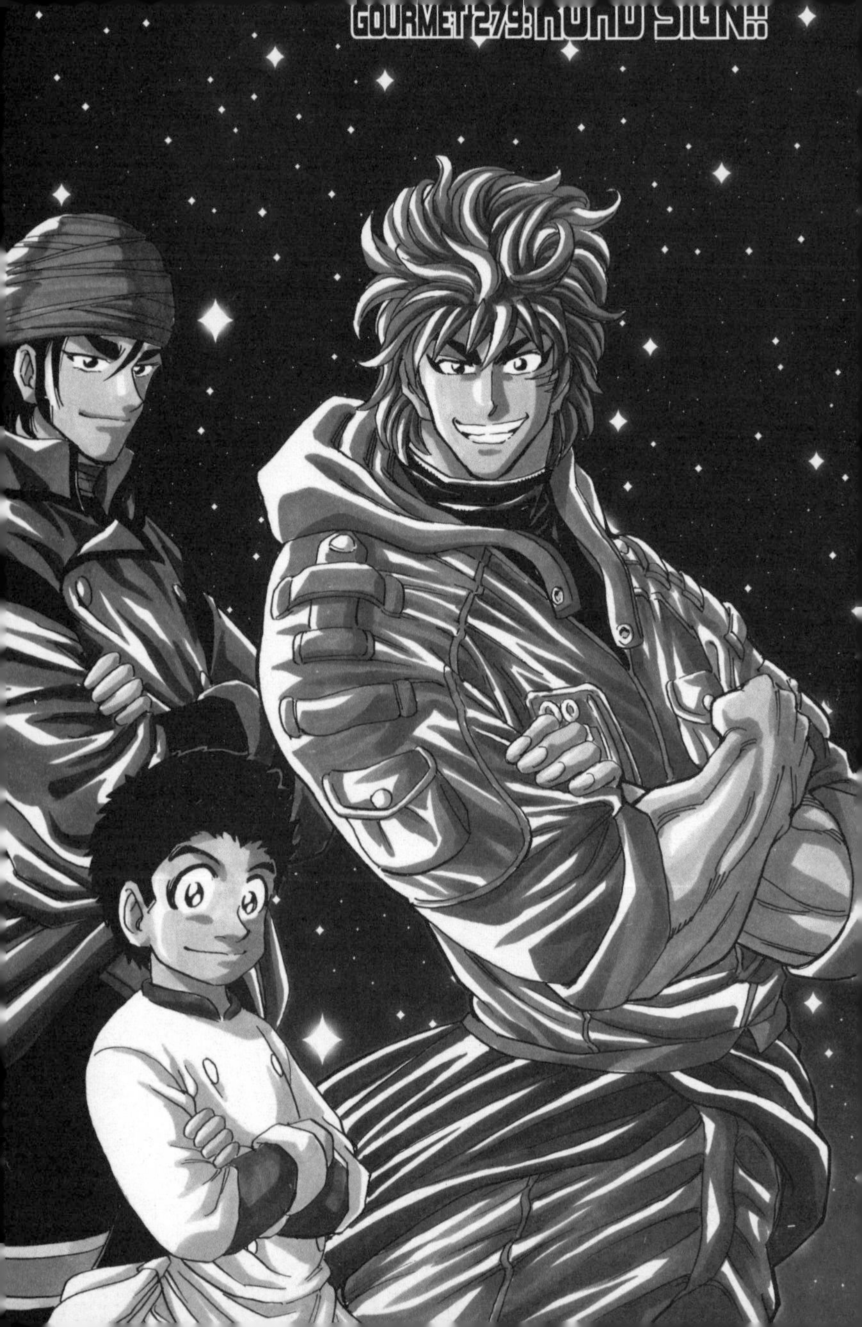

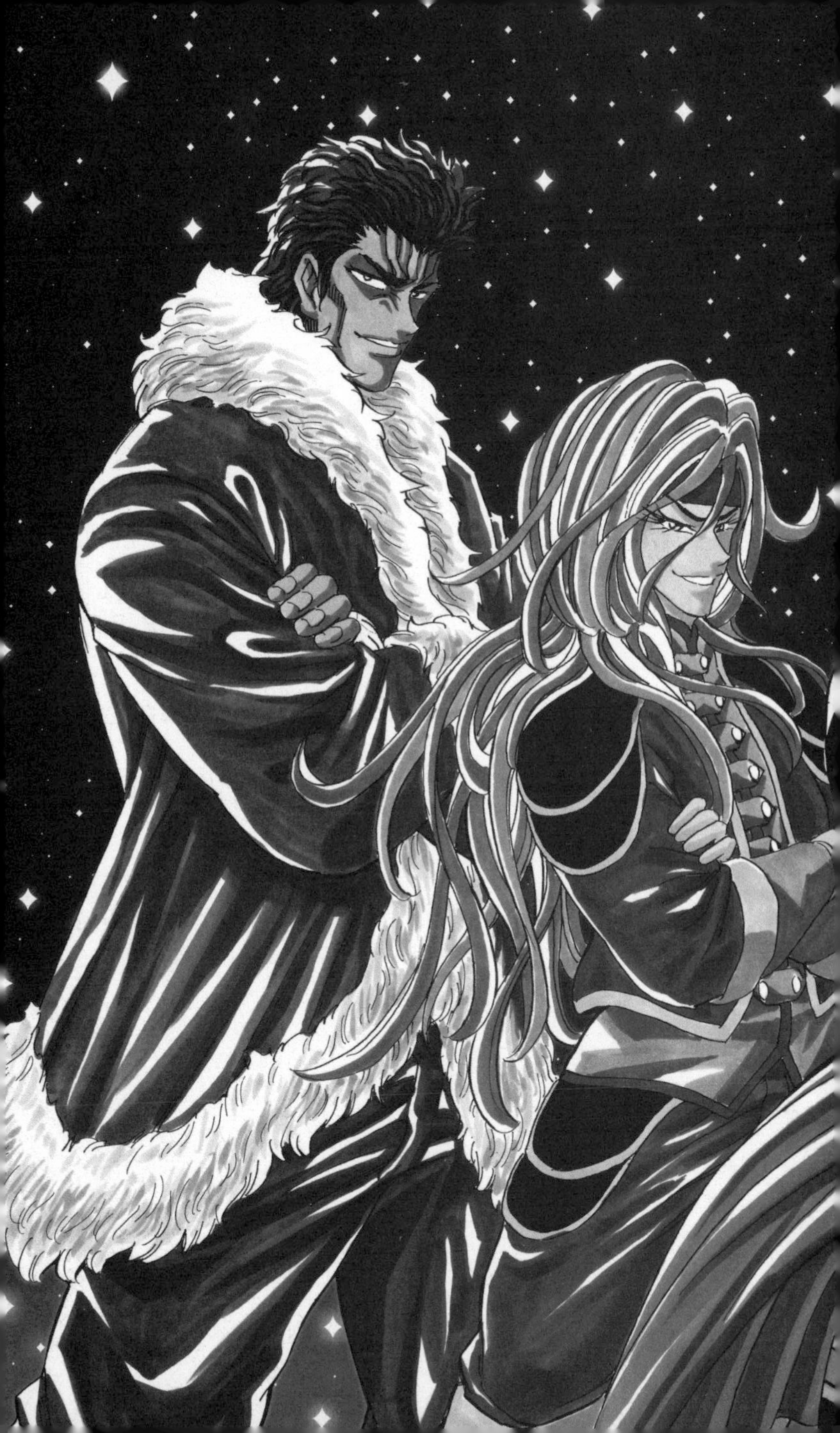

TORIKO

GOURMET CHECKLIST

Vol. 302

STAR RICE
(GRAIN)

STAR RICE.* RICE THAT TWINKLES LIKE STARS AFTER EACH GRAIN HAS BEEN WASHED AND COOKED INDIVIDUALLY.
TO EAT IT, YOU MUST GAZE INTO THE RICE WITHOUT BLINKING. BLINK EVEN ONCE, AND THE ENTIRE BOWL WILL GO BAD.

CAPTURE LEVEL: 9

HABITAT: ARTIFICIALLY PRODUCED BUT ONLY IN SMALL QUANTITIES

SIZE: 7 MM

HEIGHT: ---

WEIGHT: ---

PRICE: 9,000 YEN PER KG

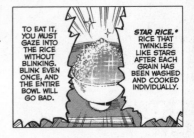

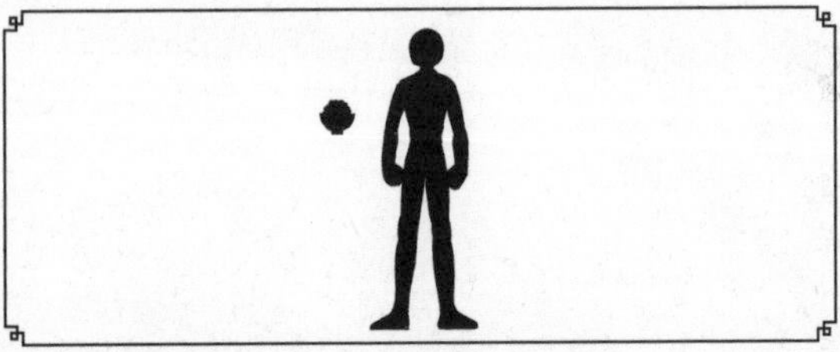

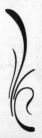

SCALE

STAR RICE GOT ITS NAME FROM THE WAY EACH INDIVIDUAL GRAIN SPARKLES LIKE STARS IN THE NIGHT SKY. THE RICE IS SO GOOD ON ITS OWN THAT IT PUTS ANY ACCOMPANYING DISHES TO SHAME. UNFORTUNATELY, RESTAURANTS ONLY OFFER IT FOR LIMITED TIMES. YOU MUST NOT BLINK WHILE EATING THIS DELICIOUS RICE OR ELSE THE FLAVOR OF THE ENTIRE BOWL WILL INSTANTANEOUSLY VANISH. ONE MUST HAVE EYES OF STEEL TO EAT THIS DISH.

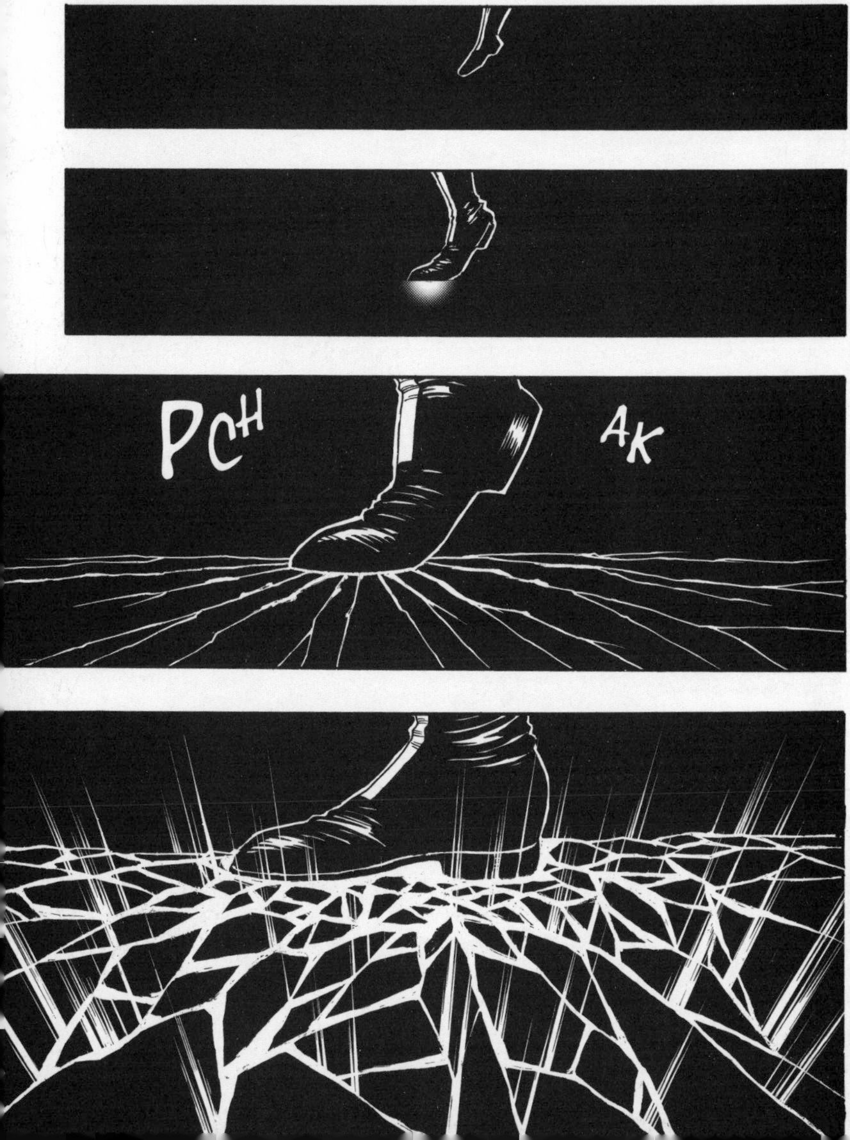
PCH
AK

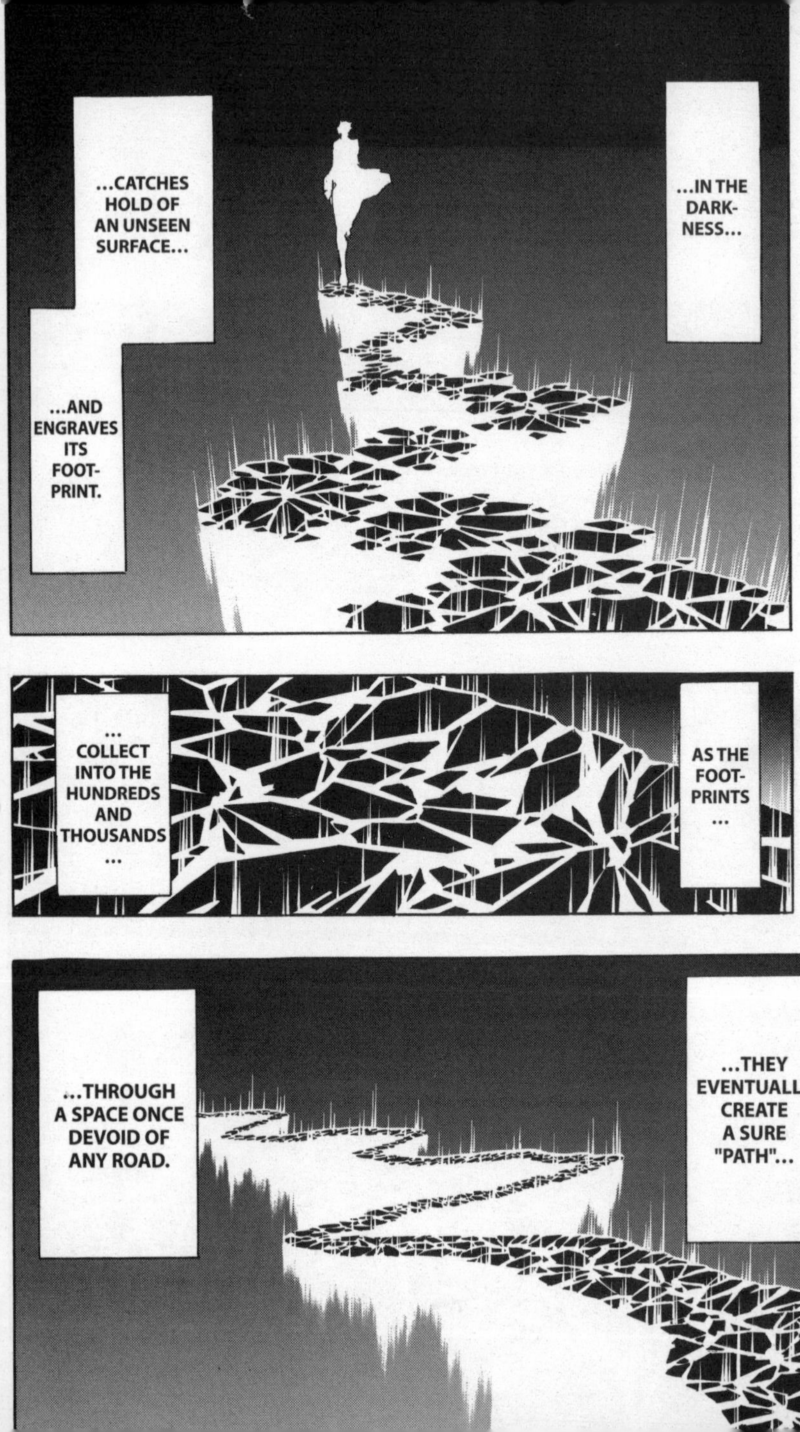
...IN THE DARKNESS...
...CATCHES HOLD OF AN UNSEEN SURFACE...
...AND ENGRAVES ITS FOOTPRINT.
AS THE FOOTPRINTS...
...COLLECT INTO THE HUNDREDS AND THOUSANDS...
...THEY EVENTUALLY CREATE A SURE "PATH"...
...THROUGH A SPACE ONCE DEVOID OF ANY ROAD.

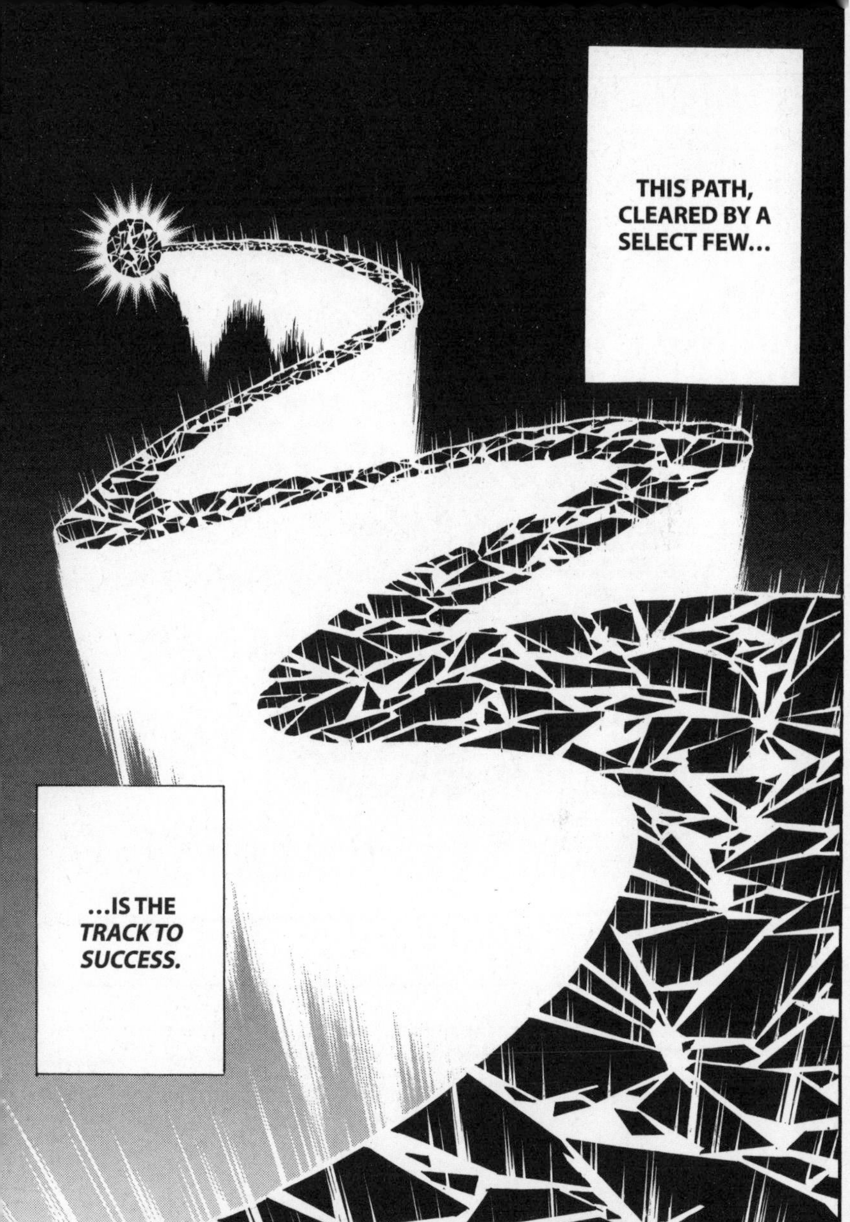
THIS PATH, CLEARED BY A SELECT FEW...
...IS THE *TRACK TO SUCCESS.*

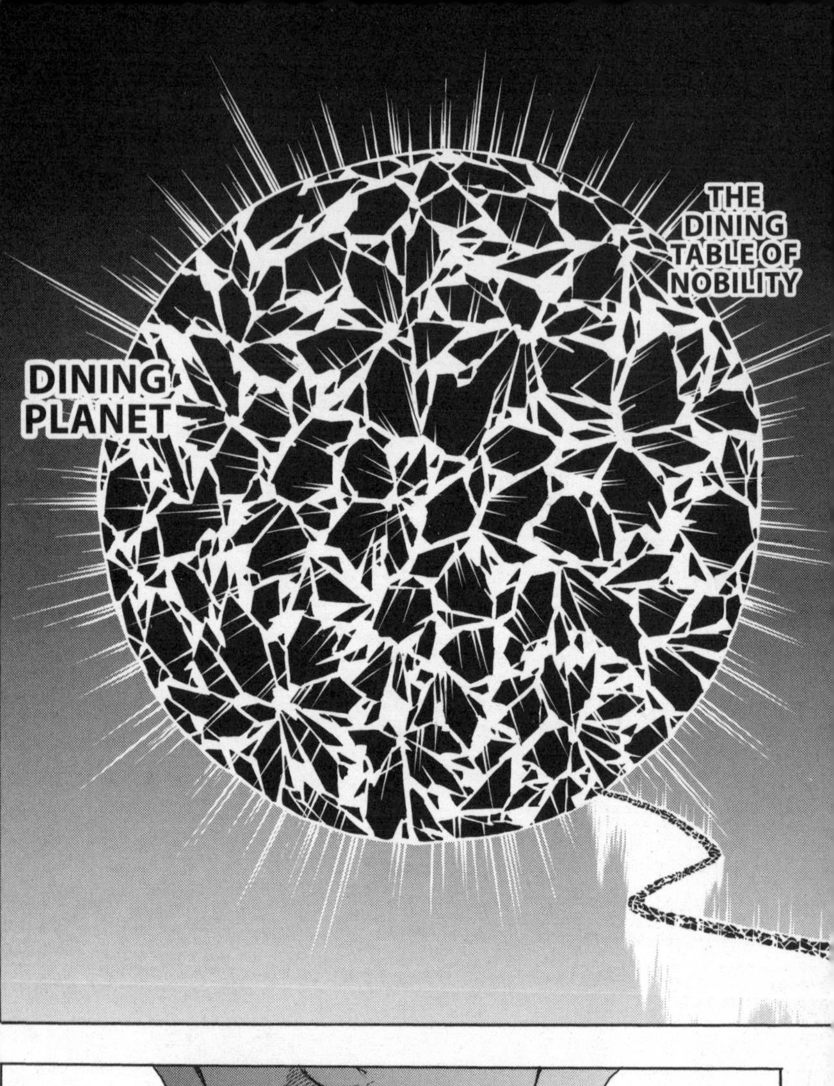
THE DINING TABLE OF NOBILITY
DINING PLANET

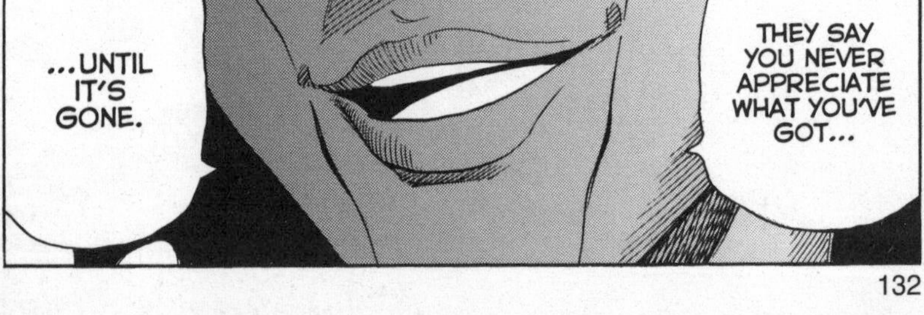
THEY SAY YOU NEVER APPRECIATE WHAT YOU'VE GOT...
...UNTIL IT'S GONE.

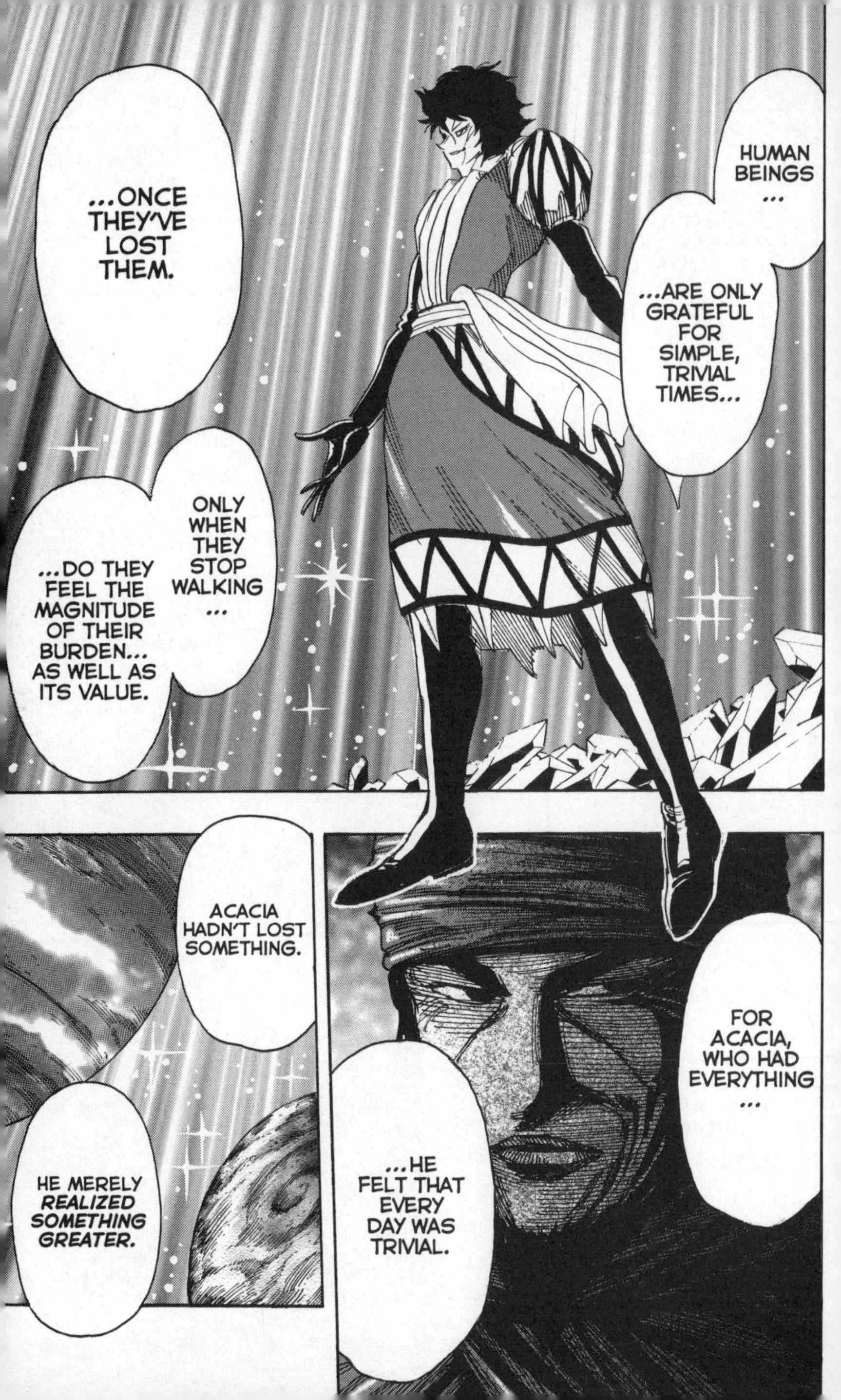
HUMAN BEINGS ...
...ARE ONLY GRATEFUL FOR SIMPLE, TRIVIAL TIMES...
...ONCE THEY'VE LOST THEM.
ONLY WHEN THEY STOP WALKING ...
...DO THEY FEEL THE MAGNITUDE OF THEIR BURDEN... AS WELL AS ITS VALUE.
FOR ACACIA, WHO HAD EVERYTHING ...
...HE FELT THAT EVERY DAY WAS TRIVIAL.
ACACIA HADN'T LOST SOMETHING.
HE MERELY *REALIZED SOMETHING GREATER.*

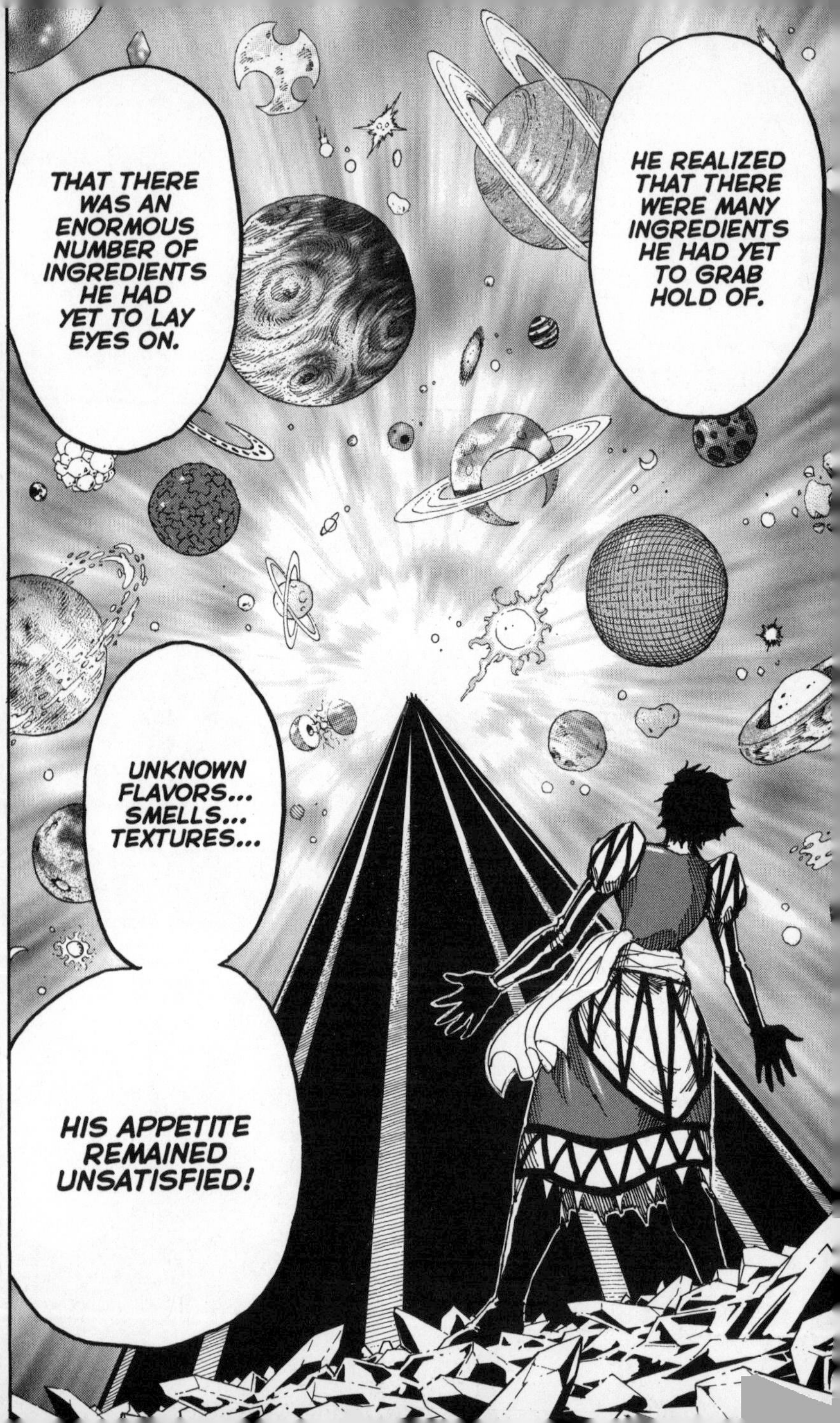
HE REALIZED THAT THERE WERE MANY INGREDIENTS HE HAD YET TO GRAB HOLD OF.
THAT THERE WAS AN ENORMOUS NUMBER OF INGREDIENTS HE HAD YET TO LAY EYES ON.
UNKNOWN FLAVORS... SMELLS... TEXTURES...
HIS APPETITE REMAINED UNSATISFIED!

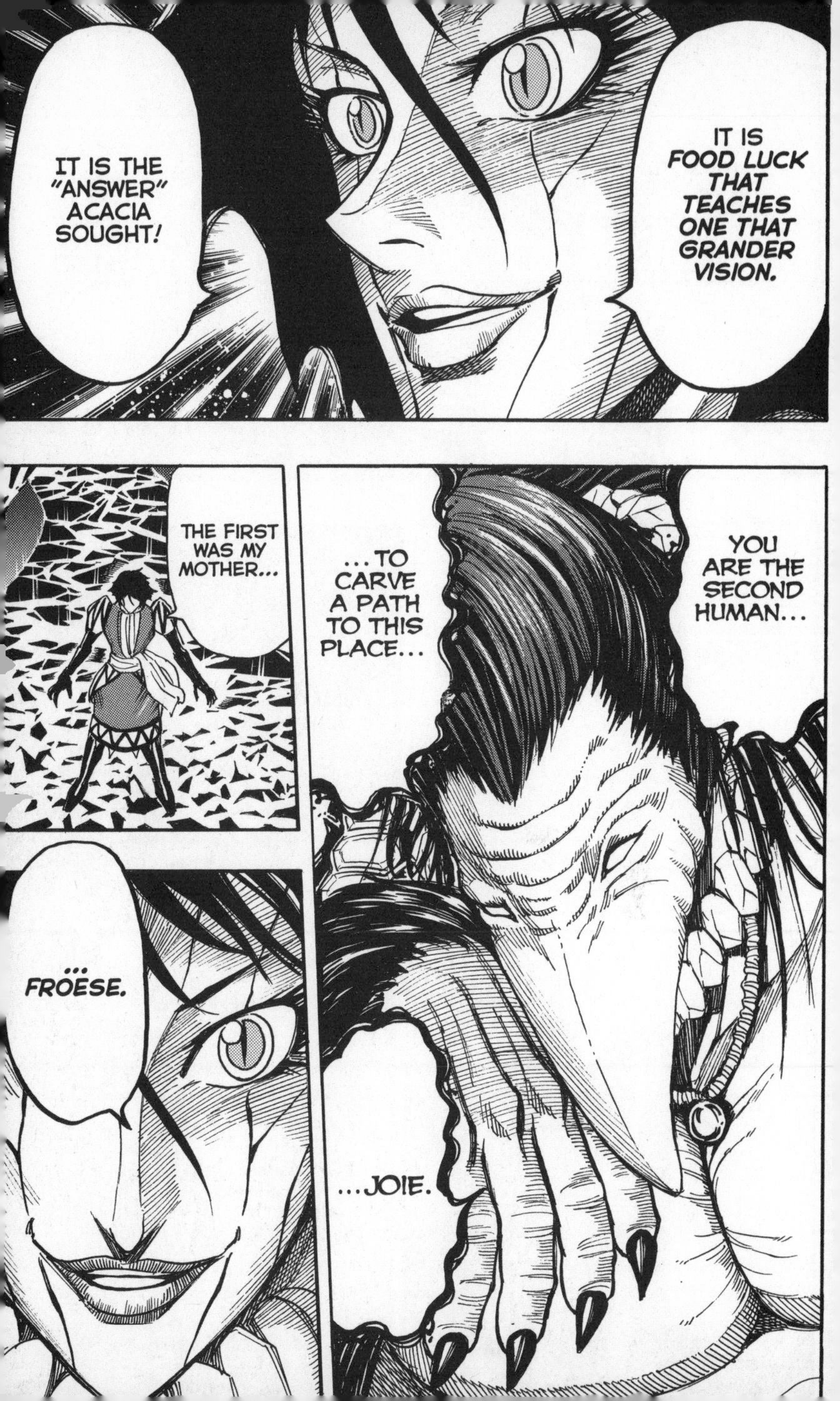
IT IS FOOD LUCK THAT TEACHES ONE THAT GRANDER VISION.
IT IS THE "ANSWER" ACACIA SOUGHT!
YOU ARE THE SECOND HUMAN...
...TO CARVE A PATH TO THIS PLACE...
...JOIE.
THE FIRST WAS MY MOTHER...
...FROESE.

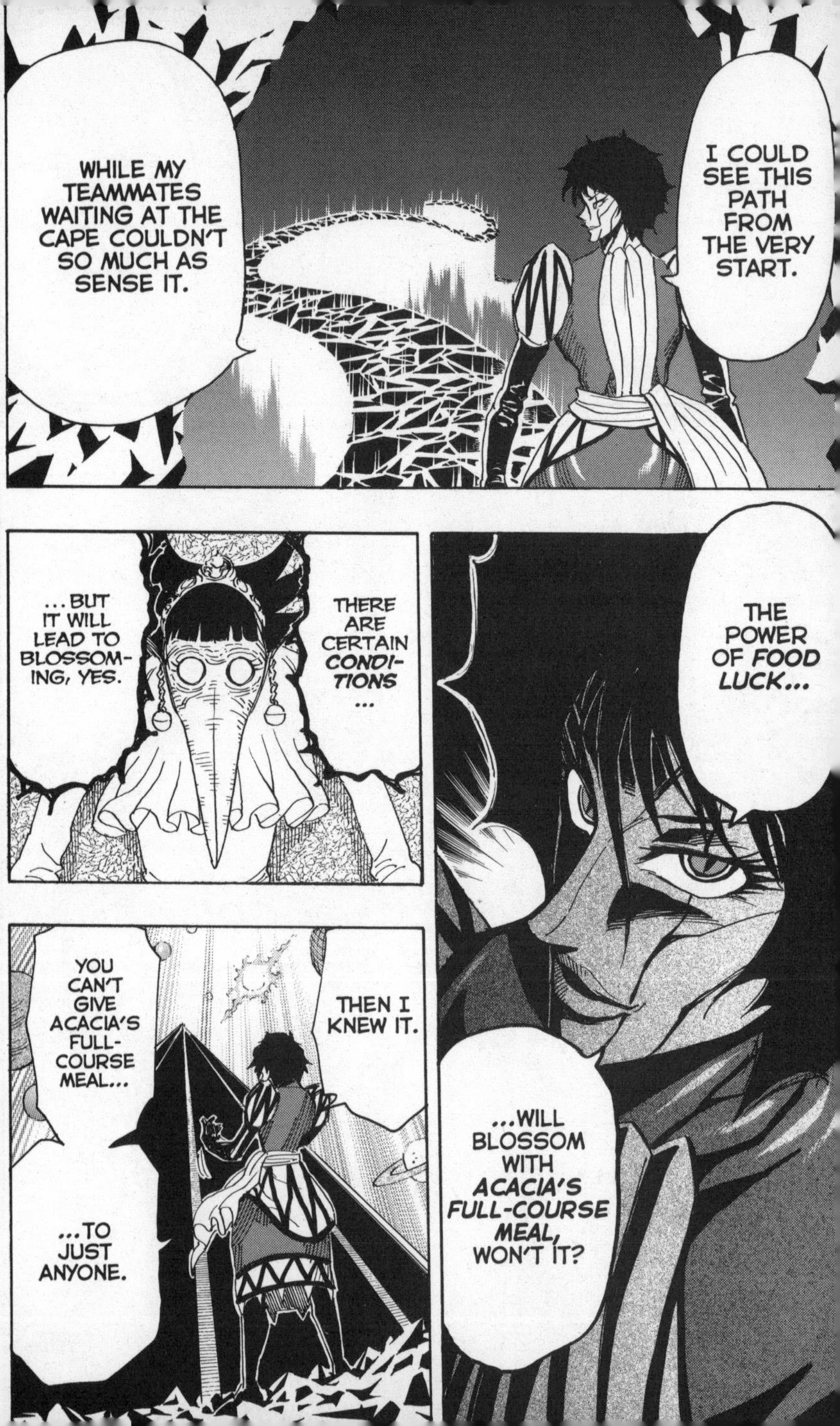
I COULD SEE THIS PATH FROM THE VERY START.
WHILE MY TEAMMATES WAITING AT THE CAPE COULDN'T SO MUCH AS SENSE IT.
THE POWER OF *FOOD LUCK*...
...WILL BLOSSOM WITH *ACACIA'S FULL-COURSE MEAL,* WON'T IT?
THERE ARE CERTAIN *CONDITIONS*...
...BUT IT WILL LEAD TO BLOSSOMING, YES.
THEN I KNEW IT.
YOU CAN'T GIVE ACACIA'S FULL-COURSE MEAL...
...TO JUST ANYONE.

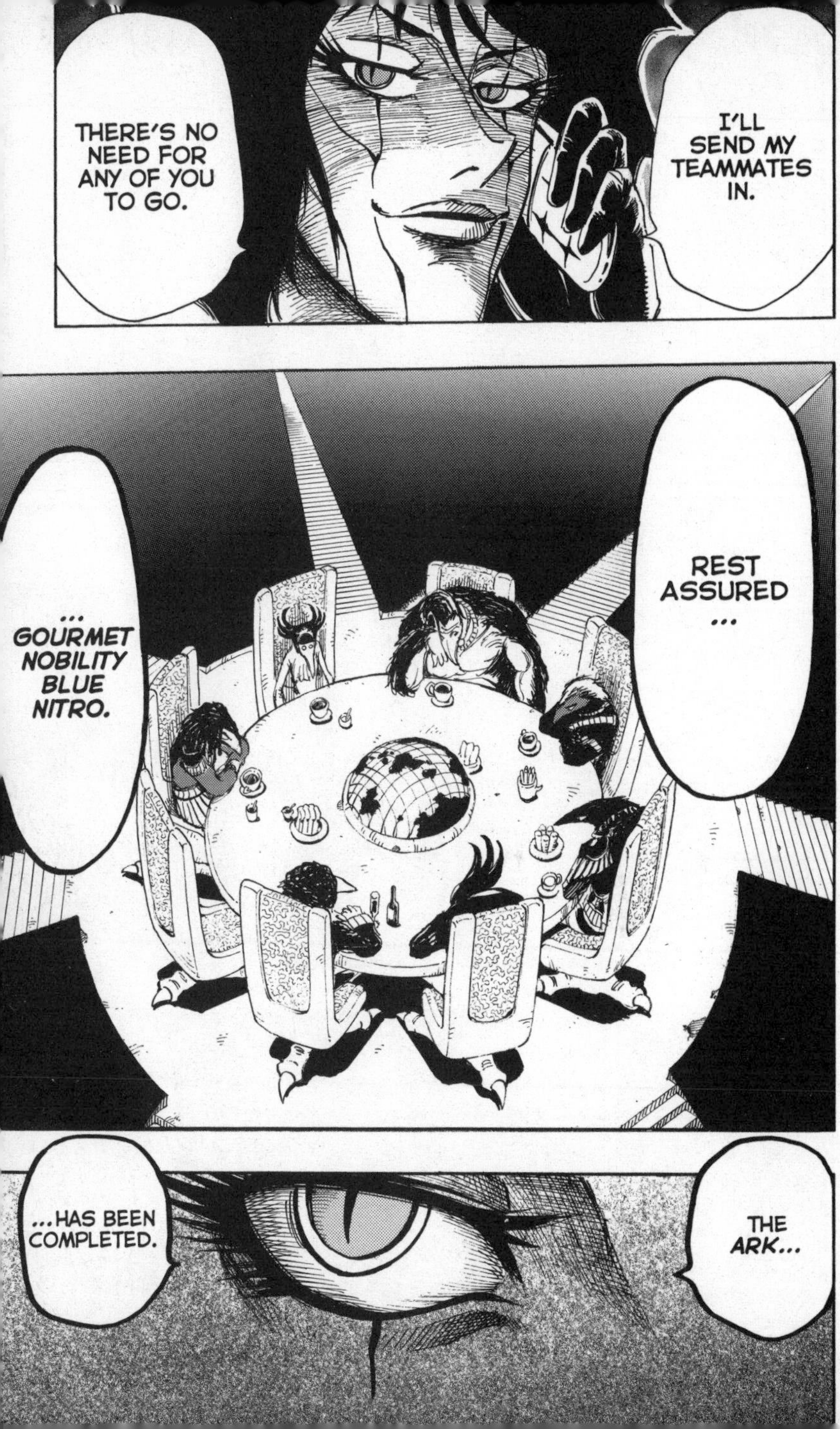
I'LL SEND MY TEAMMATES IN.
THERE'S NO NEED FOR ANY OF YOU TO GO.
REST ASSURED ...
... GOURMET NOBILITY BLUE NITRO.
THE ARK...
...HAS BEEN COMPLETED.

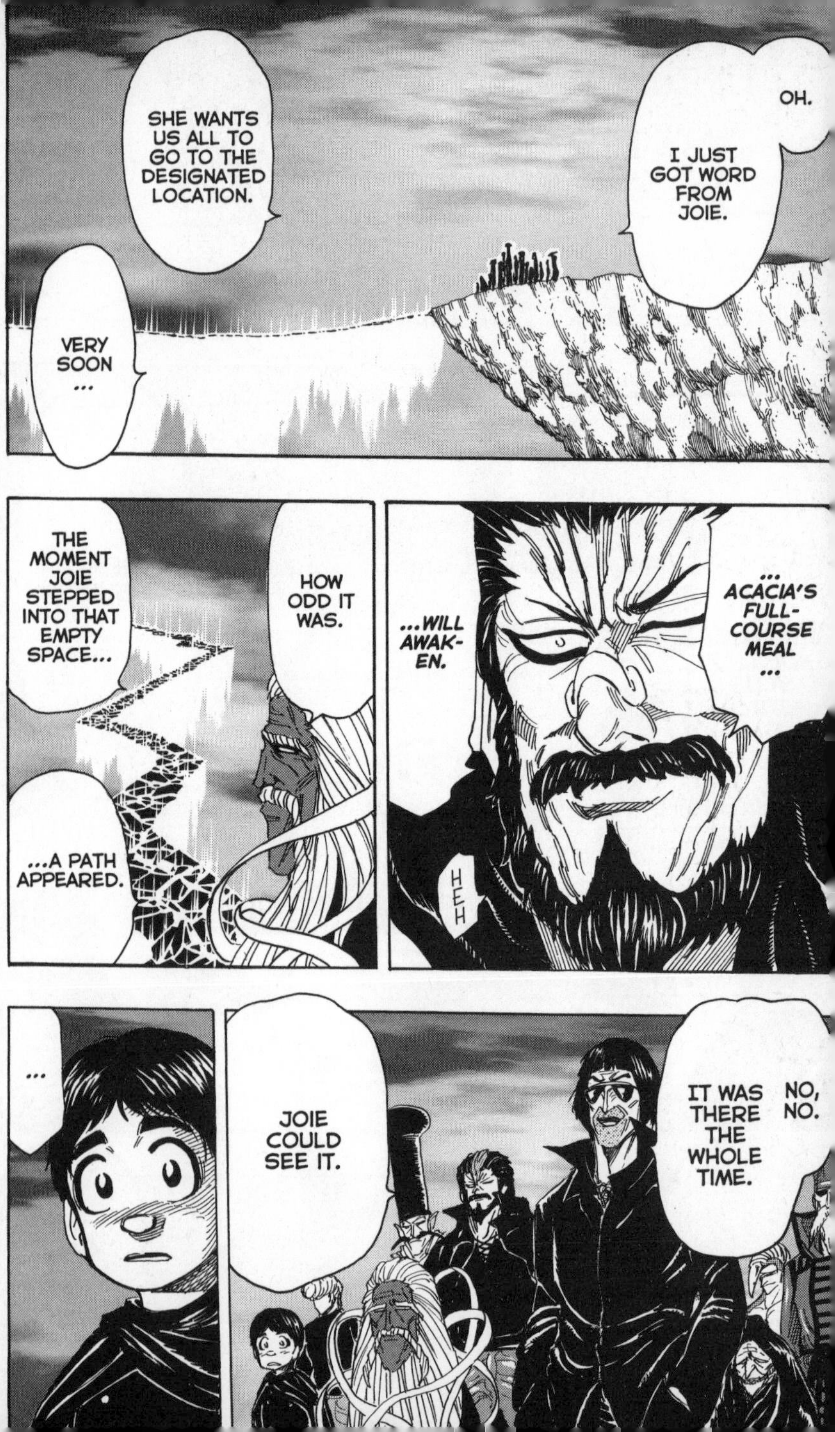

OH.
I JUST GOT WORD FROM JOIE.
SHE WANTS US ALL TO GO TO THE DESIGNATED LOCATION.
VERY SOON ...
... ACACIA'S FULL-COURSE MEAL ...
...WILL AWAKEN.
HEH
HOW ODD IT WAS.
THE MOMENT JOIE STEPPED INTO THAT EMPTY SPACE...
...A PATH APPEARED.
NO, NO.
IT WAS THERE THE WHOLE TIME.
JOIE COULD SEE IT.
...

...TO THE ANSWER!

THE ROUTE ...

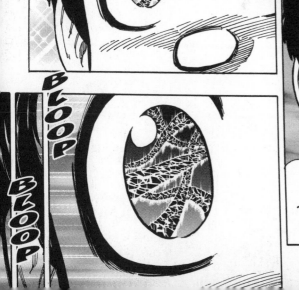

BLOOP

BLOOP

...

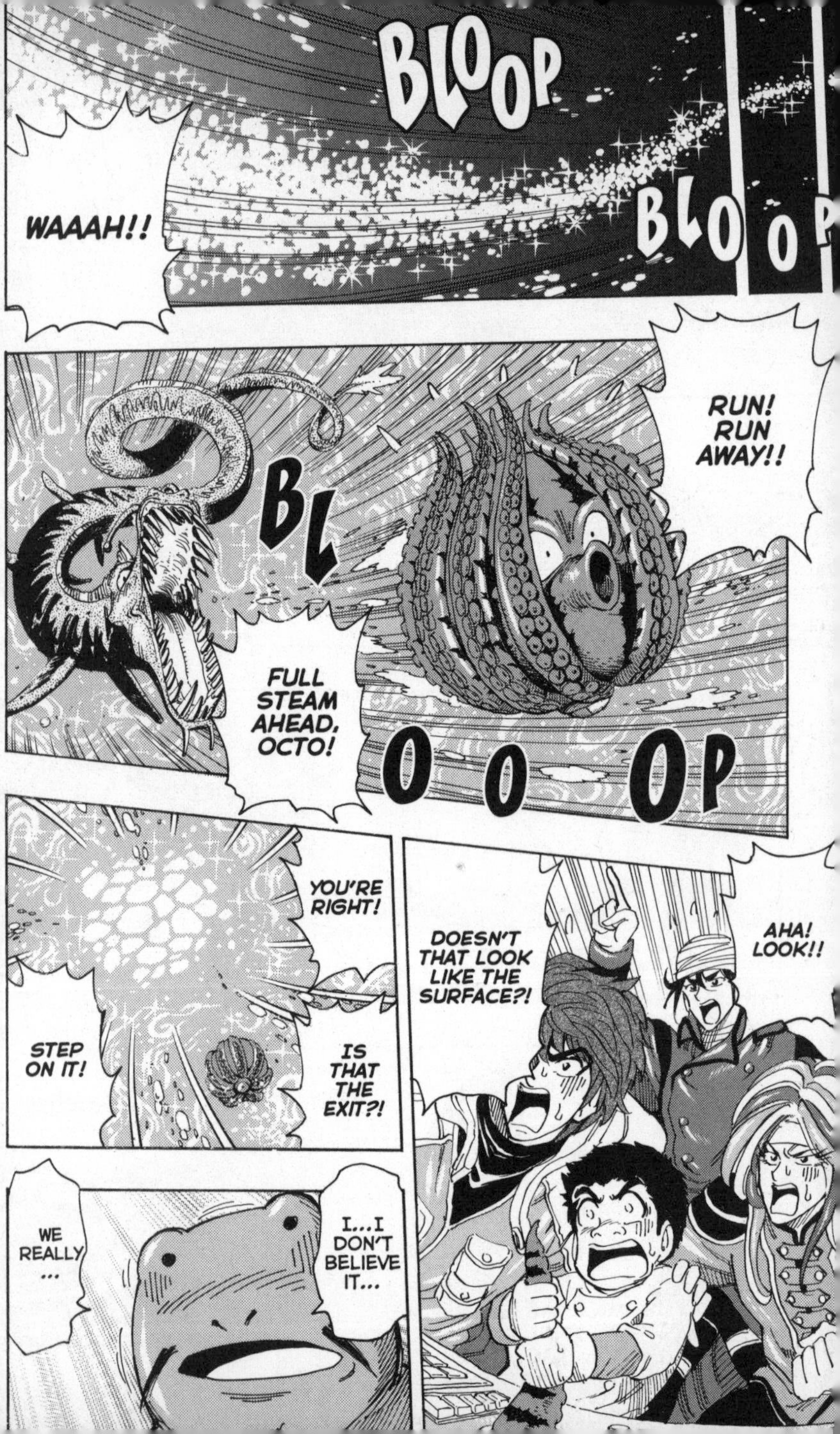
BLOOP
BLOOP
WAAAH!!
RUN! RUN AWAY!!
BL
OOOP
FULL STEAM AHEAD, OCTO!
AHA! LOOK!!
DOESN'T THAT LOOK LIKE THE SURFACE?!
YOU'RE RIGHT!
IS THAT THE EXIT?!
STEP ON IT!
I...I DON'T BELIEVE IT...
WE REALLY...

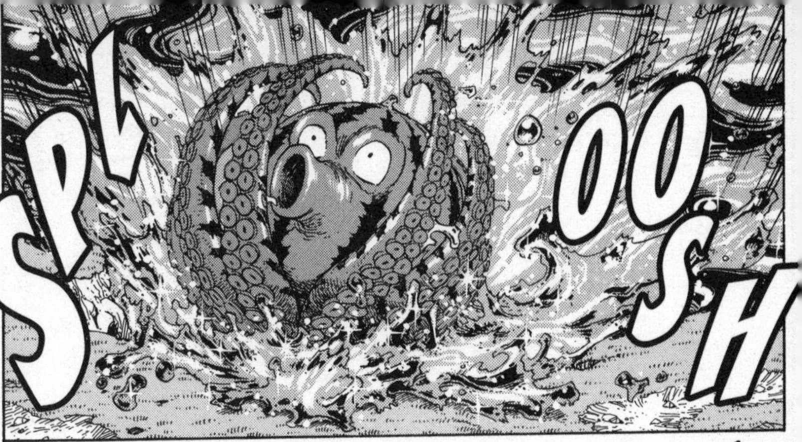
SPLOOSH

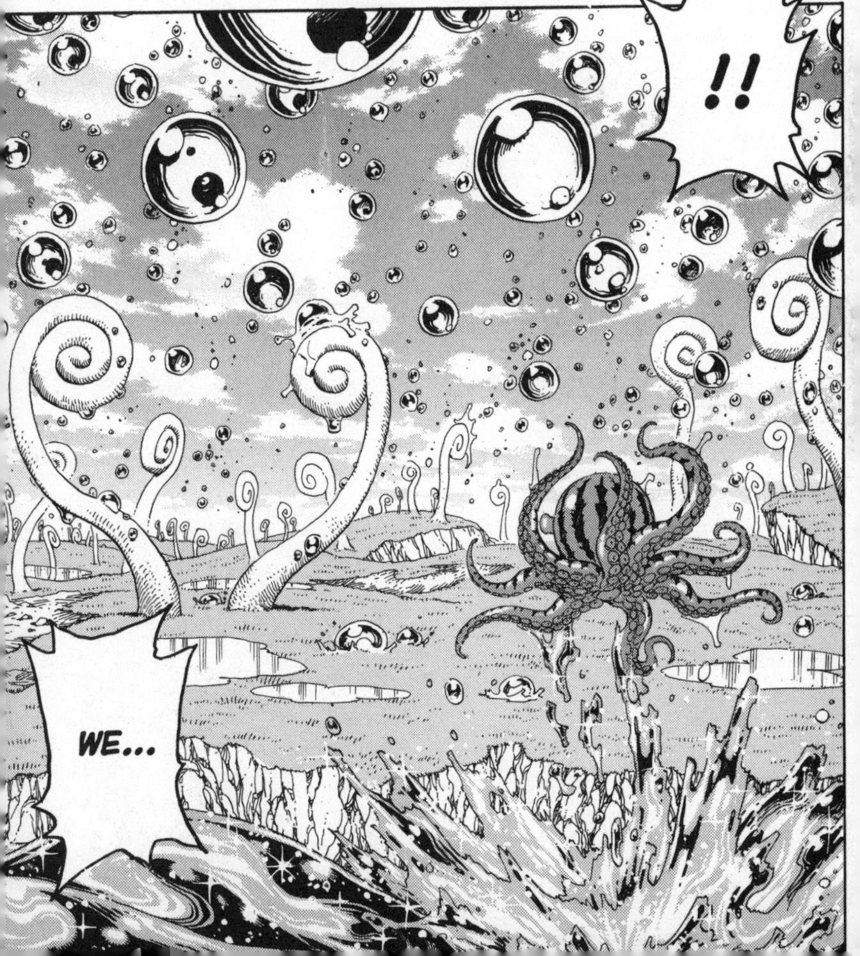
!!
WE...

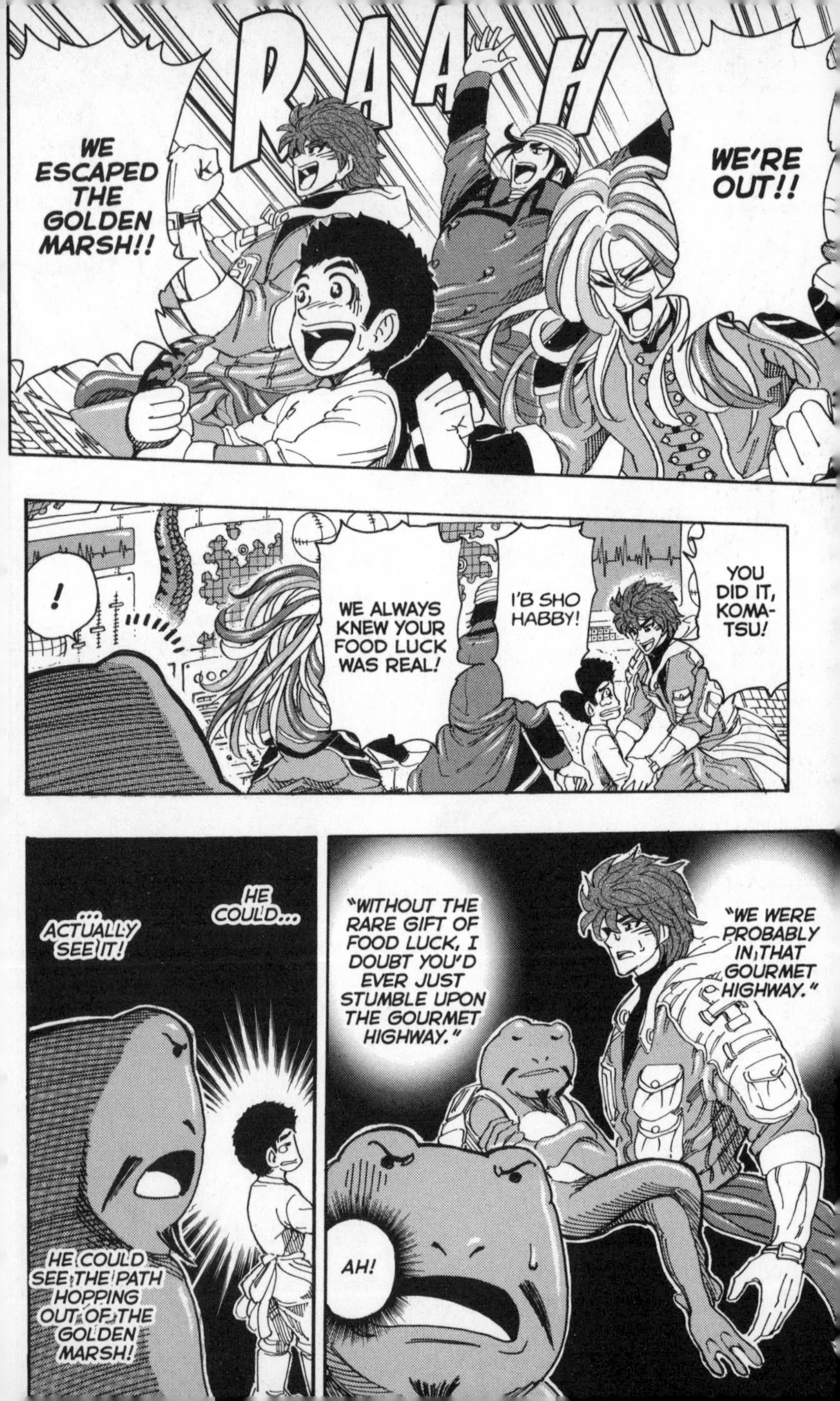
RAAH
WE'RE OUT!!
WE ESCAPED THE GOLDEN MARSH!!
YOU DID IT, KOMATSU!
I'B SHO HABBY!
WE ALWAYS KNEW YOUR FOOD LUCK WAS REAL!
!
"WE WERE PROBABLY IN THAT GOURMET HIGHWAY."
"WITHOUT THE RARE GIFT OF FOOD LUCK, I DOUBT YOU'D EVER JUST STUMBLE UPON THE GOURMET HIGHWAY."
AH!
HE COULD...
...ACTUALLY SEE IT!
HE COULD SEE THE PATH HOPPING OUT OF THE GOLDEN MARSH!

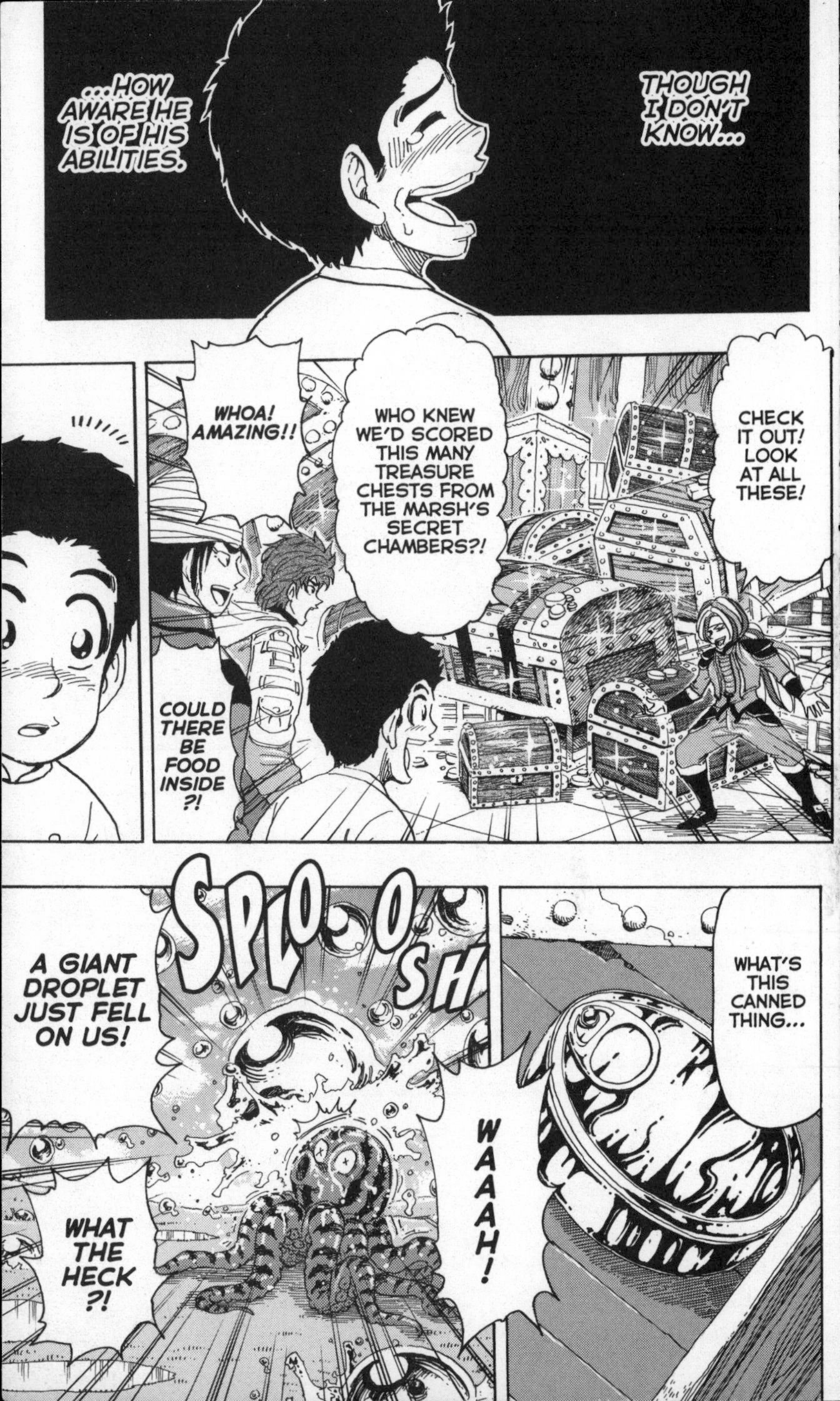
THOUGH I DON'T KNOW...
...HOW AWARE HE IS OF HIS ABILITIES.
CHECK IT OUT! LOOK AT ALL THESE!
WHO KNEW WE'D SCORED THIS MANY TREASURE CHESTS FROM THE MARSH'S SECRET CHAMBERS?!
WHOA! AMAZING!!
COULD THERE BE FOOD INSIDE?!
WHAT'S THIS CANNED THING...
SPLOOOSH
WAAAAH!
A GIANT DROPLET JUST FELL ON US!
WHAT THE HECK?!

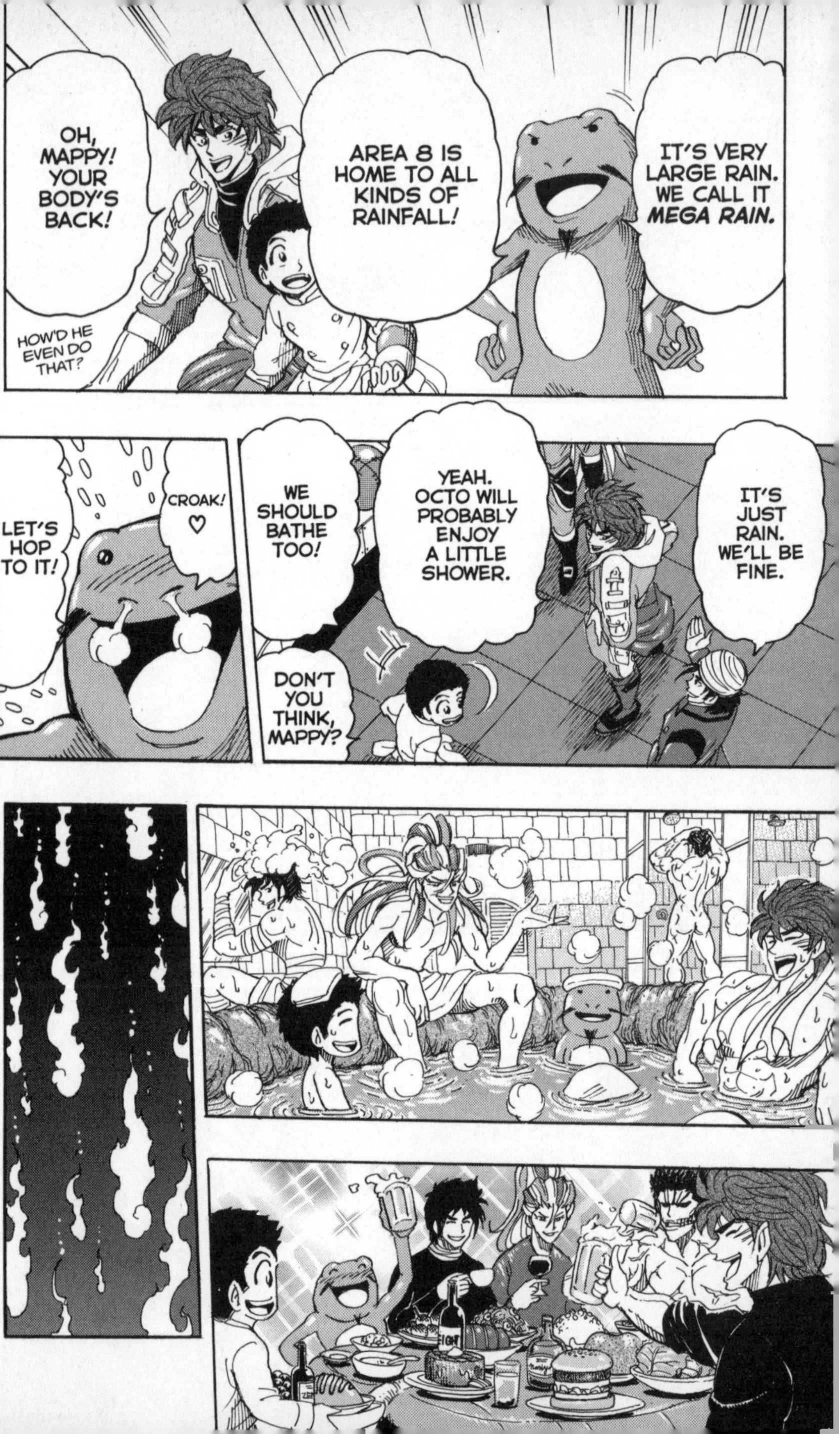
IT'S VERY LARGE RAIN. WE CALL IT *MEGA RAIN.*
AREA 8 IS HOME TO ALL KINDS OF RAINFALL!
OH, MAPPY! YOUR BODY'S BACK!
HOW'D HE EVEN DO THAT?
IT'S JUST RAIN. WE'LL BE FINE.
YEAH. OCTO WILL PROBABLY ENJOY A LITTLE SHOWER.
WE SHOULD BATHE TOO!
DON'T YOU THINK, MAPPY?
CROAK! ♡
LET'S HOP TO IT!
EIGHT

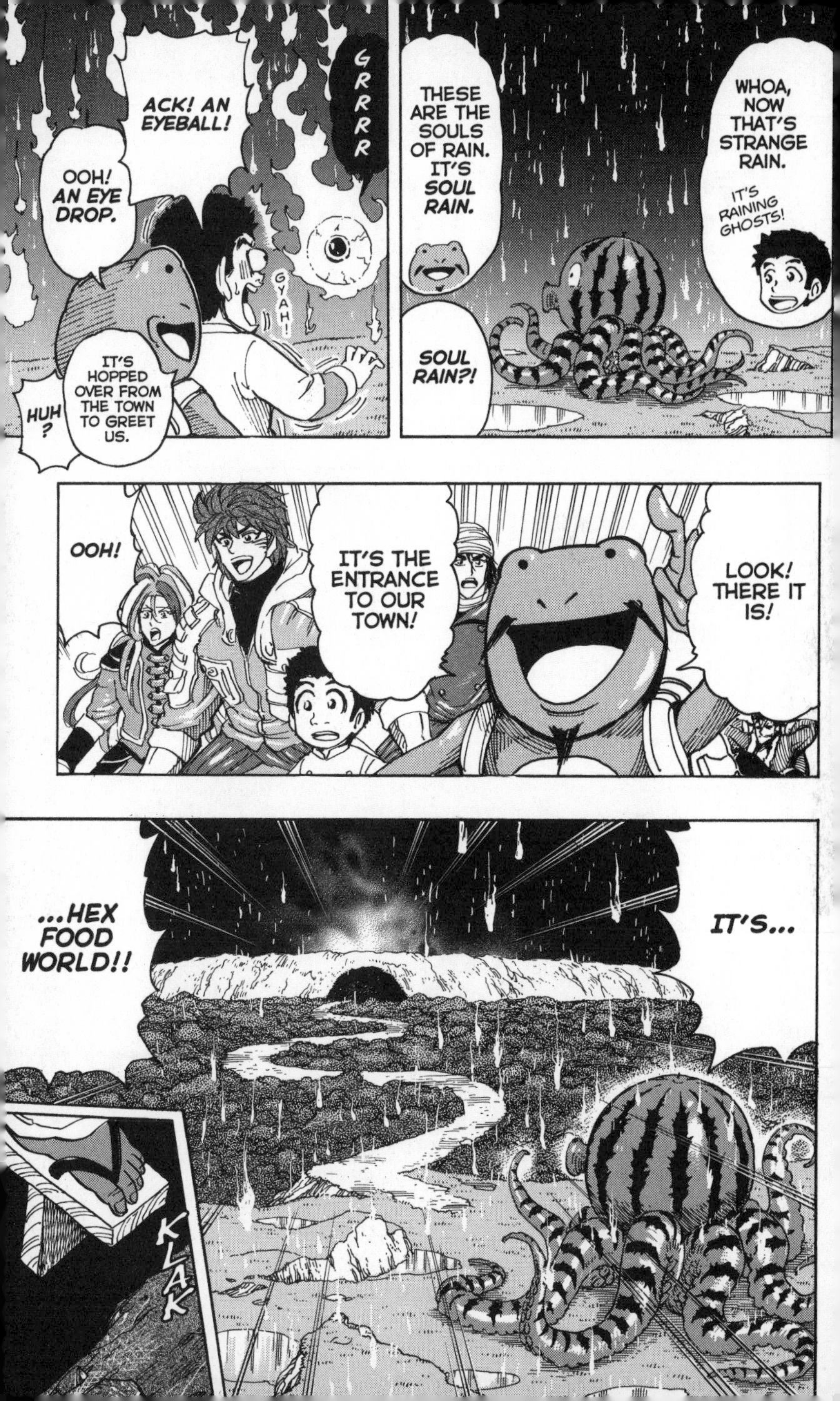
WHOA, NOW THAT'S STRANGE RAIN.
IT'S RAINING GHOSTS!
THESE ARE THE SOULS OF RAIN. IT'S *SOUL RAIN.*
SOUL RAIN?!
GRRRR
ACK! AN EYEBALL!
GYAH!
OOH! AN EYE DROP.
IT'S HOPPED OVER FROM THE TOWN TO GREET US.
HUH?
LOOK! THERE IT IS!
IT'S THE ENTRANCE TO OUR TOWN!
OOH!
IT'S...
...HEX FOOD WORLD!!
KLAK

GOURMET CHECKLIST

Vol. 303

TORCH HORSETAIL

(SPECIAL PLANT)

CAPTURE LEVEL: 1

HABITAT: CHOWLIN TEMPLE

SIZE: 35 CM

HEIGHT: ---

WEIGHT: 250 G

PRICE: 500 YEN PER STALK

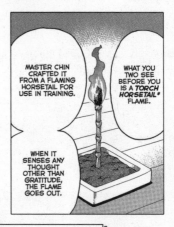

WHAT YOU TWO SEE BEFORE YOU IS A *TORCH HORSETAIL** FLAME.
MASTER CHIN CRAFTED IT FROM A FLAMING HORSETAIL FOR USE IN TRAINING.
WHEN IT SENSES ANY THOUGHT OTHER THAN GRATITUDE, THE FLAME GOES OUT.

SCALE

A UNIQUE HORSETAIL THAT CAN BE FASHIONED INTO A TORCH DUE TO ITS NATURAL OIL CONTENT. THE OIL IS SO POTENT THAT IT CAN BURN UP TO 100 HOURS STRAIGHT! THE TORCHES USED IN CHOWLIN TEMPLE WERE MODIFIED FOR MASTER CHIN'S HONOR THE FOOD TRAINING. THESE MODIFIED HORSETAILS ARE MIND READERS. WHEN THEY SENSE ANY THOUGHTS OTHER THAN SHEER GRATITUDE, THE FLAME WILL IMMEDIATELY FIZZLE. IT CAN ALSO BE USED AS AN INGREDIENT, BUT IT IS MOST COMMONLY USED FOR HONOR THE FOOD TRAINING IN CHOWLIN TEMPLE, THE MOTHER TEMPLE OF HONOR THE FOOD.

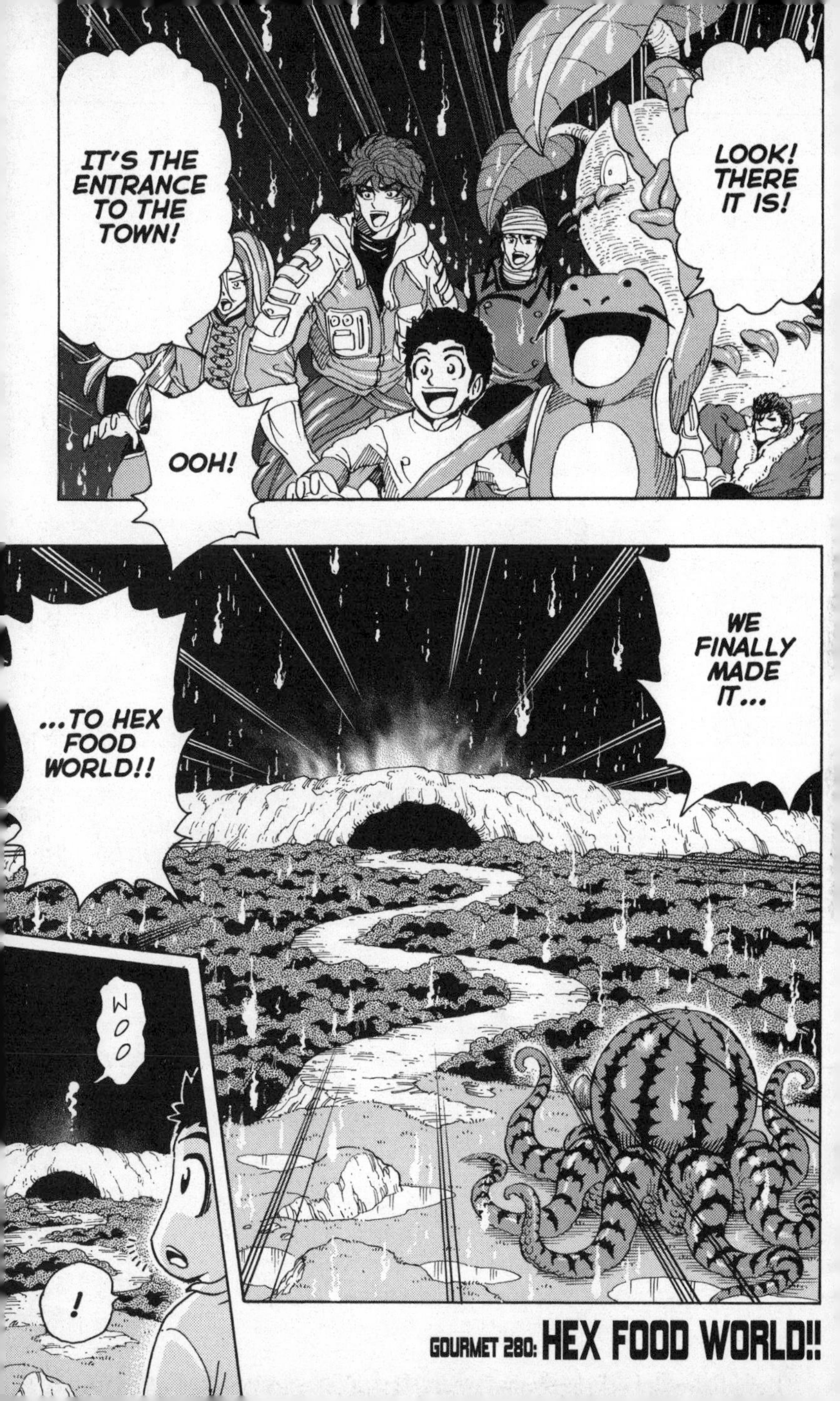
LOOK! THERE IT IS!
IT'S THE ENTRANCE TO THE TOWN!
OOH!
WE FINALLY MADE IT...
...TO HEX FOOD WORLD!!
WOO
!

GOURMET 280: HEX FOOD WORLD!!

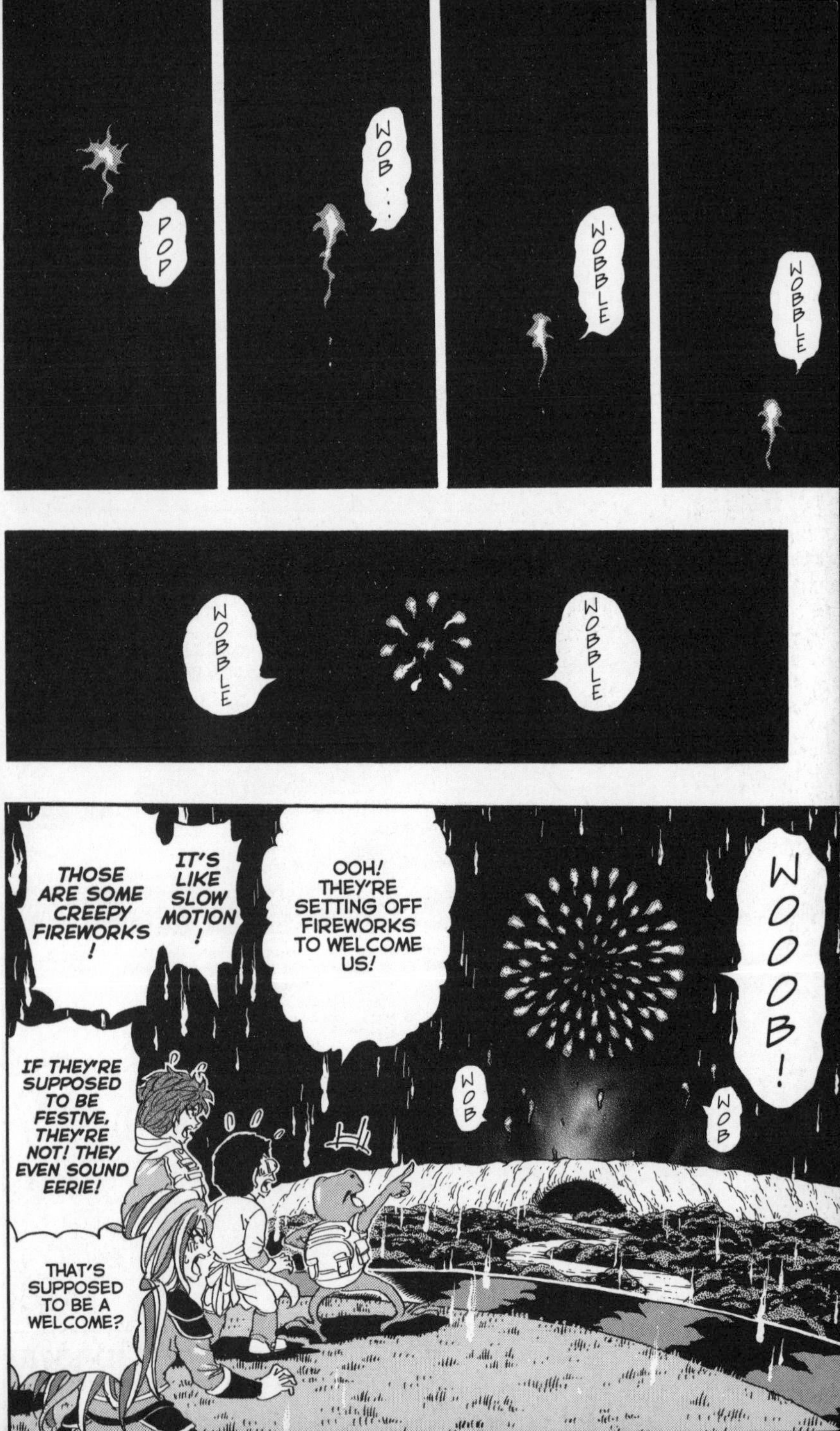
WOBBLE
WOBBLE
WOB...
POP
WOBBLE
WOBBLE
WOOOB!
WOB
WOB
OOH! THEY'RE SETTING OFF FIREWORKS TO WELCOME US!
IT'S LIKE SLOW MOTION!
THOSE ARE SOME CREEPY FIREWORKS!
IF THEY'RE SUPPOSED TO BE FESTIVE, THEY'RE NOT! THEY EVEN SOUND EERIE!
THAT'S SUPPOSED TO BE A WELCOME?

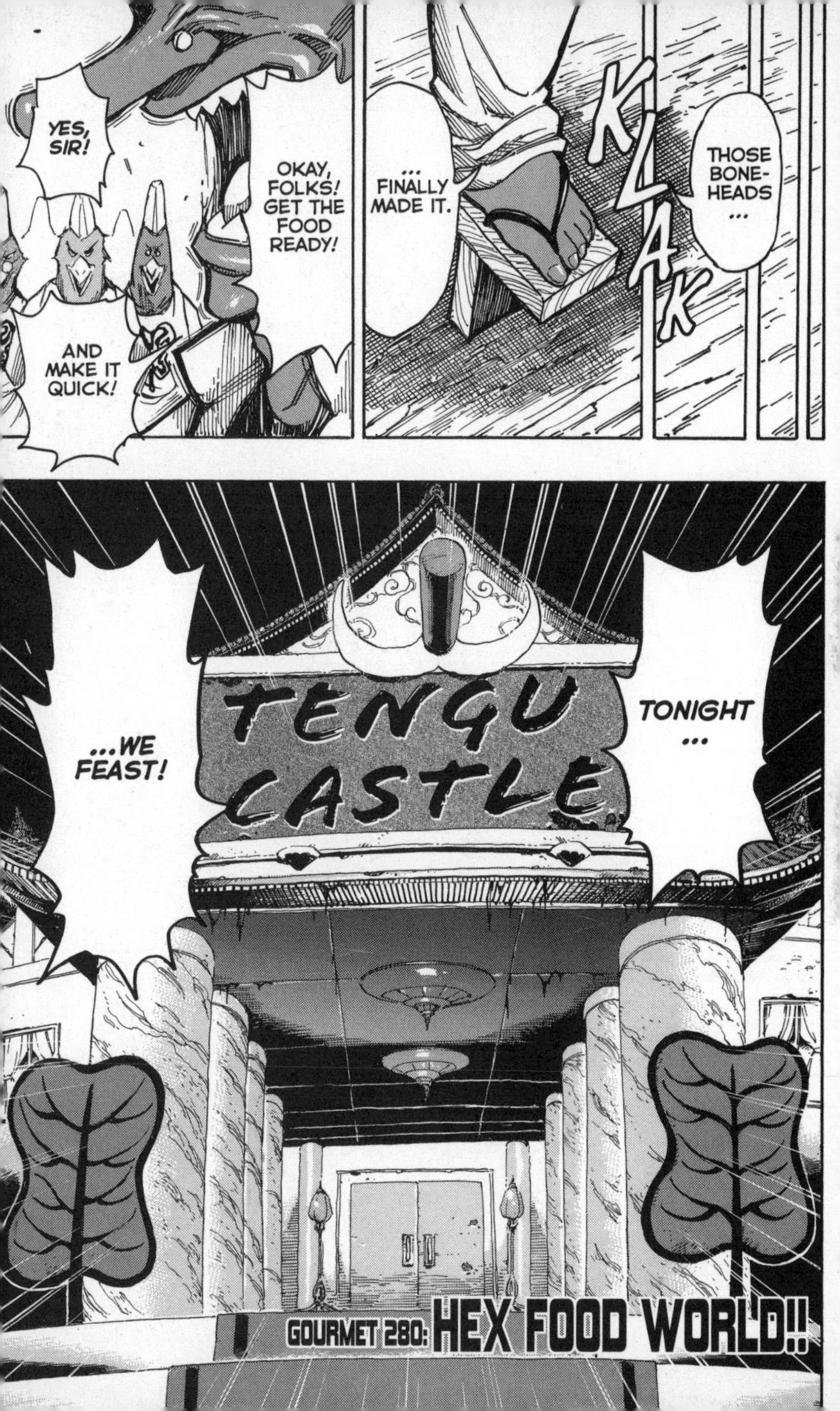
THOSE BONE-HEADS...
KLAK
...FINALLY MADE IT.
OKAY, FOLKS! GET THE FOOD READY!
AND MAKE IT QUICK!
YES, SIR!
TONIGHT...
TENGU CASTLE
...WE FEAST!
GOURMET 280: HEX FOOD WORLD!!

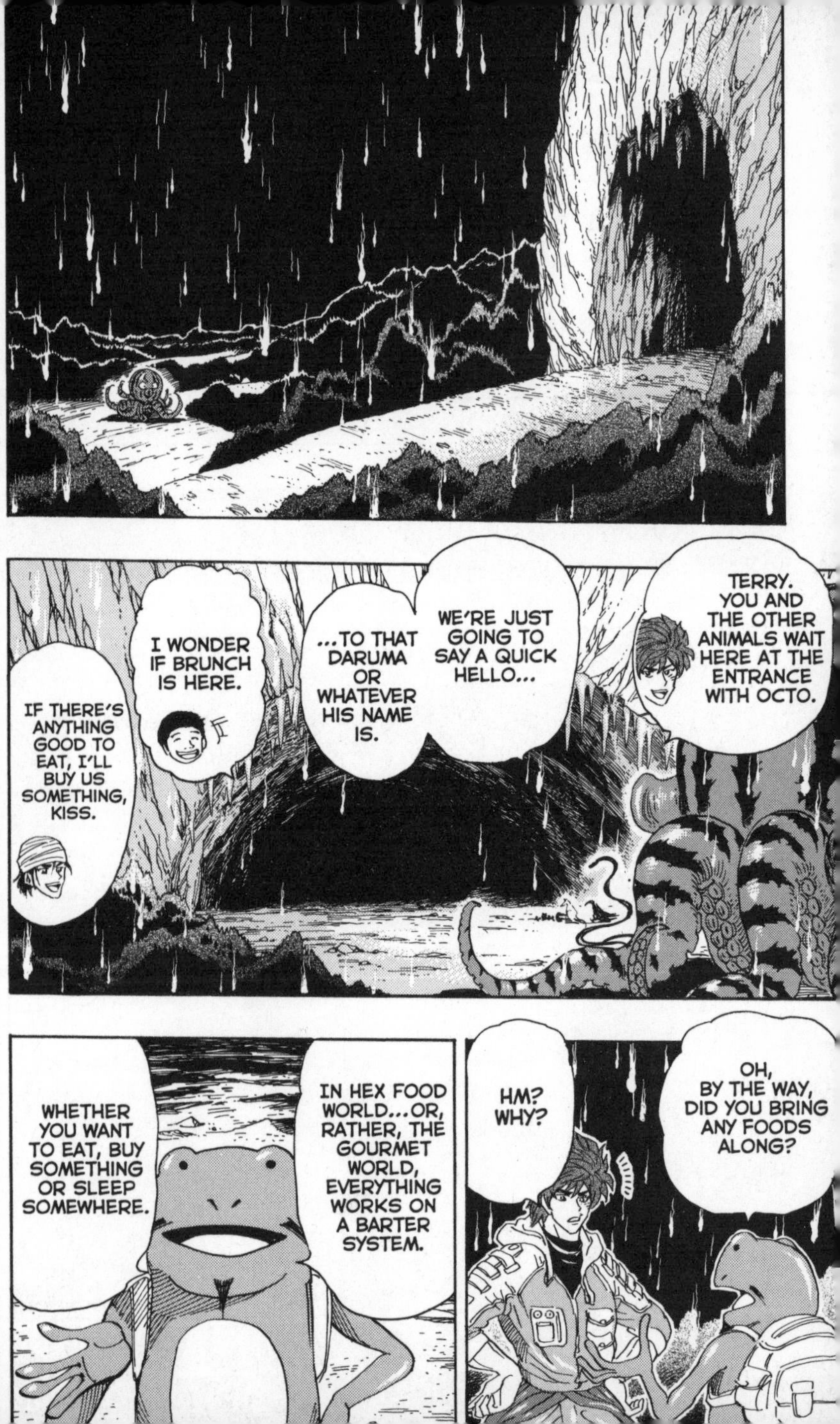
TERRY. YOU AND THE OTHER ANIMALS WAIT HERE AT THE ENTRANCE WITH OCTO.
WE'RE JUST GOING TO SAY A QUICK HELLO...
...TO THAT DARUMA OR WHATEVER HIS NAME IS.
I WONDER IF BRUNCH IS HERE.
IF THERE'S ANYTHING GOOD TO EAT, I'LL BUY US SOMETHING, KISS.
OH, BY THE WAY, DID YOU BRING ANY FOODS ALONG?
HM? WHY?
IN HEX FOOD WORLD...OR, RATHER, THE GOURMET WORLD, EVERYTHING WORKS ON A BARTER SYSTEM.
WHETHER YOU WANT TO EAT, BUY SOMETHING OR SLEEP SOMEWHERE.

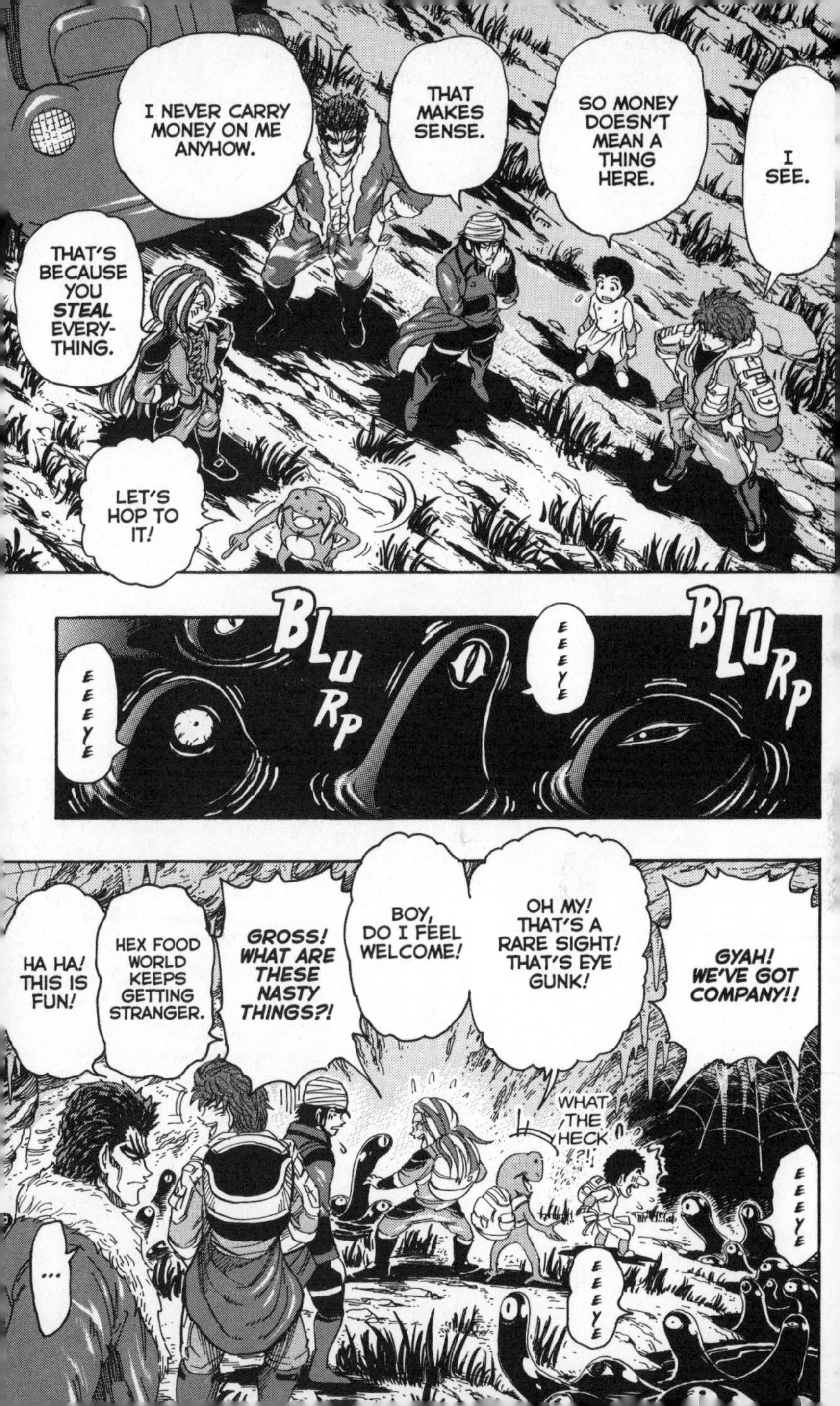
I SEE.
SO MONEY DOESN'T MEAN A THING HERE.
THAT MAKES SENSE.
I NEVER CARRY MONEY ON ME ANYHOW.
THAT'S BECAUSE YOU *STEAL* EVERYTHING.
LET'S HOP TO IT!
BLURP
EEEYE
BLURP
EEEYE
GYAH! WE'VE GOT COMPANY!!
OH MY! THAT'S A RARE SIGHT! THAT'S EYE GUNK!
BOY, DO I FEEL WELCOME!
GROSS! WHAT ARE THESE NASTY THINGS?!
HEX FOOD WORLD KEEPS GETTING STRANGER.
HA HA! THIS IS FUN!
EEEYE
WHAT THE HECK?!
EEEYE
...

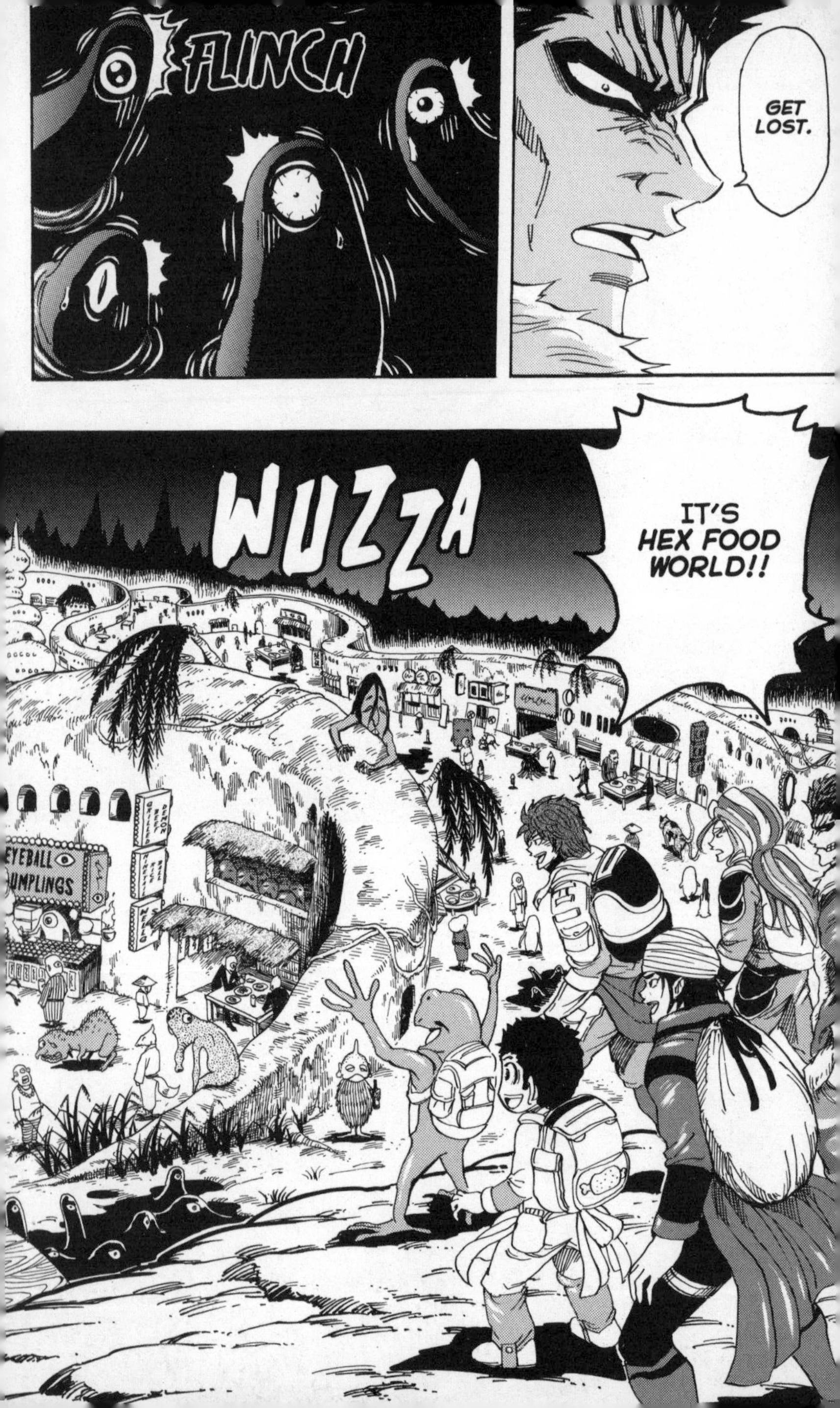
GET LOST.
FLINCH
IT'S HEX FOOD WORLD!!
WUZZA
EYEBALL
UMPLINGS

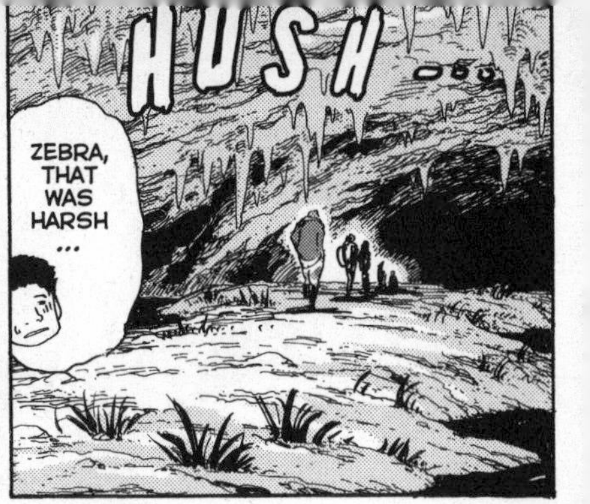
HUSH
ZEBRA, THAT WAS HARSH ...
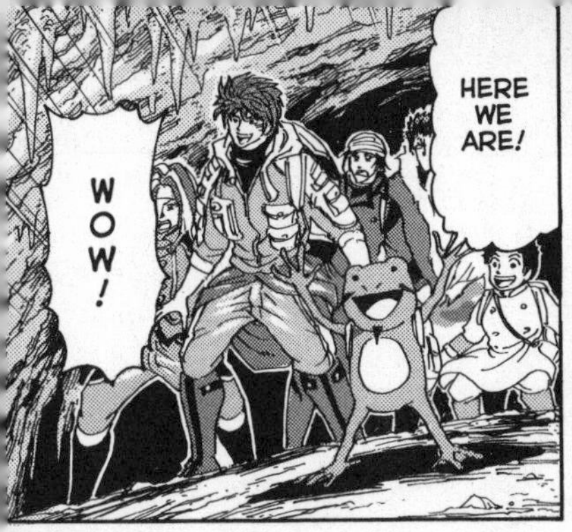
HERE WE ARE!
WOW!
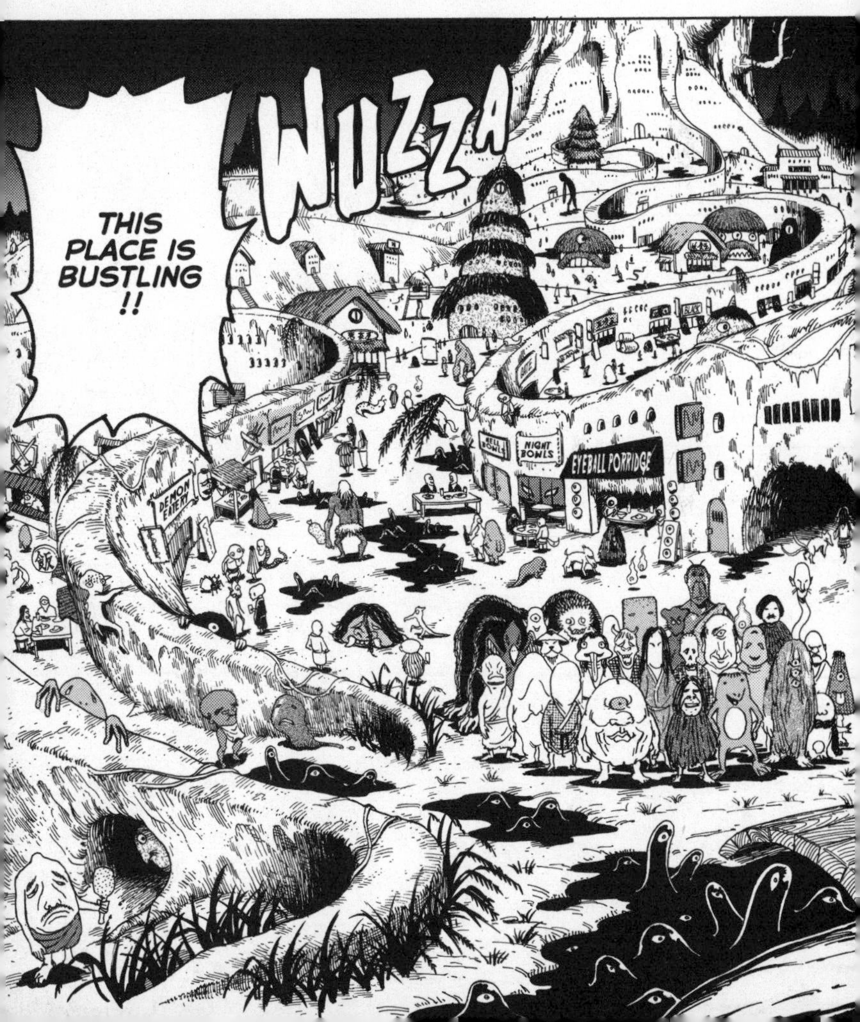
WUZZA
THIS PLACE IS BUSTLING !!
EYEBALL PORRIDGE
NIGHT BOWLS
HELL BOWLS
DEMON EATERY

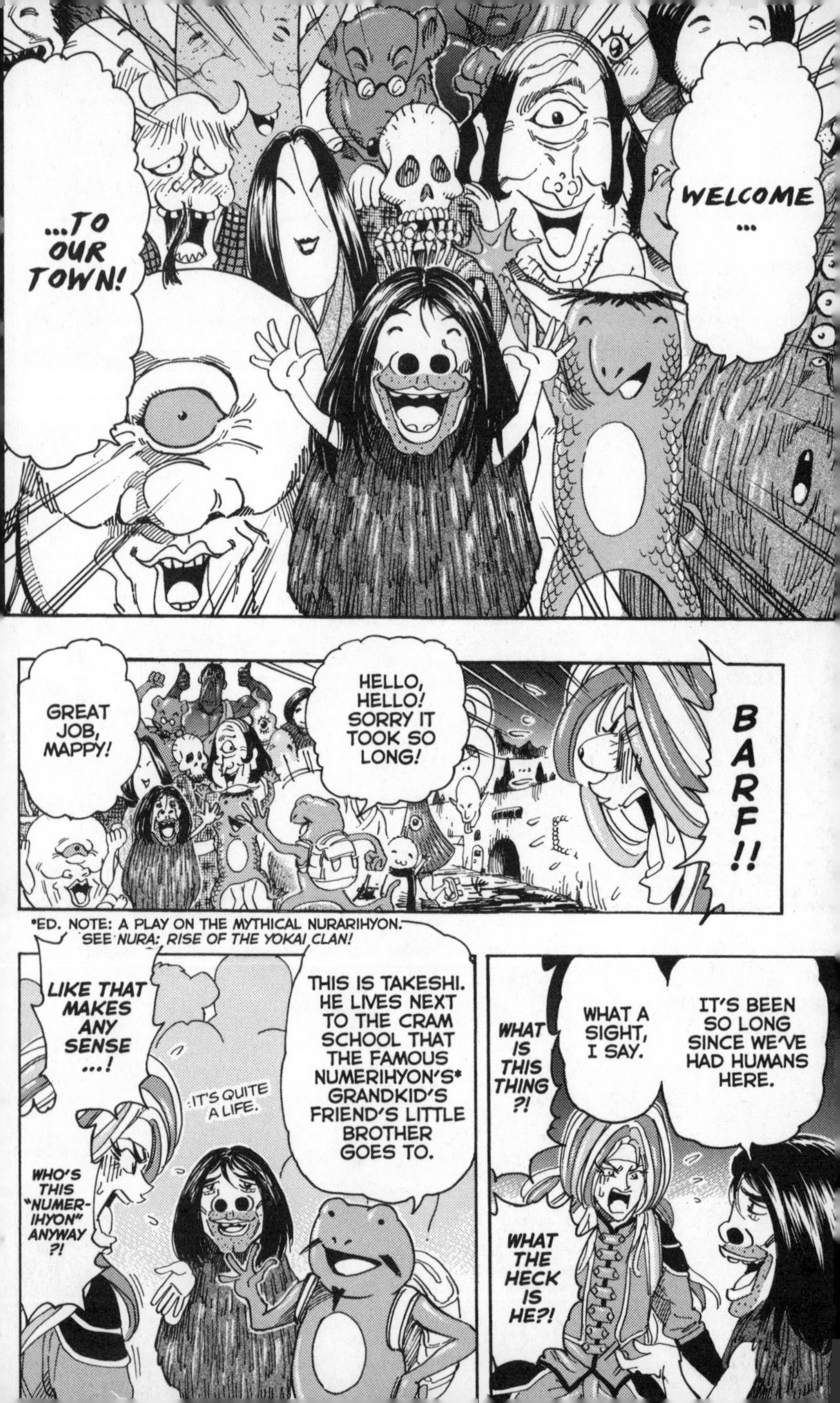
WELCOME ...
...TO OUR TOWN!
BARF!!
HELLO, HELLO! SORRY IT TOOK SO LONG!
GREAT JOB, MAPPY!
IT'S BEEN SO LONG SINCE WE'VE HAD HUMANS HERE.
WHAT A SIGHT, I SAY.
WHAT IS THIS THING?!
WHAT THE HECK IS HE?!
THIS IS TAKESHI. HE LIVES NEXT TO THE CRAM SCHOOL THAT THE FAMOUS NUMERIHYON'S* GRANDKID'S FRIEND'S LITTLE BROTHER GOES TO.
IT'S QUITE A LIFE.
LIKE THAT MAKES ANY SENSE ...!
WHO'S THIS "NUMERIHYON" ANYWAY ?!

*ED. NOTE: A PLAY ON THE MYTHICAL NURARIHYON. SEE *NURA: RISE OF THE YOKAI CLAN!*

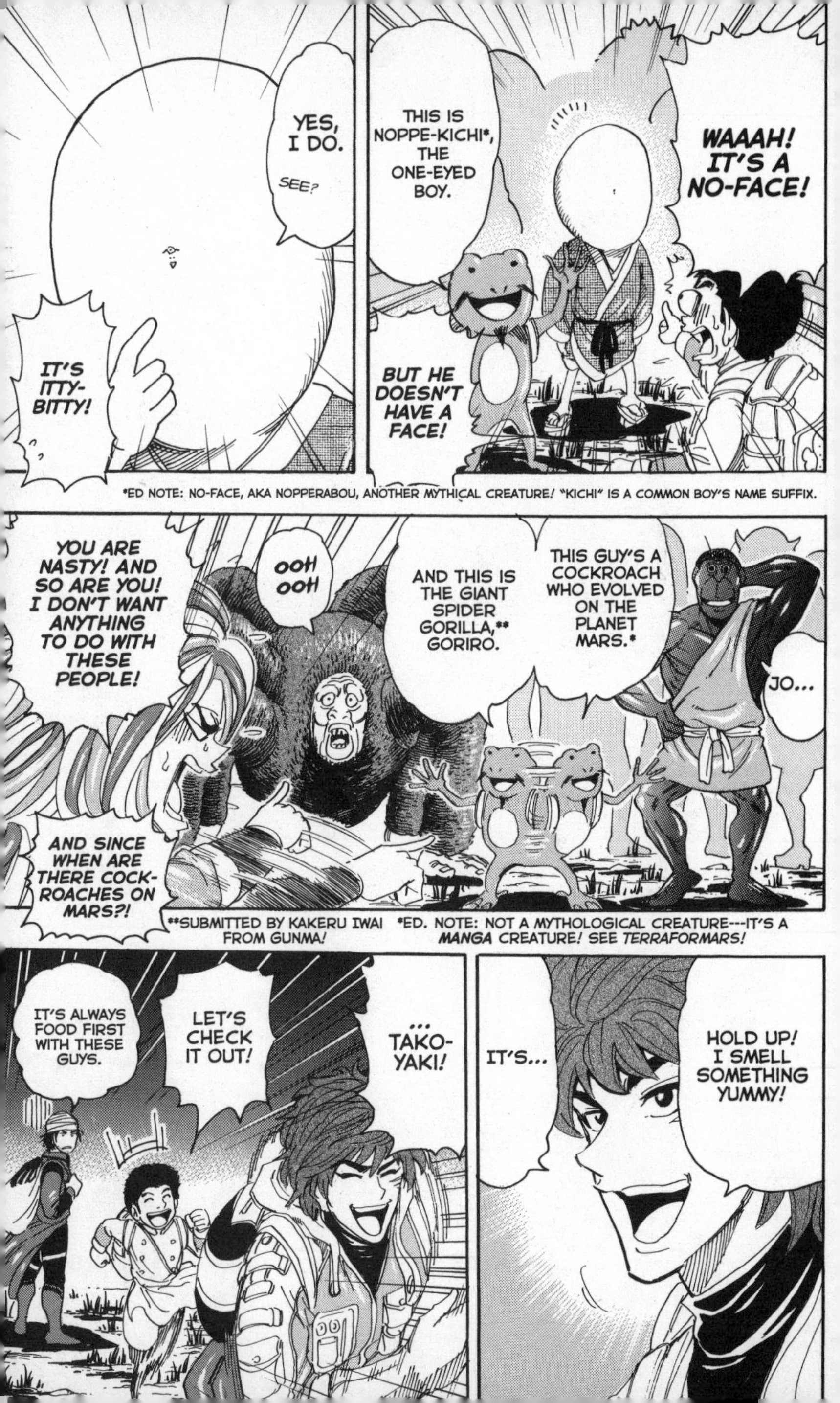
WAAAH! IT'S A NO-FACE!
THIS IS NOPPE-KICHI*, THE ONE-EYED BOY.
BUT HE DOESN'T HAVE A FACE!
YES, I DO.
SEE?
IT'S ITTY-BITTY!
*ED NOTE: NO-FACE, AKA NOPPERABOU, ANOTHER MYTHICAL CREATURE! "KICHI" IS A COMMON BOY'S NAME SUFFIX.
JO...
THIS GUY'S A COCKROACH WHO EVOLVED ON THE PLANET MARS.*
AND THIS IS THE GIANT SPIDER GORILLA,** GORIRO.
OOH OOH
YOU ARE NASTY! AND SO ARE YOU! I DON'T WANT ANYTHING TO DO WITH THESE PEOPLE!
AND SINCE WHEN ARE THERE COCK-ROACHES ON MARS?!
**SUBMITTED BY KAKERU IWAI FROM GUNMA!
*ED. NOTE: NOT A MYTHOLOGICAL CREATURE---IT'S A MANGA CREATURE! SEE TERRAFORMARS!
HOLD UP! I SMELL SOMETHING YUMMY!
IT'S...
...TAKO-YAKI!
LET'S CHECK IT OUT!
IT'S ALWAYS FOOD FIRST WITH THESE GUYS.

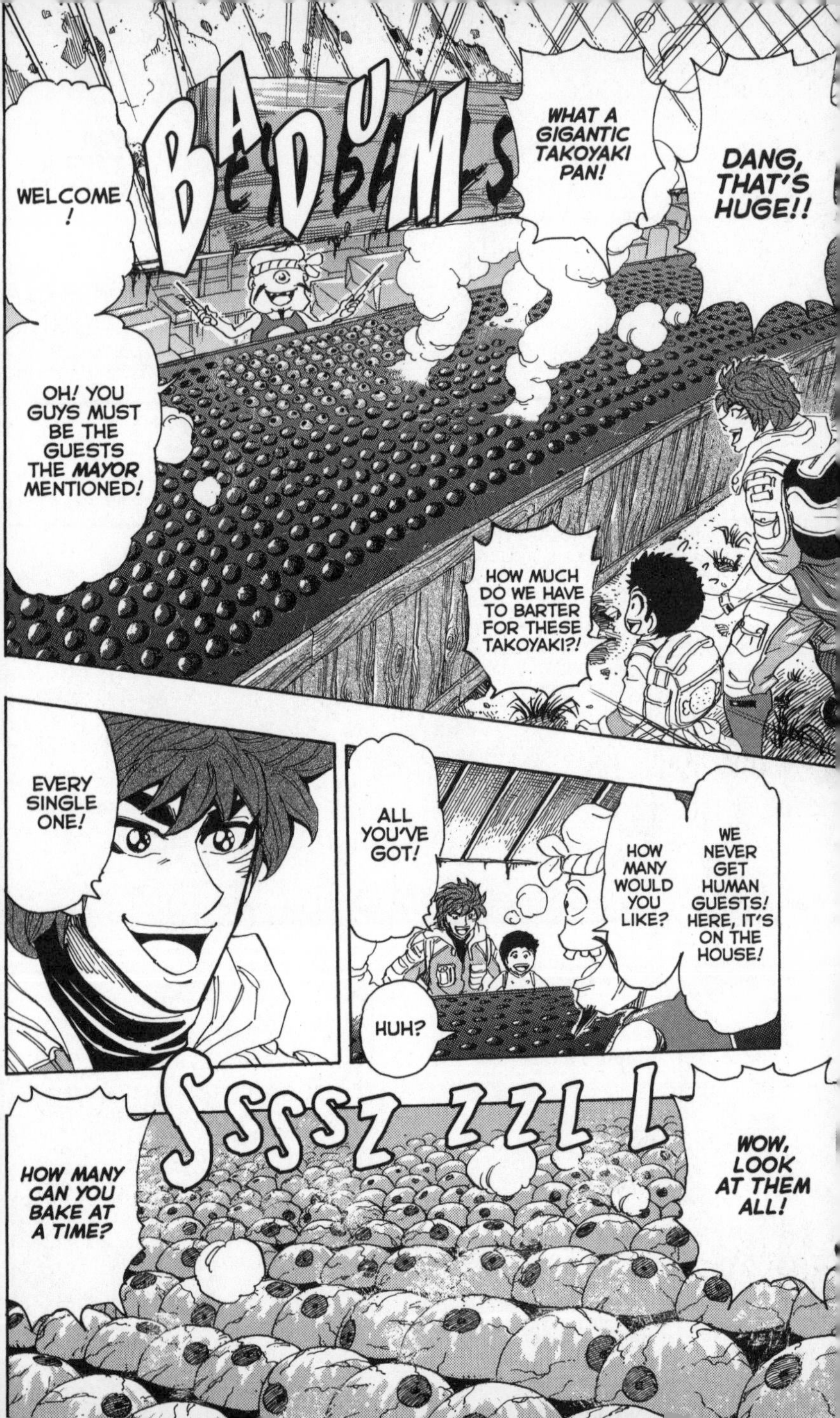
DANG, THAT'S HUGE!!
WHAT A GIGANTIC TAKOYAKI PAN!
BADUM
WELCOME!
OH! YOU GUYS MUST BE THE GUESTS THE *MAYOR* MENTIONED!
HOW MUCH DO WE HAVE TO BARTER FOR THESE TAKOYAKI?!
WE NEVER GET HUMAN GUESTS! HERE, IT'S ON THE HOUSE!
HOW MANY WOULD YOU LIKE?
ALL YOU'VE GOT!
HUH?
EVERY SINGLE ONE!
WOW, LOOK AT THEM ALL!
SSSZ ZZL L
HOW MANY CAN YOU BAKE AT A TIME?

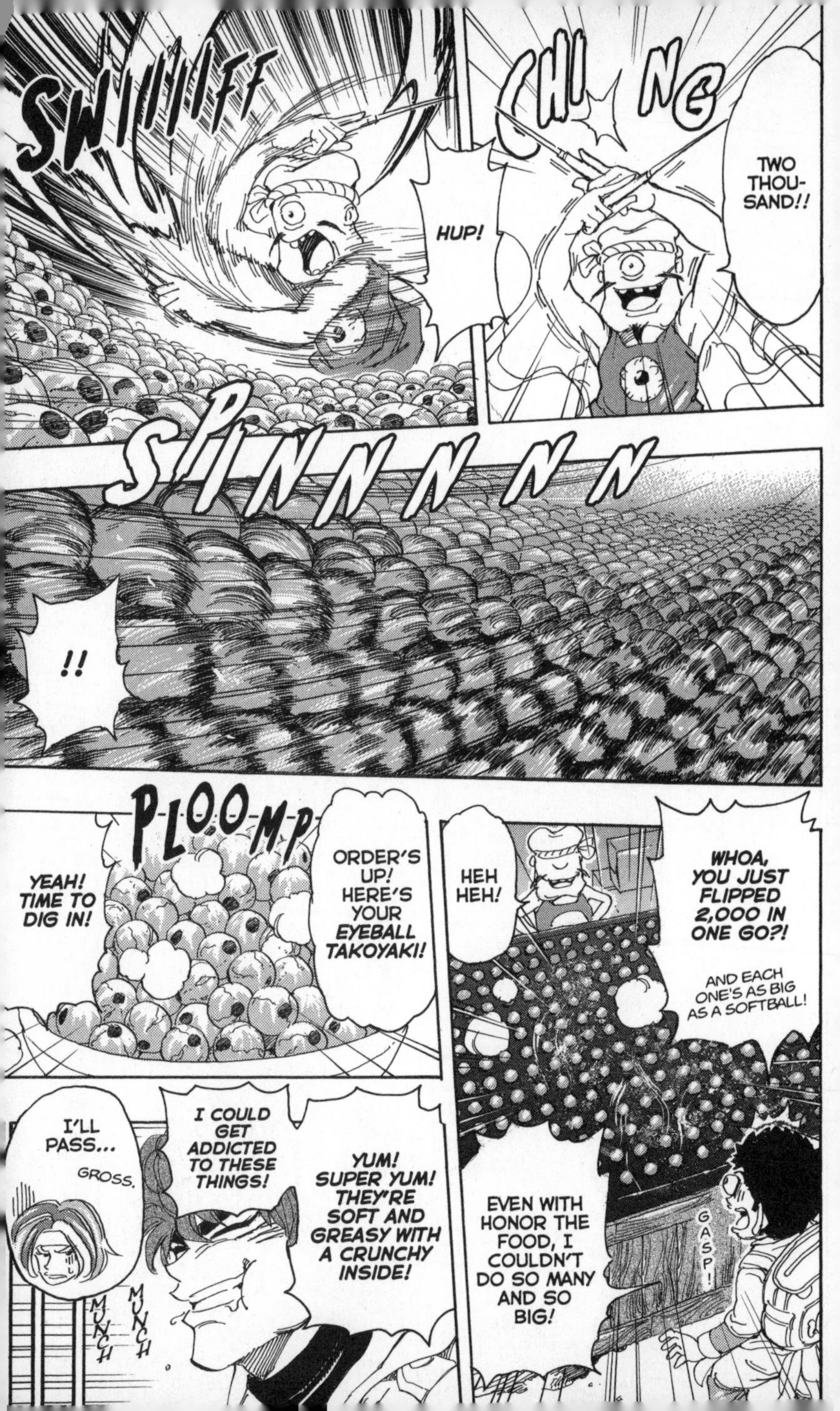
CHING
TWO THOUSAND!!
HUP!
SWIIIFF
SPINNNNN
!!
WHOA, YOU JUST FLIPPED 2,000 IN ONE GO?!
HEH HEH!
AND EACH ONE'S AS BIG AS A SOFTBALL!
EVEN WITH HONOR THE FOOD, I COULDN'T DO SO MANY AND SO BIG!
GASP!
PLOOMP
ORDER'S UP! HERE'S YOUR EYEBALL TAKOYAKI!
YEAH! TIME TO DIG IN!
YUM! SUPER YUM! THEY'RE SOFT AND GREASY WITH A CRUNCHY INSIDE!
I COULD GET ADDICTED TO THESE THINGS!
I'LL PASS...
GROSS.
MUNCH
MUNCH

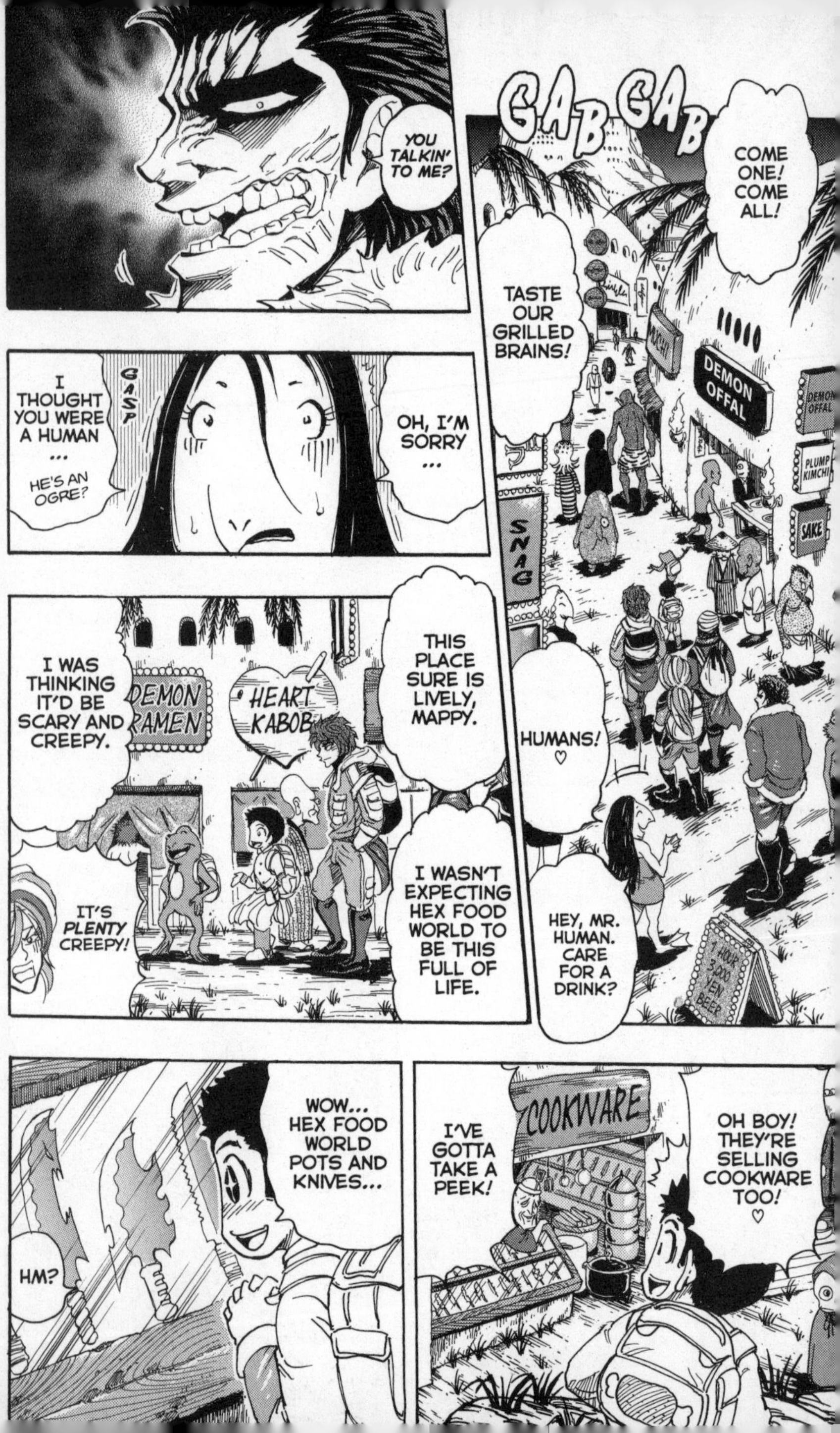
GAB GAB
COME ONE! COME ALL!
TASTE OUR GRILLED BRAINS!
DEMON OFFAL
DEMON OFFAL
PLUMP KIMCHI
SAKE
SNAG
HUMANS! ♡
HEY, MR. HUMAN. CARE FOR A DRINK?
1 HOUR 3,000 YEN BEER
YOU TALKIN' TO ME?
OH, I'M SORRY ...
GASP
I THOUGHT YOU WERE A HUMAN ...
HE'S AN OGRE?
THIS PLACE SURE IS LIVELY, MAPPY.
I WASN'T EXPECTING HEX FOOD WORLD TO BE THIS FULL OF LIFE.
HEART KABOB
DEMON RAMEN
I WAS THINKING IT'D BE SCARY AND CREEPY.
IT'S *PLENTY* CREEPY!
OH BOY! THEY'RE SELLING COOKWARE TOO! ♡
COOKWARE
I'VE GOTTA TAKE A PEEK!
WOW... HEX FOOD WORLD POTS AND KNIVES...
HM?

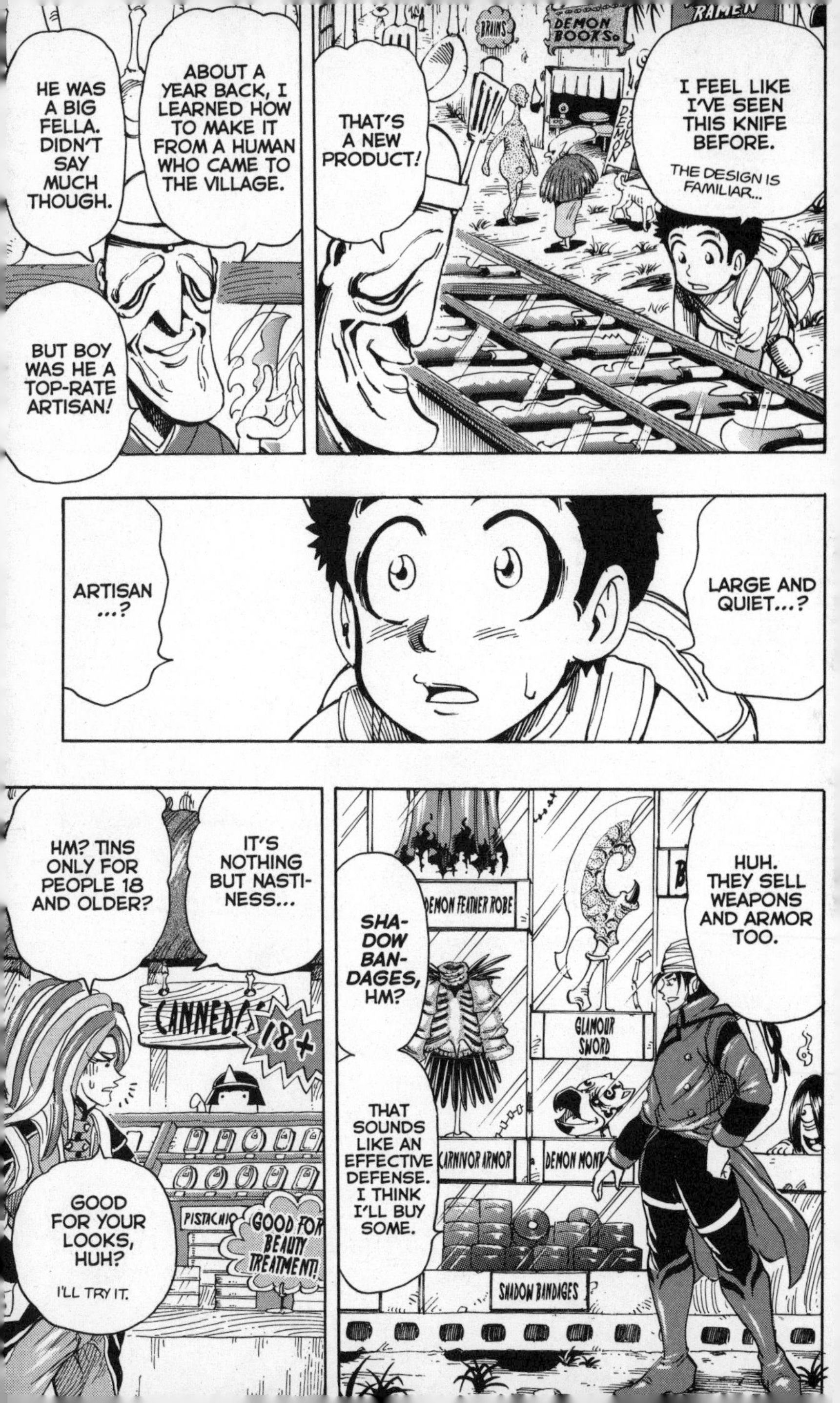
RAMEN
DEMON BOOKS
BRAINS
DEMON
I FEEL LIKE I'VE SEEN THIS KNIFE BEFORE.
THE DESIGN IS FAMILIAR...
THAT'S A NEW PRODUCT!
ABOUT A YEAR BACK, I LEARNED HOW TO MAKE IT FROM A HUMAN WHO CAME TO THE VILLAGE.
HE WAS A BIG FELLA. DIDN'T SAY MUCH THOUGH.
BUT BOY WAS HE A TOP-RATE ARTISAN!
LARGE AND QUIET...?
ARTISAN ...?
HUH. THEY SELL WEAPONS AND ARMOR TOO.
DEMON FEATHER ROBE
GLAMOUR SWORD
SHA-DOW BAN-DAGES, HM?
CARNIVOR ARMOR
THAT SOUNDS LIKE AN EFFECTIVE DEFENSE. I THINK I'LL BUY SOME.
SHADOW BANDAGES
IT'S NOTHING BUT NASTI-NESS...
HM? TINS ONLY FOR PEOPLE 18 AND OLDER?
CANNED!
18+
PISTACHIO
GOOD FOR BEAUTY TREATMENT!
GOOD FOR YOUR LOOKS, HUH?
I'LL TRY IT.

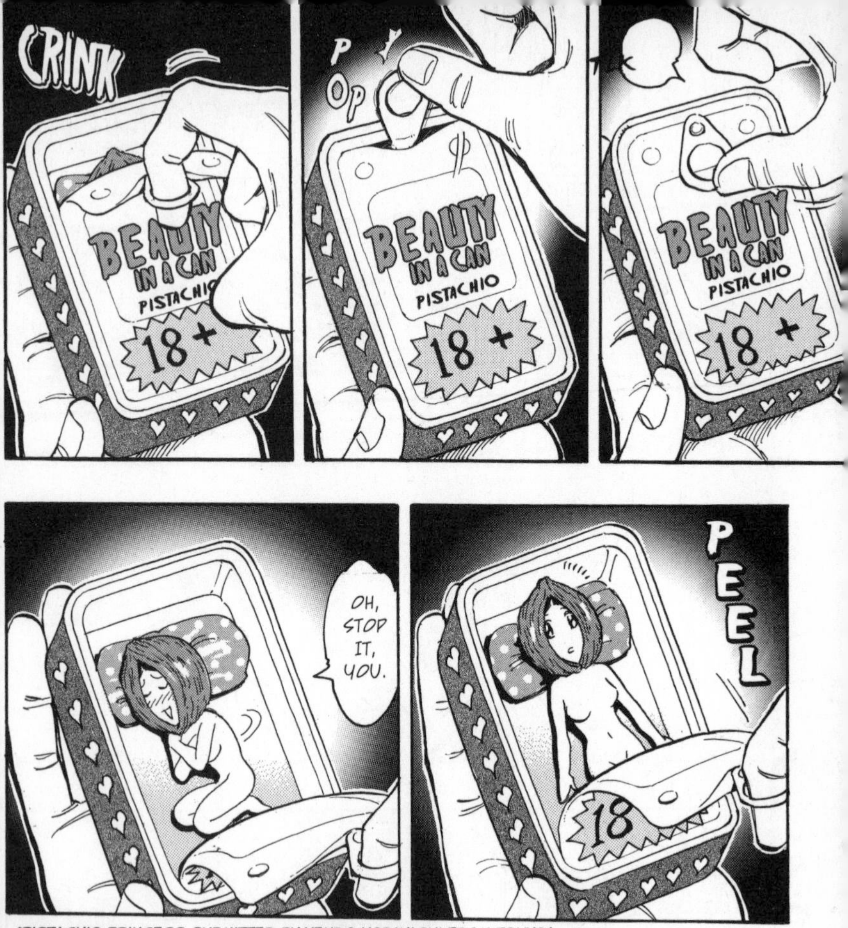
BEAUTY IN A CAN
PISTACHIO
18+
POP
BEAUTY IN A CAN
PISTACHIO
18+
CRINK
BEAUTY IN A CAN
PISTACHIO
18+
PEEL
18
OH, STOP IT, YOU.

*PISTACHIO PRINCESS SUBMITTED BY KENDO KOBAYASHI FROM TOKYO!

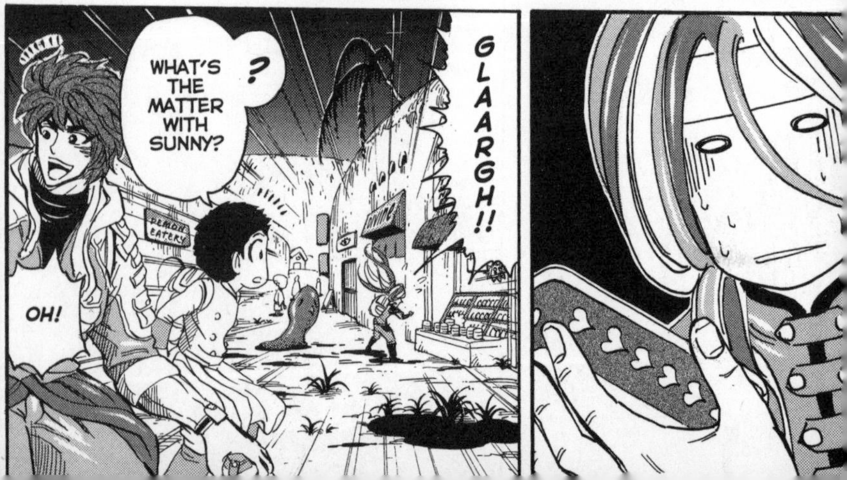
GLAARGH!!
?
WHAT'S THE MATTER WITH SUNNY?
DEMON EATERY
OH!

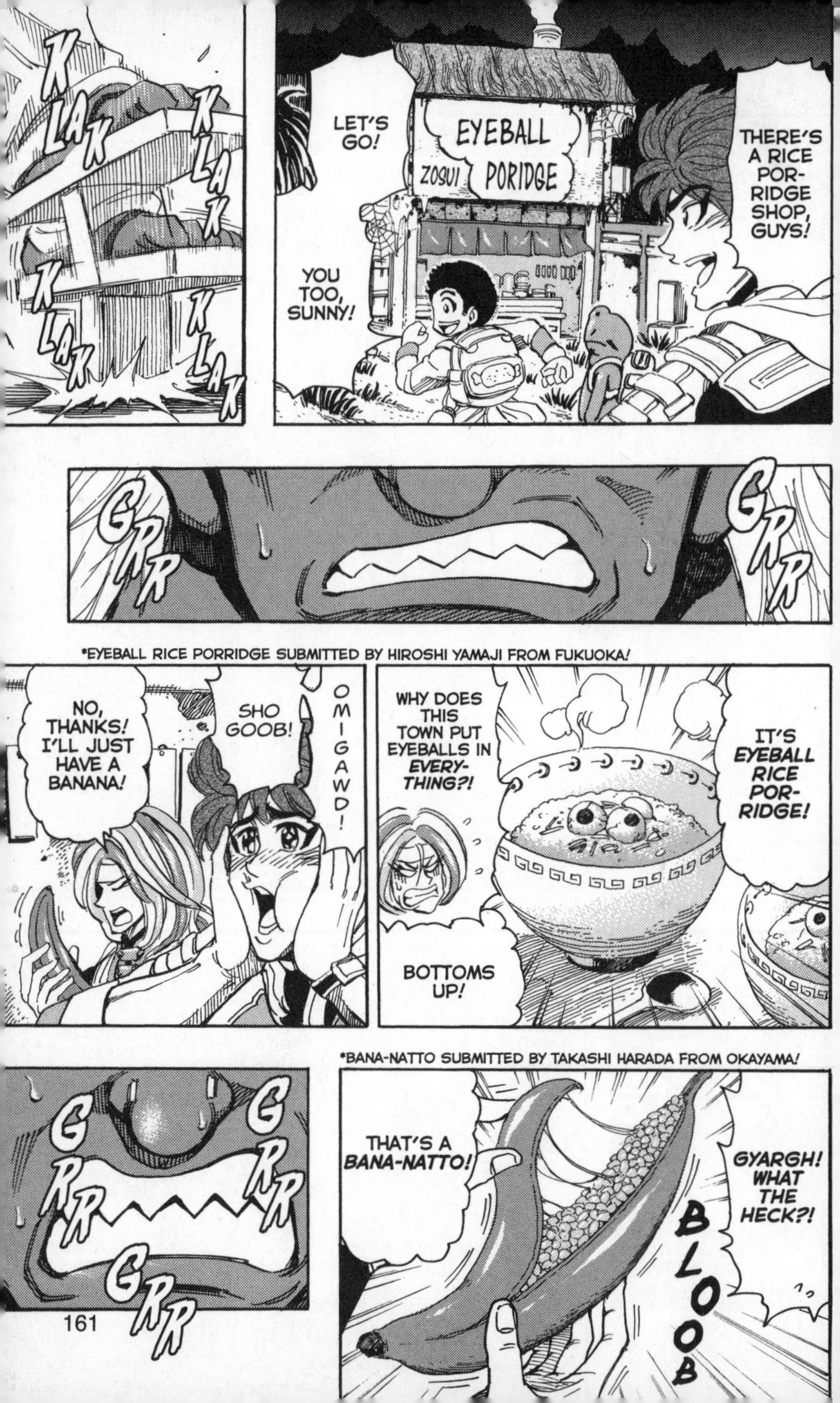
THERE'S A RICE PORRIDGE SHOP, GUYS!
EYEBALL PORIDGE
ZOSUI
LET'S GO!
YOU TOO, SUNNY!
KLAK KLAK
KLAK KLAK
GRR
GRR
*EYEBALL RICE PORRIDGE SUBMITTED BY HIROSHI YAMAJI FROM FUKUOKA!
IT'S *EYEBALL RICE PORRIDGE!*
WHY DOES THIS TOWN PUT EYEBALLS IN *EVERYTHING?!*
BOTTOMS UP!
OMIGAWD!
SHO GOOB!
NO, THANKS! I'LL JUST HAVE A BANANA!
*BANA-NATTO SUBMITTED BY TAKASHI HARADA FROM OKAYAMA!
GYARGH! WHAT THE HECK?!
THAT'S A *BANA-NATTO!*
BLOOB
GRR
GRRR
GRR

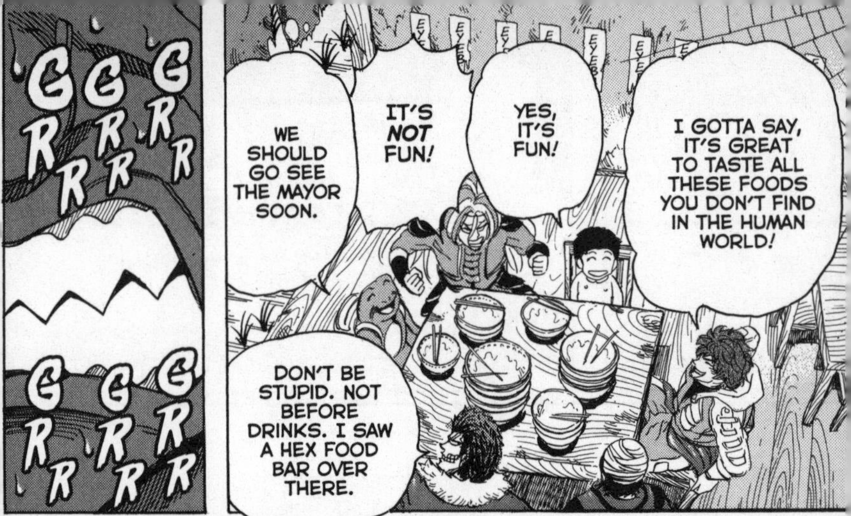
I GOTTA SAY, IT'S GREAT TO TASTE ALL THESE FOODS YOU DON'T FIND IN THE HUMAN WORLD!
YES, IT'S FUN!
IT'S NOT FUN!
WE SHOULD GO SEE THE MAYOR SOON.
DON'T BE STUPID. NOT BEFORE DRINKS. I SAW A HEX FOOD BAR OVER THERE.
GRRR GRRR GRRR
GRRR GRRR GRRR

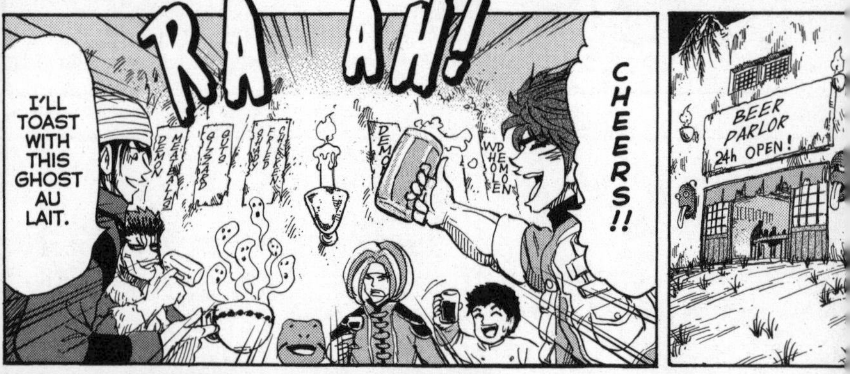
BEER PARLOR
24h OPEN!
CHEERS!!
RA AH!
I'LL TOAST WITH THIS GHOST AU LAIT.

*GHOST AU LAIT SUBMITTED BY CHEESECAKE TART FROM SAITAMA!

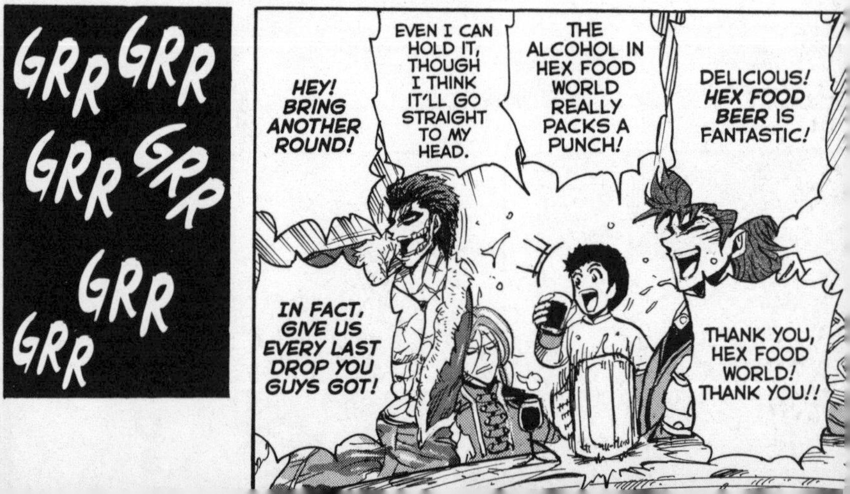
DELICIOUS! HEX FOOD BEER IS FANTASTIC!
THE ALCOHOL IN HEX FOOD WORLD REALLY PACKS A PUNCH!
EVEN I CAN HOLD IT, THOUGH I THINK IT'LL GO STRAIGHT TO MY HEAD.
HEY! BRING ANOTHER ROUND!
THANK YOU, HEX FOOD WORLD! THANK YOU!!
IN FACT, GIVE US EVERY LAST DROP YOU GUYS GOT!
GRR GRR
GRR GRR
GRR GRR

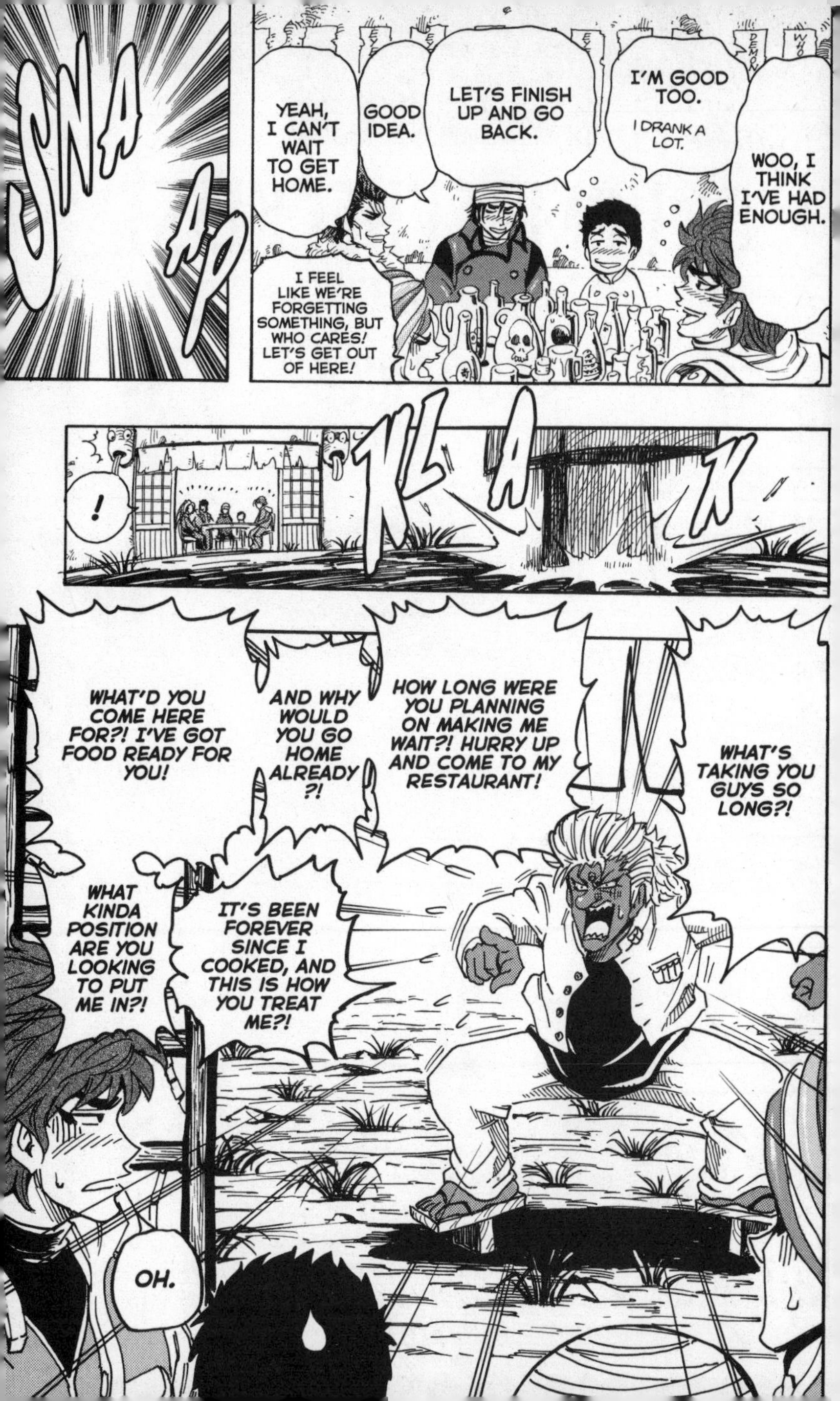
WOO, I THINK I'VE HAD ENOUGH.
I'M GOOD TOO.
I DRANK A LOT.
LET'S FINISH UP AND GO BACK.
GOOD IDEA.
YEAH, I CAN'T WAIT TO GET HOME.
I FEEL LIKE WE'RE FORGETTING SOMETHING, BUT WHO CARES! LET'S GET OUT OF HERE!
SNAP
KLANK
!
WHAT'S TAKING YOU GUYS SO LONG?!
HOW LONG WERE YOU PLANNING ON MAKING ME WAIT?! HURRY UP AND COME TO MY RESTAURANT!
AND WHY WOULD YOU GO HOME ALREADY?!
WHAT'D YOU COME HERE FOR?! I'VE GOT FOOD READY FOR YOU!
IT'S BEEN FOREVER SINCE I COOKED, AND THIS IS HOW YOU TREAT ME?!
WHAT KINDA POSITION ARE YOU LOOKING TO PUT ME IN?!
OH.

TORIKO

GOURMET CHECKLIST

Vol. 304

EGG 'N' RICE
(GRAIN)

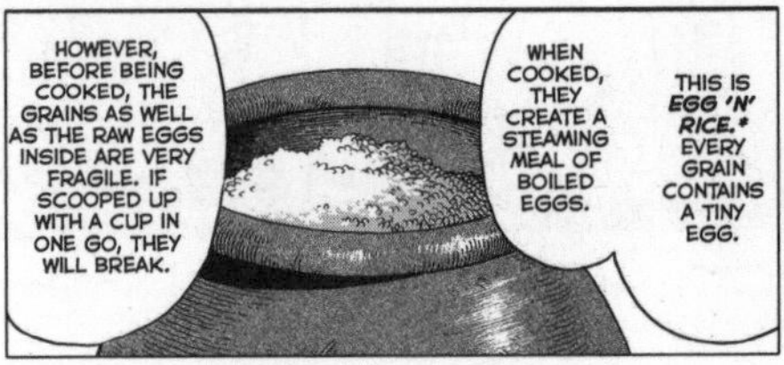
THIS IS EGG 'N' RICE.* EVERY GRAIN CONTAINS A TINY EGG.
WHEN COOKED, THEY CREATE A STEAMING MEAL OF BOILED EGGS.
HOWEVER, BEFORE BEING COOKED, THE GRAINS AS WELL AS THE RAW EGGS INSIDE ARE VERY FRAGILE. IF SCOOPED UP WITH A CUP IN ONE GO, THEY WILL BREAK.

CAPTURE LEVEL: 63

HABITAT: CHOWLIN TEMPLE

SIZE: 5 MM

HEIGHT: ---

WEIGHT: ---

PRICE: 50,000 YEN PER POT (1KG)

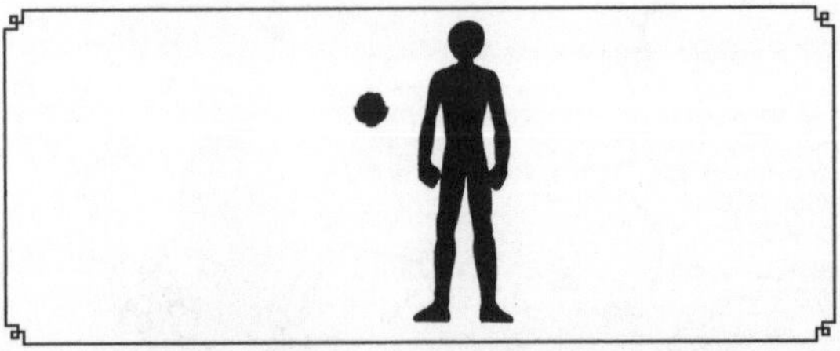

SCALE

EACH INDIVIDUAL GRAIN IS HOME TO A TINY EGG SWIMMING IN SOY SAUCE. IT IS THE ULTIMATE INGREDIENT FOR ANY EGG LOVER. WHEN BOILED, THE GRAINS BECOME THE PERFECT STEAMY EGG MEAL. BEFORE BOILING, THE RICE CAN EASILY RUPTURE, SO EACH GRAIN MUST BE HANDLED ONE AT A TIME WITH CHOPSTICKS. WHEN ONE GRAIN RUPTURES, IT SETS OFF A CHAIN REACTION AND ALL OF THE SURROUNDING GRAINS WILL ALSO RUPTURE, THUS SPOILING THE TASTE. ALL OF THE MAIN MEALS IN CHOWLIN TEMPLE ARE SERVED WITH EGG 'N' RICE WHICH REQUIRES THE UTMOST CONCENTRATION AND PATIENCE WHILE EATING.

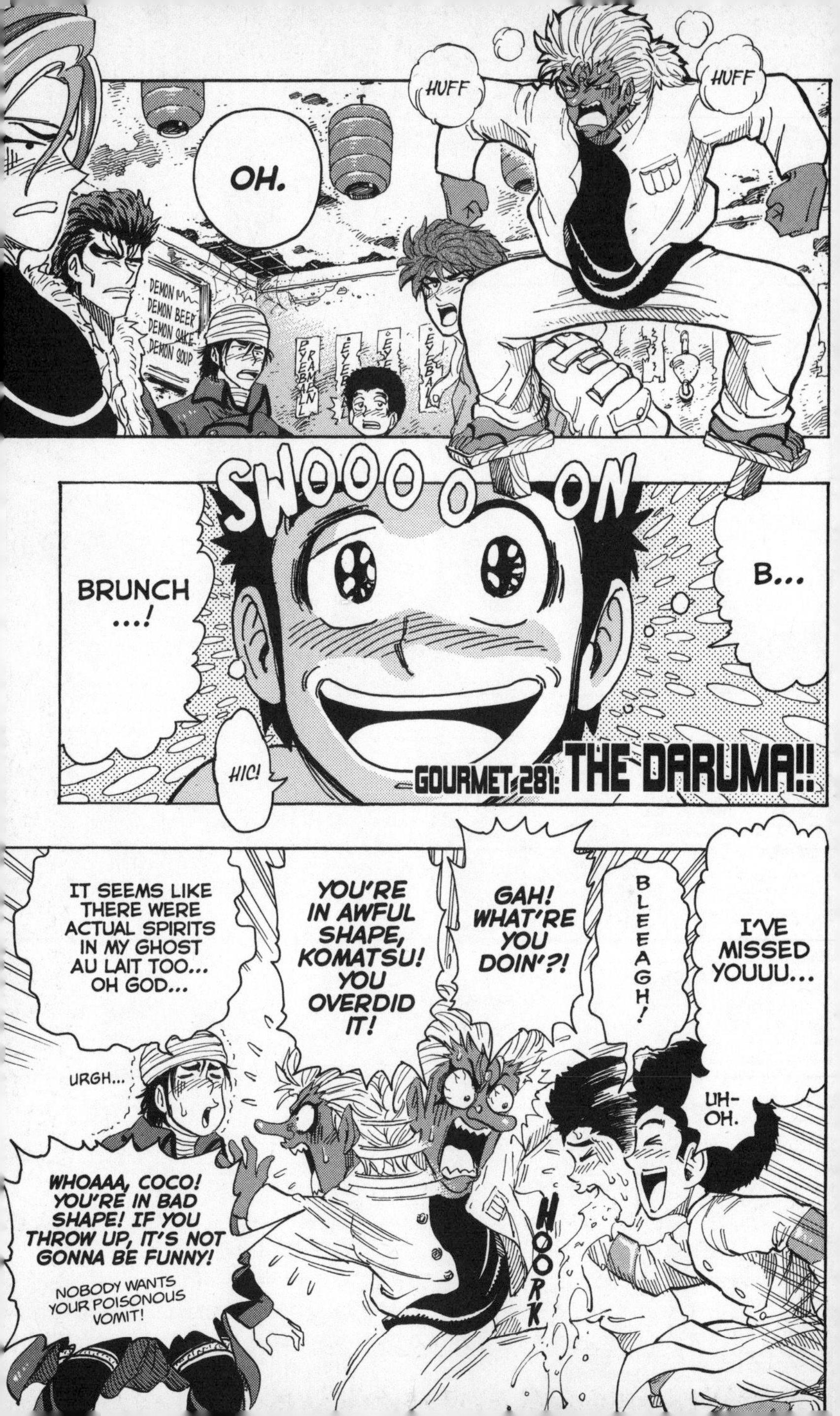

HUFF
HUFF
OH.
DEMON BEER
DEMON SAKE
DEMON SOUP
SWOOOOON
B...
BRUNCH ...!
HIC!
GOURMET 281: THE DARUMA!!
I'VE MISSED YOUUU...
BLEEAGH!
GAH! WHAT'RE YOU DOIN'?!
YOU'RE IN AWFUL SHAPE, KOMATSU! YOU OVERDID IT!
IT SEEMS LIKE THERE WERE ACTUAL SPIRITS IN MY GHOST AU LAIT TOO... OH GOD...
UH-OH.
HOORK
URGH...
WHOAAA, COCO! YOU'RE IN BAD SHAPE! IF YOU THROW UP, IT'S NOT GONNA BE FUNNY!
NOBODY WANTS YOUR POISONOUS VOMIT!

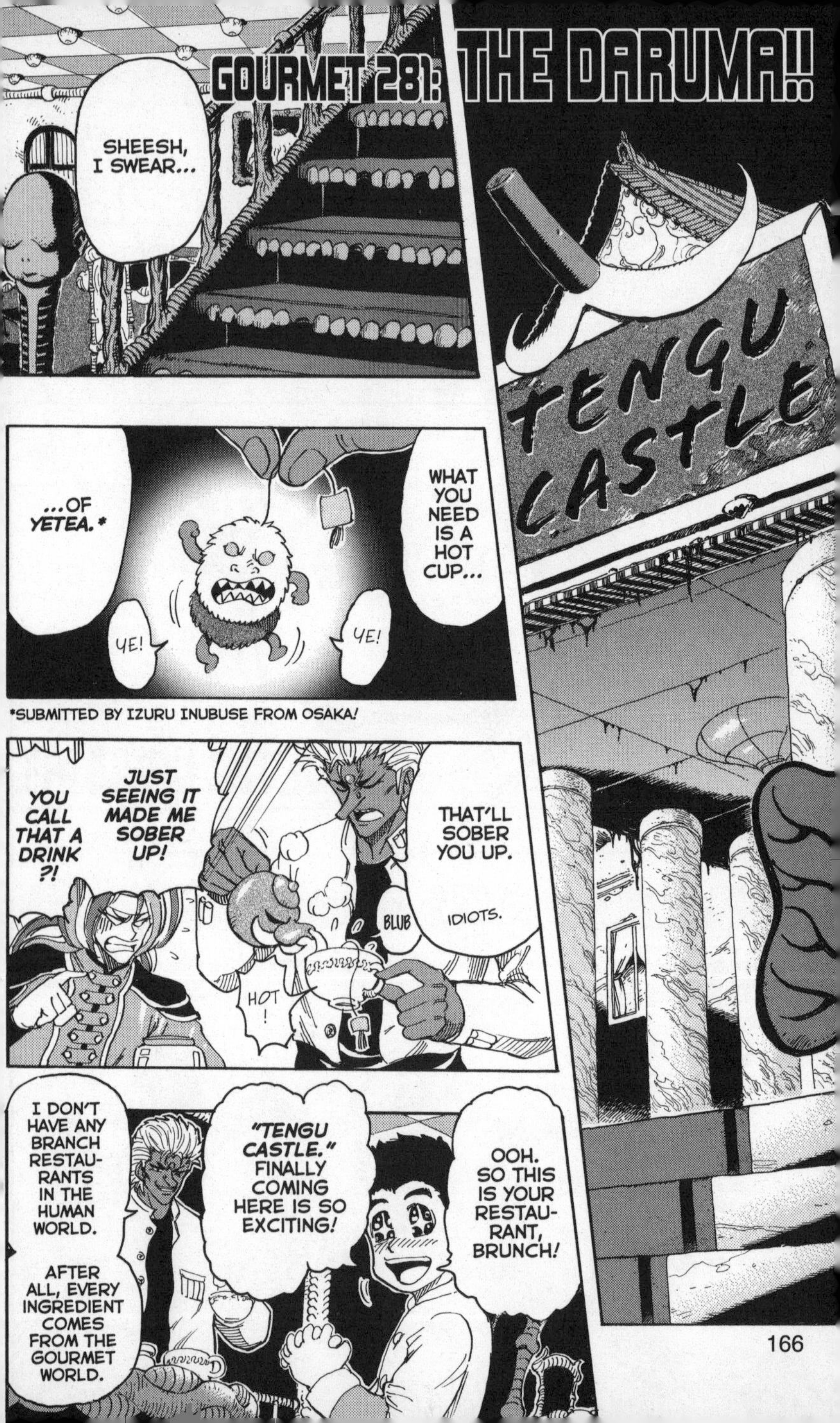
GOURMET 281: THE DARUMA!!
TENGU CASTLE
SHEESH, I SWEAR...
WHAT YOU NEED IS A HOT CUP...
...OF YETEA.*
YE!
YE!
*SUBMITTED BY IZURU INUBUSE FROM OSAKA!
THAT'LL SOBER YOU UP.
IDIOTS.
BLUB
JUST SEEING IT MADE ME SOBER UP!
YOU CALL THAT A DRINK?!
HOT!
OOH. SO THIS IS YOUR RESTAURANT, BRUNCH!
"TENGU CASTLE." FINALLY COMING HERE IS SO EXCITING!
I DON'T HAVE ANY BRANCH RESTAURANTS IN THE HUMAN WORLD.
AFTER ALL, EVERY INGREDIENT COMES FROM THE GOURMET WORLD.

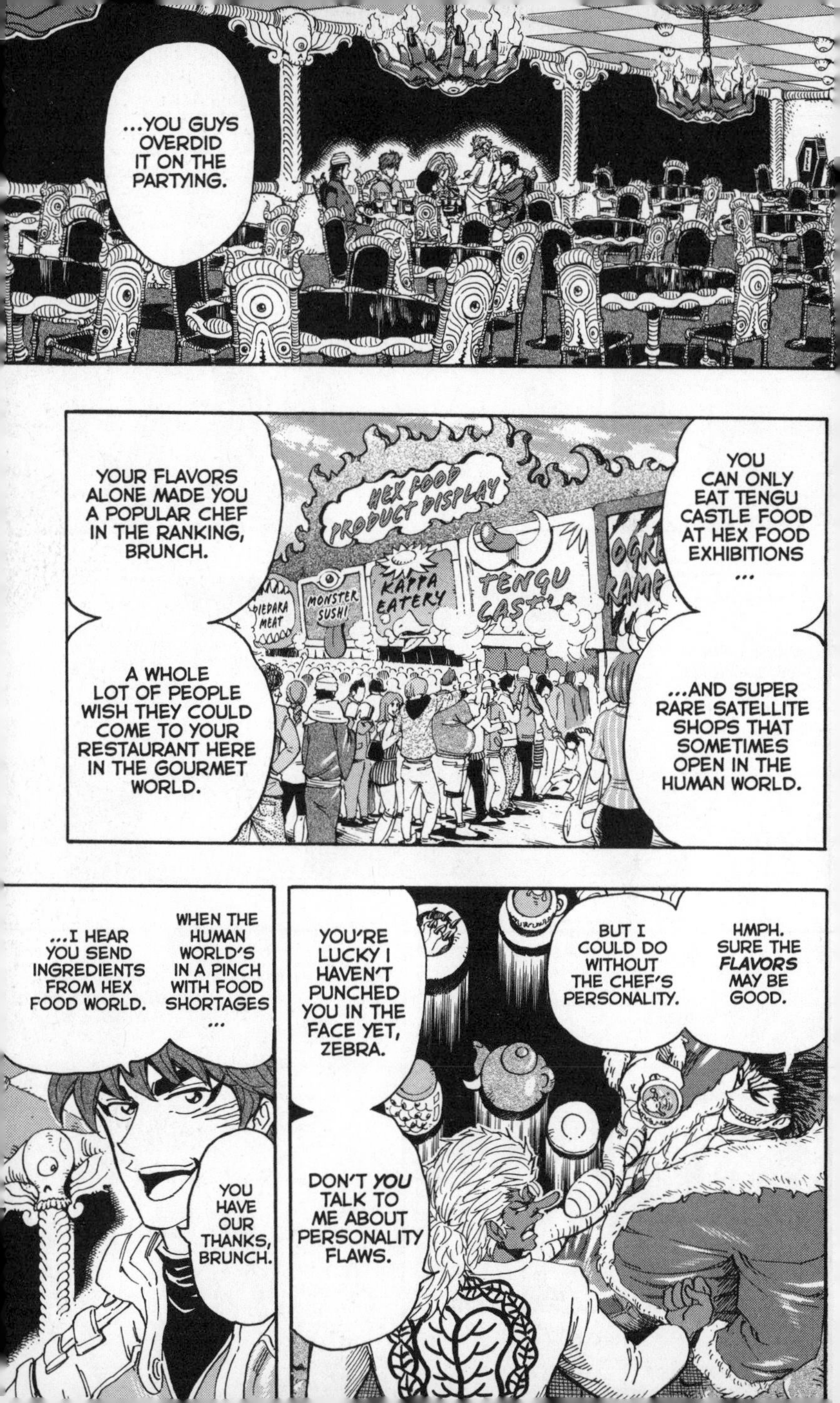
...YOU GUYS OVERDID IT ON THE PARTYING.
HEX FOOD PRODUCT DISPLAY
YOU CAN ONLY EAT TENGU CASTLE FOOD AT HEX FOOD EXHIBITIONS ...
...AND SUPER RARE SATELLITE SHOPS THAT SOMETIMES OPEN IN THE HUMAN WORLD.
KAPPA EATERY
MONSTER SUSHI
YOUR FLAVORS ALONE MADE YOU A POPULAR CHEF IN THE RANKING, BRUNCH.
A WHOLE LOT OF PEOPLE WISH THEY COULD COME TO YOUR RESTAURANT HERE IN THE GOURMET WORLD.
HMPH. SURE THE *FLAVORS* MAY BE GOOD.
BUT I COULD DO WITHOUT THE CHEF'S PERSONALITY.
YOU'RE LUCKY I HAVEN'T PUNCHED YOU IN THE FACE YET, ZEBRA.
DON'T *YOU* TALK TO ME ABOUT PERSONALITY FLAWS.
WHEN THE HUMAN WORLD'S IN A PINCH WITH FOOD SHORTAGES ...
...I HEAR YOU SEND INGREDIENTS FROM HEX FOOD WORLD.
YOU HAVE OUR THANKS, BRUNCH.

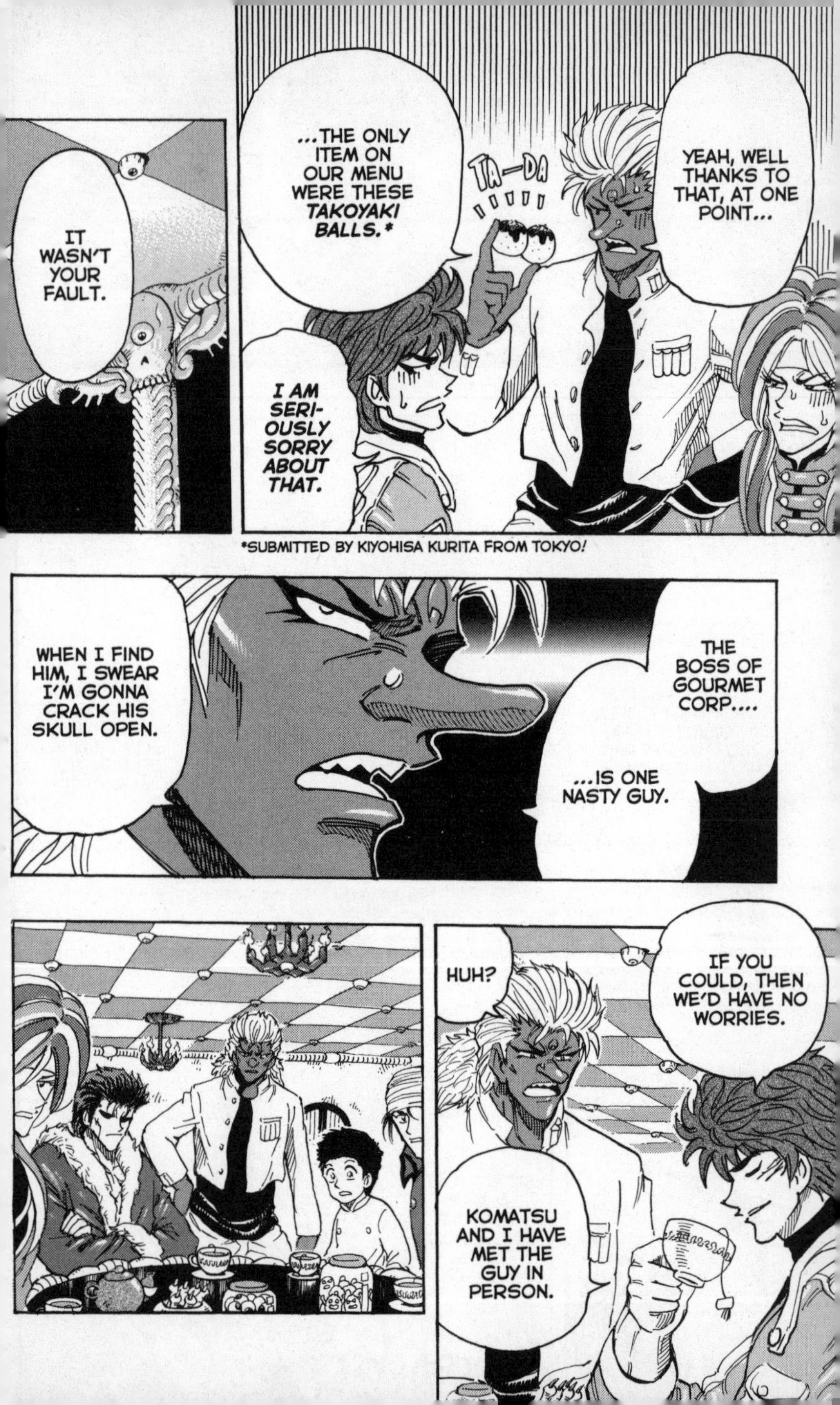
YEAH, WELL THANKS TO THAT, AT ONE POINT...
...THE ONLY ITEM ON OUR MENU WERE THESE *TAKOYAKI BALLS.**
TA-DA
I AM SERIOUSLY SORRY ABOUT THAT.
IT WASN'T YOUR FAULT.
*SUBMITTED BY KIYOHISA KURITA FROM TOKYO!
THE BOSS OF GOURMET CORP....
...IS ONE NASTY GUY.
WHEN I FIND HIM, I SWEAR I'M GONNA CRACK HIS SKULL OPEN.
IF YOU COULD, THEN WE'D HAVE NO WORRIES.
HUH?
KOMATSU AND I HAVE MET THE GUY IN PERSON.

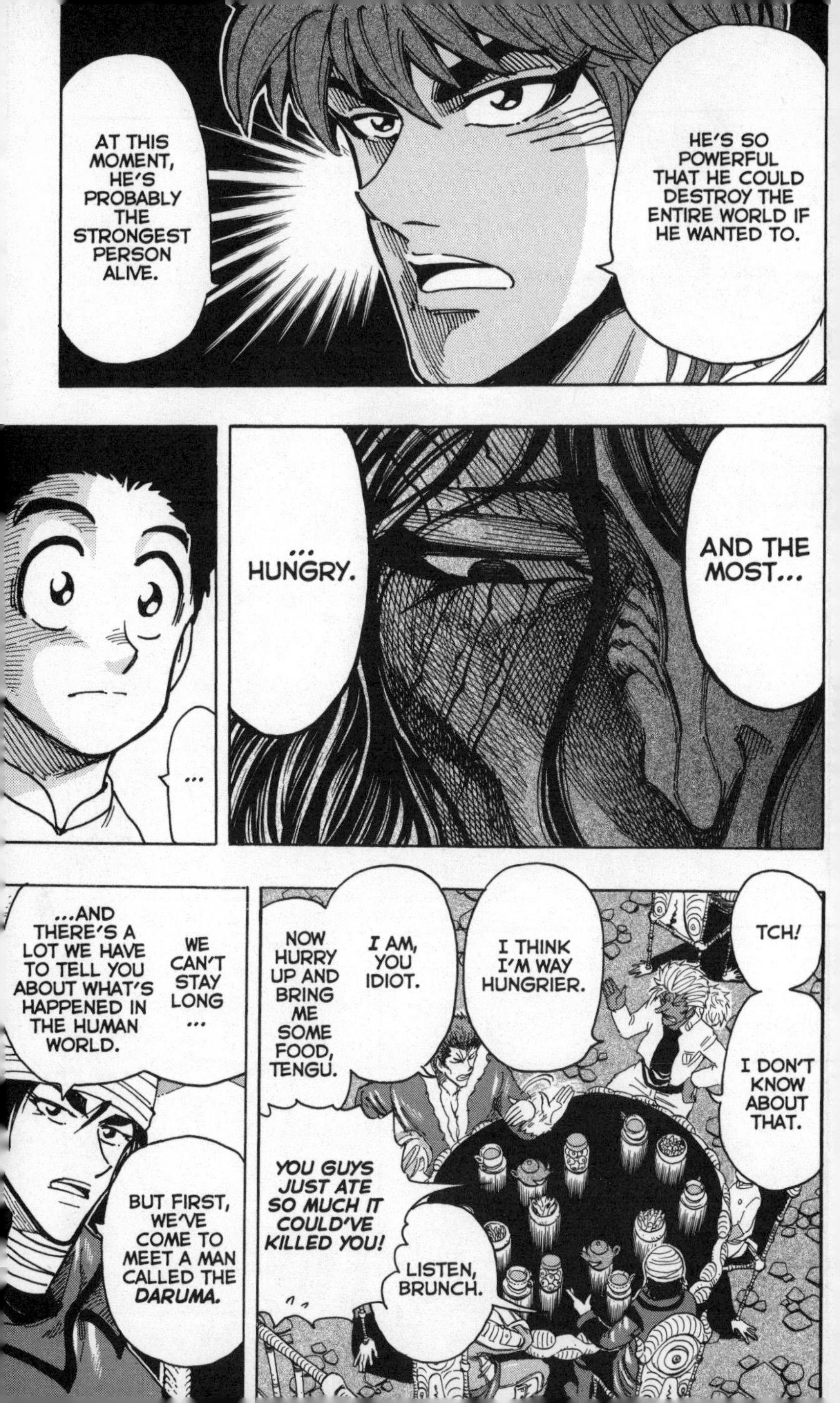
HE'S SO POWERFUL THAT HE COULD DESTROY THE ENTIRE WORLD IF HE WANTED TO.
AT THIS MOMENT, HE'S PROBABLY THE STRONGEST PERSON ALIVE.
AND THE MOST...
... HUNGRY.
...
TCH!
I DON'T KNOW ABOUT THAT.
I THINK I'M WAY HUNGRIER.
I AM, YOU IDIOT.
NOW HURRY UP AND BRING ME SOME FOOD, TENGU.
YOU GUYS JUST ATE SO MUCH IT COULD'VE KILLED YOU!
LISTEN, BRUNCH.
WE CAN'T STAY LONG ...
...AND THERE'S A LOT WE HAVE TO TELL YOU ABOUT WHAT'S HAPPENED IN THE HUMAN WORLD.
BUT FIRST, WE'VE COME TO MEET A MAN CALLED THE DARUMA.

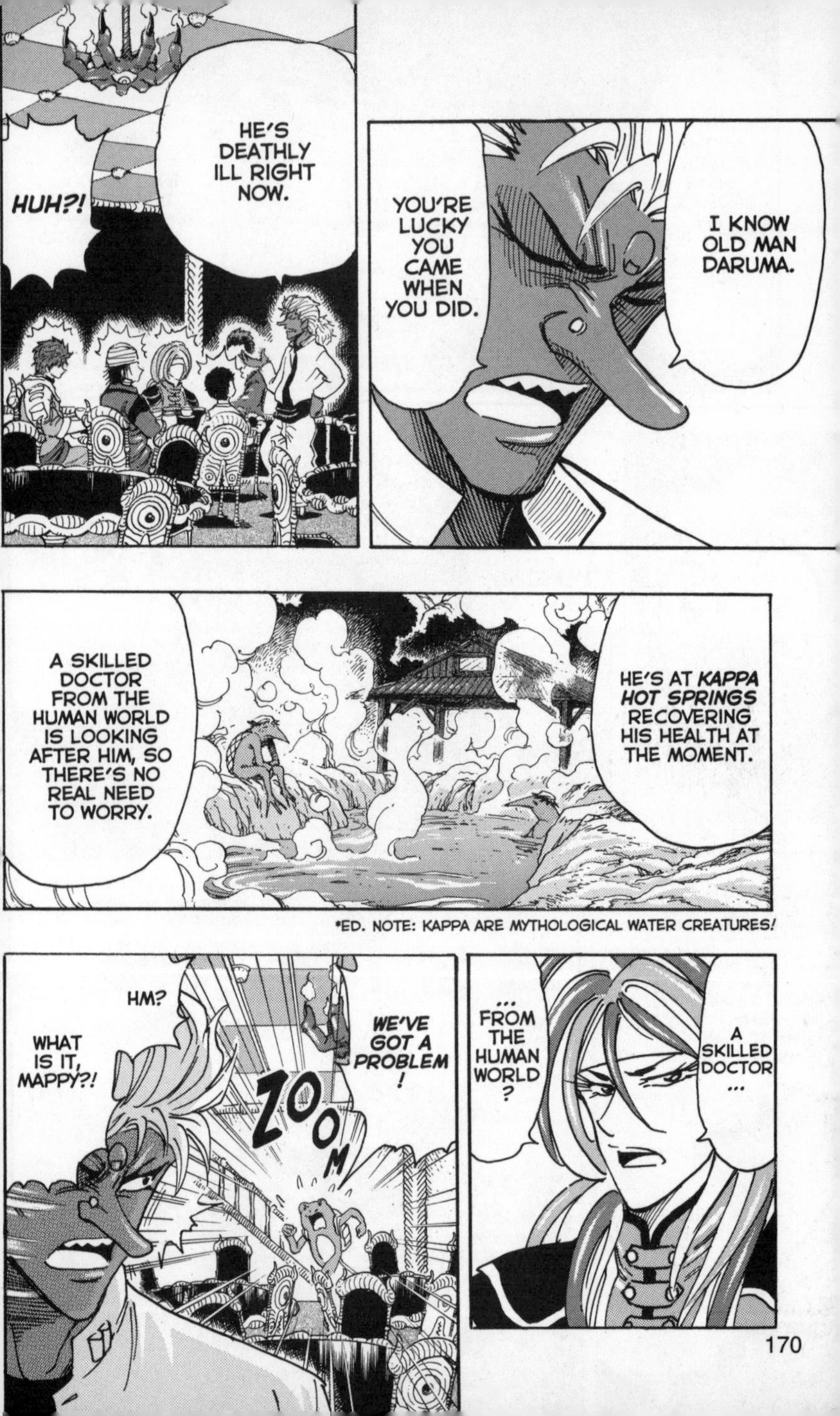
I KNOW OLD MAN DARUMA.
YOU'RE LUCKY YOU CAME WHEN YOU DID.
HE'S DEATHLY ILL RIGHT NOW.
HUH?!
HE'S AT *KAPPA HOT SPRINGS* RECOVERING HIS HEALTH AT THE MOMENT.
A SKILLED DOCTOR FROM THE HUMAN WORLD IS LOOKING AFTER HIM, SO THERE'S NO REAL NEED TO WORRY.
*ED. NOTE: KAPPA ARE MYTHOLOGICAL WATER CREATURES!
A SKILLED DOCTOR...
...FROM THE HUMAN WORLD?
WE'VE GOT A PROBLEM!
ZOOM
HM?
WHAT IS IT, MAPPY?!

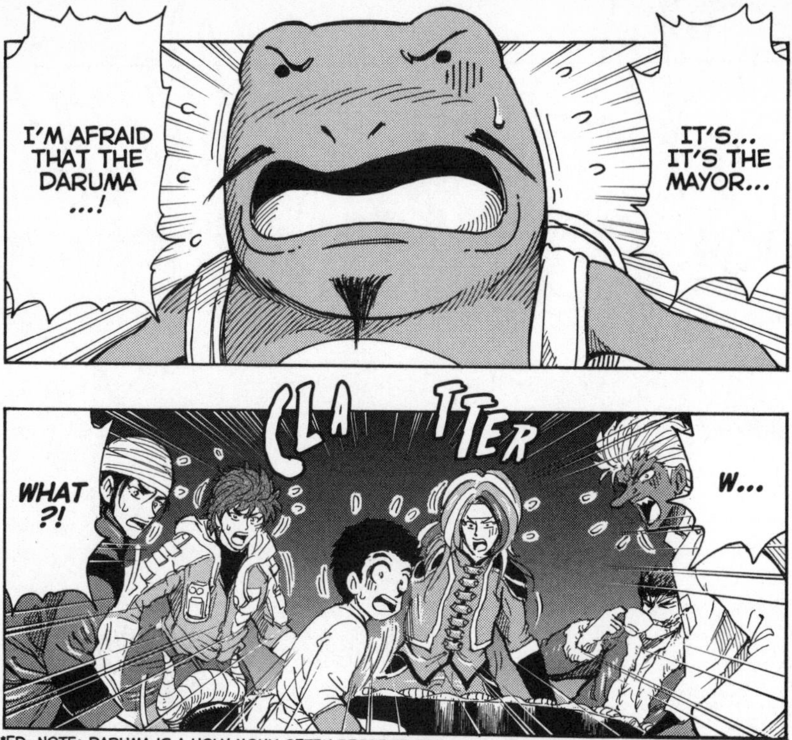
IT'S... IT'S THE MAYOR...
I'M AFRAID THAT THE DARUMA ...!
CLATTER
W...
WHAT ?!
*ED. NOTE: DARUMA IS A HOLY MONK OFTEN REPRESENTED AS A DOLL WITH A PAINTED FACE!

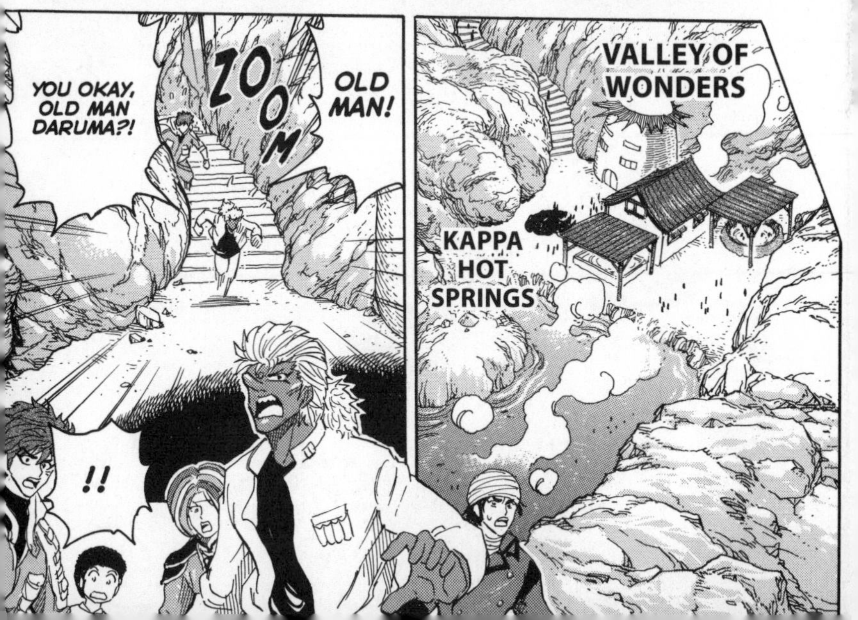
VALLEY OF WONDERS
KAPPA HOT SPRINGS
OLD MAN!
ZOOM
YOU OKAY, OLD MAN DARUMA?!
!!

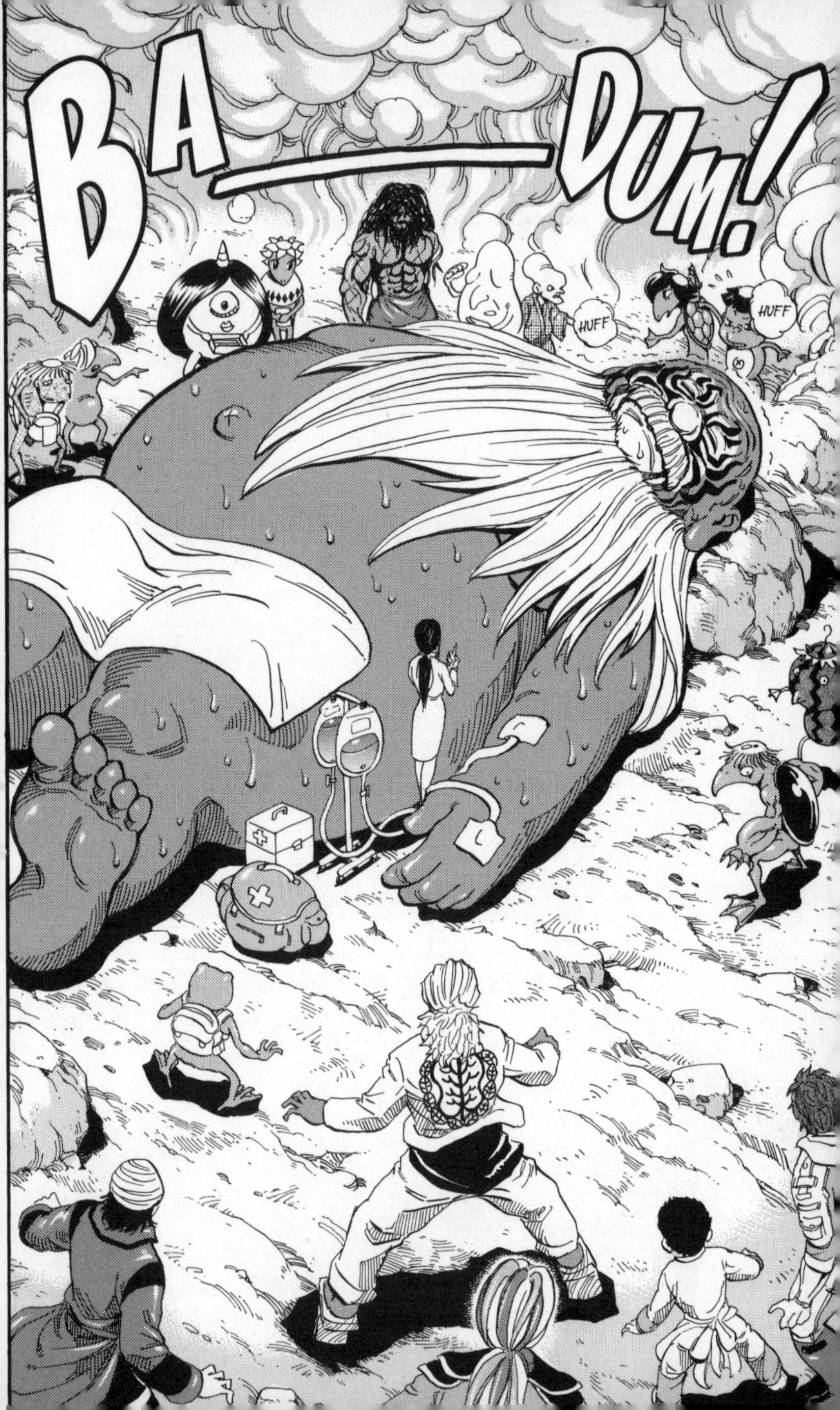
BA____DUM!
HUFF
HUFF

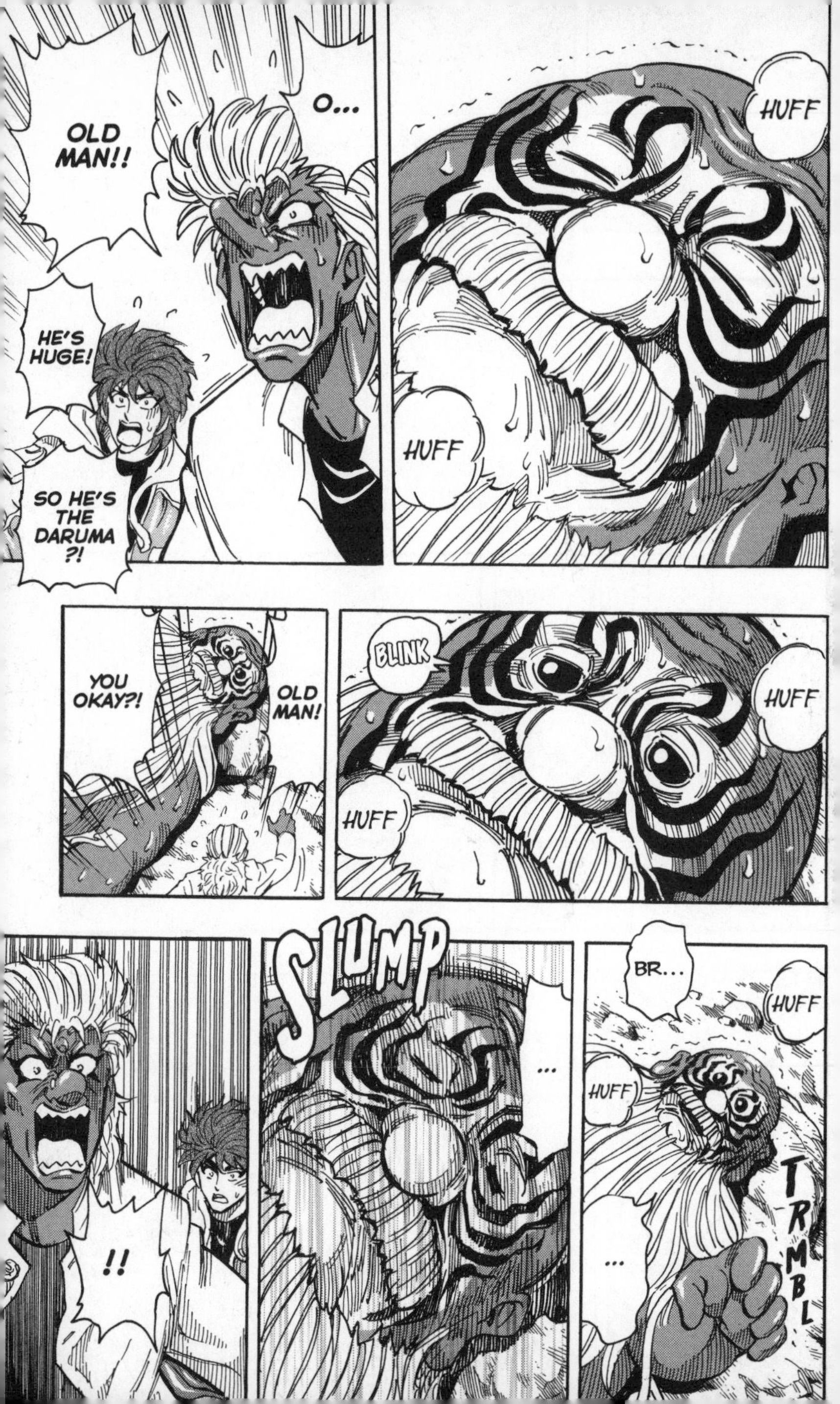
HUFF
HUFF
O...
OLD MAN!!
HE'S HUGE!
SO HE'S THE DARUMA?!
BLINK
HUFF
HUFF
OLD MAN!
YOU OKAY?!
HUFF
BR...
HUFF
TRMBL
...
SLUMP
...
!!

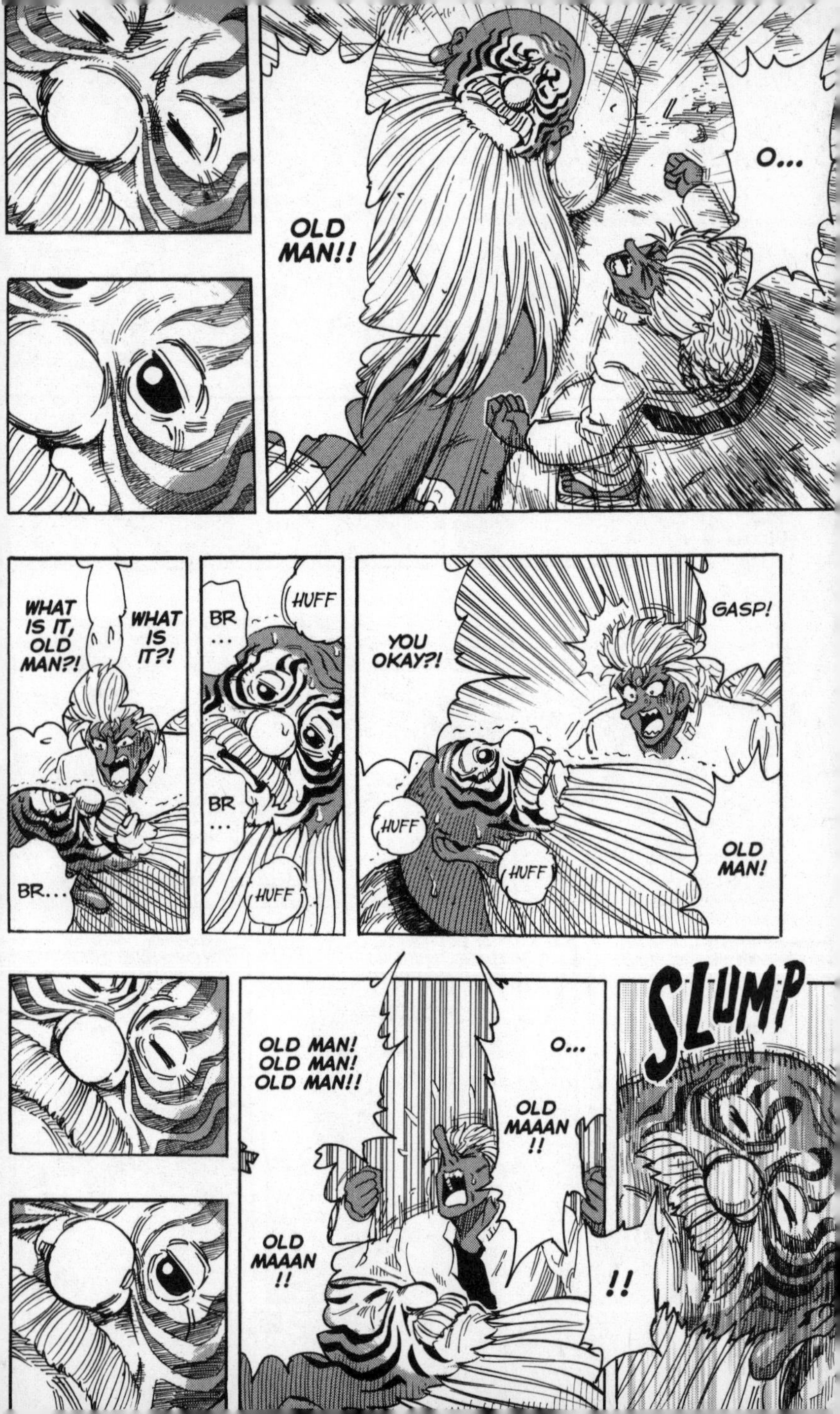
O...
OLD MAN!!
GASP!
YOU OKAY?!
OLD MAN!
HUFF
HUFF
HUFF
BR...
BR...
HUFF
WHAT IS IT?!
WHAT IS IT, OLD MAN?!
BR...
SLUMP
!!
O...
OLD MAAAN!!
OLD MAN! OLD MAN! OLD MAN!!
OLD MAAAN!!

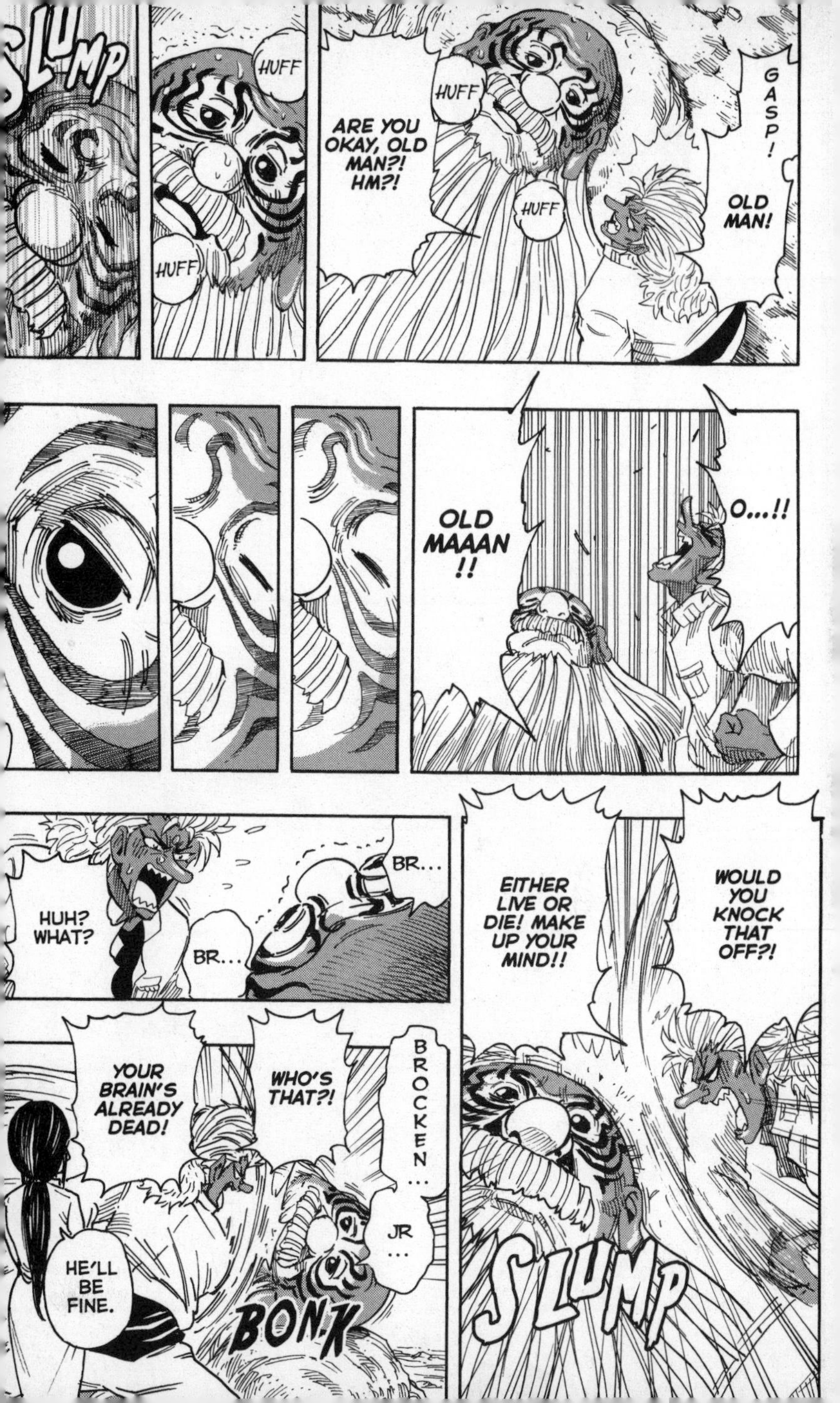
GASP!
OLD MAN!
HUFF
HUFF
ARE YOU OKAY, OLD MAN?! HM?!
HUFF
HUFF
SLUMP
O...!!
OLD MAAAN!!
WOULD YOU KNOCK THAT OFF?!
EITHER LIVE OR DIE! MAKE UP YOUR MIND!!
SLUMP
BR...
BR...
HUH? WHAT?
BROCKEN... JR...
WHO'S THAT?!
YOUR BRAIN'S ALREADY DEAD!
HE'LL BE FINE.
BONK

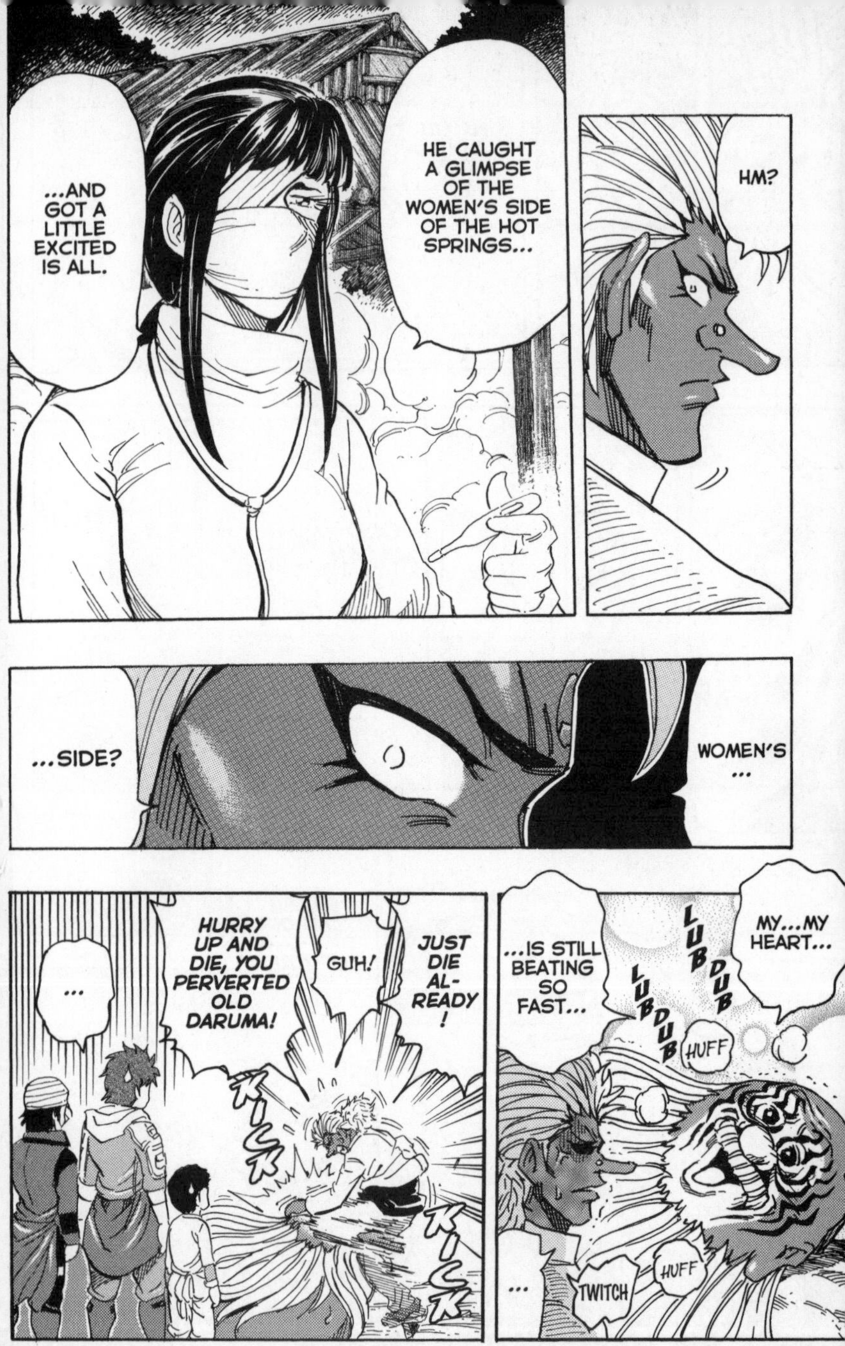
HM?
HE CAUGHT A GLIMPSE OF THE WOMEN'S SIDE OF THE HOT SPRINGS...
...AND GOT A LITTLE EXCITED IS ALL.
WOMEN'S ...
...SIDE?
MY...MY HEART...
LUB DUB
LUB DUB
HUFF
...IS STILL BEATING SO FAST...
HUFF
TWITCH
...
JUST DIE AL-READY!
GUH!
HURRY UP AND DIE, YOU PERVERTED OLD DARUMA!
KICK
KICK
...

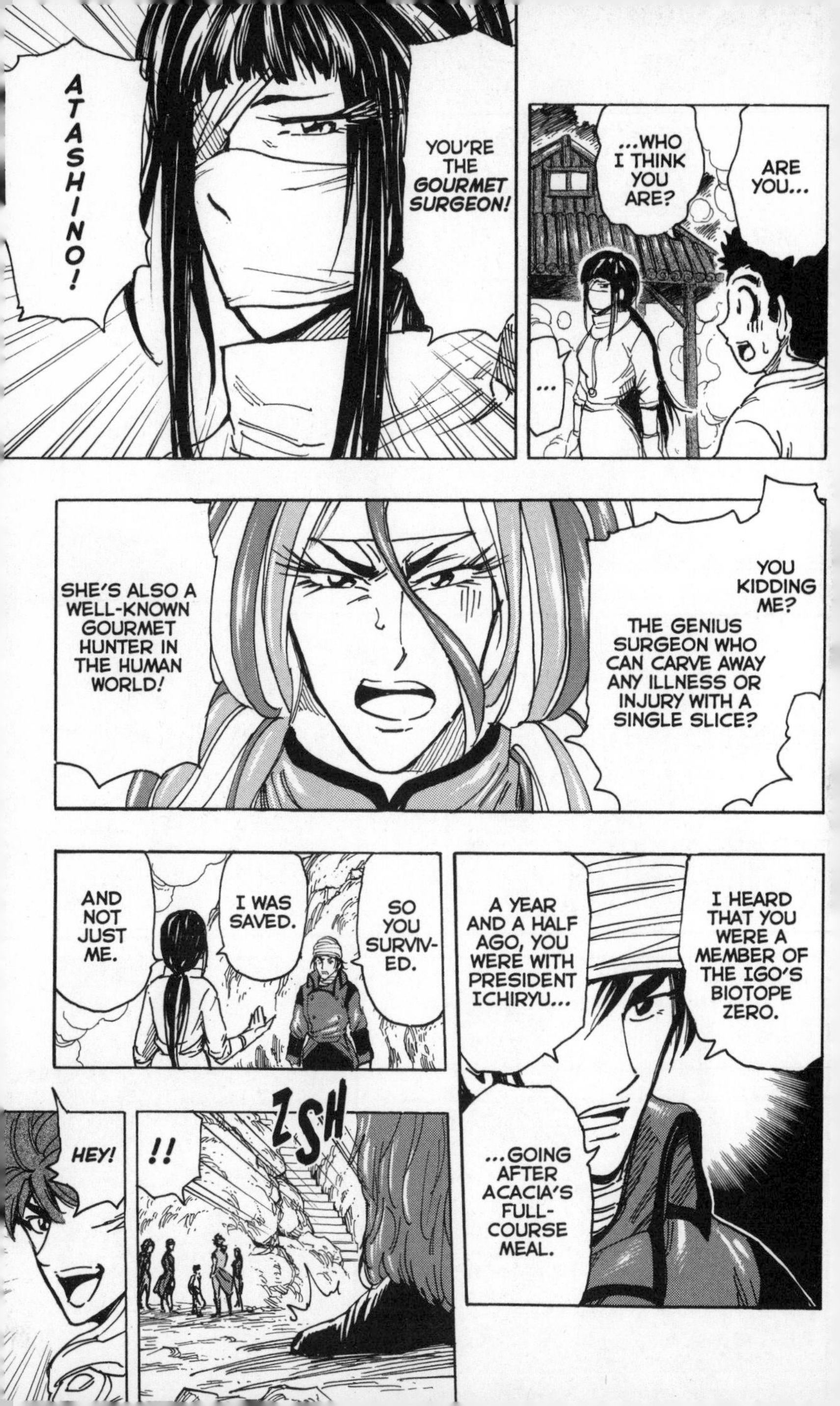
ARE YOU...
...WHO I THINK YOU ARE?
...
ATASHINO!
YOU'RE THE *GOURMET SURGEON!*
YOU KIDDING ME?
THE GENIUS SURGEON WHO CAN CARVE AWAY ANY ILLNESS OR INJURY WITH A SINGLE SLICE?
SHE'S ALSO A WELL-KNOWN GOURMET HUNTER IN THE HUMAN WORLD!
I HEARD THAT YOU WERE A MEMBER OF THE IGO'S BIOTOPE ZERO.
A YEAR AND A HALF AGO, YOU WERE WITH PRESIDENT ICHIRYU...
...GOING AFTER ACACIA'S FULL-COURSE MEAL.
SO YOU SURVIV-ED.
I WAS SAVED.
AND NOT JUST ME.
ZSH
!!
HEY!

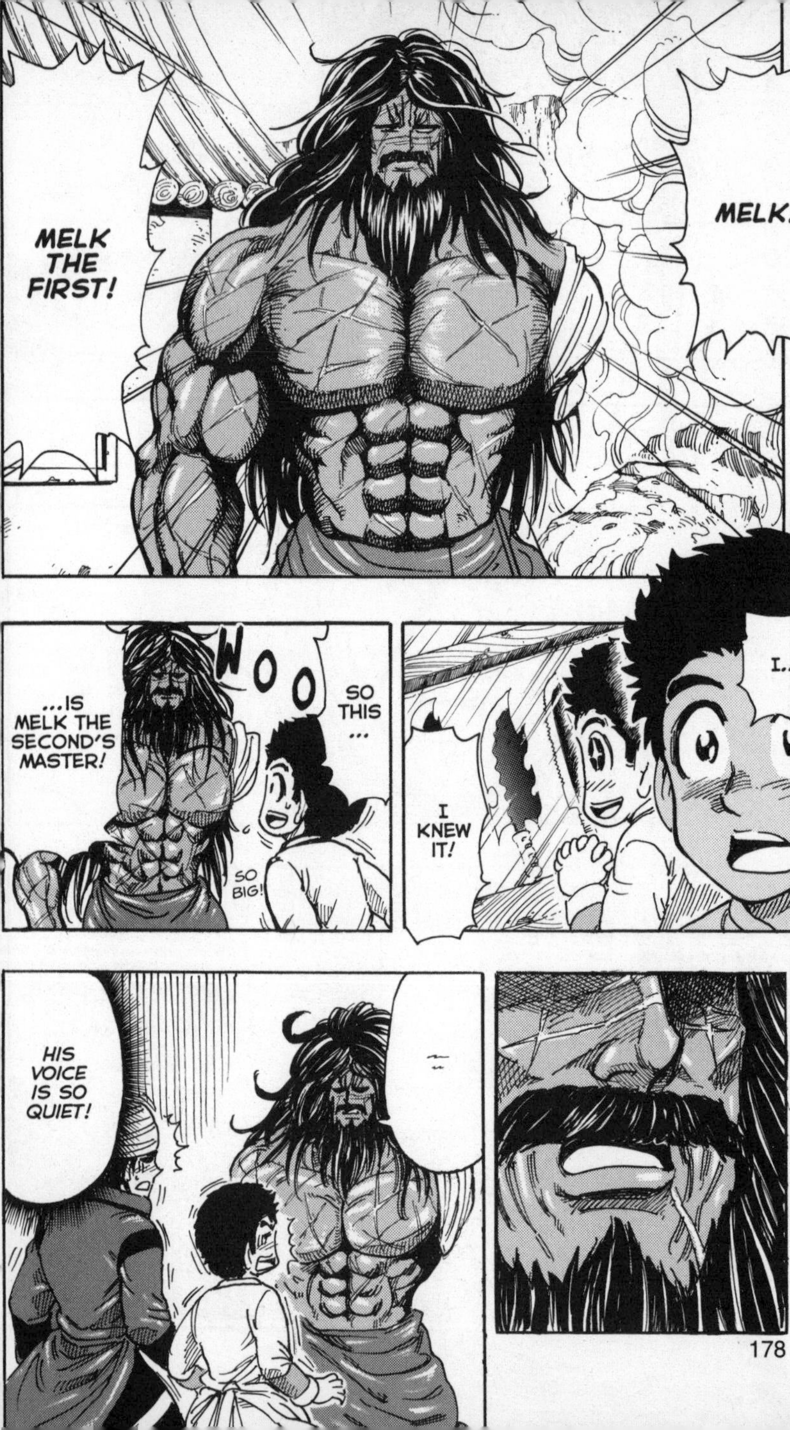
MELK!
MELK THE FIRST!
I...
I KNEW IT!
SO THIS ...
WOO
...IS MELK THE SECOND'S MASTER!
SO BIG!
HIS VOICE IS SO QUIET!

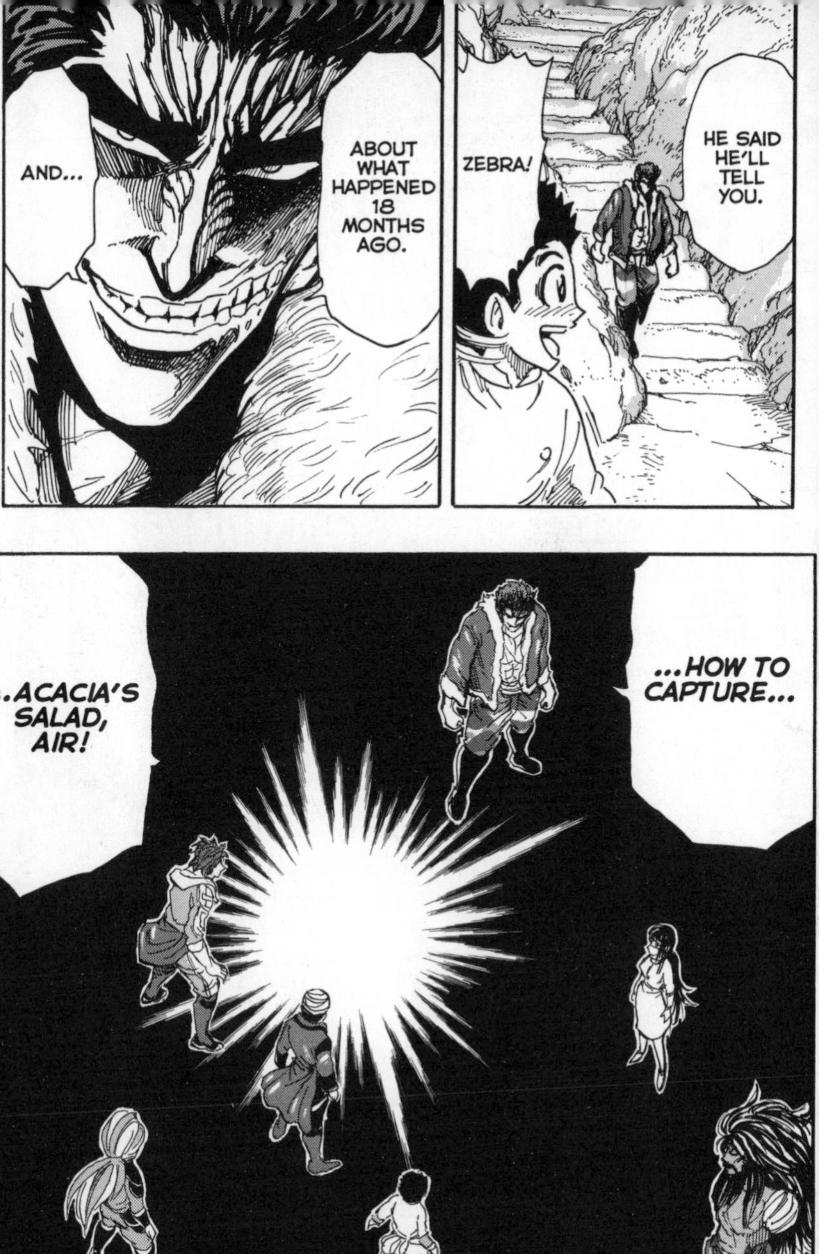
HE SAID HE'LL TELL YOU.
ZEBRA!
ABOUT WHAT HAPPENED 18 MONTHS AGO.
AND...
...HOW TO CAPTURE...
...ACACIA'S SALAD, AIR!

TORIKO

GOURMET CHECKLIST

Vol. 305

ROSE HAM
(SPECIAL PLANT)

CAPTURE LEVEL: 15
HABITAT: CHOWLIN TEMPLE
SIZE: 35 CM WHEN IN FULL BLOOM
HEIGHT: ---
WEIGHT: 400 G
PRICE: 60,000 YEN PER BLOSSOM

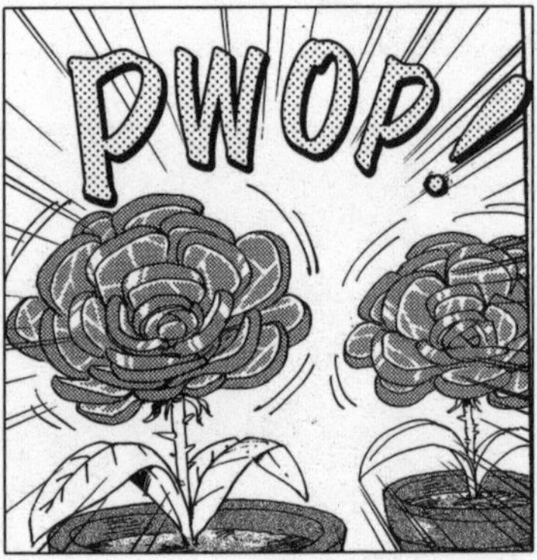
PWOP!

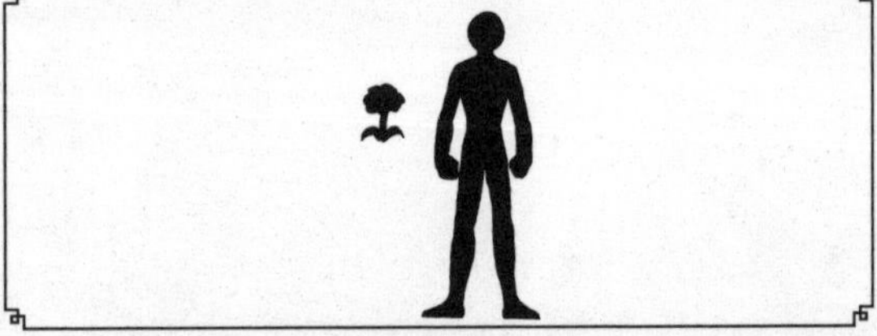

SCALE

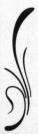

A ROSE THAT BLOOMS WITH PETALS MADE OF DELICIOUS ROAST HAM. THE LEAVES ARE AKIN TO LETTUCE AND THE STEM TO ASPARAGUS. THE FLOWER TASTES BEST SERVED WITH ALL THREE PARTS TOGETHER. IN ORDER FOR THE SEED OF THE FLOWER TO GERMINATE AND GROW, IT MUST FEEL GRATITUDE. THE STRONGER THE GRATITUDE, THE FASTER AND MORE DELICIOUS IT GROWS. IT'S A SIMPLE BUT DIFFICULT TO MASTER HONOR THE FOOD TRAINING INGREDIENT.

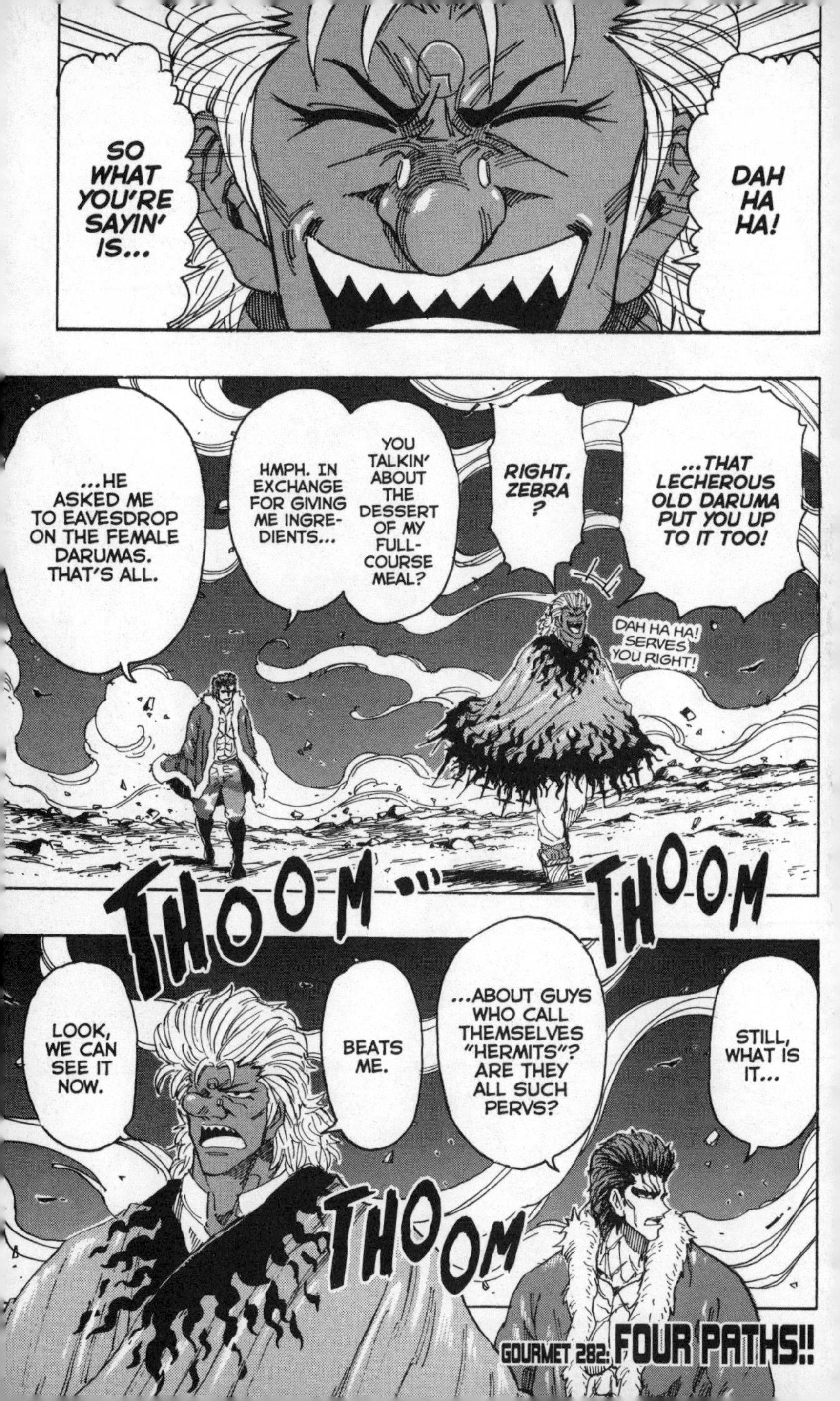
DAH HA HA!
SO WHAT YOU'RE SAYIN' IS...
...THAT LECHEROUS OLD DARUMA PUT YOU UP TO IT TOO!
RIGHT, ZEBRA?
DAH HA HA! SERVES YOU RIGHT!
YOU TALKIN' ABOUT THE DESSERT OF MY FULL-COURSE MEAL?
HMPH. IN EXCHANGE FOR GIVING ME INGREDIENTS...
...HE ASKED ME TO EAVESDROP ON THE FEMALE DARUMAS. THAT'S ALL.
THOOM THOOM
STILL, WHAT IS IT...
...ABOUT GUYS WHO CALL THEMSELVES "HERMITS"? ARE THEY ALL SUCH PERVS?
BEATS ME.
LOOK, WE CAN SEE IT NOW.
THOOM
GOURMET 282: FOUR PATHS!!

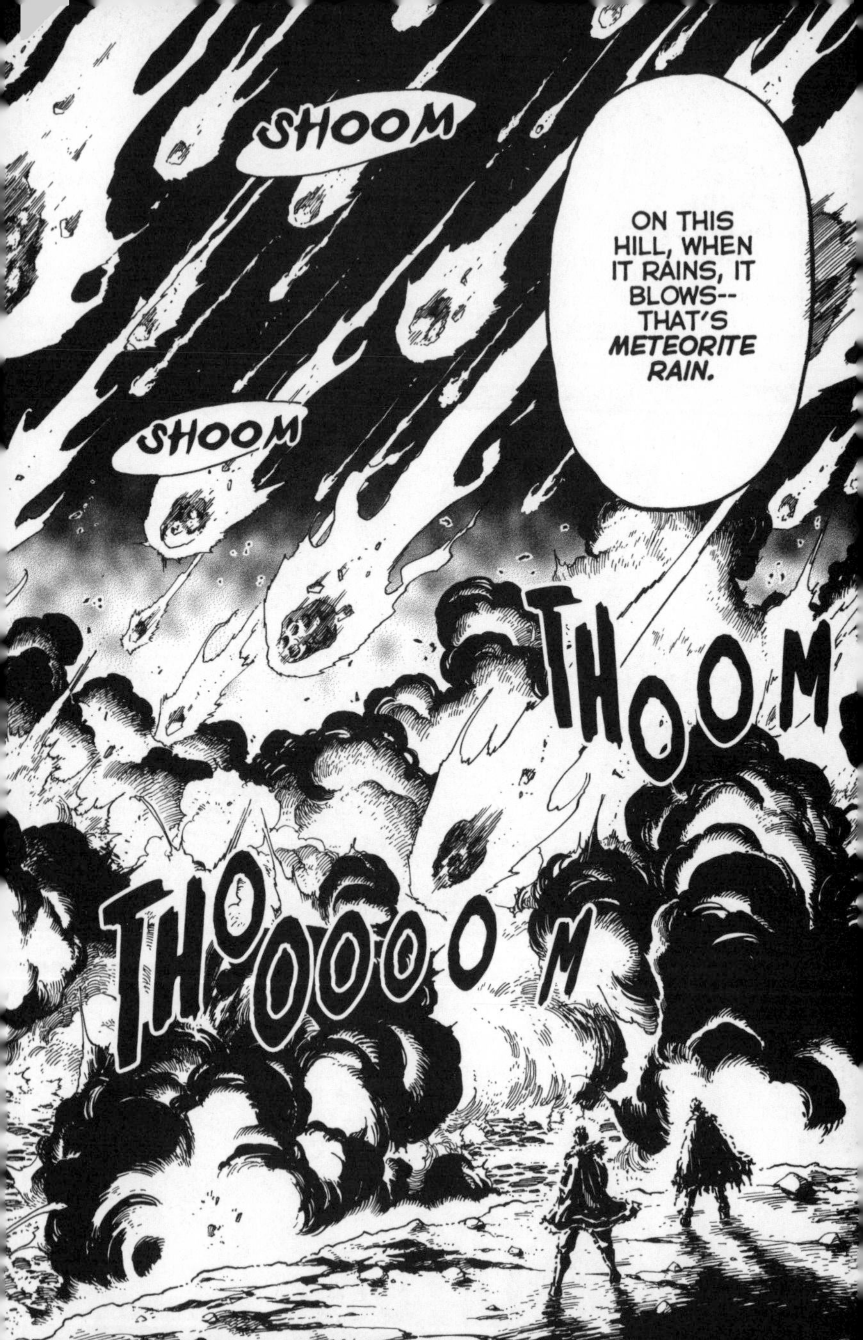
ON THIS HILL, WHEN IT RAINS, IT BLOWS--THAT'S *METEORITE RAIN.*
SHOOM
SHOOM
THOOM
THOOOOOM

GOURMET 282: FOUR PATHS!!

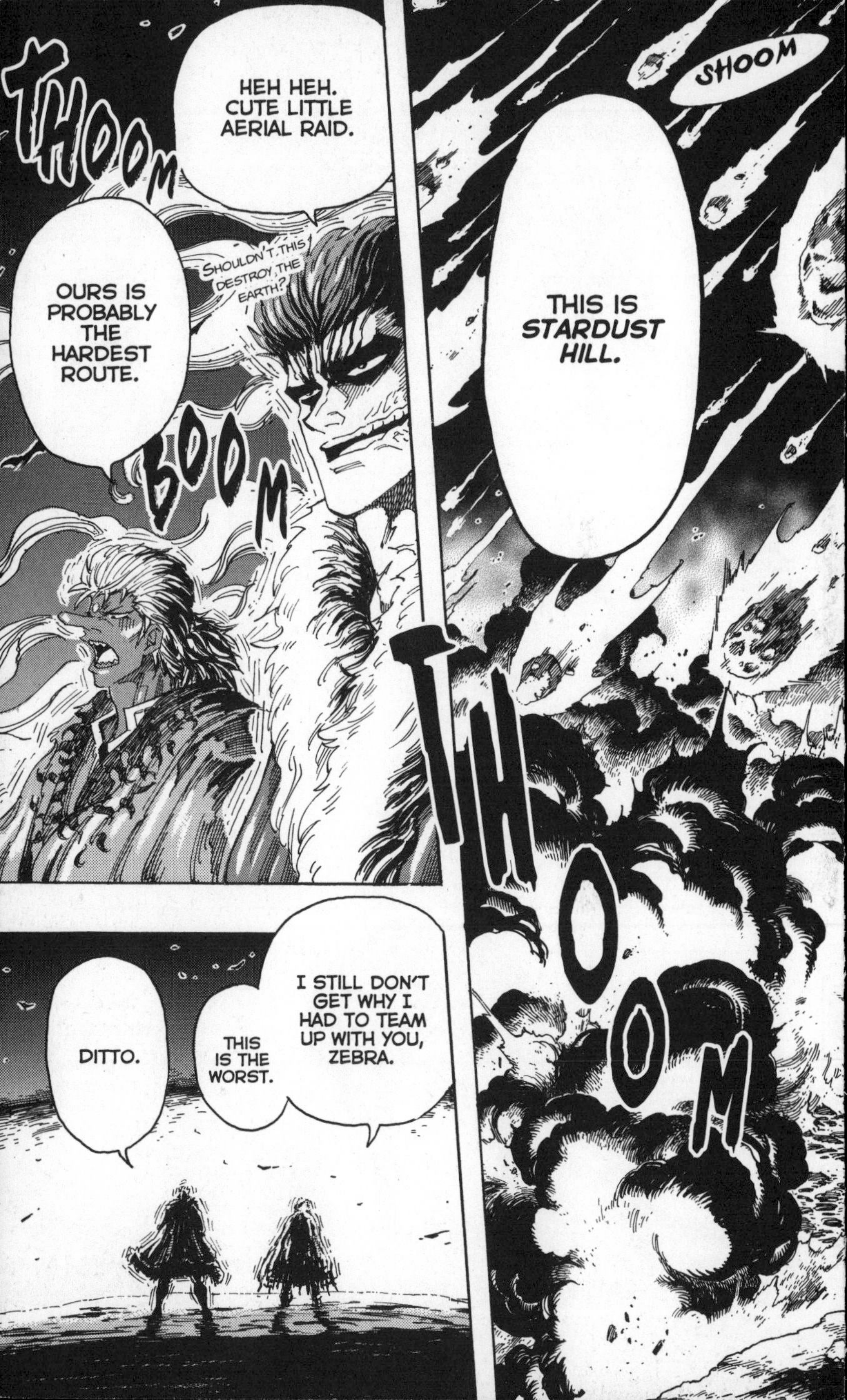
SHOOM
THIS IS STARDUST HILL.
THOOM
HEH HEH. CUTE LITTLE AERIAL RAID.
SHOULDN'T THIS DESTROY THE EARTH?
THOOM
OURS IS PROBABLY THE HARDEST ROUTE.
BOOM
I STILL DON'T GET WHY I HAD TO TEAM UP WITH YOU, ZEBRA.
THIS IS THE WORST.
DITTO.

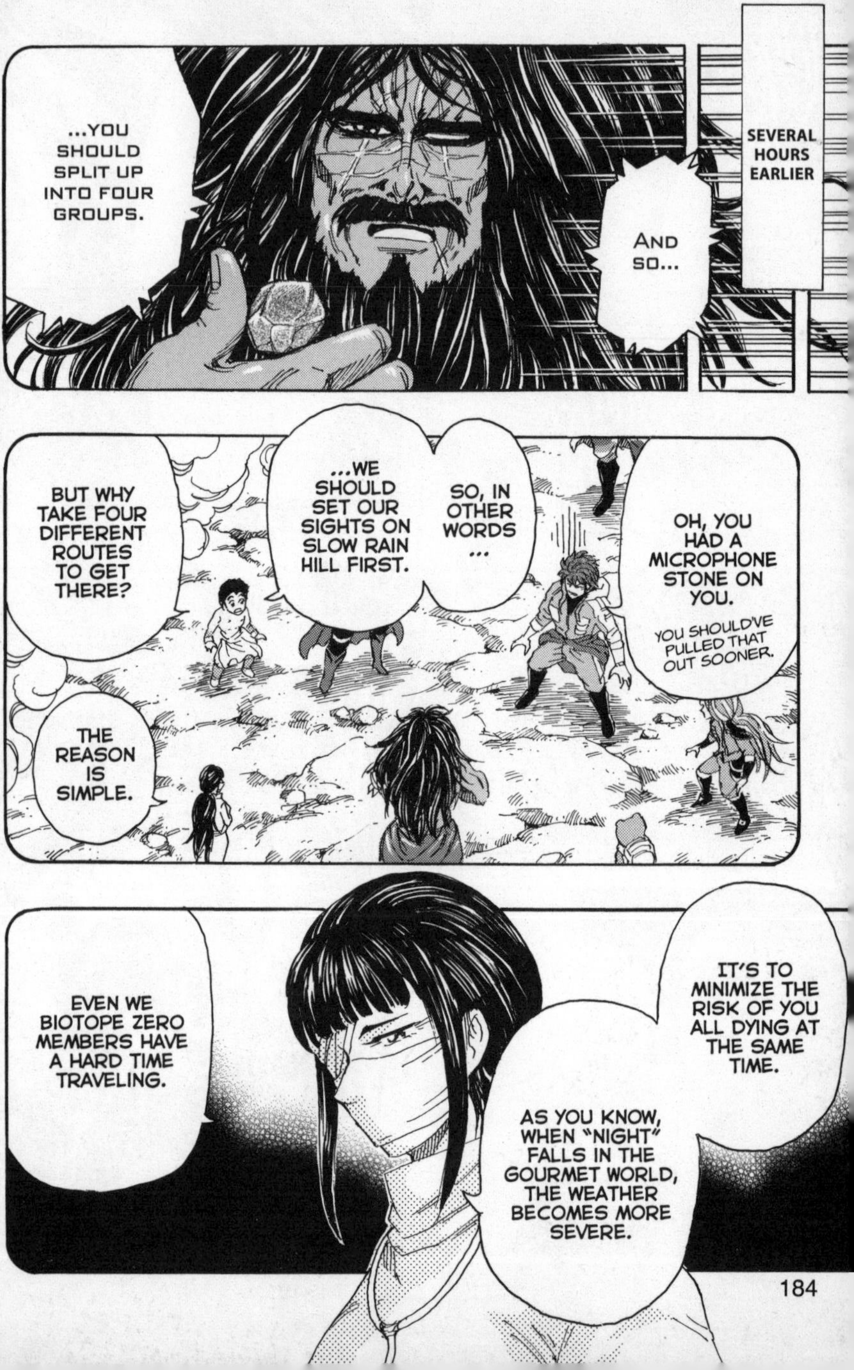
SEVERAL HOURS EARLIER
AND SO...
...YOU SHOULD SPLIT UP INTO FOUR GROUPS.
OH, YOU HAD A MICROPHONE STONE ON YOU.
YOU SHOULD'VE PULLED THAT OUT SOONER.
SO, IN OTHER WORDS...
...WE SHOULD SET OUR SIGHTS ON SLOW RAIN HILL FIRST.
BUT WHY TAKE FOUR DIFFERENT ROUTES TO GET THERE?
THE REASON IS SIMPLE.
IT'S TO MINIMIZE THE RISK OF YOU ALL DYING AT THE SAME TIME.
AS YOU KNOW, WHEN "NIGHT" FALLS IN THE GOURMET WORLD, THE WEATHER BECOMES MORE SEVERE.
EVEN WE BIOTOPE ZERO MEMBERS HAVE A HARD TIME TRAVELING.

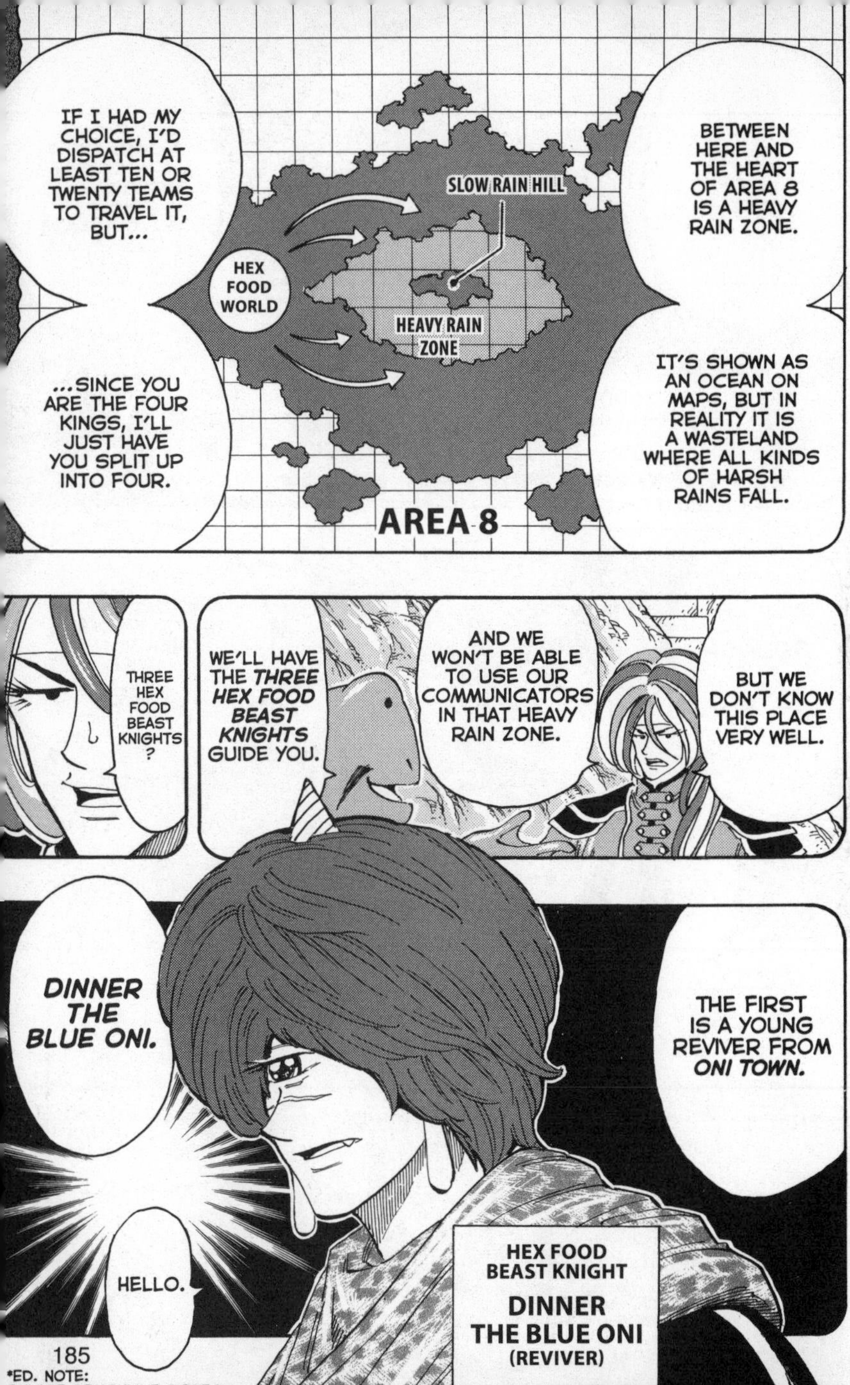
BETWEEN HERE AND THE HEART OF AREA 8 IS A HEAVY RAIN ZONE.
IT'S SHOWN AS AN OCEAN ON MAPS, BUT IN REALITY IT IS A WASTELAND WHERE ALL KINDS OF HARSH RAINS FALL.
IF I HAD MY CHOICE, I'D DISPATCH AT LEAST TEN OR TWENTY TEAMS TO TRAVEL IT, BUT...
...SINCE YOU ARE THE FOUR KINGS, I'LL JUST HAVE YOU SPLIT UP INTO FOUR.
SLOW RAIN HILL
HEX FOOD WORLD
HEAVY RAIN ZONE
AREA 8
BUT WE DON'T KNOW THIS PLACE VERY WELL.
AND WE WON'T BE ABLE TO USE OUR COMMUNICATORS IN THAT HEAVY RAIN ZONE.
WE'LL HAVE THE *THREE HEX FOOD BEAST KNIGHTS* GUIDE YOU.
THREE HEX FOOD BEAST KNIGHTS?
THE FIRST IS A YOUNG REVIVER FROM *ONI TOWN.*
DINNER THE BLUE ONI.
HELLO.
HEX FOOD BEAST KNIGHT
DINNER THE BLUE ONI
(REVIVER)

*ED. NOTE:
ONI ARE DEMONLIKE OGRES FROM JAPANESE MYTHOLOGY!

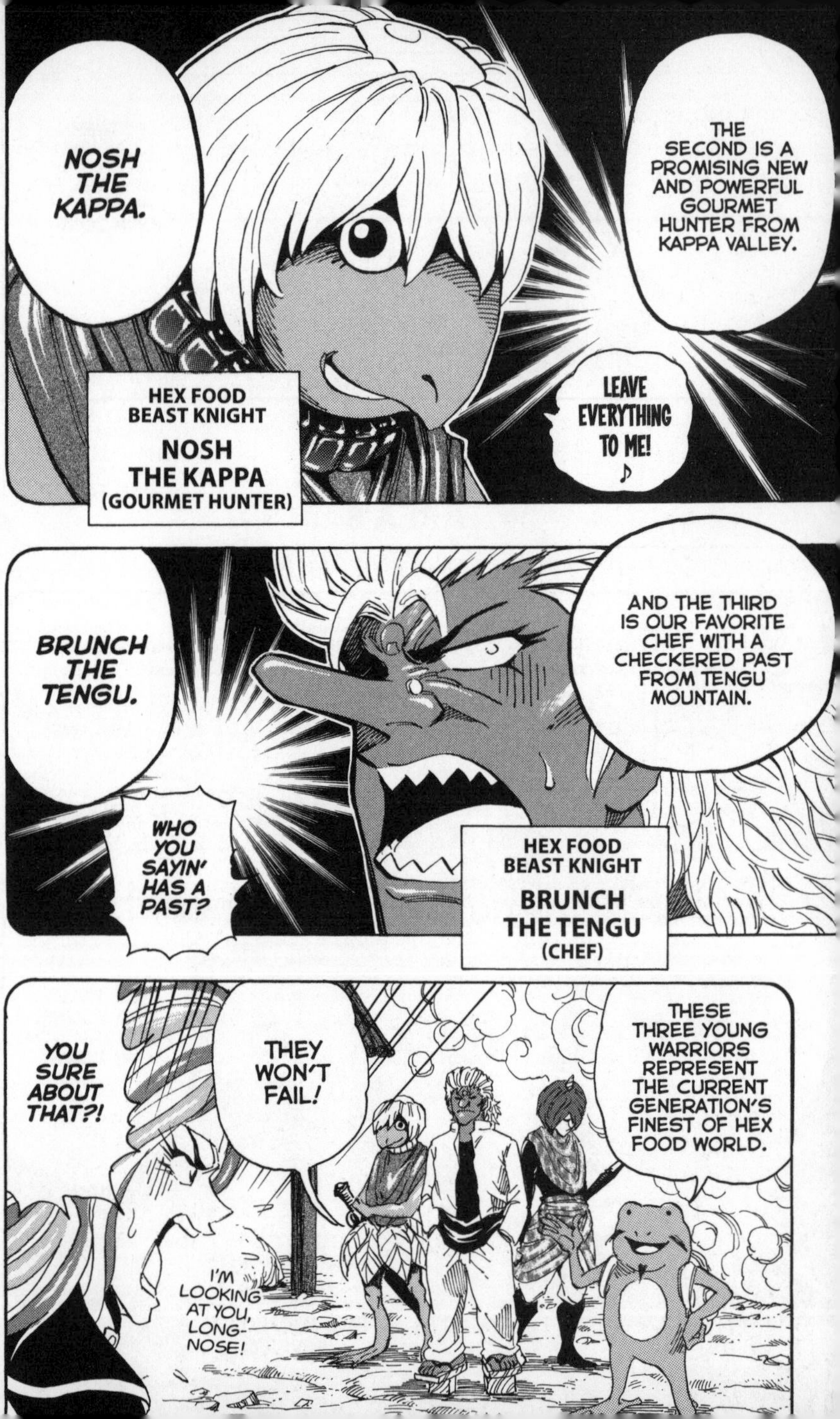
THE SECOND IS A PROMISING NEW AND POWERFUL GOURMET HUNTER FROM KAPPA VALLEY.
NOSH THE KAPPA.
LEAVE EVERYTHING TO ME! ♪
HEX FOOD BEAST KNIGHT NOSH THE KAPPA (GOURMET HUNTER)
AND THE THIRD IS OUR FAVORITE CHEF WITH A CHECKERED PAST FROM TENGU MOUNTAIN.
BRUNCH THE TENGU.
WHO YOU SAYIN' HAS A PAST?
HEX FOOD BEAST KNIGHT BRUNCH THE TENGU (CHEF)
THESE THREE YOUNG WARRIORS REPRESENT THE CURRENT GENERATION'S FINEST OF HEX FOOD WORLD.
THEY WON'T FAIL!
YOU SURE ABOUT THAT?!
I'M LOOKING AT YOU, LONG-NOSE!

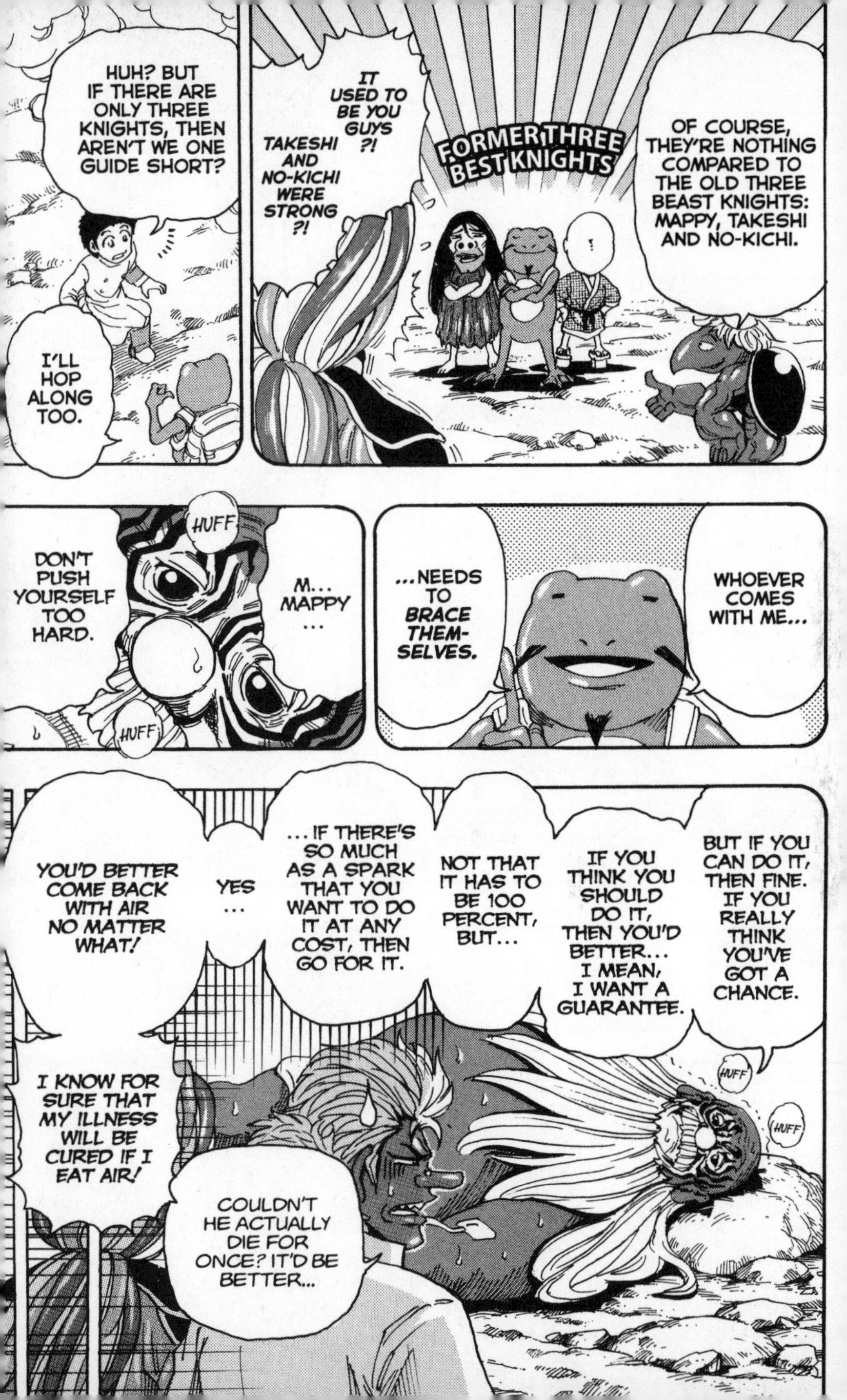
OF COURSE, THEY'RE NOTHING COMPARED TO THE OLD THREE BEAST KNIGHTS: MAPPY, TAKESHI AND NO-KICHI.
FORMER THREE BEST KNIGHTS
IT USED TO BE YOU GUYS ?!
TAKESHI AND NO-KICHI WERE STRONG ?!
HUH? BUT IF THERE ARE ONLY THREE KNIGHTS, THEN AREN'T WE ONE GUIDE SHORT?
I'LL HOP ALONG TOO.
WHOEVER COMES WITH ME...
...NEEDS TO BRACE THEM-SELVES.
HUFF
M... MAPPY ...
DON'T PUSH YOURSELF TOO HARD.
HUFF
BUT IF YOU CAN DO IT, THEN FINE. IF YOU REALLY THINK YOU'VE GOT A CHANCE.
IF YOU THINK YOU SHOULD DO IT, THEN YOU'D BETTER... I MEAN, I WANT A GUARANTEE.
NOT THAT IT HAS TO BE 100 PERCENT, BUT...
...IF THERE'S SO MUCH AS A SPARK THAT YOU WANT TO DO IT AT ANY COST, THEN GO FOR IT.
YES ...
YOU'D BETTER COME BACK WITH AIR NO MATTER WHAT!
HUFF
HUFF
I KNOW FOR SURE THAT MY ILLNESS WILL BE CURED IF I EAT AIR!
COULDN'T HE ACTUALLY DIE FOR ONCE? IT'D BE BETTER...

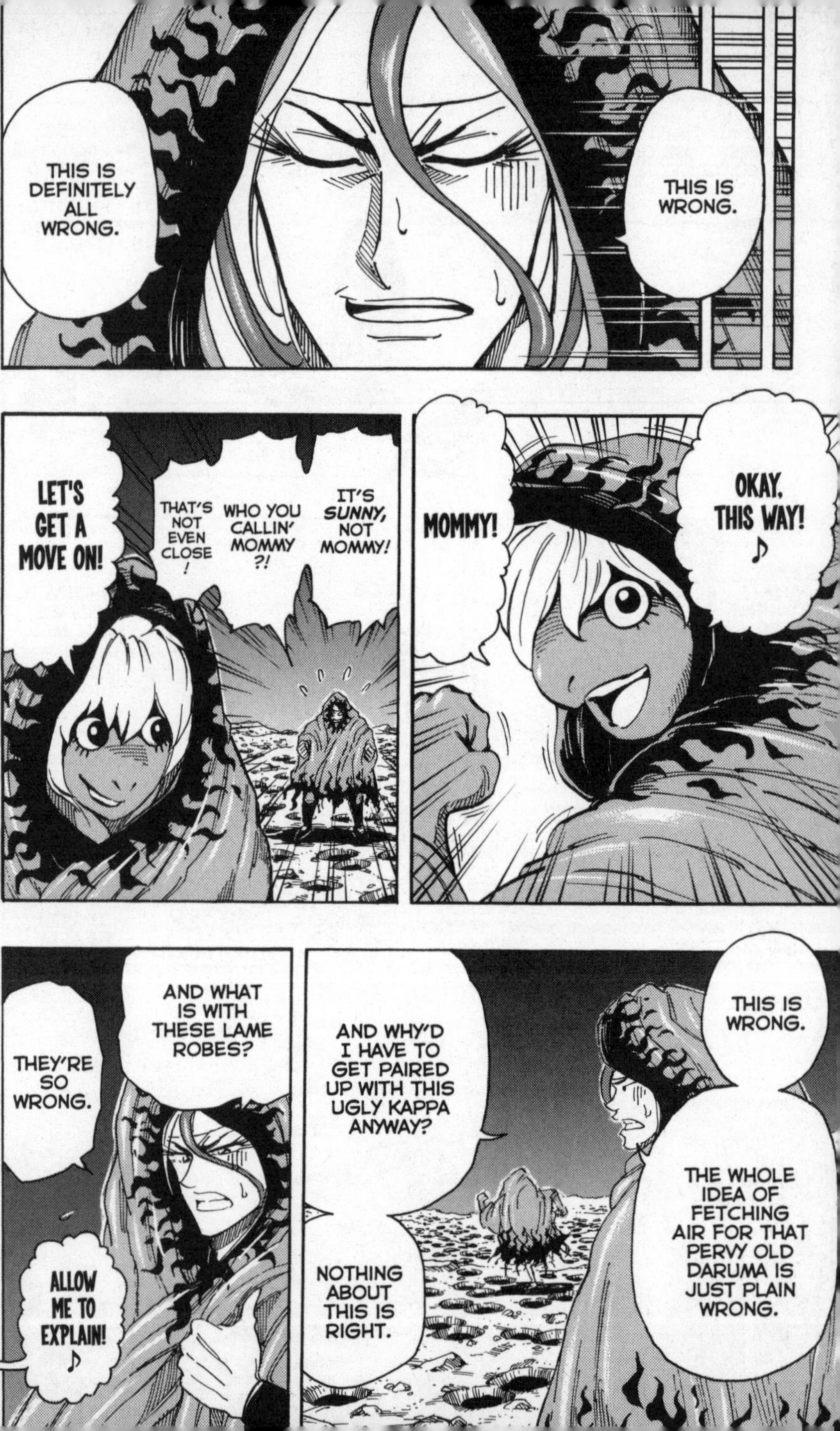
THIS IS WRONG.
THIS IS DEFINITELY ALL WRONG.
OKAY, THIS WAY! ♪
MOMMY!
IT'S SUNNY, NOT MOMMY!
WHO YOU CALLIN' MOMMY ?!
THAT'S NOT EVEN CLOSE !
LET'S GET A MOVE ON!
THIS IS WRONG.
AND WHY'D I HAVE TO GET PAIRED UP WITH THIS UGLY KAPPA ANYWAY?
THE WHOLE IDEA OF FETCHING AIR FOR THAT PERVY OLD DARUMA IS JUST PLAIN WRONG.
NOTHING ABOUT THIS IS RIGHT.
AND WHAT IS WITH THESE LAME ROBES?
THEY'RE SO WRONG.
ALLOW ME TO EXPLAIN! ♪

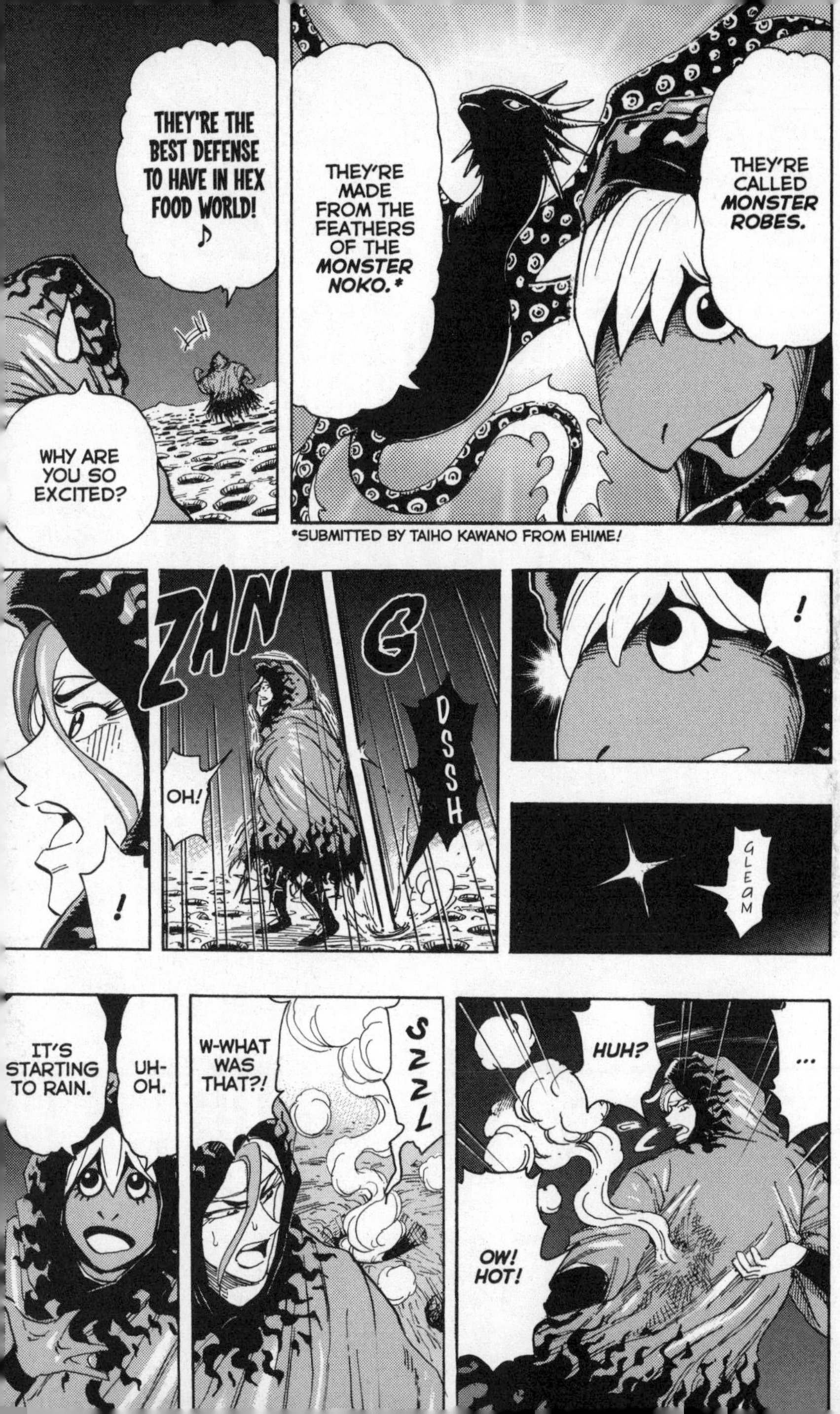
THEY'RE CALLED MONSTER ROBES.
THEY'RE MADE FROM THE FEATHERS OF THE MONSTER NOKO.*
THEY'RE THE BEST DEFENSE TO HAVE IN HEX FOOD WORLD! ♪
WHY ARE YOU SO EXCITED?
*SUBMITTED BY TAIHO KAWANO FROM EHIME!
!
GLEAM
ZAN
G
DSSH
OH!
!
...
HUH?
OW! HOT!
SZZZ
W-WHAT WAS THAT?!
UH-OH.
IT'S STARTING TO RAIN.

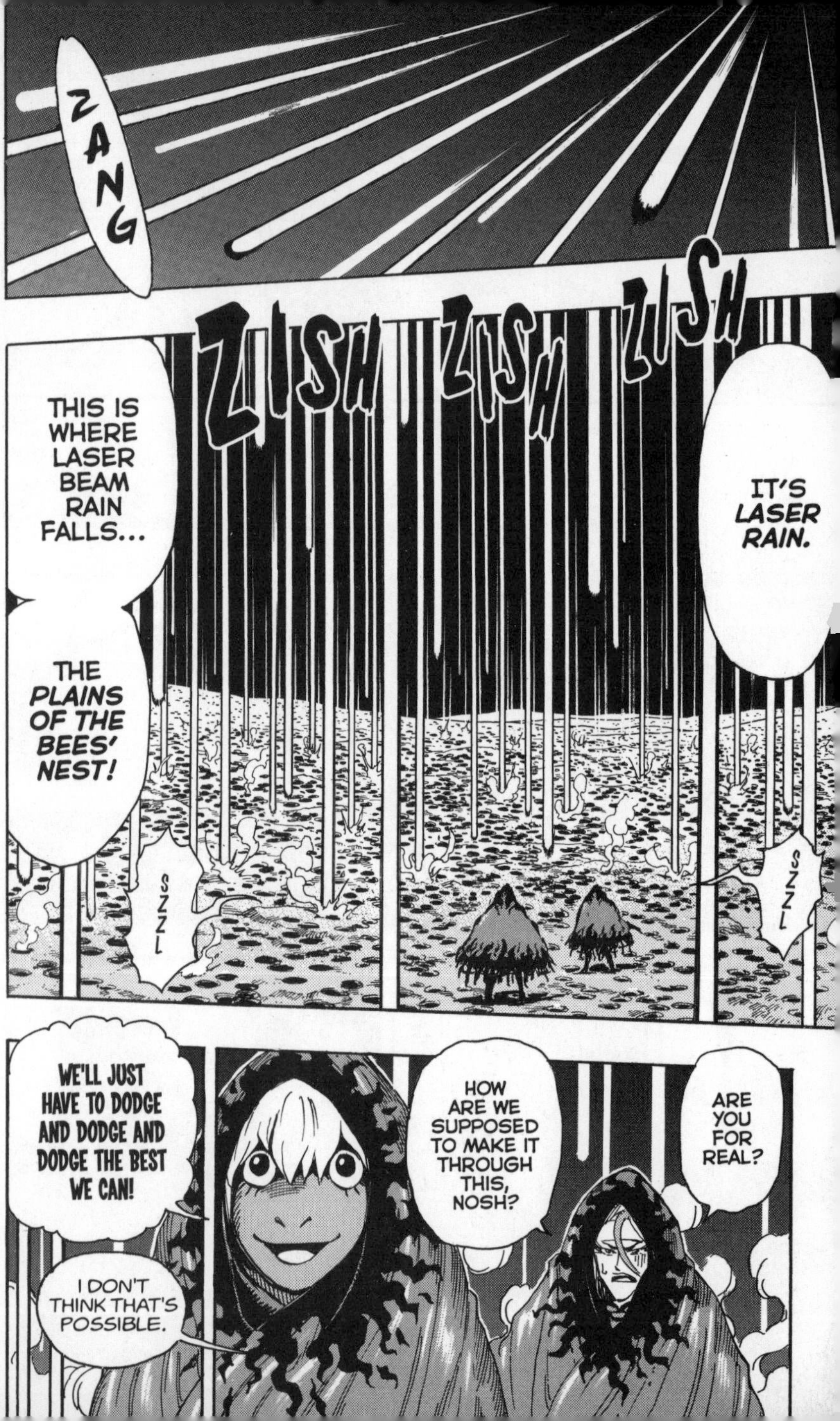
ZANG
ZISH ZISH ZISH
IT'S LASER RAIN.
THIS IS WHERE LASER BEAM RAIN FALLS...
THE PLAINS OF THE BEES' NEST!
SZZL
SZZL
ARE YOU FOR REAL?
HOW ARE WE SUPPOSED TO MAKE IT THROUGH THIS, NOSH?
WE'LL JUST HAVE TO DODGE AND DODGE AND DODGE THE BEST WE CAN!
I DON'T THINK THAT'S POSSIBLE.

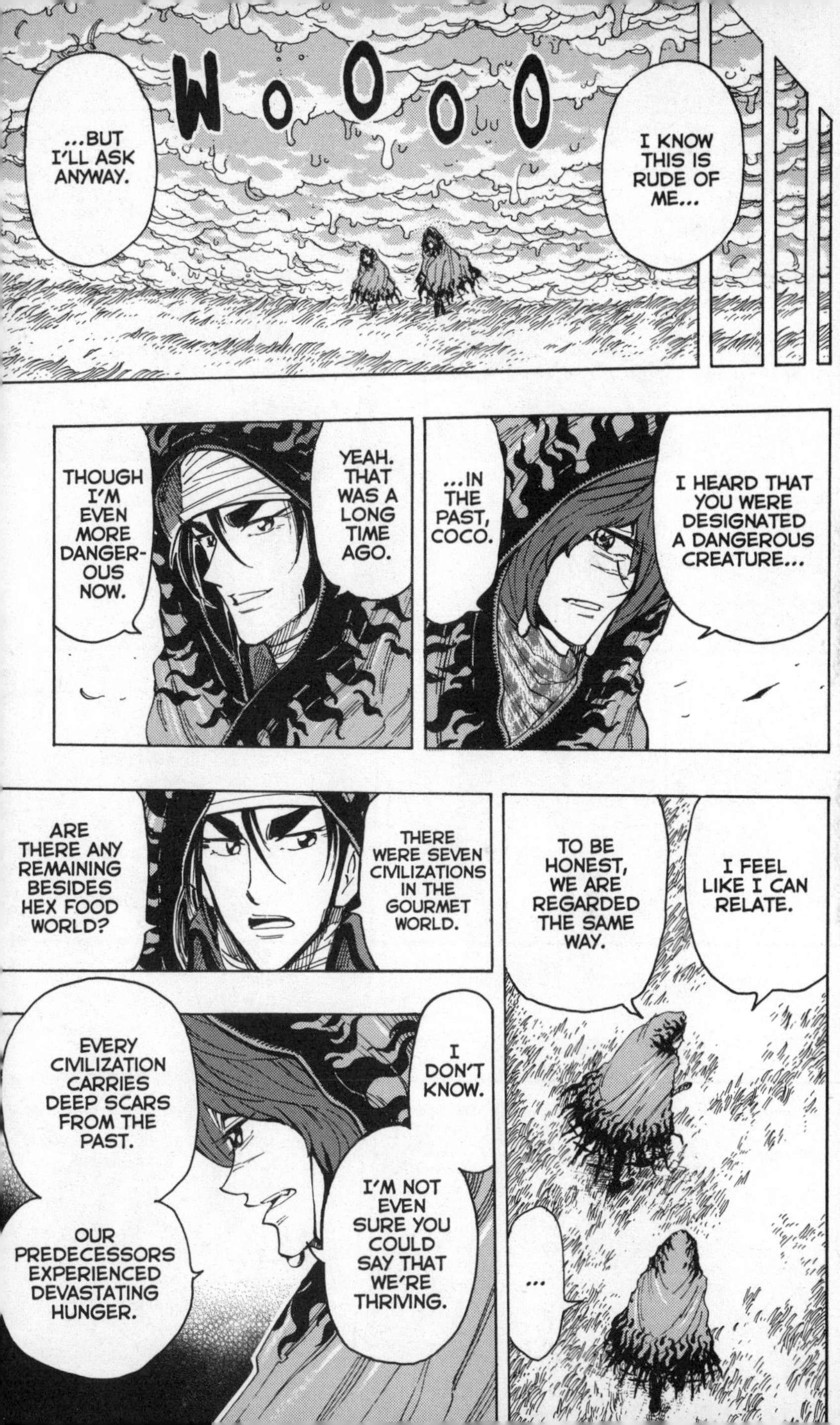
I KNOW THIS IS RUDE OF ME...
WOOOO
...BUT I'LL ASK ANYWAY.
I HEARD THAT YOU WERE DESIGNATED A DANGEROUS CREATURE...
...IN THE PAST, COCO.
YEAH. THAT WAS A LONG TIME AGO.
THOUGH I'M EVEN MORE DANGER-OUS NOW.
I FEEL LIKE I CAN RELATE.
TO BE HONEST, WE ARE REGARDED THE SAME WAY.
...
THERE WERE SEVEN CIVILIZATIONS IN THE GOURMET WORLD.
ARE THERE ANY REMAINING BESIDES HEX FOOD WORLD?
I DON'T KNOW.
I'M NOT EVEN SURE YOU COULD SAY THAT WE'RE THRIVING.
EVERY CIVILIZATION CARRIES DEEP SCARS FROM THE PAST.
OUR PREDECESSORS EXPERIENCED DEVASTATING HUNGER.

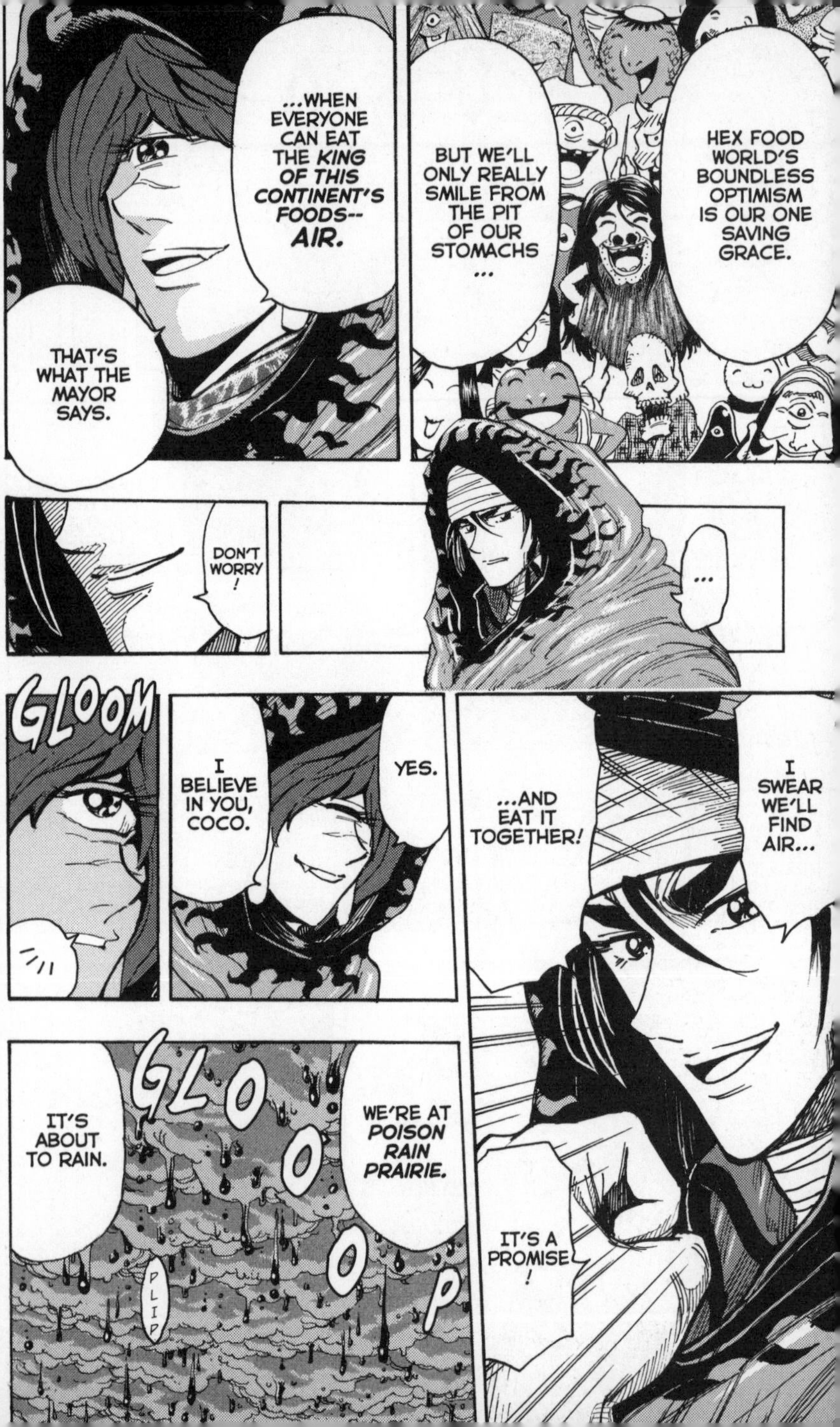
HEX FOOD WORLD'S BOUNDLESS OPTIMISM IS OUR ONE SAVING GRACE.
BUT WE'LL ONLY REALLY SMILE FROM THE PIT OF OUR STOMACHS...
...WHEN EVERYONE CAN EAT THE *KING OF THIS CONTINENT'S FOODS*-- **AIR.**
THAT'S WHAT THE MAYOR SAYS.
...
DON'T WORRY!
I SWEAR WE'LL FIND AIR...
...AND EAT IT TOGETHER!
IT'S A PROMISE!
YES.
I BELIEVE IN YOU, COCO.
GLOOM
GLOOOOP
WE'RE AT *POISON RAIN PRAIRIE.*
IT'S ABOUT TO RAIN.
PLIP

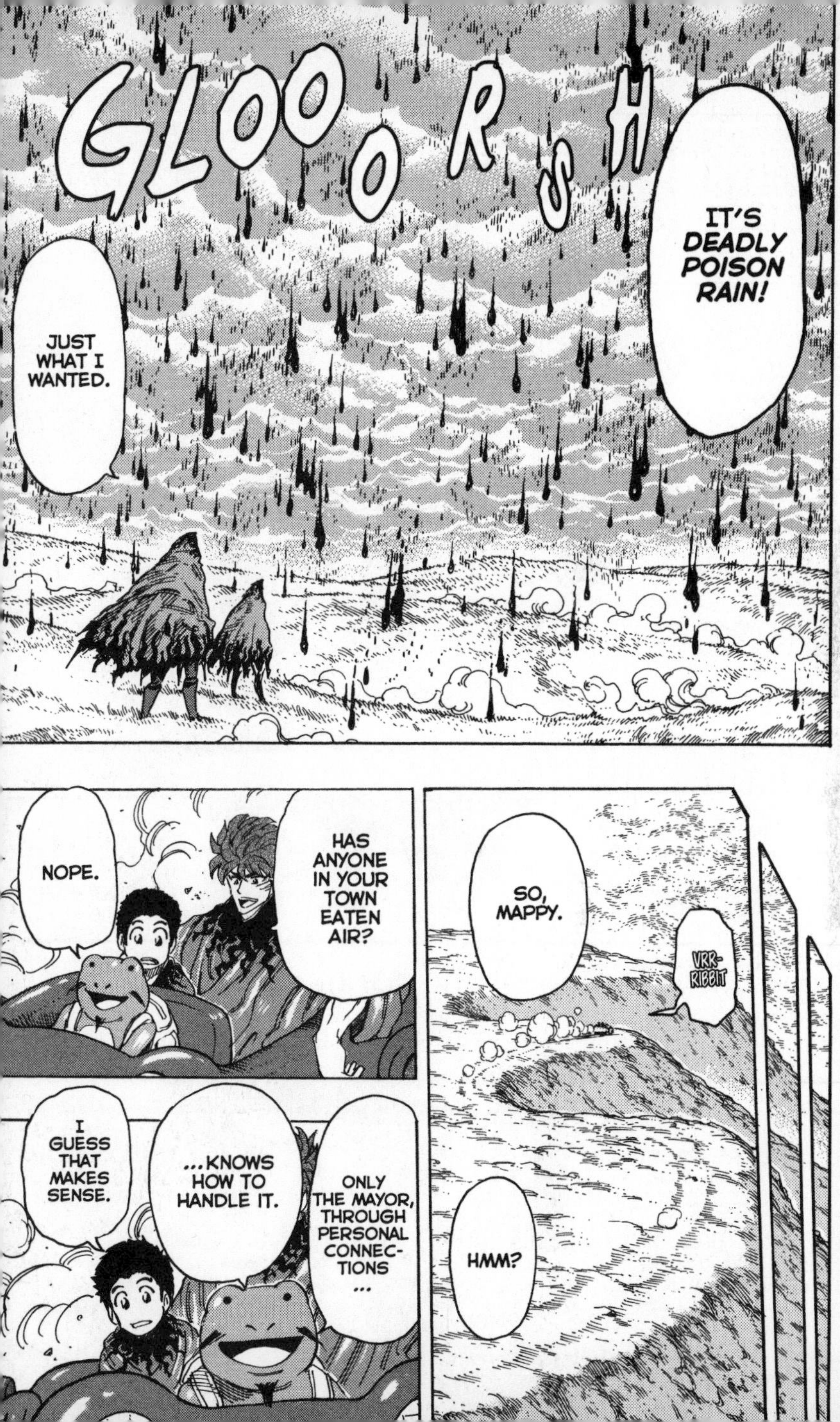
GLOOORSH
IT'S DEADLY POISON RAIN!
JUST WHAT I WANTED.
SO, MAPPY.
VRR-RIBBIT
HMM?
HAS ANYONE IN YOUR TOWN EATEN AIR?
NOPE.
ONLY THE MAYOR, THROUGH PERSONAL CONNECTIONS ...
...KNOWS HOW TO HANDLE IT.
I GUESS THAT MAKES SENSE.

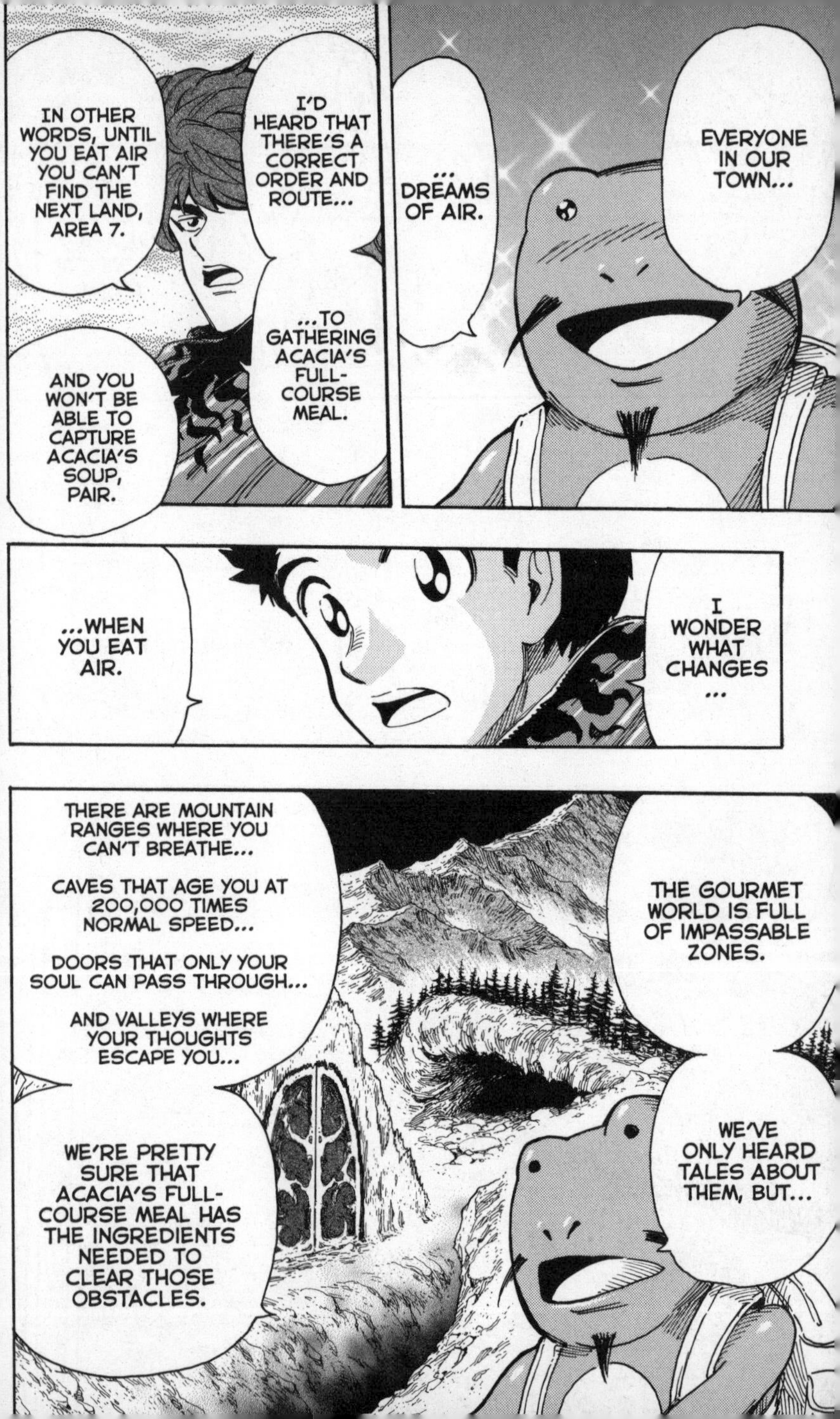
EVERYONE IN OUR TOWN...
... DREAMS OF AIR.
I'D HEARD THAT THERE'S A CORRECT ORDER AND ROUTE...
...TO GATHERING ACACIA'S FULL-COURSE MEAL.
IN OTHER WORDS, UNTIL YOU EAT AIR YOU CAN'T FIND THE NEXT LAND, AREA 7.
AND YOU WON'T BE ABLE TO CAPTURE ACACIA'S SOUP, PAIR.
I WONDER WHAT CHANGES ...
...WHEN YOU EAT AIR.
THE GOURMET WORLD IS FULL OF IMPASSABLE ZONES.
WE'VE ONLY HEARD TALES ABOUT THEM, BUT...
THERE ARE MOUNTAIN RANGES WHERE YOU CAN'T BREATHE...
CAVES THAT AGE YOU AT 200,000 TIMES NORMAL SPEED...
DOORS THAT ONLY YOUR SOUL CAN PASS THROUGH...
AND VALLEYS WHERE YOUR THOUGHTS ESCAPE YOU...
WE'RE PRETTY SURE THAT ACACIA'S FULL-COURSE MEAL HAS THE INGREDIENTS NEEDED TO CLEAR THOSE OBSTACLES.

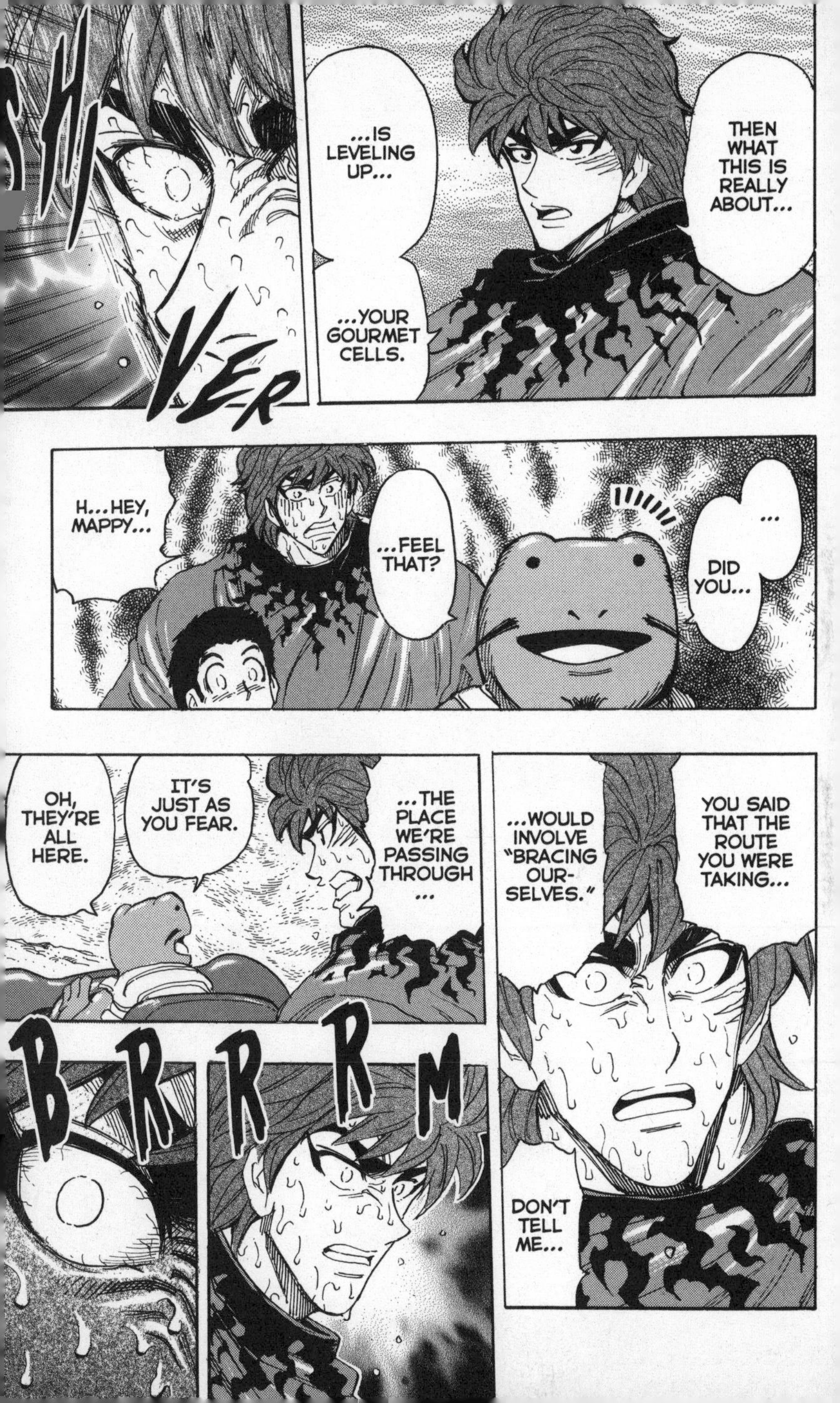
THEN WHAT THIS IS REALLY ABOUT...
...IS LEVELING UP...
...YOUR GOURMET CELLS.
SHIVER
... DID YOU...
...FEEL THAT?
H...HEY, MAPPY...
YOU SAID THAT THE ROUTE YOU WERE TAKING...
...WOULD INVOLVE "BRACING OUR-SELVES."
DON'T TELL ME...
...THE PLACE WE'RE PASSING THROUGH ...
IT'S JUST AS YOU FEAR.
OH, THEY'RE ALL HERE.
BRRRM

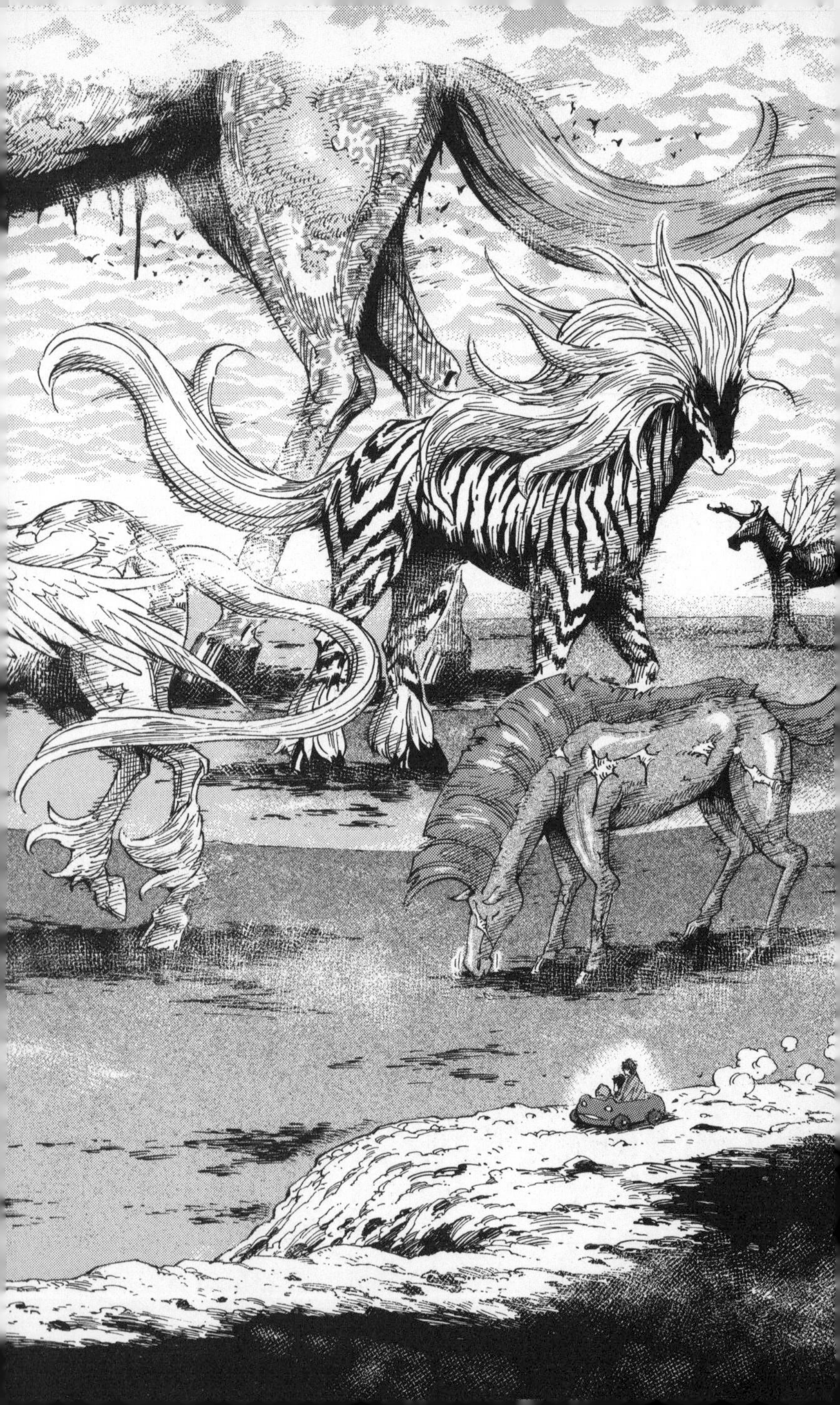

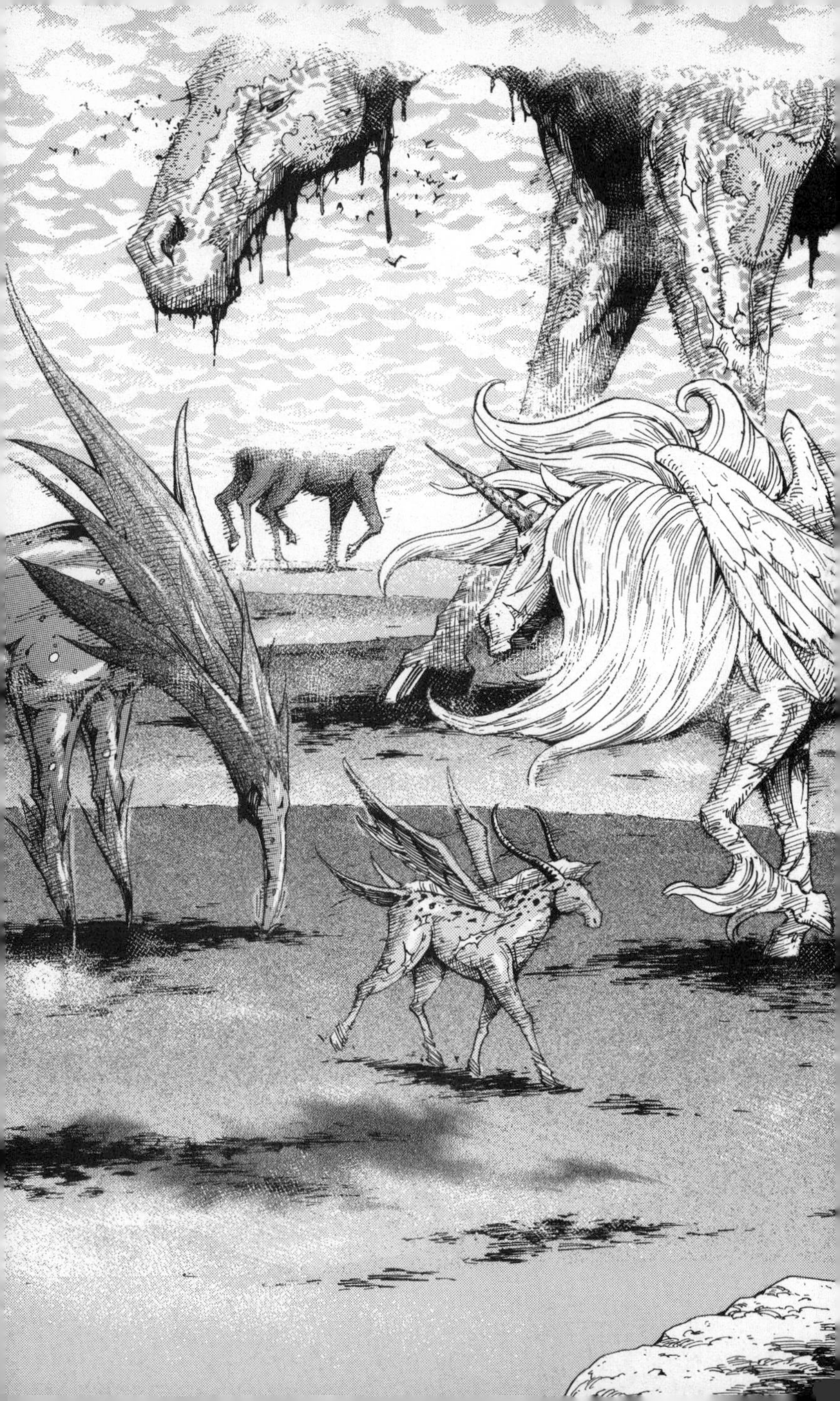

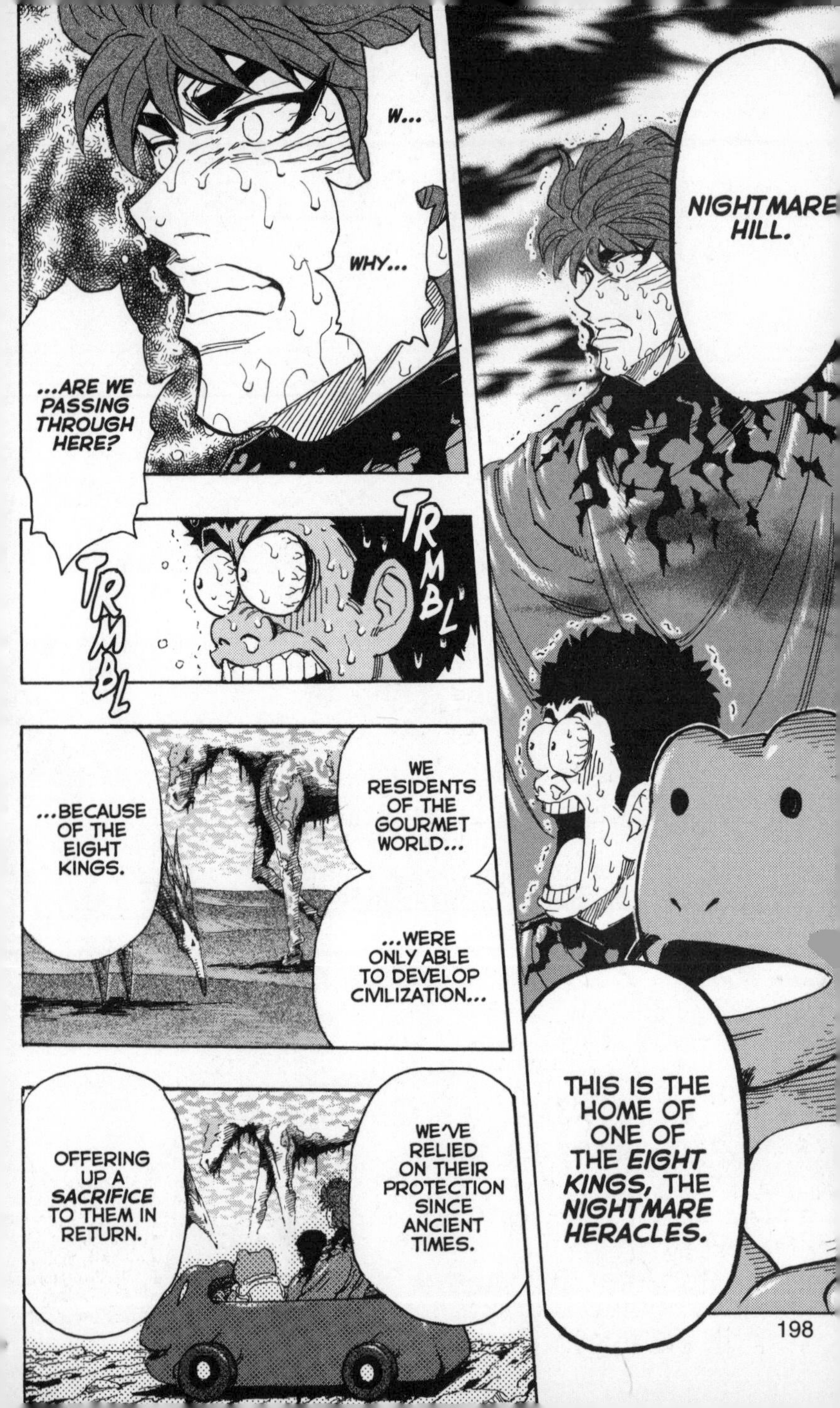
NIGHTMARE HILL.
THIS IS THE HOME OF ONE OF THE EIGHT KINGS, THE NIGHTMARE HERACLES.
W...
WHY...
...ARE WE PASSING THROUGH HERE?
TRMBL
TRMBL
WE RESIDENTS OF THE GOURMET WORLD...
...WERE ONLY ABLE TO DEVELOP CIVILIZATION...
...BECAUSE OF THE EIGHT KINGS.
WE'VE RELIED ON THEIR PROTECTION SINCE ANCIENT TIMES.
OFFERING UP A SACRIFICE TO THEM IN RETURN.

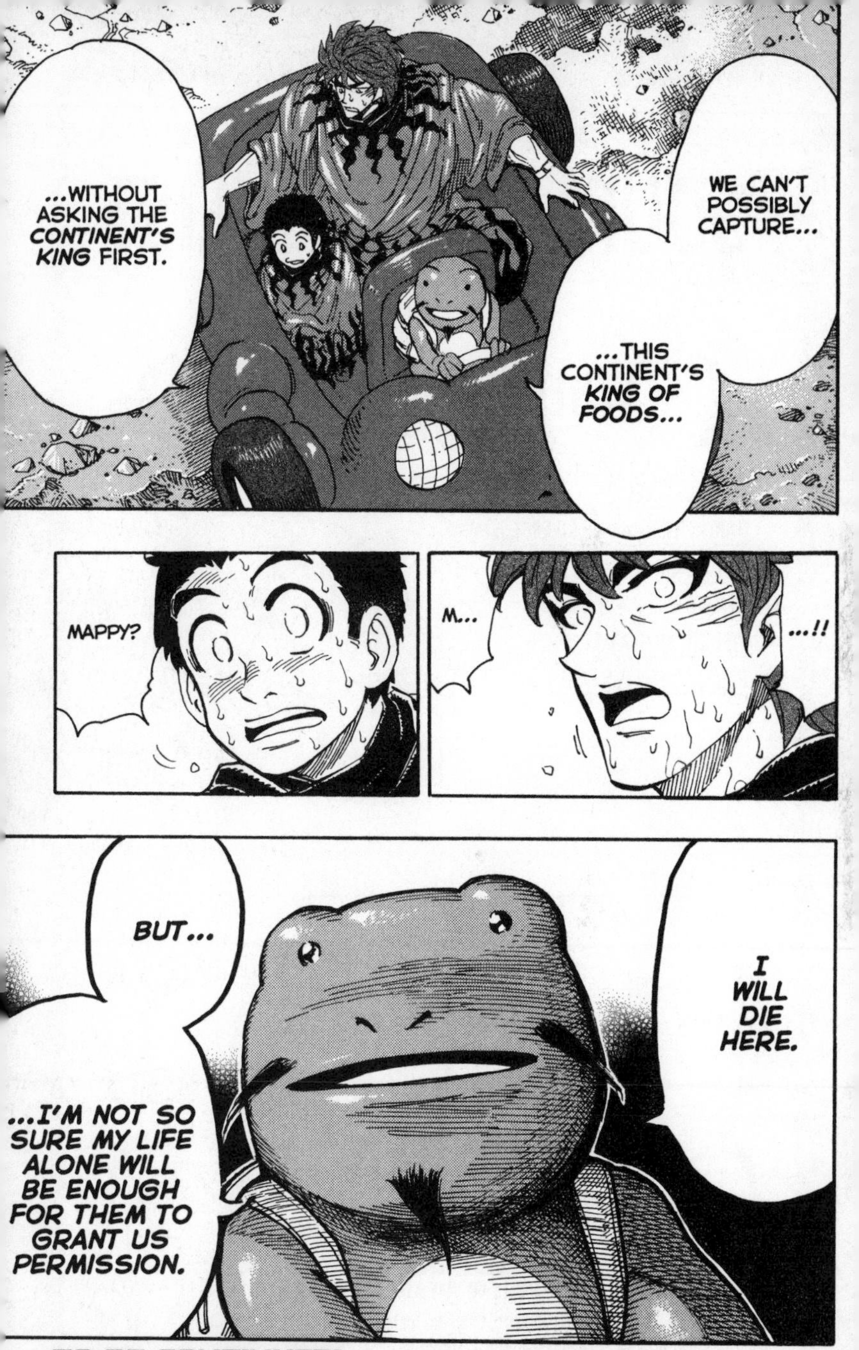

WE CAN'T POSSIBLY CAPTURE...
...THIS CONTINENT'S KING OF FOODS...
...WITHOUT ASKING THE CONTINENT'S KING FIRST.
...!!
M...
MAPPY?
I WILL DIE HERE.
BUT...
...I'M NOT SO SURE MY LIFE ALONE WILL BE ENOUGH FOR THEM TO GRANT US PERMISSION.

TO BE CONTINUED!

GOURMET CHECKLIST

Vol. 306

WHITE FISH NOODLES
(FISH)

CAPTURE LEVEL: 2

HABITAT: ESTUARINE RIVERBEDS

SIZE: 12 CM

HEIGHT: ---

WEIGHT: 10 GRAMS

PRICE: 10 YEN PER FISH

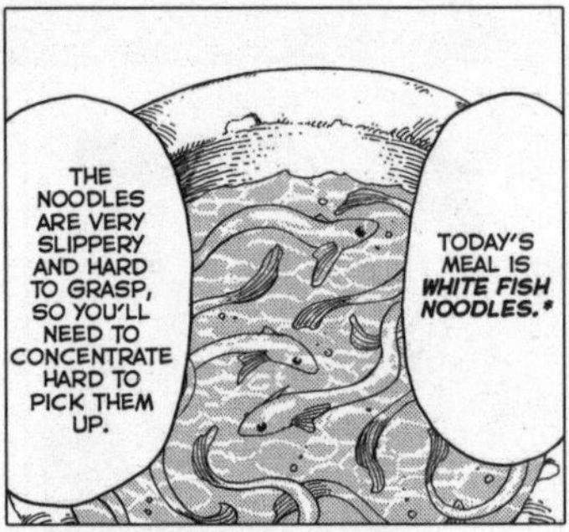
TODAY'S MEAL IS *WHITE FISH NOODLES.**
THE NOODLES ARE VERY SLIPPERY AND HARD TO GRASP, SO YOU'LL NEED TO CONCENTRATE HARD TO PICK THEM UP.

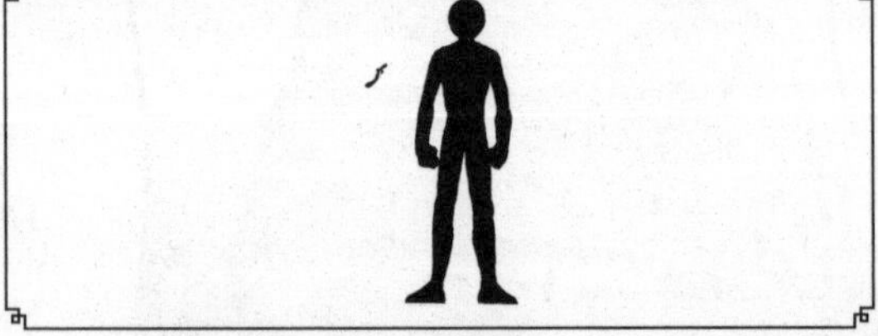

SCALE

IT TASTES AKIN TO SEA BREAM OR YOUNG SARDINES AND HAS THE TEXTURE OF SOFT, BOILED RAMEN NOODLES BLANKETING A TONGUE. THE FISH CAN BE ENJOYED HARD, WIRY, OR SLIPPERY DEPENDING ON HOW LONG THEY ARE BOILED IN WATER. HOWEVER, IF THE NOODLES ARE IN WATER FOR TOO LONG, THEY WILL BECOME SOGGY AND LOSE THEIR FLAVOR. THEREFORE, IT IS NECESSARY TO ENJOY THEM QUICKLY. WHITE FISH NOODLES ARE VERY SLIPPERY AND DIFFICULT TO GRASP, SO ONE MUST CONCENTRATE WHILE GRIPPING THEM. A CERTAIN AMOUNT OF HONOR THE FOOD IS NEEDED TO PROPERLY ENJOY THEM.

TORIKO

GOURMET CHECKLIST

Vol. 307

PUDDING CAMEL
(DAIRY)

CAPTURE LEVEL: 20
HABITAT: CHOWLIN TEMPLE
SIZE: 3 METERS
HEIGHT: ---
WEIGHT: 400 KG
PRICE: 3,500 YEN PER PUDDING

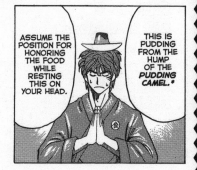

THIS IS PUDDING FROM THE HUMP OF THE *PUDDING CAMEL.**
ASSUME THE POSITION FOR HONORING THE FOOD WHILE RESTING THIS ON YOUR HEAD.

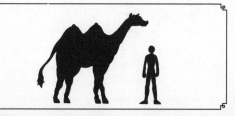

SCALE

A LUXURIOUS PUDDING CULTIVATED FROM THE HUMP OF A CAMEL. IF THE CAMEL IS ANGERED OR FRIGHTENED, THE PUDDING WILL COLLAPSE ALONG WITH THE FLAVOR. EVEN IF ONE MANAGES TO EXTRACT THE PUDDING AND TRANSFER IT TO A PLATE, EVEN THE MOST MINUTE MOVEMENT WILL DEFLATE THE PUDDING AND ALL THAT HARD WORK WOULD BE FOR NAUGHT. IT IS A PERFECT INGREDIENT FOR HONOR THE FOOD TRAINING.

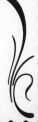

TORIKO

GOURMET CHECKLIST

Vol. 308

BUBBLE FRUIT
(TEMPLE TREASURE)

CAPTURE LEVEL: 98
HABITAT: CHOWLIN TEMPLE
SIZE: 50 CM
HEIGHT: ---
WEIGHT: 200 GRAMS
PRICE: 7,000,000 YEN PER FRUIT

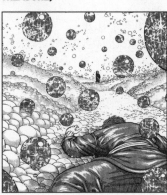

SCALE

THIS INGREDIENT IS THE TREASURE OF CHOWLIN TEMPLE. IT CAN ONLY BE FOUND ON THE HILL BEHIND THE TEMPLE KNOWN AS THE "BUBBLE WAY." HOWEVER, THE FRUIT WILL ONLY APPEAR WHEN ONE WHO IS SO UNCEASINGLY GRATEFUL FOR FOOD REACHES FOOD'S END. FOOD'S END IS CLASSIFIED AS A STATE OF BEING UTTERLY AND COMPLETELY DEVOTED TO FOOD. THIS TEMPLE TREASURE IS THE SYMBOL OF CHOWLIN TEMPLE. IT TASTES EVEN BETTER WHEN COOKED, BUT IS ALSO ENJOYABLE RAW. ALONG WITH FOOD'S END, BUBBLE FRUIT GRANTS WHOEVER EATS IT THE ENDLESS NOURISHMENT OF EVERY INGREDIENT ABSORBED INTO ONE'S BODY HENCEFORTH. TORIKO'S GRATITUDE TOWARDS THIS INGREDIENT WENT THROUGH THE ROOF WHEN HE MASTERED HONOR THE FOOD.

COMING NEXT VOLUME

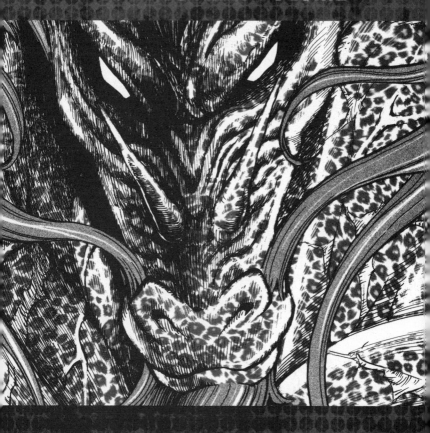

VS. HERACLES!!

Toriko, his chef partner Komatsu, and the other Four Kings finally reach the first stop on their journey to the Gourmet World. Upon arrival they learn that the Daruma, Mayor of Hex Food World, is sick and the only thing that can save him is Acacia's Salad—Air! They must travel through Hex Food World to find and prepare Air, but when Toriko comes face-to-face with a pregnant and cranky Nightmare Heracles, what is he to do? What will happen when Toriko faces off against this monstrous mother-to-be?!

AVAILABLE FEBRUARY 2016!

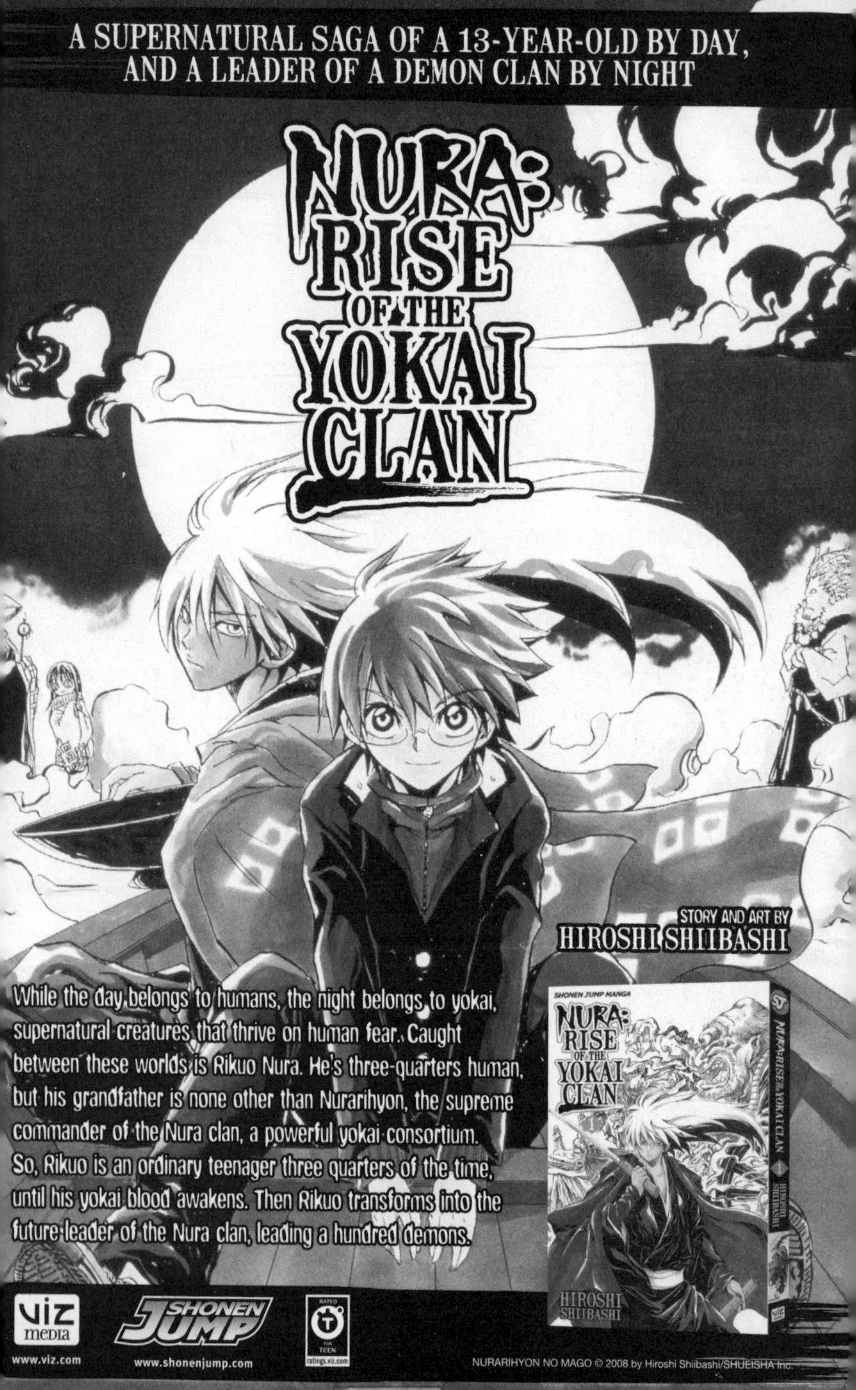
A SUPERNATURAL SAGA OF A 13-YEAR-OLD BY DAY, AND A LEADER OF A DEMON CLAN BY NIGHT
NURA: RISE OF THE YOKAI CLAN
STORY AND ART BY
HIROSHI SHIIBASHI
While the day belongs to humans, the night belongs to yokai, supernatural creatures that thrive on human fear. Caught between these worlds is Rikuo Nura. He's three-quarters human, but his grandfather is none other than Nurarihyon, the supreme commander of the Nura clan, a powerful yokai consortium. So, Rikuo is an ordinary teenager three quarters of the time, until his yokai blood awakens. Then Rikuo transforms into the future leader of the Nura clan, leading a hundred demons.
SHONEN JUMP MANGA
NURA: RISE OF THE YOKAI CLAN
HIROSHI SHIIBASHI
viz media
www.viz.com
SHONEN JUMP
www.shonenjump.com
RATED T FOR TEEN
ratings.viz.com
NURARIHYON NO MAGO © 2008 by Hiroshi Shiibashi/SHUEISHA Inc.

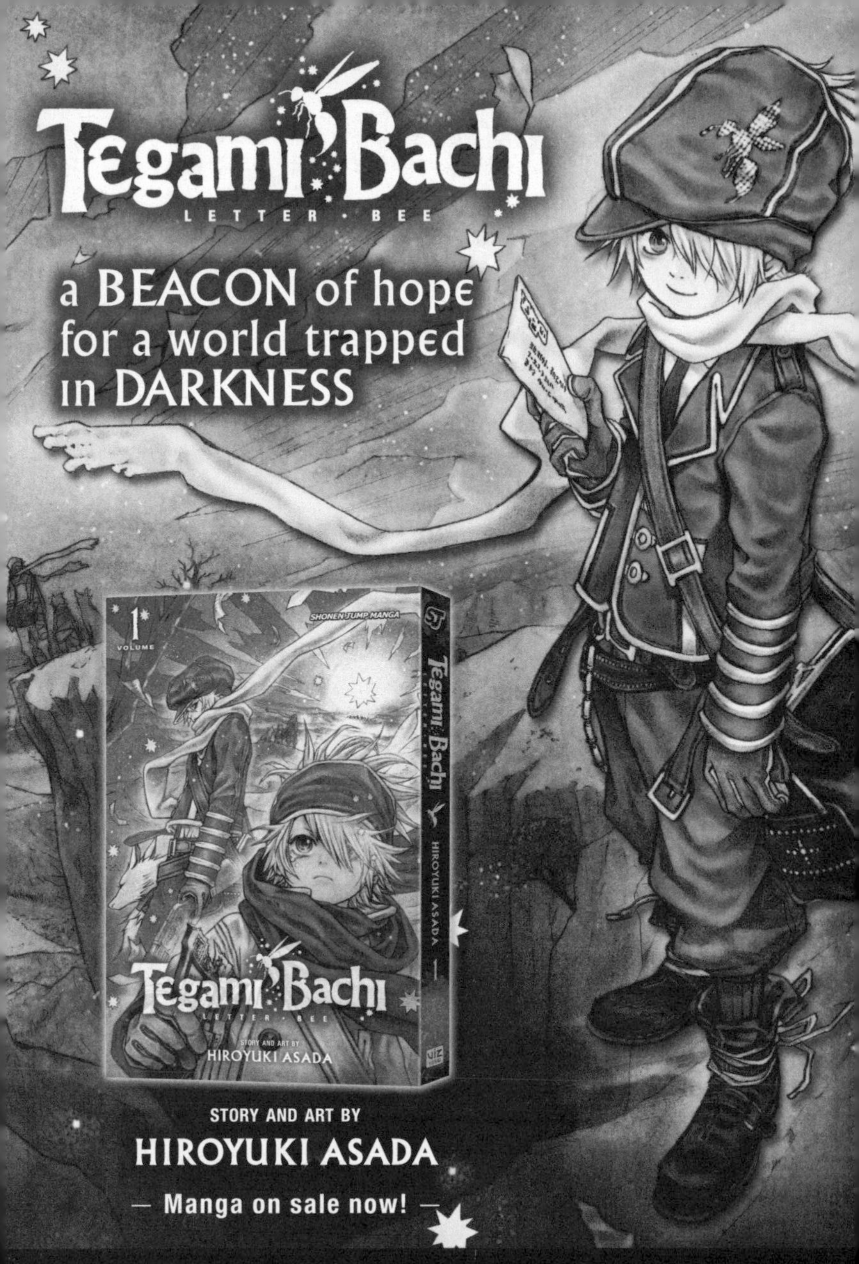
Tegami Bachi
LETTER • BEE
a BEACON of hope for a world trapped in DARKNESS
1 VOLUME
SHONEN JUMP MANGA
Tegami Bachi
LETTER • BEE
STORY AND ART BY
HIROYUKI ASADA
Tegami Bachi
HIROYUKI ASADA 1
STORY AND ART BY
HIROYUKI ASADA
— Manga on sale now! —

You're Reading in the Wrong Direction!!

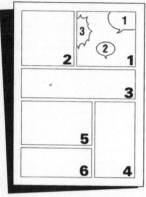

Whoops! Guess what? You're starting at the wrong end of the comic!

...It's true! In keeping with the original Japanese format, **Toriko** is meant to be read from right to left, starting in the upper-right corner.

Unlike English, which is read from left to right, Japanese is read from right to left, meaning that action, sound effects and word-balloon order are completely reversed... something which can make readers unfamiliar with Japanese feel pretty backwards themselves. For this reason, manga or Japanese comics published in the U.S. in English have sometimes been published "flopped"— that is, printed in exact reverse order, as though seen from the other side of a mirror.

By flopping pages, U.S. publishers can avoid confusing readers, but the compromise is not without its downside. For one thing, a character in a flopped manga series who once wore in the original Japanese version a T-shirt emblazoned with "M A Y" (as in "the merry month of") now wears one which reads "Y A M"! Additionally, many manga creators in Japan are themselves unhappy with the process, as some feel the mirror-imaging of their art skews their original intentions.

We are proud to bring you Mitsutoshi Shimabukuro's **Toriko** in the original unflopped format. For now, though, turn to the other side of the book and let the adventure begin...!

—Editor

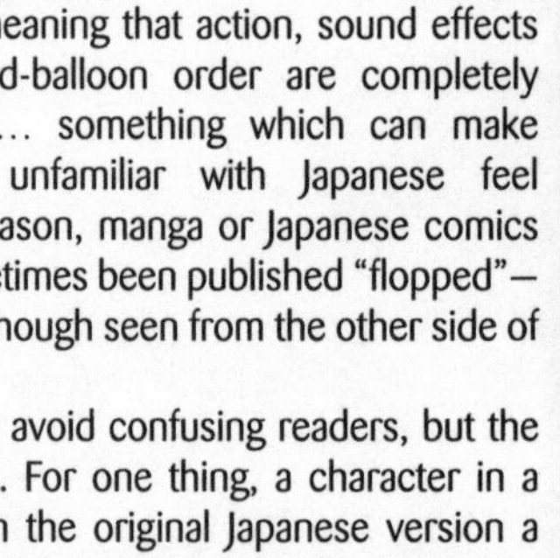